Only in Australia

Only in Australia

The History, Politics, and Economics of Australian Exceptionalism

Edited by
William O. Coleman

OXFORD
UNIVERSITY PRESS

OXFORD
UNIVERSITY PRESS

Great Clarendon Street, Oxford, OX2 6DP,
United Kingdom

Oxford University Press is a department of the University of Oxford.
It furthers the University's objective of excellence in research, scholarship,
and education by publishing worldwide. Oxford is a registered trade mark of
Oxford University Press in the UK and in certain other countries

First Edition published in 2016

Impression: 1

Published in the United States of America by Oxford University Press
198 Madison Avenue, New York, NY 10016, United States of America

British Library Cataloguing in Publication Data

Data available

Library of Congress Control Number: 2015959826

ISBN 978–0–19–875325–4

Printed in Great Britain by
Clays Ltd, St Ives plc

Acknowledgements

Almost all the chapters of this book had their genesis in a one-day conference, 'The Australian Sonderweg: Between Choice, Chance and Destiny', held in 2014 on the Fremantle Campus of the University of Notre Dame Australia (UNDA). This event constituted the annual conference of the Freedom to Choose programme, which is jointly sponsored by UNDA and the Mannkal Economics Education Foundation. Special thanks are therefore owed to the Foundation for its funding of the conference and to UNDA for providing the venue and administrative support. Thanks are also due Greg Moore, the director of the Freedom to Choose programme, for making the conference possible.

The benefit to various parts of the book from the input, criticism, and comment of Jennifer Buckingham, Max Corden, Keith Dowding, Phil Harber, Andrew Norton, and Rick Umback is gratefully acknowledged.

Table of Contents

List of Tables

Notes on Contributors

Geoffrey Blainey has held chairs in economic history and history at the University of Melbourne, and in Australian Studies at Harvard University. He has published over thirty-five books, including *The Rush That Never Ended: A History of Australian Mining* (1963), *The Tyranny of Distance: How Distance Shaped Australia's History* (1966), *Triumph of the Nomads: A History of Ancient Australia* (1975), *A Short History of the World* (2000), and *A Short History of Christianity* (2013). He has been chairman of the Australia Council, the Australia-China Council, the Commonwealth Literary Fund, the Australian War Memorial, and the National Council for the Centenary of Federation. In 2000 he was made a Companion of the Order of Australia.

Nick Cater has a long and varied career in journalism in Australia and Great Britain. He directed the BBC documentary *Bridge Builders*, comparing the construction of the Tyne and Sydney Harbour Bridges. From 2007 to 2013 he was editor of the *Weekend Australian*. His book *The Lucky Culture and the Rise of an Australian Ruling Class* was published in 2013. He has co-edited *A Better Class of Sunset: The Collected Works of Christopher Pearson* (2014) and is working on a second book, provisionally entitled *Delusions: A History of Bad Ideas*.

Stephen A. Chavura has lectured in political thought and history at Macquarie University and Campion College. His book *Tudor Protestant Political Thought, 1547–1603* was published in 2011. He is currently co-authoring a book about the emergence of the secular state in Australia.

William O. Coleman, Reader in economics at the Australian National University, has written extensively on inflation, the history of economic thought, and the contested position of economics in society. He has authored, or co-authored, several books, including *Giblin's Platoon: The Trials and Triumph of the Economist in Australian Public Life* (2006), and *Economics and Its Enemies: Two Centuries of Anti-Economics* (2002).

Adam Creighton began his career at the Reserve Bank of Australia before completing a Master of Philosophy in economics at Oxford University. He has since worked as an economist at the Centre for Independent Studies, has contributed to *The Economist*, and since 2012 has been the economics correspondent for *The Australian*. He authored a chapter in *The Oxford Handbook of Pensions and Retirement Income* (2006).

Henry Ergas, Professor of Infrastructure at the University of Wollongong, is a prolific author and columnist on public affairs. Ergas's early career was with the Organisation for Economic Co-operation and Development (OECD) in Paris, serving ultimately as

Counsellor in its Economics Department. He has subsequently held professorial positions at Monash University, the University of Auckland, and the Kennedy School of Government of Harvard University. His service to government reviews and long experience in telecommunications provided the material for his book, *Wrong Number: Resolving Australia's Telecommunications Impasse* (2008). In 2016 he was made an Officer in the Order of Australia.

Phil Lewis is Professor of Economics and Director of the Centre for Labour Market Research at the University of Canberra. He is among the best-known economists in the area of the economics of employment, education, and training in Australia, and is the author of over a hundred publications, including journal articles, book chapters, and books, such as the successful introductory text *Essentials of Economics* (2013). He is currently the editor of the *Australian Journal of Labour Economics*, and is a past president of the Economic Society of Australia.

Greg Melleuish has taught Australian politics, political theory, and history at the University of Melbourne, the University of Queensland, and the University of Wollongong. He is the author of *Cultural Liberalism in Australia* (1995), and co-authored the entry on 'Australian Political Thought' for the *Oxford Companion to Australian Politics*. His most recent books are *Australian Intellectuals: Their Strange History and Pathological Tendencies* (2013) and *Despotic State or Free Individual?* (2014). He is currently writing a book that will evaluate the contribution of James McAuley to Australian intellectual life.

J. R. Nethercote, Adjunct Professor at the Australian Catholic University, has served on the staff of the (Coombs) Royal Commission of Australian Government Administration, the Public Service Commission of Canada, and the Australian Public Service Board. A past editor of the *Australasian Parliamentary Review*, he has also edited or co-edited numerous books, including *The Menzies Era* (1995), *Liberalism and the Australian Federation* (2001), *The 'Whig' View of Australian History and Other Essays* (2007) and *Restraining Elective Dictatorship: The Upper House Solution?* (2008).

Jonathan Pincus, Visiting Professor of Economics at the University of Adelaide, is a scholar of the intersection of economics, politics and history. From 2002 through 2007 he was Principal Adviser Research at the Productivity Commission. He has written scholarly works in public choice, fiscal federalism, and economic history, including *Pressures and Politics in Antebellum Tariffs* (1977) and, as a co-author, *Government and Capitalism: Public and Private Choice in Twentieth Century* (1982). He is the 2015 Distinguished Public Policy Fellow of the Economic Society of Australia.

Richard Pomfret is Professor of Economics at the University of Adelaide, following previous appointments at the Johns Hopkins University, Bologna, and Nanjing. He has also acted as adviser to the Australian government, the World Bank, the OECD, and the Asian Development Bank. He has written seventeen books, including *Investing in China: Ten Years of the Open Door Policy* (1990), *Constructing a Market Economy: Diverse Paths from Central Planning in Asia and Europe* (2002), and *The Central Asian Economies since Independence* (2006). His most recent books include *The Age of Equality: The Twentieth Century in Economic Perspective* (2011), and *Public Policy and Professional Sports: International and Australian Experiences* (2014).

Keith Rankin is a lecturer in economics at Unitec, Auckland, having previously taught at the University of Auckland, Victoria University of Wellington, and Massey University. He has published on New Zealand economic history, macroeconomic crises and imbalances, and on taxation and welfare issues. His credits include widely used estimates of historical economic growth in New Zealand, estimates of unemployment in the 1930s, and an economics textbook, *Economic Concepts and Applications* (2008).

Peter Yule, of the University of Melbourne, is a fertile historian of the nerves and sinews of the Australian economy. Best known for his well-received biographies of business magnates (*William Lawrence Baillieu: Founder of Australia's Greatest Business Empire* (2012) and *Ian Potter: A Biography* (2006)), he has also authored histories of the Victorian Auditor-General's Office, the Collins Class submarine project, Australian National Airways, the Commerce Department of the University of Queensland, and the Warrnambool Agricultural Society. A Fellow of the Royal Historical Society, he has recently published an economic history of Australia in the First World War in the co-authored *The War at Home* (2015).

1

The Australian Exception

William O. Coleman

1.1 The Question

To invoke the unusual about Australia is usually to evoke the outlandish: black swans, flying foxes, flying doctors, Ned Kelly's armour, Christmas on Bondi beach, a prime minister vanishing without a trace while surfing. Weird, curious, and unimportant.

This book is concerned with something more significant. In the early twenty-first century Australia appears to be drifting from the tendency of the English-speaking world in matters of economic and social policy. Australia seems to be following a 'special path' of its own that it laid down more than a century ago. It is constituting an 'exception' to the common course of societies to which it could be obviously compared.

Perhaps the five most salient features of this Australian exceptionalism are:

1. A tightly regulated labour market.
2. A tax-transfer system heavily reliant on direct taxation and means testing.
3. A 'facade federalism', where an appearance of a federal structure belies the reality of a unitary state.
4. A lofty prominence in public life of an 'official family' of senior bureaucrats, complemented by proliferation of the 'independent' statutory bodies possessing a state-within-a-state aspect.
5. Certain electoral peculiarities: including compulsory and preferential voting, an unassailably independent Electoral Commission, and a distinct rural party (the Country Party and its later incarnations).

These phenomena make themselves felt in everyday life; a minimum wage of $A17.29 per hour, which is sternly enforced;[1] an unemployment benefit that requires no previous employment history of its recipient;[2] state governments—more bereft of revenue sources than any other such tier in the world[3]—struggling with hospital expenditure; a compulsion to vote in a plebiscite on same-sex marriage; an income tax in 2015/16 of 49 cents in the dollar from about two and quarter times average weekly earnings (see Table 1.1).[4]

Table 1.1 Top Marginal Tax Rates, 2014

	Australia	New Zealand	Canada	USA	UK	Germany	Japan
Rate	46.50	33.00	49.50	46.25	45.00	47.48	51.08
threshold of top rate, as multiple of average earnings	2.26	1.28	4.45	8.23	4.21	5.66	4.57

Source: OECD.

In Australia career public servants daily claim a public profile and prestige that elsewhere only central bankers could hope for. Only in Australia could a suite of public servants have enjoyed the policy heft of the 'Seven Dwarfs' of the post-war period (Nethercote 2012). Today their successors preside over the 'more or less self-contained administrative satrapies' (Encel 1960, p. 75) that constitute much of the Australian state; including the Australian Competition and Consumer Commission, the Australian Broadcasting Corporation, the Commonwealth Grants Commission, and others.

It is easy to add other things that single Australia out, at least by the standards of anglophone countries: a state 'broadcasting corporation' funded by general taxation; a massive compulsory saving scheme secured through

[1] Measured at market exchange rates, in 2014 Australia had the highest legislated minimum wage rate in the world, bar Luxembourg (OECD 2015). One 2014 study ranked Australia 132 out of 144 countries surveyed in terms of wage determination flexibility and 136th in hiring and firing flexibility. 'Australian businesses, year after year, have named the restrictive labor regulations the most problematic factor for doing business in their country by a wide margin' (Schwab and Sala-i-Martin 2014, p. 27).

[2] Australia and New Zealand are the only Organisation for Economic Co-operation and Development (OECD) countries where to be eligible for an unemployment benefit does not require any history of previous employment.

[3] Repeated international comparisons have revealed that Australian states raise from their own revenue resources a substantially smaller proportion of their spending than the same level of government in Canada, Germany and the United States (Dollery 2002). One American observer has judged: 'I cannot help but be struck by how little most [Australian] public servants and economists appear to care about fiscal federalism' (Gramlich 1984, p. 273).

[4] In one judgement, 'the Australian tax system has one of the most progressive structures of all OECD countries, and... the social security system is the most progressive of all countries' (Whiteford 1998, p. 211). The concessionary taxation of compulsory saving qualifies this conclusion to some degree.

workplace relations law; a taxation of tobacco of a severity unmatched anywhere else (see Table 1.2).

Table 1.2 Tobacco Taxation Revenue, 2013, $US

	Australia	New Zealand	Canada	USA	UK	Germany	Japan
Per adult	427	226	249	133	284	268	210
Per smoker	2375	n/a	1244	632	1289	787	582

Notes: Adults are measured as population over 14. Smokers are measured as population over 14 multiplied by the proportion of men who smoke. USA, New Zealand, and Canada, 2012/13. Australia and Japan 2013/14.[5]
Sources: World Health Organization, World Bank.

But perhaps the best illustration of Australia's tendency to keep pressing along a path it has cut for itself is in school education. From the start of the government school system in the 1870s, Australia's administration has been unusually centralized. The 'boards of education' which governed Australia's government schools at the very foundation of the system—themselves 'feeble parodies' of British school boards (Fairfield 1891, p. 177)—had been by 1880 abolished, and the entire conduct of schools vested in the education departments of the states under identical arrangement (Barcan 1995). In the late nineteenth century church school systems were being constructed, but through funding and regulation these were eventually assimilated, in effect, into 'the elaborate State systems which are now the central fact of Australian educational life' (Partridge 1968, p. 9).[6] But in the second decade of the twenty-first century the Australian presumption that a government-funded school must be remote-controlled by an education department has been challenged by the explosion in the number of 'charter schools' in the USA, 'academy schools' in England, and 'free schools' in Sweden. In Australia, however, this movement to maximize the autonomy of government funded schools has only been slightly felt, if at all.[7] Instead, the chosen response to failing government schools was, amid massive publicity, a scheme to substantially increase 'funding' and create new national school authorities; a scheme which promptly won a pledge of support from all major parties (Department of Education and Training 2011).[8] Commensurate with the *froideur* shown

[5] The Australian figure does not reflect the 50 per cent increase in tobacco excise rates that is taking place between 1 September 2014 and 1 September 2016.

[6] In 2010 government grants provided half the funding of non-Catholic non-government schools, and three quarters of Catholic non-government schools. Elaborate registration requirements also keep 'independent' schools under tight rein.

[7] The one parallel to charter schools in Australia is the 'Independent Public Schools' programme in Western Australia and Queensland (Jha and Buckingham 2015). A move to the same in Victoria was reversed by a change in government in 2014.

[8] The 319-page statement of this policy mentions charter schools once. It is sometimes suggested that in Australia non-government schools assume the function of charter schools. But for many reasons non-government schools are far from perfect substitutes for government schools.

charter schools, still more radical initiatives overseas to accommodate schools beyond the superintendence of education departments, such as the recent growth in Sweden and the UK of for-profit schools, have been utterly frozen out: for-profit schools are expressly disallowed federal funding, and in some states are illegal.

These departures from the tendency of anglophone countries are, evidently, not mere curiosities.

Neither are they the vagaries of some passing sway, or the precarious edifice of some creaking ascendancy. I would venture they enjoy the sympathy and indulgence of the Australian public. And for that reason Australia's special path has in its essentials complete bipartisan support; as one political scientist has put it, Australia's political 'competitors are offering only slightly different brews of the same ideological ingredients' (Collins 1985, p. 154).[9] There is a durability and resilience in the approach, which, in the eyes of critics, amounts to something stuck.

Neither are these departures miscellaneous. They appear to share a common character; a character that is approached by terms such as 'egalitarian', collectivist, *dirigiste*—three concepts that, for all their differences, are frequently found in each other's company. If we think of a spectrum running from collectivism to individualism, from 'public' action and concerns to 'private' action and concerns, from left to right, and plot societies on this spectrum, it would appear that most anglophone countries cluster together, while Australia is an outlier.

The aim of this book is to get an understanding of this situation.

1.2 Questioning the Question

The remit of this book's undertaking might be denied.

Sceptics of the existence of Australian exceptionalism might point to international surveys of values and institutions that purport to show that Australia floats in an unremarkable proximity with other anglophone countries.

Other sceptics might instance counter-examples to the suggestion that Australia is unusually collectivist: the entrenched National Health Service in the UK; the impregnable regulation of the sugar sector in the USA; or enduring agricultural subsidies in the European Union.

Others will use the distance between Australia and some comparators to confer an abnormality on the comparators, rather than Australia. The USA is

[9] 'The fact is that the Liberal party has made the policies of the Labor party its own' (Métin [1901] 1977, p. 71). A century after this was written in 1899 the same could be said. And the sentence could be truthfully reversed.

perhaps the only developed country to not have a statutory entitlement to annual leave: let the USA be deemed 'the outlier', and be puzzled over (Archer 2007).

Others will press a lack of distance between the two poles of the relevant spectrum. After all, there must always be 'a largest', and there must always be 'a smallest'; but, it might be maintained, the absolute distance between is so slight that they hardly merit being termed 'extremes'.[10]

None of these attempts to discount Australian exceptionalism have much force.

The existence of Australian exceptionalism is not greatly tested by international comparisons constructed from the arbitrary selection and weightings of institutions; or by the manipulations of survey results, that can only measure circumstantial judgements and rarely general values. Neither is Australian exceptionalism controverted by other countries exemplifying values which are not being claimed especially for Australia. Thus Australia's specialness certainly does not lie in any European-style elevation of the state into some autonomous regnant force; an 'indomitable entity' (de Gaulle), the 'divine idea as it exists on Earth' (Hegel). Neither is Australia's specialness refuted by an incoherence of the policy suite of more polycentric countries, such as the USA. Nor is Australian exceptionalism extinguished by the existence of other exceptionalisms. Any spectrum will have two ends. An American exceptionalism is consistent with an Australian one. Finally, who would say the distance between the spectrum's two ends is so slight it is not worth noticing?

But to give sceptics their due, Australian exceptionalism is not capable of demonstrative proof. For all that, proof is not needed: it will be generally allowed.

Something that would more deeply undermine the point of this work would be a scepticism about the significance of Australian exceptionalism, rather than its existence.

'Isn't every country exceptional?' is a question that might be asked. Isn't every society possessed of its own particular flavour? In this objection, there exists no *spectrum* (left to right, light to dark) which can capture policy differences. Rather, differences are held to be differences in kind not quantity; in hue, not shade. The upshot of this irremediable individuality is every country constitutes a special case of some sort. We have a British way, a New Zealand way,

[10] A methodologically-based scepticism of claims to exceptionalism is also sometimes maintained. This requires that anything deemed exceptional must amount to an anomaly; the 'exceptional' must constitute a disconfirming case of a general model that is otherwise predictively successful. Thus the height of Australia's minimum wage, in this conception, is not 'exceptional' if a model that successfully predicts the minimum wage across countries also successfully predicts the considerable height of Australia's minimum wage. In reply it may be observed that there is no model, generally successful in prediction, that predicts the height of Australia's minimum wage; or any of the other salient features recorded at the opening of the chapter.

an American way, just as much as an Australian way. This objection—that all difference is a difference in kind—is tenable. But differences in kind crave explanation. Let all these kinds be explained, and not omit Australia's.

'Isn't every country unexceptional? Isn't every country the same in what matters?' This objection, too, contends that differences are a matter of kind, not degree or quantity, but additionally charges that 'nations' do not constitute kinds. Thus, this objection, instead of elevating national individuality, reduces it to the stuff of quirks, idiosyncrasies, and trivialities. Briefly, only non-national categories count. Thus Marxism will reduce the radical variety of market institutions to a single identity, 'capitalist'. A more current tendency of thought supposes that whatever is important will be captured by some category that is supranational and cultural: 'neo Europe' or 'neo Britain'. This last thought has a particular tug on Europeans and Britons unacquainted with Australia, who incline to perceive it as a wholly derivative society; a dim provincial echo of its British source. But this presumption runs afoul of the many differences in those two societies. Thus Australia's industrial relations system—the platypus of Australia's institutional menagerie—owes nothing to any British inheritance.[11] Australia is different.

Perhaps the most cogent mode of demoting the national is a historicism that holds the things that make up the world are 'ages' rather than 'cultures'. This 'historicism' draws an authority from the distinct tendency of all countries to swing one way or another simultaneously in their policy regimes. The worldwide movement towards deregulation in the 1980s is the stuff of history. The international spasm of protectionism of the 1930s is the stuff of lore. The Progressive era of the USA is the stuff of massive scholarship, and has very plain parallels in the New Liberalism of the United Kingdom, and the Deakinism of Australia.[12] Therefore, in trying to understand and explain policy, our first point of reference should not be 'nation', but 'period'. We should be, for example, contrasting the Age of Keynes versus the Age of Friedman, and not contrasting the antipodes—where people stand on their (policy) heads—with a supposed normality ruling on the other side of the earth. But the believer in Australian exceptionalism can retort that Australia has caught most of these

[11] With a handful of baroque or insipid exceptions, the mass of British legislation on industrial relations was neither drawn on nor imitated in Australia (see Quinlan 1998). Thus, the first footling in the rising Australian edifice of workplace regulation—the Servants and Labourers Act of 1828—rightly begins with the avowal of a fresh start, 'WHEREAS many of the Acts of the British Parliament relating to servants and laborers are not applicable to the Colony of New South Wales . . . '. To the same effect, one historian of Australian labour law opines, 'We are, I think, correct in stating that no anti-combination laws for the purpose of regulating industrial bargains were ever passed in this country . . . ' (Thomas 1962, p. 27). The claim that UK 'Combination Acts' were deployed in the turmoil of the 1890s is a myth (Bolton and Gregory 1992).

[12] Beyond mere parallels, there were some direct links between Deakinism and Progressivism: for example, Inglis Clark's friendship with Oliver Wendell Holmes, and Henry Bournes Higgins' friendship with Felix Frankfurter (Lake 2013).

international swings, yet barely rode their roundabouts. Thus, the Progressivist outlook managed to endure successfully into interwar Australia—and to leave an enduring impress—despite it rapidly becoming a thing of the past elsewhere.

A different historicism that tames the Australian difference, but without obliterating it, would deploy the contention that the development of all societies is characterized by a sequence of stages. Australia, in this telling is a young country, its differences arise from its youth, and it will retrace the history of its older and more mature siblings (Goodrich 1968). This cues the objection to Australian exceptionalism that probably has the most resonance with contemporary commentators:

'Australian exceptionalism is just a passing historical aberration.' In this criticism the Australian way is just the diminuendo of the 'Australian Settlement' of the early twentieth century, so closely associated with the three-time prime minister, Alfred Deakin, 'the great phenomenon of Australian history, even Australian experience' (Roe 1984, p. 18). But that Settlement, says this criticism, was undone in the second generation after the Second World War, and from 1980 Australia quickly began to normalize (Kelly 1994). Therefore, while, once upon a time, Australia was fiercely protectionist, over the past thirty years trade barriers have been massively reduced. Once Australia's banking system consisted of a clutch of government banks (and insurers) plus a suite of regulated and collusive private ones; now government ownership in the financial sector has disappeared, and sixty-six banks compete with one another. Once wages and conditions were decided by judicial legislation; now business and unions decide these matters by bargain, with tribunals merely present (it is said) to provide a benediction. And, most pointedly, whereas once Australian immigration policy sought with some rigour to secure a White Australia, Australia is now an ethnically diverse society on account of an official immigration policy that has accommodated diversity.

To recapitulate the contention: once Australia was floating down its own little stream, but now it has rejoined the Big River.

Perhaps the most ambitious rebuttal to this attempt to dispose of exceptionalism is that the cited shifts are more a matter of form than nature. Yes, tariffs have fallen, but 'budgetary assistance' has ballooned. Yes, banks were deregulated in the 1980s, but at about the same time a massive system of regulated saving was instituted ('superannuation'). Yes, a racist White Australia is now remote history, but it might be argued the policy was, in nature, a drastic economic regulation, and that nature remains unchanged. Australia still drastically regulates immigration on economic grounds: the Department of Immigration has the air of a Soviet planning department in determining, through its Skilled Occupations List, how many antique dealers, sonographers, and welders (first class) Australia will annually admit. But perhaps it is in industrial relations that the appearance of change is most illusory. 'Enterprise bargaining' is in several ways simply the old 'consent awards' procedure in a new bottle. Bargaining remains the legal monopoly of 'registered' trade unions. And if tribunals cannot now be obliged to arbitrate the wages and conditions of 'enterprise bargains', a swathe of matters that could once be altered by application to a tribunal are now entirely beyond even their arbitration, and require the resolve of two chambers of national parliament to change.[13] Tribunals themselves remain directly occupied in determining wages and conditions in contexts ranging from Alpine Resorts to Wool Sampling. Some 935 pages of legislation govern the whole system.

There is, then, a great deal of 'changing same' in Australia (Macfarlane 1978). Rather than being temporary aberration, the present work maintains that Australian exceptionalism is better described as enduring. This endurance is underlined by the contrast of Australia with two countries that, until recently, seemed to have travelled in parallel with Australia over the most of the twentieth century: Sweden and New Zealand. Both were—like Australia—small, marginally located, trade-dependent economies, composed of well-educated populations working on favourable resource endowments, committed to egalitarianism, with very significant labour parties, and with large state involvement. And both—like Australia—began pruning state structures in the 1980s.

Australia differs from Sweden and New Zealand in that the shift, since 1980, to 'the market' has been deeper and more enduring in the two smaller economies. New Zealand today has highly deregulated financial, product, and labour markets, a cleanly floating currency, and substantially lower income tax. 'The streets of Stockholm are awash with the blood of sacred cows' (Micklethwait and Wooldridge 2014, p. 171), and 'Sweden and Denmark... now lead the world in privately run hospitals...and...schools...run by profit-making companies' (Moore 2014, p. 21).

In this writer's analysis it is Australia's much vaunted period of 'microeconomic reform' of the 1980s that has been temporary and passing. That period was more of a holding, or stalling, manoeuvre than an embrace of the new. Australia is the country that won't move on, which is stuck in its way. Australia is not the world's 'social laboratory'; it is a sacred grove dedicated to the dogged observance of customary gods.

But must this inertia be for the bad? The merit of Australian exceptionalism has been episodically contested, and, in turn, hotly defended. But this volume is not directly concerned with whether the way is good or bad; or whether it

[13] Maximum weekly hours, redundancy pay, long service leave, parental leave, annual leave, public holidays, notice of termination.

has made Australia richer, or poorer; fairer or unfairer; wiser or stupider.... The ultimate concern of this volume is with *why* Australia is like that.

1.3 Planet Australia

Why Australia is 'exceptional' has received only intermittent scrutiny. This inattention is doubtless in part the human failing of taking for granted what endures. More than a century ago Australia was most conspicuously distinguished from its parent society by the provision of railways by government. This had significant impacts (see Chapters 9 and 13, this volume), but it seems to have provoked more scrutiny from outside of Australia than within (Acworth 1892), and was explained away to British visitors as simply a matter of applying to railways the method of supplying postal services. Today the contrast endures—with passenger railways (outside metropolitan Victoria) remaining a matter of government administration—yet the difference is even less remarked, even if the Post Office of the UK (now a market institution) will no longer serve to normalize it.

But the lack of scrutiny is not just a consequence of inattention; it is also the effect of a certain system of proprieties having established itself in Australia. Any system of proprieties reigns by silences as much as by pronouncements: some things are not to be spoken of. And so it is with Australian exceptionalism. Thus, A. F. Davies records publicly the simple truth that Australia is acutely bureaucratized, and for this is 'never forgiven' by some of his peers (Walter 2007). Thus Australia's most learned scholar of legislation, Geoffrey Sawer (1952, p. 213), writes of the 'conspiracy of silence' regarding the intensity and extent of judicial legislation in the Australia. Similarly, the impact of unions is somehow never mentioned in the studies of Australian public administration (see Chapter 14, this volume), or even superannuation (see Chapter 10, this volume). The corruption ('rorting') that blights state utilities and agencies may make news, but never scholarly journals. Indeed, unlike the USA, the public's offence at corruption seems mild.

A silencing effect can also come from being preoccupied with Australia to the exclusion of other societies. The past cultivators of the Australian difference have been reasonably described as 'obsessed' with Australia (Boyd 1972); an obsession epitomized by that 'map of Australia' that any book on Australia once seemed of necessity to begin with, and which excised all trace of the neighbouring world. Thus there was a 'guiltless incuriosity' about New Zealand (Davies 1985, p. 248); and comparative studies were cautioned against as potentially 'very dangerous' (Gollan 1965, p. 1).

This incuriosity about alternatives in space is matched by a parallel incuriosity in time: Australian historians seem to have had little interest in the counterfactual.[14] The counterfactual serves the sense that 'other histories' are possible; that events need not of necessity turn out as they did; and things are not the way they are from some deep (grand?) necessity, but instead have arisen from chance, a chance that might be trivial and low. Perhaps the only extended examination of the counterfactual in Australian history is by Portus (1944)—an adherent of Australia exceptionalism—and, tellingly, his message was how little difference different happenstance would have made to the long-run course of affairs in Australia.

Another form of silence is to not talk about those who have talked about it. W. K. Hancock's *Australia* has remained unreprinted in fifty years. Despite being known, read, and saluted, it seems to constitute a samizdat.

The present work's overriding purpose is to breach this silence, and to increase the awareness of Australian non-conformity. For that purpose, this book brings together a diverse range of authors, united by the view that the topic is important and worth pondering. No deeper unity amongst the authors need be looked for: this book is not a manifesto, and its authors are not some company of 'the undersigned'.

In serving its overriding purpose, the book ranges widely, and begins with the unparalleled encounter between the Aborigines and Europeans that marked the genesis of modern Australia (Chapter 2). Yet the present work is not committed to finding exceptionalism wherever it ranges: thus one chapter argues that the temptation to see Australia as unusually secular is misplaced (Chapter 4). Neither does it commit itself to look for exceptionalism everywhere: Australia's economy and politics are this work's primary focuses. Even within the confines of the economic and political, the volume does not attempt to comprehensively survey the territory, but instead takes the measures of some prominent features of the terrain. Chapters are devoted to accounting for the vacuity of Australian federalism (Chapter 6); charting the industrial relations maze (Chapter 7), along with one of its strange progeny—compulsory superannuation (Chapter 10); dispelling the lazy-minded characterization of Australian governance as 'Westminster' (Chapter 14); pondering the 'poverty of discourse' in Australian social affairs (Chapter 5); uncovering the legacy of government ownership of railways on politics and administration (Chapter 9); puzzling out how Australian agriculture could be both so laggard and dynamic (Chapter 13); identifying 'the difference' from New Zealand, that—after so long tracing a parallel path—has now diverged so much from Australia; and furnishing a biographical insight into H. B. Higgins, one the most significant 'hero-villain-fools' of Australian history (Klapp 1954) (Chapter 12).

[14] One exception is found in Blainey's speculations on the consequences of the creation of a state of North Queensland (1980, pp. 200–4).

The constrained focus of the work entails that it is not hunting for some national spirit that would holistically explain all. And wisely so: such a quarry may not exist. What could be more idiosyncratic than Australia's intensity of labour market regulation? And what could be 'more Australian' than sport? Yet Australian sport eludes Australia's mass of labour legislation and unionization, and (unlike in the USA) is an oasis of industrial peace (Chapter 11).

Nevertheless, the present work inevitably confronts the nature of Australian society, and in doing so it may resemble the flood of books that appeared in the 1960s (Horne, Pringle, Boyd, Phillips, McGregor, Coleman . . .). But the present book is not a revival of that literature.

The 1960s literature was distinctly 'newist'; whether cautiously hailing what seemed to be coming around the corner, or impatiently hastening its advent, the whole literature had the air of a 'modern' Australia purposefully interring a traditional one. The present work, in contrast, is gripped not by a sense of the new but by the repetition of the same old story. But, it might be retorted, surely traditional Australia has, in fact, expired? A country in which in 1911 over 42.5 per cent of the population resided in rural areas has become one in which barely 11 per cent does; one where the sentimental memorializations of pre-war rustical Australia—preserved in the post-war period by Russel Ward—have mutated into a cold hatred of that terrain (Conrad 2003). One in which, in 1901, just 4.6 per cent of its inhabitants were born outside of Australia or the British Isles becomes one where 21.5 per cent have been. A country that, at time of Federation, was three-quarters Protestant becomes, by 2006, one where one third is. One, where two generations ago 70 per cent of the Catholic population voted Labor, is now one where 70 per cent of the ten most Catholic seats in New South Wales (NSW) are won by anti-Labor parties.[15] The progeny of yesterday's 'Seven Dwarves' are now the futile officialdom of various policy fiascos,[16] or are reduced to playing Polonius to Hamlet's antic disposition. Most fundamentally, characteristic Australianness just isn't what it used to be. The 'broad' Australian accent ebbs from a third of the population to barely one tenth. The masculine, nonchalant, blunt, Wild Colonial Boy (Digger, Crocodile Dundee) has been supplanted (at least in the minds of some—see Greer 2013) by the mealy-mouthed and meekly 'compliant'—or the crudely criminal.[17] Russel Ward cherished the fact that Australia only experienced its first kidnaping in 1960; from the vantage point of 2015 that fact bespeaks how far traditional Australia has receded. Are these not transformations? Or is it more remarkable that so little has changed in the face of them?

[15] See <http://www.abc.net.au/news/nsw-election-2015/guide/census/#Religion> (accessed 20 November 2015).

[16] See, for example, the Royal Commission into the Home Insulation Program 2014.

[17] Paul Hogan (2015): Australia 'is not as unique as it was. There was a spirit here that has disappeared, a bit of larrikin spirt, a bit of pioneer spirit.'

The expansion in higher education is surely a symbol of the new Australia. In 1939 14,000 students were enrolled in higher education in Australia: by 2014, domestic enrolments were a touch under 1 million. But this expansion underlines the persistence of the old, as the expansion is a replication of the format laid down for school education a century before: massive state universities, with a parallel-funded Catholic system, largely free-to-user,[18] all under a Department of Education exercising a degree of control unseen in universities in any other anglophone country (Corden 2000; Lane 2013). In Australia, history keeps on keeping on.

The 1960s literature was, additionally, overly 'Australianist'. It functioned—like all twentieth-century theorists of Australian exceptionalism—under a distinct sense of an integral 'national community'. All explanation was to arise from an integral Australia; none, it seemed, from sub-national or supra-national categories. A reaction against this false unity of an integral Australia had begun in the 1960s with the emergence of regional history. Regrettably, that regional history neglected the greatest geographical fracture of all: that between 'the two cultural and intellectual regions into which the country has always been divided' (Davies 1984, p. 57), 'the cold south' and the 'uncouth' north (Ward 1988, p. 2); a fracture that had been noted by visitors from the late nineteenth century,[19] was underlined by Sydney's rejection of Federation in the referendum of 1899,[20] and was felt throughout the subsequent century (Clark 1962; Docker 1974; Davidson 1986). Yet the existence of that fracture does not repudiate Australian exceptionalism. On the contrary, one of the unusual features of Australian society is that a vital north–south dualism has failed to truly develop, and instead the 'cold south' carves out 'all her desires and will brook no interference' (Adams 1892, p. 60). Thus, part of the understanding of Australian exceptionalism will not be locating some national essence but understanding a regional sway.

The reaction to the history of 'national community' that did eventually prevail was an overreaction to that history, and an overreaction that would have Australian exceptionalism extinguished. In the succeeding historiography, all contention would be focused on sub-national (indigenes, 'ethnics') or supra-national categories of (women, 'settlers'). There was no more

[18] No payment is required up front of Australian tertiary students, but graduates are liable to a supplementary tax on any income in excess of a certain amount. The revenue of this tax is about one fifth of the cost of current domestic students. This type of scheme was first mooted by Milton Friedman (1962, p. 105), and was first implemented by Australia.

[19] See Adams (1892, p. 59) on Sydney vs Melbourne, and Richard Twopeny on the 'Whiggism' of New South Wales and Queensland and the 'radicalism' of Victoria and South Australia. Also Dilke (1890, vol. 2, p. 484) on the greater fellow feeling with the USA in NSW and Queensland.

[20] The referendum of 20 June 1899: Sydney 'No's 35,457, Sydney 'Yes's 34,765 (Legislative Assembly of New South Wales 1899). 'Sydney' means 'Greater Sydney' as according to the usage of Clifford et al. (2006, p. 33).

Australian Legend, or Australian exceptionalism, or anything else. Australia was a postcode of international capitalism; a postcode variously inhabited by Unionists, Convicts, Militarists, Irishmen, Racists, and Pianists, but not 'Australians' (McQueen 1970).

Here is a paradox. Never has Australia been closer to constituting a postcode in a quasi-universal global society. Never has it been so palpably integrated into a globalized world: beyond the familiar technological miracles that soak it deep in the realities and attitudinizing of the rest of the world, one may note that the country saw almost 7 million visitors in 2013; 422,000 foreign students lived there; and, in 2013, 27.7 per cent of the Australian permanent population was born elsewhere, twice the proportion in the USA. But Australian exceptionalism, it appears, is strengthening rather than fading. This speaks of Australia possessing an enveloping climate of opinion as much as its own physical climate. The existence of such a climate is not premised on some homogeneity or cohesion of its components, or any consciousness of itself at all. This volume, if it hopes to achieve anything, hopes to restore some of that consciousness.

1.4 The Australian Moment

The issue of Australian exceptionalism obtains an added significance in the light of Australia's situation—not only the country's economy's exhilarating performance since the turn of the twenty-first century, and, even more, in the recently growing sense that the country has finally reached a climacteric. Australia economic history may be construed as a sequence of long booms of a duration of thirty-five to forty-five years, each followed by severe depression (McCarty 1973). Could the hour of severe depression be nigh?

Australia may be judged to have been in a long boom since 1979. In the *treize glorieuses* from 2000, Australia glided through the 'dot com' bust and through the Great Recession. The performance since 2007 has been especially remarkable (see Table 1.3).

Table 1.3 Growth Rate in GDP, 2007–13, Percentage change in $US GDP

Australia	New Zealand	Canada	USA	UK	Euroland	Japan
55	37	26.1	15.8	−9.6	2.6	12.9

The motor behind this economic feat was the 101 per cent increase in Australia's terms of trade between September 2000 and September 2011, itself driven by the explosion in China's steel production from 128 million tons in 2000 to 701 million tons in 2011, an explosion that defied sophisticated forecasts of the day. Had 'the lucky country' ever got luckier?

Yet the sentiment has now burgeoned that her luck is running out (see Garnaut 2013). The most recent data on performance is discouraging: despite her exemption from the Great Recession, Australia's measured unemployment rate in 2015 materially exceeded that of the USA.[21] Even more remarkable, despite her economy racing ahead while that of the USA crept, Australia's government deficit, as a proportion of national income in the current year, is projected to be barely different from that of the USA.[22] Looming over public discourse is the apprehension that Australian exceptionalism amounts to an indulgence of simplicity and fancy, made possible only by lenient economic circumstances; and in this sunny ease, the adult organs of calculation and restraint have atrophied, and a regression into a national infantilism has begun (see Kelly 2014). This sort of diagnosis has been challenged (see Edwards 2014). Yet whatever the correct diagnosis, in the current precarious circumstances, it is worth taking the measure of the nature of Australia's mettle.

References

Acworth, W. M. 1892. 'Government railways in a democratic state', *Economic Journal*, vol. 2, no. 8, pp. 629–36.

Adams, F. 1892. *Australian Essays*. Melbourne: William Inglis.

Archer, R. 2007. *Why Is There No Labor Party in the United States?*, Princeton, NJ: Princeton University Press.

Barcan, A. 1995. 'The state and education in Australia', *Education Research and Perspectives*, vol. 22, no. 1, pp. 22–38.

Blainey, G. 1980. *A Land Half Won*. Melbourne: Macmillan.

Bolton, G. and Gregory, H. 1992. 'The 1891 shearers strike leaders: railroaded?', *Labour History*, no. 62, pp. 116–26.

Boyd, R. 1972. *The Great Great Australian Dream*. Rushcutters Bay, NSW: Pergamon Press.

Clark, C. M. H. 1962. 'Faith' in P. Coleman (ed.), *Australian Civilization: A Symposium*. Melbourne: FW Cheshire.

Clifford, E., Green, A., and Clune, D. 2006. *The Electoral Atlas of New South Wales, 1856–2006*. Bathurst, NSW: NSW Department of Lands.

Collins, H. 1985. 'Political Ideology in Australia: The Distinctiveness of a Benthamite Society', *Daedalus*, vol. 114, no.1, pp. 147–69.

Conrad, P. 2003. *At Home in Australia*, London: Thames and Hudson.

[21] During 2015, the unemployment rate averaged at 6.1 per cent in Australia, and 5.3 percent in the USA.

[22] Australia's federal government deficit is projected to be 2.3 percent of GDP in 2015/16; that of the USA, 2.2 percent in fiscal 2016.

Corden, M. 2000. 'Australian universities: Moscow on the Molongolo', *Quadrant*, vol. 49, no. 11, pp. 7–20.

Davidson, J. (ed.). 1986. *The Sydney-Melbourne Book*. Sydney: Allen & Unwin.

Davies, A. F. 1984. 'Mass communications' in S. Encel (ed.), *Australian Society: Introductory Essays*. Melbourne: Longman Cheshire.

Davies, A. F. 1985. 'Small country blues: advantages and disadvantages of living in a small country like Australia', *Meanjin*, vol. 44, no. 2, pp. 243–52.

Department of Education and Training. 2011. *Review of Funding for Schooling: Final Report*. Canberra: Department of Education and Training.

Dilke, C. 1890. *Problems of Greater Britain*, 2 vols. London: Macmillan.

Docker, J. 1974. *Australian Cultural Elites: Intellectual Traditions in Sydney and Melbourne*. Sydney: Angus and Robertson.

Dollery, B. 2002. 'A century of vertical fiscal imbalance in Australian federalism', *History of Economics Review*, no. 36, pp. 26–43.

Edwards, J. 2014. *Beyond the Boom*. Sydney: Penguin.

Encel, S. 1960. 'The concept of the state in Australian politics', *Australian Journal of Politics and History*,vol. 6, no.1 pp. 62–76.

Fairfield, C. 1891. 'State socialism in the Antipodes' in T. Mackay (ed.), *A Plea for Liberty: An Argument against Socialism and Socialistic Legislation*. London: John Murray.

Friedman, M. (with R. Friedman). 1962. *Capitalism and Freedom*. Chicago: University of Chicago Press.

Garnaut, R. 2013. *Dog Days: Australia after the Boom*. Melbourne: Redback.

Gollan, R. 1965. 'American populism and Australian utopianism', *Labour History*, no. 9, pp. 15–21.

Goodrich, C. 1968. 'State in, state out: a pattern of development policy', *Journal of Economic Issues*, vol. 2, no. 4, pp. 365–83.

Gramlich, E. 1984. '"A fair go": fiscal federalism arrangements in Australia' in R. E. Caves and L. B. Krause (eds.), *The Australian Economy: A View from the North*. Washington, DC: Brookings Institution.

Greer, G. 2013. 'Cut it out', *Australian Financial Review*, 25–28 January.

Hogan, P. 2015. 'I'm the last larrikin left, says Hoges', *Sunday Telegraph*, 7 June, p. 25.

Jha, T. and Buckingham, J. 2015. *Free to Choose Charter Schools: How Charter and For-Profit Schools Can Boost Public Education*, CIS Research Report no. 6. Sydney: Centre for Independent Studies.

Kelly, P. 1994. *The End of Certainty: Power, Politics and Business in Australia*. St. Leonards, NSW: Allen & Unwin.

Kelly, P. 2014. 'The politics of denial', *The Australian*, 5 July, p. 16.

Klapp, O. E. 1954. 'Heroes, villains and fools, as agents of social control', *American Sociological Review*, vol. 19, no. 1, pp. 56–62.

Lake, M. 2013. '"This great America": HB Higgins and transnational progressivism', *Australian Historical Studies*, vol. 44, no. 2, pp. 172–88.

Lane, B. 2013. 'Quality regulator "at the extreme end"', *The Australian*, 19 June, p. 33.

Legislative Assembly of New South Wales. 1899. *Submission of the Australasian Federal Constitution to the Electors of New South Wales under the Australasian Federal Enabling Act*. Sydney: Legislative Assembly of New South Wales.

McCarty, J. 1973. 'A general approach to Australian economic development 1845–1895', *Historian*, no. 25, pp. 50–9.

Macfarlane, A. 1978. *The Origins of English Individualism: The Family, Property and Social Transition*. Oxford: Blackwell.

McQueen, H. 1970. *A New Britannia: An Argument concerning the Social Origins of Australian Radicalism and Nationalism*. Melbourne: Penguin.

Métin, A. [1901] 1977. *Socialism without Doctrine*, trans. R Ward. Chippendale, NSW: Alternative Publishing Co-operative.

Micklethwait, J. and Wooldridge, A. 2014. *The Fourth Revolution: The Global Race to Reinvent the State*. London: Allen Lane.

Moore, C. 2014. 'Are freedom's enemies being proved right?', *Daily Telegraph*, 1 June, p. 21.

Nethercote, J. 2012. 'Unearthing the Seven Dwarfs and the age of mandarins', *National Centre of Biography*, Australian National University, <http://adb.anu.edu.au/essay/5/text26981> (accessed 5 October 2012).

OECD (Organisation of Economic Co-Operation and Development) 2015. 'Real minimum wages', 'http://stats.oecd.org/Index.aspx?DataSetCode=RMW, 14 December 2015.

Partridge, P. H. 1968. *Society, Schools, and Progress in Australia*. New York: Pergamon Press.

Portus, G. V. 1944. *They Wanted to Rule the World: Studies of Six Dictators, and Other Essays*. Sydney: Angus and Robertson.

Quinlan, M. 1998. 'Regulating labour in a colonial context: maritime labour legislation in the Australian colonies, 1788–1850', *Australian Historical Studies*, vol. 29, no. 111, pp. 303–24.

Roe, M. 1984. *Nine Australian Progressives: Vitalism in Bourgeois Social Thought, 1890–1960*. Brisbane: University of Queensland Press.

Sawer, G. 1952. 'The record of judicial review' in G. Sawer (ed.), *Federalism: An Australian Jubilee Study*. Melbourne: FW Cheshire.

Schwab, K. and Sala-i-Martin, X. 2014. *The Global Competitiveness Report 2014–2015*. Switzerland: World Economic Forum.

Thomas, L. M. 1962. *The Development of the Labour Movement in the Sydney District of New South Wales*. Canberra: Australian Society for the Study of Labour History.

Walter, J. 2007. 'Alan Fraser Davies', in *Australian Dictionary of Biography*, vol. 17. Melbourne: Melbourne University Press.

Ward, R. 1988. *A Radical Life*. Crows Nest, NSW: Allen & Unwin.

Whiteford, P. 1998. 'Is Australia particularly unequal? Traditional and new views' in S. Paul and B. Cass (eds.), *Contesting the Australian Way: States, Markets and Civil Society*. Melbourne: Cambridge University Press.

2

Australian Exceptionalism

A Personal View

Geoffrey Blainey

Australia is marvelled at because of its unique fauna and flora, and its unusual 'natural history'. Australia is also exceptional in its human history. Few other countries have had so many important episodes or events that, by world standards, are exceptional.

Most Australians familiar with their country's history might well protest: what precisely has been exceptional? In fact Australia has been unusual in the length of its recorded human history and in the magnitude of the most influential event of that history—the rising of the seas, which drowned a huge area of inhabited land, completely changed the map, and isolated all Australians from the outside world. (Mulvaney and Kamminga 1999, pp. 103, 331–2). Australia is exceptional because it experienced perhaps the most insoluble confrontation of cultures and economies so far recorded in human history; because of the tug it exercised on the world's economy in the mid-1850s, when its population was tiny; because it is one of the oldest, continuous democracies in the world; and because its people achieved, in the modern phase of their history, the highest standard of living in the world, only to quickly lose that claim when it experienced, perhaps through overconfidence, one of the gravest financial crashes known in the nineteenth century.

After the Second World War, Australia commenced an unprecedented switch, in its commerce and its people, from a nation of European ancestry to, prospectively, a European–Asian nation. An earlier exceptional trend, persisting for more than a century and a half, was the degree to which males outnumbered females. Also unusual were the geographical influences: the long isolation of Aboriginal Australia from the outside world; the remoteness of modern Australia, in time and distance, from the European homeland that was for long the source of nearly all of its institutions and ideas; and the extreme variability of Australia's long-term climate—a powerful fact which is perhaps glimpsed more than realized by many historians.

Some of these exceptional changes and episodes have evoked praise, others have been deplored, but together they shaped not only a vanished Australia but also the one we know today.

2.1 Worlds Apart: Nomads and the Industrial Revolution

Australia has experienced a human history that is much longer than any other New World nation or society. Nearly all of Australia's long history has centred on the hunters and gatherers, who arrived from South-East Asia as the first settlers when Australia and New Guinea formed one continent. For some 50,000 years they continued to practise a semi-nomadic way of life. In the face of several setbacks of a magnitude not experienced in the modern history of this land, Aborigines survived, succeeded, and sometimes triumphed.

The rising of the seas—commencing fewer than 20,000 years ago—largely isolated the Aborigines. The present continent of Australia, in full view of generations of its inhabitants, was slowly cut off from New Guinea, and severed from Tasmania. The rising seas created or shaped many of the landmarks of the east coast of the continent, including the Torres Strait and its islands, the Great Barrier Reef, Sydney Harbour, and Port Phillip Bay. The higher sea levels also created Kangaroo Island, the Swan River estuary, the Kimberley archipelago, the Gulf of Carpentaria, and the Derwent estuary (Blainey 2015, ch. 6). These tumultuous changes were part of an astonishing period of global warming that spread the eucalyptus over a huge area of Australia (Pyne 1991, ch. 1), shaped the fern gullies of Gippsland and the wide expanse of Mallee scrub, landscaped the Kakadu swamps, and altered the main deserts of the interior for better or worse.

By isolating Australia from the outside world, the rising seas largely deprived the Aborigines of the benefits—and the drawbacks—of the first major economic revolution in human history: the slow birth of agriculture and pastoralism in the Middle East and other parts of the northern hemisphere. In most of the world—but not in Australia—the farmers and the keepers of flocks and herds eventually supplanted the hunters and gatherers (Burroughs 2005, pp. 188–92). The food supply of the world was augmented, and its population multiplied. In Australia, in contrast, economic change, though present, was slower and less decisive.

The domestication of plants and animals was even more a political than an economic revolution. There can be no farms, no agriculture, without a disciplined workforce, and a strong army that protects the whole territory from invaders. There can be no agriculture without the help of new customs and institutions that safeguarded crops and herds, and new granaries and other places for storing food. The revolution was marked by the centralizing of power, the rise of strong despots ruling a far bigger area than was normally controlled by a typical nomadic tribe or 'nation', and the rise of professional soldiers, larger armies, and permanent forts. The new way of life encouraged the division of labour. It was marked by the growth of knowledge specialists, including metallurgists, potters, bureaucrats, and priests. It led to specialist occupations such as gardeners, shepherds, millers, builders, and metal workers—for the invention of iron and bronze is a later part of what is called the Neolithic Revolution. In 1788, there were no signs of these new rulers, specialists, and institutions in Australia, though they could be seen everywhere in Asia and Europe.

Thus Australia was 'exceptional' in standing, for such a long span of time, outside the economic and political revolution created by the domesticating of plants and animals. No other large part of the world stayed outside. No other large territory, with considerable areas of favourable climate and soil, escaped this revolution for so long. In contrast, New Guinea and the Torres Strait Islands, and, of course, New Zealand (Belich 2001, ch. 2), became, at different stages and in varying degrees, some of the beneficiaries of the Neolithic Revolution.

When the first British settlers landed in Sydney in 1788 they unknowingly faced one of the sharpest contrasts in the recorded history of the world. Two distinct cultures, ways of life, and political and economic systems came face to face, and could not comprehend each other. A country embarking on the Industrial Revolution and the age of steam suddenly confronted several hundred mini-republics that practised many impressive skills but could not boil water. Aborigines possessed no agriculture and metallurgy as we know them, and could not read and write. The British and the Aboriginal attitudes to land tenure, to personal possessions, and to family, marriage and child-rearing, and death were far apart. One simple contrast: a nomadic people usually do not accumulate possessions, for they were usually a burden; and likewise nomadic people do not occupy the land in the same way as agriculturists. Moreover, the new British and the old Aborigines had no common language, and the first meetings were often marred by simple misunderstandings. Their mutual puzzlement, in some facets of daily life, would persist, even as the twenty-first century dawned (Blainey 2015, pp. x, 215).

2.2 Making Peace: Australia and New Zealand

There was no prospect of signing a treaty between Britain and, say, five, let alone several hundred, Aboriginal tribes or nations. Even if, in 1788, a treaty had been miraculously signed—between Governor Phillip and, say, the tribes on or nearest Sydney harbour—it would not have lasted long. Aborigines could not envisage the effects of the intrusion in their homelands of large numbers of alien livestock. The British could not envisage the effects of the multiplying flocks of sheep on the Aborigines' traditional food supplies and ceremonies. It is hard to envisage four Aboriginal tribes or nations agreeing amongst themselves, let alone with a British governor. Intermittent warfare soon broke out between the new settlers and local Aborigines. The nomads had no hope of an ultimate victory. Unlike the native North Americans and the New Zealand Māori, they did not often adopt firearms nor use them effectively. The Aborigines also fought intermittently amongst themselves. Traditional enmities persisted even in the face of an alien invader.

In warfare with the British invaders, deaths were numerous. But they were small compared to deaths caused by the spread of unfamiliar diseases. Aborigines had no immunity to smallpox, influenza, measles, and other imported diseases (Blainey 2015, pp. 323–4). The population so declined that, by 1910, it was widely predicted that full-blood Aborigines would completely disappear.

New Zealand too suffered a less drastic decline in native population, and also displayed a more decisive and effective leadership structure when faced with warfare. The Māori spoke a common Polynesian language whereas the Aborigines were divided by several hundred languages. The Māori had larger tribes and held more fighting men in each, they had forts to which they could retreat, and they acquired firearms (Belich 2001, pp. 75–81). Against the same British invader they fought more effectively, if no more bravely, than the Aborigines. Indeed the British had to land a large army in New Zealand to ensure victory. More significantly, the Māori knew how to negotiate. They understood to an impressive degree the society that was trying to take them over or occupy large areas of their traditional lands. They also won begrudging respect. By 1867 Māori men had received the right to vote, a specific quota of seats in parliament, and the retention of large areas of their homeland (Moon 2013, p. 228). In these gains the Māori generally were far ahead of Australia's Aborigines.

2.3 Australia: an Early Showplace of Mass Prosperity

Measured by some criteria, Australia was the world's surprise packet for much of the nineteenth century. Between 1830 and 1850 its standard of living increased, thanks to the output of wool, and then for another twenty years when gold provided more wealth than wool.

The four decades from 1851 to 1890 saw fast economic development. The population multiplied by almost ten. Just imagine today's Australia displaying a similar pace of growth in the next forty years. It would mean that the present population of 23 million would exceed 200 million before the year 2055. In the initial gold era, Victoria was the leader and Melbourne, its capital, passed Sydney in population; but every colony enjoyed one or more phases of fast economic growth: Western Australia was the exception, lagging until the 1890s. The most backward of the seven Australasian colonies, it came alive through gold in the 1890s, trebling its recorded population in the space of ten years. As a trigger of growth, gold was dynamic over a far larger geographical area in Australia than in the comparable gold countries of North America and South Africa. Furthermore, Australia's rushes—and New Zealand's too—began when the local economy was tiny and therefore was more easily transformed by a dynamic new activity.

In the first forty years after the initial discoveries, gold's impact on Australia was formidable. Most historians—persuaded by the calculations of Noel G. Butlin—now believe that, for about four decades, the Australian people enjoyed the highest—or close to the highest—standard of living in the world (White 1992, p. 155). Even at the first peak of the gold output, in the mid-1850s, Australia's standard of living probably was amongst the highest. The Australian ports and gold-diggings were heavy consumers of luxuries, including natural ice imported in sailing ships from Boston at high prices (Blainey 1966, pp. 275–6). This was simply one of many mirrors of a high standard of living. By 1889, urbanization and the kind of consumer life lived in the cities were others (Frost 2015, p. 250). Of the declining population of Aborigines, most did not share noticeably, and many did not share at all, in these gains. Large numbers, of course, lived totally outside the European-style economy and had barely heard of it.

In explaining Australia's high per capita standard of living, especially in the period 1850–90, the exploitation of grasslands and mineral deposits and other new natural resources was vital. Also important were the high flow of British capital at low rates of interest, the adoption of new British technology in many fields, the introduction of suitable livestock and crops from the northern hemisphere, and the presence for four decades of relatively favourable weather in the south-eastern quarter of the continent. Ample rain was a boon in an era when rural production was vital to the standard of living. A little-recognized asset was that in the nineteenth century most immigrants came from the British Isles, which, at that time, were, compared to most other peoples, sympathetic to new technology. After 1890, as we shall see in section 2.8, Australia's relatively high income began to fall on the international ladder.

2.4 Australian Gold Glitters across the Seas

There was another exceptional hallmark in the 1850s. Australia was perhaps more important in the world economy than ever before or after. Australians—though few in numbers—represented one of the main global markets at a time when Britain was the world's leading manufacturer. A heavy exporter and importer, Britain's cargoes from England to the wealthy Australian cities were on a very large scale, and included enormous quantities of shoes and boots, alcoholic spirits, and other costly or luxurious items that were in high demand. In 1853 a total of 15 per cent of Britain's exports went to Australia. Was there ever, in modern history, another example of so few people exercising such purchasing power and, in the process, helping to revive the world's most influential economy? (Blainey 1963, ch. 5).

The global economy in the mid-1840s had been depressed, and its revival in the following decade owed much to the enormous purchasing power generated by the two main goldfields, California and south-east Australia. One characteristic of the 1850s was rapid inflation globally, which came after one-third of a century of falling prices (Blainey 1963, pp. 62–3). There has long been debate about the major causes of that decade of unusual inflation, but one cause was the world's mental reaction to the soaring output of gold. The conviction was strong that the astonishing surge in the world's annual gold output would lead to a fast rise in the general price level. In short, the anticipation of higher prices became, in the inflationary 1850s as in the inflationary 1970s, a cause of higher prices.

The parallels between those two decades of extreme inflation—decades 120 years apart—deserve a brief comment. Central to the inflation was the behaviour and influence of two strategic commodities, New World gold in the first period and Middle East oil in the second (McLean 2013, ch. 9). Now that gold is no longer a pivot of the financial and banking systems we forget how pivotal it once was. Gold was then, like oil is today, a strategic commodity.

In essence, Australia in the 1850s—perhaps for the only time in its history—held an unusually powerful role. In the two world wars it held no such role. Even its long-term pre-1980 role as a vital source of wool for the world, and its recent role as a vital supplier of minerals to a powerful China, cannot realistically be compared to its dynamic influence on the world's economy in the 1850s.

2.5 Wool and Gold: Two Commodities that Wed

Between 1851 and about 1910 Australia had two dominating but rival exports—gold and wool. Probably no other country held such a mix of exports; one (gold) with a static price, and the other (wool) with a fluctuating price. Whereas the price of wool rose when the world economy was prospering, the nominal price of gold was static. In Australia, gold-mining, though such a cyclical industry, tended to flatten out the economic fluctuations in a way not visible in North America and South Africa. When the price of wool was low on the world markets, the price of gold in real terms tended to be relatively high. Thus the exploration for gold and the mining of gold were stimulated at the very times when wool was producing less income.

2.6 From Despotism to Democracy: a Swift Transition

Australia, though commonly described as a young nation, owns an unusual political pedigree. It is one of the oldest, continuous democracies in the world. It became a democracy in the 1850s, when such a political system was operating in no more than a handful of countries. Even to designate these countries as democratic is open to dispute. The UK in 1860 was perhaps not a democracy. Only a small fraction of adults had the right to vote, and because all those entitled to vote had to declare their vote in public—there was no secret ballot—they could be intimidated. A tenant farmer or the employee of a big manufacturer or merchant could easily be pressed into voting for the candidate favoured by his master. Even in the USA, one of the grandfathers of modern democracy, important groups had no right to vote. For example, slaves had no vote, and long after the end of the American Civil War most Afro-Americans could not vote. France could be called a democracy in revolutionary 1792, but not for long. Democracy in France was frail and sometimes tottering until 1875 when adult male suffrage was endorsed; but French democracy collapsed again in 1940.

Britain was far behind Australia in achieving adult male suffrage, and so, too, was almost every country in Europe. Even in the British overseas colonies, with their sympathies towards democracy, New Zealand, though a slow starter, became one of the few stars. Canada, seemingly so democratic and operating a vigorous form of parliamentary government after the forming of the Confederation in 1867, did not introduce universal adult-male franchise until years after Australia became a federation in 1901.

Australia became a full-blooded democracy in the late 1850s, achieving it with lightning speed. Only thirty years previously it had consisted of two convict colonies, ruled by governors whose personal power was magnified because most of their subjects were prisoners or ex-prisoners. Moreover, the governors were so remote geographically that Britain's control of them and their decisions was loose. One year might elapse between the governor writing an urgent despatch to London, and the arrival of an official reply. And yet, from this prison-like regime, democracy speedily emerged. This was an exceptional outcome.

In 1860 almost nine of every ten white Australians lived in those colonies where every man had the right to vote. Perhaps only one other country of the world—the USA—had a higher proportion. Furthermore, Australian parliamentary elections were held every three years, and a local politician was more accountable than his counterpart in any European or North American parliament. Victoria and South Australia in 1856 became the first territories in which elections were conducted by secret ballot: a reform which prevented an employee from being intimidated or unduly influenced by his employer or landlord at the public polling-place. Slowly the remainder of the semi-democratic world adopted this device, calling it either the Australian or Victorian Ballot. Here, in Australia, was an infant democracy, eager to experiment.

Another leap forward in Australian democracy was made at the end of the century. New Zealand became the first country in the world to give women the vote, and Australia was the first to give them both the vote and the right to stand for parliament.

Even then, in the main Australian colonies, democracy was still hampered. An upper house or legislative council was dominated usually by the wealthier sectors of society; but it had to be wary of blocking any legislation which had massive popular support. The big sheep-owners were powerful in these upper houses but often they lowered their colours to the lower house in a political crisis. Slowly the upper houses surrendered much of their power. A more important impediment to Australian democracy in the long term was the long absence of full rights for Aborigines. It is difficult to summarize, even in two pages, the position of Aborigines, for their civic rights differed from colony to colony, from state to state, and decade to decade. Thus, in the two most populous states, many Aborigines exercised a right to vote long before and long after 1901. But in Queensland and Western Australia—the two biggest states in area—few Aborigines had the right to vote even as recently as 1945. Throughout the twentieth century, the Aborigines, whether enfranchised or not, represented only a tiny proportion of Australia's population.

For many well-informed British people, Australia's first democratic experiment had been a dangerous piece of political chemistry. Many of London's more conservative politicians feared that Australia might adopt universal adult suffrage (Hirst 1988, p. 71). In 1851 *The Times*, a daily journal of high prestige, argued that in a democratic system, 'the lowest types were elected to parliament, governments were unstable, inefficient and corrupt and sanctioned the wildest prejudices of the mob.' At its birth Australian democracy was definitely an example of exceptionalism. Yet the fact that Australia today is one of the oldest continuous democracies may owe much to the sad fact that

Hitler's conquests temporarily snuffed out most of the vigorous democracies in Europe.

Why did the colonies move so quickly from despotism to an advanced kind of democracy at a time when democratic states in the world were few? The great majority of immigrants, especially in the 1840s and 1850s, came from the British Isles where a restricted and highly cautious form of democracy was already being practised. Moreover, these immigrants were largely people who possessed no vote at home but believed—more perhaps than any previous generation—that they should be entitled to a vote.

The quick rise of an advanced democracy in Australia also owed much to a group of British politicians and critics. Recalling the breakaway of the North American colonies and the outbreak of the American War of Independence in the 1770s, they tended to believe that overseas colonies would inevitably break away unless they were treated sensitively and favourably. Indeed, the seven colonies in Australasia might eventually secede, even if they were humoured and courted by the mother country. These more radical British politicians and critics were sympathetic to the creation in both Canada and Australasia of self-governing colonies with a franchise and structure notably more democratic than that prevailing in the British Isles. In line with the decay of the mercantilist vision of empire, such countries received a kind of economic freedom not usually accorded to colonies: the right to impose a protective tariff against goods exported from the motherland.

2.7 How a Populist Democracy Flavoured Economic Life

As one of the earliest democracies, Australia, in the second half of the nineteenth century, might have been expected to pursue distinctive economic policies. The poorer people exercised more political weight than in almost any other country, and so certain equalitarian trends were evident in new laws. The state could interfere more often: it could take on additional duties; it could occasionally redistribute wealth.

This kind of exceptionalism did occur, though on a moderate more than a sweeping scale. For example, in England, the USA, and many other countries, the private companies operated nearly all the railways. In contrast, after the first private railway companies in Victoria and New South Wales (NSW) failed in the 1850s, the governments became the dominant builders and operators of railways (Ergas and Pincus 2015, pp. 234–5). By 1900 the government-owned railways were the biggest business enterprises in Australia and dwarfed any single mining and manufacturing and financial company in their revenue, and in the number of their employees. In Australia, government railways were pace-setters in providing secure employment, in paying higher wages, and even in providing—at the government's request—work for the unemployed in a time of recession.

That Australia was a leader in providing free and compulsory and secular education was partly a result of the ultra-democratic parliaments. Victoria passed the first of these reforms in 1872, when it was the most populous Australian colony, and NSW soon copied Victoria. The steady move away from government subsidy for fee-paying denominational schools, towards the total government financing of free secular schools, was, in effect, the nationalizing of the largest sector of the education system in every colony. Only the Catholics objected emphatically. Henceforth, until the 1960s, they paid for their own primary schools—a financial burden for those numerous Catholic families who stood near the bottom of the income ladder.

The ultra-democratic parliaments—especially in NSW, Victoria, and South Australia—affected economic and social life in other ways, whether spectacularly or quietly. Even before 1900 they initiated the compulsory arbitration of industrial disputes; they initiated the setting of a minimum wage in certain industries; they permitted shorter working hours in certain major industries; and they tended to favour the small landholder at the expense of the large. They provided fertile ground for the rise of trade unions, and for the rise of a Labor Party which became perhaps the first in the world to hold the reins of government. Labor held office for one week in the colony of Queensland in 1899 and won its first, if brief, federal term in 1904; the first national Labor government anywhere. Here was a triumph in exceptionalism.

2.8 After the Panic

Australia, from 1851 to 1890, passed through an exceptional phase of achievement. Then came depression and an unpredicted era of economic setbacks.

It has been customary to view Australia's depression of the 1890s as essentially the effect of the speculative boom and the economic hysteria of the late 1880s. Without doubt, the 'property bubble' of the 1880s and the cracks already visible in the banking system were dangerous and ultimately damaging (Maddock 2015, pp. 272–4). Add to these weaknesses the global decline in the prices of wool, the country's main export. These, however, were not the cause. The depression was made deeper by the liquidity crisis of 1893 and the absence, in every Australian colony, of that mechanism available in London, Washington, Vienna, and many other capital cities for speedily halting a run on the banks. The mechanism was simply to declare that bank notes were temporarily the legal tender. Through overconfidence, however, the various Australian banking laws had no such provision.

No stampede for gold, no pressure on liquidity, had endangered a major bank in Australia until the early 1890s. Minor banks had fallen, but not major banks. The stampede of 1893 was almost unthinkable—such was the outward success of the banking system in Australasia. The unthinkable occurred. Half of all the deposits in the Australian financial system were in banks which had to close their doors and then reconstruct their business. Many of those deposits were partly or fully locked up for years. The panic of 1893 made the depression deeper and it severely damaged, in the medium and long term, Australasia's reputation as a safe and attractive haven for money. The banking crash in Australia was probably more damaging than that in any other country in the 1890s (Blainey, 1980, p. 328).

Then came a long drought. The pre-1890 optimism about the climate had been breath-taking (Blainey 1980, pp. 352–3). The Federation Drought was devastating. A little-known statistic from the Commonwealth Bureau of Meteorology is that since 1900, when a nationwide annual rainfall could be calculated, the two years of lowest rainfall were not in the vividly remembered drought of the twenty-first century, but in 1902 and 1905. The population of sheep was almost halved. In essence, the bank crashes and the drought initiated the long-term decline of Australian incomes relative to American incomes (McLean 2013, p. 139).

2.9 Where Would Socialism First Sprout? Australasia or Russia?

The federation of the six colonies—stirred mainly by those colonies suffering most severely from the economic slump of the 1890s—was achieved in 1901. In the next twenty years, a new round of political experiments was made, the states initially being the busiest experimenters. Compulsory and preferential voting (PV) were amongst the innovations.

After the 1890s interventionism became almost normal. Regulationism soared as a general ideology, especially in the years 1900 to 1925. Many governments set up state business enterprises. Queensland, for example, founded state butcher's shops and even planned a state steel industry which would ship its iron ore from Yampi Sound in Western Australia. The federal government created its own shipping line in the First World War, but sold it in the 1920s. Expensive reservoirs and irrigation or hydroelectric schemes became a priority of state governments. Welfare schemes, ranging from old-age pensions to a basic wage, also became the vogue in the period 1895–1914.

Free trade, which was a semi-religion preached more than it was practised in the late nineteenth century, declined during the first decade of the twentieth. The economists remained true believers; those who managed the economy acquired other ideas. In the new federal parliament that first met in Melbourne in 1901, two of the three political parties usually advocated free trade, but Labor soon became protectionist, and the Free Trade Party of George Reid fused with the protectionist Liberals under Alfred Deakin in 1909 and joined the protectionist movement. In 1909 the federal protective tariff became high, and manufacturing soared. A new political party, the Country Party (now called the Nationals), was strong enough in 1923 to become almost an equal partner in S. M. Bruce's right-wing government. Initially free trade in sympathies, it joined the protectionist orchestra as the new conductor. Aid to a wide variety of rural industries became federal policy. In the 1930s even the gold-mining industry, less influential than in 1900, gained government subsidies.

The federal government penetrated far into the field of taxation, which, in 1901, had been largely the realm of the six states. Soon there was a federal income tax and a federal land tax, as well as federal old-age pensions. A minor borrower on the British loan market before 1914, the federal government became the main borrower and never looked back—except to observe occasionally the mounting public debt. Some of these changes are the themes of detailed chapters in this book. Matching the more radical mood in Australia, beginning in the 1890s, was a second wave of parliamentary reforms, including votes for women. They form part of Australia's exceptionalism, in the eyes of political scientists.

Just before 1914 the question was increasingly posed: which would be the world's first country to practise a form of socialism. Czarist Russia was rarely mentioned. New Zealand and Australia were widely predicted to become the first semi-socialist states in the world. The Russian revolutions in 1917 ended that prediction. The high point of economic radicalism in Australia was the decision of the federal Labor government in 1947 to nationalize the banks—a decision thwarted first by the High Court, and then by the electors. The definite swing away from this long era of interventionism and state activism probably began in the 1970s.

2.10 Immigration: an Exceptional History

Australia was first colonized by Western Europe, a half-continent which was exceptionally remote from Australia. The British Isles, with a little help from Germany, supplied most long-term migrants, and they, in turn, shaped nearly every facet of Australian life, whether law, politics, religion, sport, or the arts. The composition of Australia's population for at least sixteen decades differed from that of other New World lands settled increasingly by Europeans. It lacked the Spanish and Portuguese intake in Latin America and the French intake in Canada. It lacked the Dutch inflow in South Africa. For at least 170 years it lacked the more diverse inflow of Europeans into the USA.

A characteristic of Australasia was that, for a long period, a high proportion of its immigrants arrived only because their shipping fares were subsidized or fully paid for. The 160,000 convicts arriving before 1868, when the last British convict landed in Western Australia, were fully paid for. More than half of the free migrants—known usually as assisted migrants—arriving before 1970 came in chartered migrant ships or in the mail steamships, and were enticed into the country by subsidies from the Australian or British governments. In contrast, it was cheaper for European emigrants to go to the Americas than to Australia. Moreover, they had a higher chance of returning home if they were disappointed by the new pioneering life in North America. The climate and vegetation of North America, especially, was also more to their liking (Blainey, 1966, ch. 7).

Cheap land in North America was another magnet. In the face of these attractions, Australia, in the period 1788 to, say, 1914, could not compete. A subsidy was vital. Naturally the government which paid the subsidy selected the migrants: naturally they preferred British migrants. In the period 1840 to 1900, South Australia and Queensland chose a minority of German migrants, but elsewhere migrants from the British Isles were the dominant category amongst the assisted incomers.

The assisted migrants typified Australia and New Zealand. That had exceptional consequences. The British and Australian governments regulated shipboard health and living conditions, and food supplies on the long voyage to Australia and New Zealand: most migrants were their responsibility. In contrast, transatlantic migrants were not treated so benevolently. When the assisted migrants landed, they expected the government to provide work for them, if the economy was struggling. Moreover, at very lean times, governments arranged to recruit fewer immigrants or none. In the depressed 1890s, assisted as well as free migration to Australia almost ceased.

It is reasonable to suggest that this distinctive long-term recruiting scheme not only increased the tendency of migrants to expect and encourage an activist government in the new land of hope, but also helped to pave the way for the rise of trade unions, which, by 1890, held unusual power in many Australian industries. The trade unions' power ultimately depended more on their ability to retain members in bad times than in good times. The distinctive immigration policy often prevented an inrush of newcomers in bad times. The unions' power also helped the rise of the Labor Party, which vigorously and gladly accentuated this trend towards regulationism after 1900.

The gold rushes of the 1850s attracted a very high proportion of unassisted migrants. Most were men, especially single men. This initially aggravated the serious shortage of women that was a hallmark of British Australia. In 1830, about 75 per cent of Australia's white population was male, and in 1851 there were still 138 males for every 100 females, though the ratio was much higher in Victoria (Vamplew 1987, pp. 23–33). The First World War marked the first time that females equalled males in an official Australian population count. This unique statistic was made possible largely because several hundred thousand men were away—they were fighting in Europe. After the surviving soldiers returned, the male ascendancy returned and was quite pronounced in the 1930s. Without a long-term policy of assisted migration, the shortage of women would have been larger, and persisted longer. Traditionally, the scarcity of women had been larger in the countryside and outback than in the big towns. Thus it was notable in Western Australia and its booming goldfields, where, in 1901, there were 158 males for every 100 females. In the same year, the Northern Territory's tiny population consisted of 558 males for every 100 females (Vamplew 1987, ch. 3). In that total, the ubiquitous Chinese—mostly males—were systematically counted but not the Aborigines, who mostly lived in remote places.

The high proportion of men, especially single men, in the population in the mid-nineteenth century helps to explain the nation's increasing premium on leisure. Many workmen with a high standard of living now called for shorter working hours rather than for higher pay, and they were more likely to win their claims if they were government employees or builders working on government contracts. Many of Sydney and Melbourne's building workers, especially the stonemasons, achieved an eight-hour day in 1855 and 1856. The hot summers spurred their demand. The movement for a shorter working day and for a half-holiday on Saturday (as well as the traditional religious holiday for Sunday) was also strong in public works, the government-owned railways, and also the gold mines. The rise of Australian Rules football in Melbourne by 1880 to be one of the most popular winter spectator sports in the world owed much to the abundance of public parklands and to the new Saturday half-holiday. It was not, strictly speaking, a half-holiday, for many workplaces opened early and closed only at 2 p.m. Therefore, football matches did not usually begin until 3 p.m., and in midwinter they finished in near-darkness.

Indeed, the mania for spectator sport—and its rising role as an avenue for Australian nationalism—would have been impossible but for the shorter working hours in many city and town occupations. Likewise, the crowds attending horse races were enlarged by the public holidays which were more frequent in Australia than in the British Isles. As early as 1877, Melbourne enjoyed a public holiday on the Tuesday of the Melbourne Cup. The spread of the eight-hour day, however, was not as quick as is commonly believed, and in 1900 probably half of the workforce in Australia worked more than 48 hours a week.

2.11 The Compass Needle Swings from Britain to Asia

The impact of the British Isles on Australia, for more than a century and a half, was powerful. Britain was the main source of the democracy, the language, new technology, education methods, the system of justice, and all but one of the major religious denominations—the Lutherans. In defence and commerce, Britain and Australia were tightly linked, though the trading ties were slowly loosening after about 1880, when Germany and France increased their share of Australian commerce. The First World War and the opening years of the Second World War temporarily enhanced those British ties. In population, defence, and political and many other ties, Britain remained central.

Proximity to South and East Asia made Australia unlike the typical British-settler colonies and dominions. Thus, in the 1850s, Victoria attracted an early wave of Chinese migration. Other waves followed, to NSW, Queensland, Tasmania, and South Australia's own Northern Territory. On at least five occasions in the period 1857–77, Chinese diggers on the goldfields, their favourite destination, were attacked by mobs.

Not once in the nineteenth century were the Chinese as an ethnic group entirely banned from entering Australia, but they were heavily taxed at the point of arrival. Such taxes increasingly prevented them from arriving in a faster stream, and sometimes prohibited them from working on new goldfields. Western Australia was the last to receive Chinese migrants in some numbers, but, like the other colonies, it firmly restricted them in 1897.

Finally, in 1901, the new federal parliament resolved, with a few trivial exceptions, to admit no Chinese, Indians, Pacific Islanders, or other forms of cheap and energetic labour. The decision, for decades, had strong economic consequences. Australia, in effect, declared itself to be a dear-labour country. Henceforth, any natural resources or industries that required very cheap labour tended to be neglected or abandoned.

Hitherto, much of the economic development inside the four tenths of the nation which lay in the tropics had been fostered by cheap labour. The economy in the tropics had relied on the Afghan camel-drivers, the Chinese railway builders and gardeners in the Northern Territory, and the Chinese gold miners in most of the new goldfields. It had also depended on the Pacific Islanders working on the sugar plantations on the Pacific coast, and the Japanese and other Asians who manned the pearling fleets in a few Australian tropical ports. The pastoral industry before 1900 had also relied on imported low-wage labour as well as the local Aborigines. With the decline of imported labour, the Aborigines were the main workers on numerous cattle stations, but they had little interest in sheep stations and sugar farms and—until recent years—in most of the semi-skilled and unskilled occupations in tropical Australia.

It is reasonable to suggest that if, after 1900, there had been a colony covering all tropical Australia, with its own seat of government guiding its special economic interests, and a right to select cheaper forms of labour, the tropical north would have advanced more rapidly. Instead, the entire and vast region of tropical Australia was ruled by capital cities, which lay in the 60 per cent of the nation standing to the south of the Tropic of Capricornia.

The failure to create any new fully-fledged colony or state after 1859, when Queensland was founded as a breakaway from NSW, was a vital event or non-event. Whereas many new states were created in the USA after 1859, not one was created in Australia—except the large Northern Territory and tiny Australian Capital Territory, which, at best, are half-states. A new colony or state, created in, say, 1860 or 1889, and based entirely in the tropics, would have formed its own policy on immigration, and probably would not have been a democracy in the Australian style. Whether such a colony would have resolved to enter—or been permitted to enter—the Australian federation in 1901 is doubtful.

Australia had remained in ancestry, for much of its history since 1788, a child of the British Isles. On the other hand, largely hidden from sight was an Aboriginal component which increasingly intermarried with the Anglo-Celtic component. After 1945, and the shock of Japanese military victories so close to Australia, came a population somersault. Australia sought a higher population and a strong industrial base. Deliberately its population mix was transformed, first by migration from continental Europe and, after the late 1970s, by increasing migration from Vietnam, China, India, and other parts of South and East Asia, with lesser intakes from Africa, the Americas, and Pacific Islands. Australia became cosmopolitan—'multicultural' is the more popular label but is clumsy because it carries too many rival meanings. Few countries had voluntarily changed their population mix so quickly. Here was yet another episode in Australian exceptionalism.

At the same time, Britain ceased to be the main trading partner, being surpassed by Japan in the 1960s and then by South Korea, Taiwan, and a cluster of East Asian nations (McLean, 2013, p. 228). China almost propped up, indeed galvanized, Australia's economy after the global financial crisis in 2008.

2.12 The Balance Sheet

Australia had provided a mixture of unusual experimenting, and unusual rigidities and conservatism. What is the balance sheet? All in all, it is one of the most experimental, and one of the most exceptionalist, countries in the history of the modern world. But historians cannot readily agree on the question: which exceptional episodes should be applauded or regretted?

References

Belich, J. 2001. *Making Peoples: A History of the New Zealanders: From Polynesian Settlement to the End of the Nineteenth Century*. Auckland: Penguin.

Blainey, G. 1963. *The Rush that Never Ended: A History of Australian Mining*. London: Melbourne University Press.

Blainey, G. 1966. *The Tyranny of Distance: How Distance Shaped Australia's History*. Melbourne: Sun Books.

Blainey, G. 1980. *A Land Half Won*. Melbourne: Macmillan.

Blainey, G. 2015. *The Story of Australia's People: The Rise and Fall of Ancient Australia*. Melbourne: Viking.

Burroughs, W. J. 2005. *Climate Change in Prehistory: The End of the Reign of Chaos*. Cambridge: Cambridge University Press.

Ergas, H. and Pincus, J. 2015. 'Infrastructure and colonial socialism' in S. Ville and G. Withers (eds.), *The Cambridge Economic History of Australia*. Melbourne: Cambridge University Press.

Frost, L. 2015. 'Urbanisation' in S. Ville and G. Withers (eds.), *The Cambridge Economic History of Australia*. Melbourne: Cambridge University Press.

Hirst, J. 1988. *The Strange Birth of Colonial Democracy: New South Wales, 1848–1884*. Sydney: Allen & Unwin.

McLean, I. W. 2013. *Why Australia Prospered: The Shifting Sources of Economic Growth*. Princeton, NJ: Princeton University Press.

Maddock, R. 2015. 'Capital markets' in S. Ville and G. Withers (eds.), *The Cambridge Economic History of Australia*. Melbourne: Cambridge University Press.

Moon, P. 2013. *Encounters: The Creation of New Zealand*. Auckland: Penguin.

Mulvaney, J. and Kamminga, J. 1999. *Prehistory of Australia*. Washington, DC: Smithsonian Institution Press.

Pyne, S. J. 1991. *Burning Bush: A Fire History of Australia*. New Lambton, NSW: Elephant Press.

Vamplew, W. 1987. *Australians: Historical Statistics*. Broadway, NSW: Fairfax, Syme and Weldon.

White, C. 1992. *Mastering Risk: Environment, Markets and Politics in Australian Economic History*. Melbourne: Oxford University Press.

3

Theories of Australian Exceptionalism

William O. Coleman

How to explain the distinguishing, the singular, and the exceptional of Australian society? To ask this question is to bring to mind Australia's physical environment—the ultimately remote, dry and level landscape; or, even more quickly, to conjure up Australia's Hogarthian historical origins. But these flights of thought reach too deeply, too quickly. The investigator's first task is to diagnose, and only then to pathologize. The first task of this enquiry is to identify the condition that underlies Australian exceptionalism, and then to explain how that condition came about.

There are several contrary diagnoses of the condition that lies beneath Australian exceptionalism. The most popular turn on the alleged slightness of vertical relations ('egalitarianism') and the supposed thickness of horizontal ones ('mateship'). But other investigations have repudiated these analyses, and have located the source of exceptionalism in quite different provinces of life; in bureaucracy, or even in the strength of economic calculation operating in an abnormal context.

The rival theories of Australian exceptionalism may be usefully organized by taking each to amount to a claim over the location in the social organism of the condition that produces exceptionalism. It is argued in this chapter that the key theorists of exceptionalism—Russel Ward, Louis Hartz, W. K. Hancock, and A. F. Davies—were identifying one province of life as yielding exceptionalism on account of its supposed atrophy, or hypertrophy, relative to 'normal' conditions. These include 'status', 'fraternity', 'autonomy', 'societal technology'. Why these social arenas were atrophied or hypertrophied was typically then traced by these authors to one of two possibilities: either an enduring physical reality, or some cultural legacy of Australia's historical origins.

It might be said the advocates of these alternative analyses both too much agreed, and too much disagreed. There is too much disagreement in that the enlargement of one province clearly need not exclude the enlargement of another. Taking up that truth, this chapter suggests it is the hypertrophy of two arenas—fraternity and societal technology—that captures the incongruities that characterize much of Australian life. At the same time, there is also too much agreement in that, whatever their differences, the diagnosticians of Australian exceptionalism concur that Australia has now been shaped, for good or ill, and its cast is rigid. History for the Australian exception is, indeed, over. This belief implicitly infers a latent strength from its manifest rigidity. The chapter ends by imputing instead a potential brittleness to the hardened figure of the Australian exception. This possibility is entertained on account of a third potential shaping force; neither rational adaptation to a physical reality, nor the non-rational impress of culture, but the good sense in obeying the reverberating edicts of past events until new events countermand.

3.1 Status and Station

A former highway man is the personal physician of the governor; the owner of the colony's sole copy of Blackstone's *Commentaries* has been convicted of stealing calico from Sir Robert Peel; and the Chief Constable of Bathurst has been previously found guilty of high treason.[1] And then, in the space of ten years, Botany Bay becomes, to use the Chinese lexicon, the New Gold Mountain, and is flooded by emigrants—disproportionately young, Irish, and Scottish[2]—welcoming, in Anthony Trollope's judgement—the 'overthrow' of the state of the world.

Australia's particular origins evidently played mayhem with the customary vertical gradations of society, and the manifestations of that were copiously noted by British visitors: how traditional relations were unsettled between women and men (Adams 1892, p. 49), children and adults (Fraser 1910, p. 123), and sons and fathers (Twopeny [1883] 1973, p. 102), and how the subordination of the Dissenter and Catholic to the effectively disestablished Church of England was broken.[3] Most conspicuously, class relations were dislocated, as the reliance on birth and refinement would jar too badly with imperatives of pioneer existence. In this aspect Australia was 'English, with a thick slice cut off the top, and a thin slice at the bottom' (Martineau 1869, p. 56); Great Britain with the 'upper classes left out' (Dilke 1890, vol. 2, p. 236).

[1] D'Arcy Wentworth, Simeon Lord, and John Strange.

[2] In 1891, the population of Ireland and Scotland amounted to 30 per cent of the population of England and Wales. In New South Wales (NSW) in 1891 the number the Irish and Scots born amounted to 72 per cent of its English and Welsh born.

[3] The Church of England itself could not, in Australia, reproduce in its own governance the vertical structures of its metropolitan.

So much for the fact: what did it spell for the bent of policy regime? Perhaps the decomposition of social structure meant less of a protective mantle was cast over wealth. The pangs of economic disparity were now less benumbed by a congruence of that disparity with distinctions in social standing. These pangs would now be more palpable as social ambitions and gratifications receded. Economic conflict became more blatant,[4] and equalizing policies were the upshot: 'selection' intended to share land; later, the first taxation on Georgist principles, designed to break up large estates;[5] and, in 1915, income taxation devicefully contrived to be progressive.[6] Social egalitarianism, in brief, was the basis of economic egalitarianism.

Any explanation of economic egalitarianism by social egalitarianism is sapped by the fact there was, inevitably, an accepted gradation of status in Australia. The presence of social mobility is obviously not the same thing as the absence of social gradation. And the fact that the social structure of the parent society was not transferred *holus bolus* hardly implies its absence in the child. One immigrant complained, 'There is no place in the known world where the different grades of society are so strictly marked as here' (Neil Black quoted in Kiddle 1961, p. 100).

The suggestion that social egalitarianism is the basis of economic egalitarianism is even more embarrassed by the observation that the society that had still more social egalitarianism than Australia had much less economic egalitarianism: the USA. And this is not surprising: prestige, birth, refinement, and culture are obviously no necessary ally of the pursuit of wealth, and in many instances are hostile to it. Which is doubtless why the USA was socially egalitarian: the pursuit of wealth was strong enough to secure a prestige system that was squarely congruent with it, and was, in the minds of critics, simply a stencil of wealth. This never happened in Australia: squatters' economic success did not win for them esteem, but hatred.[7] Why the difference? Perhaps because social disarticulation went deeper in the USA. Australia inherited a considerable part of traditional status system; a pocket facsimile of feudal structures;[8] the object of wealth as a means to secure or cement a

[4] One British visitor at the beginning of the twentieth century saw 'a bitterness, a vindictiveness, almost a savagery between class and class' (Fraser 1910, p. 213). Another may have put their finger on the root of this estrangement: 'the [middle and upper] "classes" cannot exact deference from the masses, but neither can the masses exact social recognition from the [middle and upper] "classes"' (Rowland 1903, p. 21).

[5] The Georgist creed has been popular in Australia, and it is one of the very few countries that taxes unimproved land values. New Zealand enacted the first such taxation. Queensland followed in 1879.

[6] In 1915 the Commonwealth Statistician contrived an elaborate system of constantly rising marginal rates of income tax, which was duly instituted and lasted in revised form until 1974.

[7] 'In Australia there is little respect for wealth as such' (Eggleston 1953b, p. 11).

[8] In a telling contrast of the 'great America on the other side of the sphere, Australia' (Melville [1851] 1972, p. 206) with the real America, Section 9:8 of the US constitution proscribes the receipt by American citizens of any 'Title, of any kind whatever, from any King'.

gentlemanly status; and the prejudices against 'trade' so characteristic of the professions—law, medicine, civil service, and engineering—which predominated among the 'massive' immigration of mid-nineteenth-century bourgeois to Australia.[9] In 1911 not one manufacturer held a place in Victoria's Upper House (Serle 1967), and, remarkably, there was just one in the lower chamber between1856 and 1881 (Parnaby 1967, p. 89). Could Australia's inheritance of traditional status structure in a truncated form have been less congruent with wealth than the traditional structure in its complete form? The matter is speculative.

The relative scrappiness of social structure may be a case where an absence is not explanatory, and social structure might be best treated a blank card in the explanation of Australian exceptionalism. The inscrutability—or vacuity—of Australia's social structure may be why, despite massive effort (Encel 1970), the country still awaits its scientific divination or, indeed, its novelist or playwright.[10]

3.2 Fraternity

If the awry angles of Australia's vertical gradations are of arguable significance in explaining her exceptional aspects, perhaps the strength of horizontal bonds is more useful. In taking this hypothesis we turn from a striving for status to another province of human existence, 'fraternity'; a province born of an impulse for comradeship, fostered by shared if perhaps distinctive experience, directed by the common sense of the average mind, constrained to spurn the renegade, and precipitated by collective actions that amount to rituals of oneness (meals, ceremonies, marches, strikes). The province has a particular valency with youth; it is congruent with an uninhibited, extrovert disposition. It in no essentials conflicts with the quest for status. But as vertical relations can be confounding of horizontal ones, the repudiation of vertical relations can mean fewer potential obstructions to live out fraternity. Thus, while the province of fraternity is not specific to the working class, it lives more easily there. The repudiation of vertical ties that accommodate the province also obviously correlates with an 'anti-authoritarian' (i.e. anti-authority) posture, and the province of fraternity tends to leniency of group

[9] In 1891 three of the six colonies' Chief Justices were Anglo-Irish. See O'Farrell (1993) for the leading role of the 'Anglo-Irish professional classes' in Melbourne in the nineteenth century. One biographer of H. B. Higgins notes 'Anglo-Irish of Dublin of those days despised commerce as a career' (Palmer 1931, p. 23).

[10] American social pundits seem to conjure easily with issues of status (for example, Brooks 2001). By contrast, the most memorable Australian critic of the subject is a comedian, Barry Humphries.

lawlessness and corruption. Clearly, this department of life is in fundamental antagonism with the sphere of autonomy as expressed in the market. On account of that antagonism, this department of life forebears to be ambitious of the material prizes of that sphere, without unnecessarily sacrificing any corporeal satisfactions. As it has no truck with that sphere's justifying premise of self-determination, it is consequently acquiescent to the rule of 'time and chance'.

Not surprisingly, political expressions of fraternity have appeared under the banner of 'socialism'. But, for all the company it keeps with philosophers of brotherhood, the province in no way amounts to some ethic of indefinitely diffuse sociality; to be everyone's ally is to be no one's ally; and fraternity to some ends in enmity to others—and, as sociologists repeatedly stress, fans the flames of partisanship, sectarianism, and racism. 'Community' becomes tribe; cooperation is collusion; the seemingly social ends in the truly anti-social.

For 'fraternity' may be read 'mateship', and this realm looms so large in the definition of Australianness it might seem to explain all of the Australian difference. It can certainly explain the permeation of life by the state: a sense of solidarity goes some distance to solving the 'collective action problem' of any group (Olson 1965), and such a solution will spawn in its wake the creations of law to advance that group. Whether it issues in an extensive ethos of equality—let alone equalizing policies—is not so clear: every fraternity has boundaries, and dispenses disregard, contempt, and even oppression towards those beyond them. Yet the fact that a fraternity will have boundaries doesn't reduce its strength within these boundaries.

The fact and import of fraternity seems so obvious that the brilliant theorists of fraternity, Russel Ward (1914–1995) and Louis Hartz (1919–1986), took its significance for granted, and instead devoted their energies to explaining its strength.

3.2.1 *Russel Ward*

In the *Australian Legend* Ward (1958) unhesitatingly traced one source of the strength of fraternity to Australia's convict population. They constituted a ready-made 'compulsory fraternity', which, in Ward's telling, grew old educating, by example and instruction, the freeborn out of any bourgeois notions.[11] But this contention is dubious. Convicts under 'tickets of leave' (or parole) were notoriously shunning of the free (Harris [1847] 1953, p. 87; Smith 2010). And on the expiration of their sentence they appear not have formed the propertyless throng of Ward's perception. The telling fact is that most convicts

[11] A common conservative complaint: Martineau (1869, p. 67).

accepted land grants (Martin 1973). Or, as one voice of 1825 stated, 'when they become free they generally begin business' (Dyster 2007, p. 13).

But to Ward a deeper foundation of fraternity lay in the material circumstances of the new country. To Ward, the strength of fraternity sprang not from 'socialist or collectivist theories' but from 'conditions of Australian geography and history' (Ward 1967, p. 13). Australia's harsh frontiers had taught the 'virtue of cooperation'. If all frontiers are harsh, including that of the USA, then, in Ward's contention, the arable agriculture of the USA produced a 'peasant' individualism of log cabins and sodbusters, while the pastoral agriculture of Australia produced a 'nomad' collectivism of canvas camps and bushmen. In Australia the especially abundant land 'diminished individualistic tendencies by diminishing competition for land', and constituted 'sundering distances' that taught men 'to help one another' (Ward 1965, p. 9). Following Frederick Jackson Turner, it was the frontier—the most idiosyncratic and most extreme environment in any New World society—and not the globalized cities that was the forcing ground of the characteristic national type. To Ward, the epitome of the Australian frontier was the landless shearer of the pastoral outback.

Ward's account may appear to be wholly apiece of the one-dimensional materialism of the pre-war Marxism that he would have absorbed at the Hunters Hill Communist Group; the only creative features of human existence are technology and geography (Ward 1954).

But in Ward's telling the material also fermented an intangible but active agent, culture, that ensorcelled the broader public. To Ward, the palpable Australian reality was not as important as the Australian Legend. The bush proletarian—the shearer of the nineteenth-century reappearing in the world wars in the form of the Australian Digger—came to constitute an almost Jungian archetype for Australians, city bred and rural alike, serving as an object, not so much for literal emulation, but for admiration (Ward 1976). The key vehicle disseminating this image was, in his opinion, the nineteenth-century 'bush ballad', which he championed in *The Australian Legend.*

It is troubling for Ward's purpose that bush ballads have an 'inauthenticity' in origin. The best-known bush ballad—*The Wild Colonial Boy*—seems not to have originated in Australia, and was probably introduced to it by a global music industry (Anderson 2002). And whatever the ballads' origins, their hold on the imagination of the populace was feeble. The denizens of Australia's cities in the last decade of the nineteenth century crowded to hear Mendelssohn's *Elijah*—or the Georgia Minstrels—not bush balladeers.[12] And, despite his partly rural upbringing, Ward himself only became acquainted with the

[12] In 1967 a historian closely questioned seventy-five octogenarians and nonagenarians about their youth in 1890s Brisbane: not one could recall singing an Australian song (Lawson 1980).

existence of these ballads thanks to some Scottish neighbours of his in Sydney (Hirst 1996). There is an uncomfortable sensation that the mid-twentieth-century vogue of these ballads was not much more than an exercise in revivalism and fakelore (Davison 2012).

If the current of Ward's cultural electricity is weak, the pat functionalism of his material account of the foundation of collectivism is wholly inadequate. Ward assumes that a certain practice will spring into existence if it is useful to the group. But as long as Old Adam prevails, no decision is taken simply because it is advantageous to the group that it advantages. It is taken because it is advantageous to the decision-maker who makes it; and decisions with such advantages may, notoriously, be costly to the group. Old Adam may have expired on the frontier. But Ward gives no argument as to why individual motivations would so shift on the frontier, and no evidence that Old Adam did not prevail in point of fact. The undisputed social aspects of bush life—such as mutual assistance in bush fires—have equivalents in coastal environments. The anti-social dimension in bush life, from cattle doffing to bush ranging, is notorious. The rural unions of the workers Ward lionized were constantly dogged by the calculus of the individual.

Ward's use of the shearer as both the epitomization and the proof of bush mateship has been undercut by the work of historians who have demythologized the legend of shearer unity (Merritt 2008, O'Malley 2013). Shearing was ridden with division and rivalry,[13] reflecting an 'urge to compete with one another' on the 'highly competitive environment' of the shed floor (Merritt 2008, pp. 64, 83). Most damaging to Ward is the value set that underlay these behaviours. 'Many rural workers [adopted an] "ideology of self-help"' (Merritt 2008, p. 57) and 'hoped to become the equal of their employers, or their masters, not the equal of shed hands, burr cutters and sundowners' (Merritt 2008, p. 63). Such ambitions may have drawn on the ambiguity of the impact of those 'sundering distances' that Ward invokes. The author of 'Waltzing Matilda' was also the author of 'The Man from Snowy River'. Ward's account of the bushman as independent and self-reliant easily lends itself to the individualist 'pioneer legend', and in several accounts to *individualism* (for example, Spate 1968, p. 47; Pike 1962).

3.2.2 *Louis Hartz*

If Ward invoked the aesthetic to rivet the supremacy of fraternity, Louis Harz, in *The Foundation of New Societies*, used the 'realm of meaning' to secure the

[13] 'While the work that shearers did... left them with much in common, the bonds so created did not produce a fraternity that held together across districts or even within sheds' (Merritt 2008, p. 64).

primacy of the same. Contrasts between the two men can be pursued further. To Ward, the material/economic was primary, and the historical/cultural supplementary; Hartz supposed the reverse; Ward (like F. J. Turner) deemed exceptionalism was functional; Hartz saw it as dysfunctional. More personally, Ward's path in life took him from a coastal city to the provincial interior; Hartz journeyed from the interior to the metropolitan coast, and thence to 'traversing random international roads in a disquieting quest for the meaning of world history' (Barber 1986, p. 355). Ward took the nation to be *sui generis*, while Harz adopted a comparative method. Ward was fixated on Australia; Harz cultivated a general theory of New World exceptionalism.

Hartz conceived New World societies, such as Australia, to be amputee Old World societies (Hartz 1964). To Hartz the limbs of the Old World are Marxian-like class categories: feudal, bourgeois, proletariat, and so on. But in the creation of New World societies only one of these limbs is transferred. Thus, what is important in the New World is not the new environment confronted, but what travels to confront it; and what was left behind was as important as what actually made the journey. In this passage—and this was his key point—the dynamic of European culture was lost; the thesis had left its antithesis behind in the Old World, and in the New World history ceases the moment it begins, with the transplanted fragment in solitary and sterile possession: 'French Canada becomes more feudal than France ever was' (McCarty 1973, p. 155).

In the specific case of Australia, R. N. Rosecrance, Hartz's collaborator, contended, 'Australia's uniqueness is a result of settlement by a particular fraction of British society' (Rosecrance 1964, p. 276). A 'fragment' of Great Reform Bill England, Chartism, 'lodged in Australia' (Rosecrance 1964, p. 280), and 'in isolation from social and political movements elsewhere, it congealed', and ruled through its 'philosophy of the alehouse bench'. Australia, then, was 'born radical' and must remain so.

General theories invite general criticism. Might not an amputee social organism reconstruct itself, as a fish regenerates fins and tail? Hartz's thesis denies the possibility. And his denial might be correct—the squattocracy did not succeed in establishing itself as a ruling elite—but nothing in Hartz explains why. Rosecrance proposed the explanation lay in the bourgeois mentality of the squatters. This conjecture brings us to Hartz's basic presumption: ideas make the world go round. His three 'estates' are at bottom ideologies—conservatism, liberalism, and radicalism—with classes simply the incidental material bodies of ideological soul. Ideas, then, are the inhabitants of the world. These inhabitants contend, breed, and sometimes are stranded solitary upon a far shore. On these far shores they may be accompanied by matter in the form of other class categories, but these other forms lack soul, and will be dominated, just as the physical environment will be dominated by any body with a soul.

Hartz's triumph of mentality over materiality may be plausibly denied.[14] Even if it is accepted, the representation of Australia as a sundered limb, or a fragment ('incomplete part') of the idea-population of the parent culture can also be refused. Australia, at least until the end of the nineteenth century, was not the sundered limb of some denizen of the European pantheon, but a cell of global cultural entity; not a fragment, but an epitome. At least until the end of the nineteenth century Australia remained an integrated, if incompletely participating, province of the British cultural world. In the humanities, a persisting integration is indicated by Samuel Alexander, V. Gordon Childe, and Gilbert Murray, all alighting in Britain without a feather ruffled, or a sign to show their Antipodean origin; or, going in the other direction, the instant assimilation by Australian political life of various florets of British learning (Charles Pearson, Francis Adams, B. R. Wise). Australia at the end of the century seemed utterly open to the *fin de siècle.* Hartz's formulation of his thesis for Australia amounts to a denial of the relevance for Australian events of any currents from Europe felt later than, say, 1860, whatever visibility they may have had. Thus, for all the unusual prominence of British immigrants in the creation of the Labor Party in the 1890s, they didn't make a difference; or, for all the protectionist ideas that the same British unionists brought with them, these didn't make a difference. However wrong Hartz may have been in these denials, he at least had a vision that yielded them: just as bodies without soul are without an influence, so are souls without bodies. The intellectual societies that shape material events consist of a population of bodies with soul, and this population had been established, according to Hartz, by 1860. Yet the choice of cut-off date is not important. To Hartz the foundation of Australia was concluded at some point, and an oversimplicity in the social contents of that foundation precluded any intellectual combustion, leaving a stable ideological ascendancy. An inert one,[15] but an ascendancy all the same.

3.3 Autonomy and W. K. Hancock

Ward and Hartz's common presumption of the hypertrophy of fraternity as the characterizing feature of Australian life was challenged by Hancock's

[14] Contrary to a triumph of the ideal over the material, 'fragments' appear protean in their subsequent development: Ulster, the West Indies, and North America took roughly equal shares of British immigration in the twenty years before 1642 (Bolton 1973).

[15] 'Australia has not got a mind' (Horne 1964, p. 16). See the same sentiment in Grattan (1940, p. 7), Edwards (1979, p. 43), MacKenzie (1961, pp. 146–9). 'The poverty of theoretical notions is astonishing' (Métin [1901] 1977, p. 180).

Australia of 1930. Where in Australia, asked Hancock, were the manifestations of 'civil society' that would surely be one fruit of such a sense of bond and identity? The only example he could find was the Australian Natives Association, a Fabian-like pressure group for state action, and hardly an expression of self-contained community activity. To add to his case, he could have pointed out that the then newly established Parents and Citizens Associations had been created 'top down', at the behest of school inspectors, who sadly contrasted the indifference of Australian parents with the vitality of US school associations.[16] And he may have observed that the one fragment of civil society in Australian education that did exist—the Australian Council of Education Research, founded in 1925, was established by the Carnegie Foundation. In the same vein, he could have noted that all Australian universities were state foundations; instrumental 'public utility' universities.[17] Or that trade unions of twentieth-century origin, as distinct from those of the nineteenth century, were the deliberate growths of the legislative hothouse.[18] Finally, Hancock might have added that local government—surely an indication of the strength of tendency to form associations—is feeble in Australia. First instituted in 1842 by imperial edict in the face of a wary colony, only in 1906 was local government expanded to encompass the great bulk of New South Wales, and then only over the strenuous opposition of local residents.[19]

In Hancock's analysis, the Australian condition is diagnosed not as hypertrophy of fraternity but a distortion of the very different 'sphere': that arena of life in which self-assertion, guided by private reason and constrained to 'walk reputably towards those without, and have need of no one' (1 Thessalonians 4:12), results in wealth. This might be referred to as 'the economy', but may just as well be identified with the 'modern liberty' discerned by Benjamin Constant. It will be called here 'the sphere of autonomy', and it was the key to Hancock. According to Hancock, Australia's foundation amounted to an eruption of individual self-assertion in the wake of the eclipse of social deference. Australia began with an 'enrush of a horde' of 'individualistic', 'self-assertive', 'egotistical' 'invaders' who were 'held together by nothing' and, driven by 'greed', 'imposed themselves' on the continent to draw its wealth, 'forcing',

[16] The relative rarity of cooperatives in Australia may also betoken a weakness in civil society. Dilke (1890, vol. 2, p. 296) notes their 'disappointing' state. 'There is very little co-operative enterprise in Australia' (Eggleston 1953a, p. 54).

[17] 'The notion of the school as being a kind of society... has not been very conspicuous in Australia' (Partidge 1973, p. 82). Partridge suggests the goal of the government school system in Australia is to dispense a 'basic wage' of education.

[18] A historian of one of Australia's largest unions has judged 'undoubtedly, arbitration... was largely responsible for the union's growth' (Merritt 1986, p. 363).

[19] As in NSW, local government in South Australia and Victoria was very much the creature and dependent of state governments (see Hirst 1973, p. 147).

'fighting' 'pushing' 'south... north' (Hancock 1930, pp. 32–3). How, then, could such a raging wellspring conclude in the tame runnel of economic enterprise that he surveyed three generations later in 1930? When visitors could note 'no noisy self-assertiveness' (Fraser 1910, p. 9), an inclination to only 'grumble', a 'singular absence' of 'commercial ambition' and 'initiative' (Moffat in Edwards 1979, p. 49); an evident unwillingness or inability to 'impose' themselves on newly available lands, which Italian immigrants were managing to prosper on (Hagan and Turner 2007); a lengthy patience with a rapidly expanding web of economic controls, both formal and informal.

To Hancock the key to explaining this transition of Australian history lay in the configuration that the sphere of autonomy had come to assume in the face of Australia's abnormal circumstances. Australians were economic individualists: six million little 'silos'. But they had been taught, by experience of their country's circumstances, that each silo could be best filled by extensive collective action. Australia's collectivism, then, was not an ethos *(à la* Ward and Hartz) but a strategy; it was a collectivism of actions and means, rather than one of ends and values. 'Mateship' was not an ethic of sociality, but a technique for filling the swag of each mate to the full. ('A fair go usually means money': Horne 1964, p. 24). Thus, individualist ends were to be sought by social means; the reverse of the outlook of Australia's economists of Hancock's day—who sought the public interest (a 'social' end) through individualist means—and who were, as Hancock stresses, the object of a special ire in Australia.

Hancock appears to subscribe to the rationality of Australia's 'collectivism of means', as he frequently repeats that Australia could not have developed without extensive government action and control. Whence, then, the grimace of distaste and disappointment with Australia that pervades his book? It partly arises from Australia's abuse of the potential for collective action: as the size of 'government failure' through the overprovision of infrastructure was at least comparable with the underprovision that would have taken place under a free market. But why was collective action abused rather than used? Hancock could have answered by observing that self-assertion in the context of collective provision will manifest itself in accepting benefits but refusing costs. But rather than simply relying on self-assertion in such a context, Hancock cuts deeper against the significance of fraternity, by asserting that a kind negative sociality was tainting Australian society. In Hancock's mind, Australian jealousy at one's brother's favour was a stronger feeling than any concern for their ill fortune. Australia's 'collectivist strategy' was not so much a solipsist individualism as the issue of a resentful ménage: an anti-social socialism. This amounts to an ethic that the placings in life's race should never alter, no matter how the course might evolve (Hancock 1930, p. 183); a 'socialist conservatism'.[20] It was in such a vein that Martineau had, long before, sourly observed that Australian rum drinkers insisted on also receiving any reduction in duty that wine drinkers received (Martineau 1869, p. 141). But the looming illustration of 'socialist conservatism' is the intense legislation for 'wage margins for skill' across the Australian labour force. We come back to paradox of fraternity: we cannot all be members of the 'in' group.

Hancock successfully addressed a paradox: that Australia appears to be simultaneously preoccupied by the economic and flouting of the economic.[21] It is preoccupied with the economic as an individual end, but flouts it as an aggregate goal.[22]

3.4 Societal Technology and A. F. Davies

Hancock's starting point was that the bureaucratized systems so distinctive of Australia—the massive state-owned utilities in transport, communication, and water—were instrumental to her economic development. Yet, before many pages, he was allowing they were not instrumental to the economy but burdensome to it. Perhaps these bureaucratized systems are not instrumental to the economy, or anything else, but only to themselves. We are drawn to Alan Fraser Davies's *aperçu* that 'the characteristic talent of Australians is not for improvisation, it is for bureaucracy' and 'the gift is exercised on a massive scale' (Davies 1958, p. 3). This characteristic talent is the epitomization of that province of human existence born of an impulse to order and organize, steered by the considerations of the objective and quantifiable, and constrained to bristle at the anomalous, which ultimately precipitates in procedure and regimen that may or may not have a social value. The concrete

[20] The 'Austrawlsian' social welfare function of 'socialist conservatism' should be distinguished from the Rawlsian social welfare function. The 'Austrawlsian' states,

$$SW = \min(y_i - y^*_i)$$

where y^*_i is the normal income of the ith person. Thus, contrary to Rawls, a policy which increases the size of the lowest income, but does not increase the size of the highest, is not an improvement.

[21] 'Australia is a thriving country to which capitalists come to increase their wealth and workers come to find higher wages' (Métin [1901] 1977, p. 10).

[22] The maximization of the aggregate of utility:

$$U = u(y_1) + u(y_2) + \ldots u(y_N) \qquad u'>0, u''<0$$

subject to an 'income possibility frontier', $f(y_1, y_2 \ldots) = 0$, will plausibly be costly to the size of aggregate income, $y_1 + y_2 + y_3 + \ldots$. But the maximization of the aggregate of *envious* utility functions:

$$U = u(y_1 - EY) + u(y_2 - EY) + \ldots u(y_N - EY)$$

subject to $f(y_1, y_2 \ldots) = 0$ and $EY \equiv [y_1 + y_2 \ldots]/N$, will surely be still more costly.

illustrations of this 'societal technology' variously include: systems of nomenclature; street numbers; sporting rules; time zones; road conventions; electoral systems; the rationing of goods and immigrants; conscription; land registration; all manner of codes and regulation; and bureaucracy.

Societal technology culminates in well-wrought machines, *human* machines, in which, unlike ordinary machines, the material ('paperwork') is relatively trivial, however notorious. For all their human elements, these human machines are greatly complemented by material technology. Societal technology and material technology often run together, and meet in 'public health' and 'preventative medicine', which might be the paradigmatical of societal technology. Or, even more, the 'safety' ethic, of which Australia has been such a vigorous 'early adopter' (Jessop 2009).[23]

Societal technology is more naturally midlife rather than adolescent, more suburban rather than rural. It is palpably Scandinavian (Daun 1996) and, with the two clocks of railway Ballyhough station in mind, not obviously Irish. Societal technology appears to be the inevitable adversary of the sphere autonomy; it was hugely important to twentieth-century socialism as a means of filling a void created by the retrenchment of that sphere. Yet in Australia it has sometimes tolerated 'the market' as a device of societal technology.

Societal technology waxes fat in Australia. It is seen everywhere, literally, in the pointless road signs that festoon roadways. It is seen in specific and favoured creations of state, such as the Commonwealth Scientific and Industrial Research Organisation (CSIRO). It is seen, perhaps, in the overambitious hopes for computing technology by Australian governments, and the recurrent catastrophic consequences of that misplaced faith.[24] It is seen in the language; it has been claimed the term 'public servants' originates in Australia (Richards 2015). It is seen, above all, in the bureaucratic; in the treatment of the civilian by the state that has maddened visitors, both recent and long past (Martineau 1869; Brûlé 2015);[25] in the warping of the state so that 'Federation' becomes a bureaucracy in three layers; and in formations outside the state. Unions, with their 'tentacular grip' on Australian life (Davies 1958) are, of course, elaborate bureaucracies, and have been so from their origin. Their most important product is policies; policies that at best only obliquely serve equality and fraternity but gratify the quest for control, such as compulsory peacetime

[23] Victoria was the first jurisdiction in the world to introduce the compulsory wearing of motorcycle helmets and seat belts, and random breath tests. 'Safety' can, of course, be dangerous (Peltzman 1975). For safety, read 'regimen'.

[24] See Chesterman (2013) on how a $6 million IT contract became a $1.2 billion cost.

[25] The talent for bureaucracy sometimes impressed visitors: 'It would be difficult to find a higher type of public servant anywhere in the world' (Nelson T. Johnson quoted in Edwards 1973, p. 85).

military service. Originating in Prussia, it was first introduced in the British Empire by Australia, as the *Commonwealth Year Books* for years proudly recorded.

Why is this province so overgrown? A possible historical–cultural base of the hypertrophy of societal technology might be sought in the 'worldly Presbyterianism'—the secularized, rationalistic puritanism—that so dismayed Francis Adams about Australia (Adams 1893, p. 28). An alternative environmental–economic foundation for Australia's 'talent' for societal technology might be sought in the benefits of a human machinery, in that it is the 'world's first and most suburbanised nation' (Clarke 1965, p. 63);[26] and in the low costs of human machinery in Australia on account of the country's homogeneity in language and culture. The cost of human machinery is doubtless reduced still further by the country possessing 'the least diversity of surface of any of the continents' (Taylor 1945, p. 316) and the sort of well-defined and formidable natural borders that facilitate the close organization of a society. To illustrate that thought, Australia has had a penchant for rigorous quarantine (books, the sick, alien races, exotic pests, asylum claimants, film stars' dogs) because it can have such a penchant.

There are several other candidate causes with broader historical roots.

3.4.1 *Colonial Origins*

Australia's penchant for bureaucracy might be traced to the fact that Australia was a colony:

> Possibly the most enduring feature of any colonial regime, one of the first to appear and the last to leave, is the administrator, the colonial bureaucrat, high, middle and low. (Stein and Stein 1970, p. 68)

The highest stratum of the original bureaucratic management of Australia was another bureaucracy, the Colonial Office, presided over in the key years 1825–45 by James Stephen, a 'strict legalist' with a 'passion for system and uniformity' (Pike 1957, p. 35). The next stratum consisted of the governors, who, too, were public servants, in as much that they were accountable to the Colonial Secretary. The example of elevated and conscientious colonial governors—Macquarie, Bourke, King ('bursting with plans and policies': Roe 1963, p. 7)—may have provided archetypes for the procession of industrious, intelligent, and overweening public servants that have been conspicuous in Australian history. The third stratum was the local staff, and the excellence and profusion in Australian of that useful tool of government—government

[26] Dilke opines that Australian town democracy is attracted to state socialism, while the small agricultural proprietors of the USA are repelled by it (Dilke 1890, vol. 2, p. 265).

statisticians, or 'statists'—may be ultimately traceable to the recurrent tyre-kicking by Great Britain of her doubtful colonial asset.[27]

3.4.2 *Authoritarianism*

Perhaps the *authoritarianism* with which societal technology is implicitly laden was instilled by the parade-ground character of original European settlement. Given the poverty of communications, for its first thirty-five years the governors of NSW, unlike North American governors, ruled as might an absolute monarch, and with a mercantilist apparatus. Thus, Edward Shann—surely the most eloquent critic of Australian exceptionalism—wrote that more of Australia than the crooked streets of Sydney can be traced to the period's military rule.

Shann's command society vision of the first generation of European settlement has been challenged. NSW, it has been said, was a 'convict colony' rather than a penal colony (Hirst 2009b); one which barely had a prison as such for its first thirty five years, and in which there reigned the rule of law, not the rule of man. Yet its texture was highly authoritarian, as the rule of law sanctioned one man to make the rules. Governor Macquarie could ordain thirty-one lashes for any deserting (free) seaman (Quinlan 1998). Furthermore, 'The state had no compunction in separating mother and child' (Belcher 1999, p. 17), and 'the minutest details of civil life' were controlled by the state (Hartwell 1955, p. 51). NSW exhibited the aspect of a military station quite beyond literal barrack walls; until 1825, every free person was required to present themselves at an appointed place and time for each 'population muster'.

But Shann's stress on Australia's early command society might also be faulted on the grounds that this authoritarianism actually fostered liberalism, by way of provoking a reaction: it was the *ancien régime* of Old Sydney Town that provided a foil to a nascent liberalism. 'A government official in your eyes', it was complained to W. C. Wentworth, 'is a tool of power, the unblessed offspring of tyrannous rule' (Roe 1965, p. 78). By contrast, to the busy bourgeois of the convict-free colonies to the south, a government official was, from an early date, something else entirely. *L'État, c'est nous*.[28]

An entirely different objection to tracing Australia's engrossment by social machinery to its early command society will press that the early command society expired after two generations. Australia, in this objection, was

[27] 'Victoria has almost from her very birth been at the head of all countries in statistics, and the Year-Book of the Government statist and other productions of his office are as nearly as perfect as such works can be' (Dilke 1890, vol. 1, p. 187).

[28] Thus Grant (1975) has noted the contrast between nineteenth-century Victoria's intelligentsia and the oppositional role commonly attributed to such formations. Victoria's intelligentsia was not resisting 'society', it was shaping it.

effectively re-founded, by wool and gold, in the image of the liberalism and capitalism of Industrial Revolution Britain, a highly individualist and rights-conscious society. These forces remade Australia by dissolving the older military state.

3.4.3 *Legal Constructivism*

Alternatively, the strength of social machinery might be traceable to the very legality that characterized both the original military society and the liberal civilian society that succeeded it. In the beginning was the law: Australia began with an Act of parliament: Transportation Act 24 Geo 3 c56 1784. Within six months of the establishment of Sydney, 'There was not... even a bridge over the Tank Stream but there was already a flourishing legal system' (Kercher 1996, p. xix). In a new society such as this, lawyers, as Tocqueville stressed, will constitute its sole aristocracy.[29] No aristocratic class is renowned for its humility, and the bench in Australia has been ready to 'slaughter' legislation under various principles of judicial review, with a 'devastating effect... on the balance of constitution' (Hancock 1930, p. 118);[30] on occasions to virtually claim the right to choose the Chief Justice; to subject entire dimensions of economic life to judicial legislation; and several times to construe the mere criticism of a court decision as contempt of court, while at the same time bearing 'contempt for the judgement of parliament and Executive' (Sawer 1952, p. 240). One Chief Justice declared in the early 1970s that more important decisions had been taken in the Court House than the Parliament House (Hirst 2009a, p. 8); he was soon to become Governor-General,and construe the position in entirely juristic terms, with unfortunate consequences for parliament and Executive

Australia, then, has been a rich field for the 'empire of law'—the cultivation of prerogatives, refinements, extensions, and ramifications of law. But 'legalism' so defined hardly defines a social philosophy. One can imagine a legalism of contract, of property, and of tort; a legalism of individualism; the legalism characteristic of the USA, which is indisputably a legalistic society, but one where legalism serves individualist values. In Australia, legalism has done

[29] Conformably, the law in Australia has produced legal dynasties of a strength and lustre unknown in politics, the arts, or business (Fox 2015). One dynasty, the Stephens, provided justices of the NSW Supreme Court for four successive generations. The first of the dynasty was a brother of James Stephen, the 'uncompromising legalist' Under-Secretary of the Colonial Office (Pike 1957).

[30] For much of the twentieth century the High Court was one of the world's very few genuine courts of constitutional review; between 1900 and 1950 fifty-three laws in the USA were declared unconstitutional, while sixty-seven laws were so declared in Australia (Davies 1958, p. 75). But, unlike the American stance towards the US Supreme Court, 'in Australia it is still considered very largely as being "bad form" to criticise judicial attitude and actual judgements' (Sawer 1952, p. 238).

otherwise. It is *legal constructivism* that captures best the significant 'legalism' of Australia; the presumption that the law is the best tool to make the world a better place. So, whereas positivists might pin their hopes on science in making the world a better place; and moralists on morality; and liberals on freedom, in confronting any problem legal constructivists will reach for a new law. Is a low voter turnout a problem? A law making voting compulsory is the answer. Are strikes are a problem? Make them illegal.[31] Being dismissed arbitrarily is undesirable; clearly that action should be outlawed. The uncompetitiveness of Australian business is costly to national welfare: its illegalization will be the remedy.

This legal constructivism is essentially 'Benthamism', the philosophy of societal technology on legal stilts. Thus, the prospect arises of Australian exceptionalism being the issue of one of the most celebrated and censured of social philosophies (see, for example, Collins 1985); one flourishing in Europe at the very time of the European settlement of Australia, although unknown at that time—let it be marked—in the USA. Trollope (1873, p. 239) observed 'our colonists of Australasia are... as impatient of the doctrine of natural rights as the editor of the Quarterly Review'. He should have added, 'or Bentham'.

3.5 Disharmony in the Spheres

None of the various 'provinces of life' that have been the units of analysis of previous sections constitute a candidate for the explanation of Australian exceptionalism to the exclusion of the others. They all may be operative. They may actually be complementary in effect. Thus, the labour movement draws strength from both 'human machines' and from fraternity (or, at least, its mythology); here the spheres of fraternity and societal technology are reinforcing. Yet the tension between fraternity and societal technology may be still more important. They easily make for a set of contrasts: efficiency versus equity; authoritarian versus anti-authoritarian; high-minded versus broad-minded; humourless versus humour-filled; doctrinal versus attitudinal; productivity versus pleasure; Albert Jacka VC versus Sir John Monash GCMG, KCB, VD; the paltry rationalism and frigid sanctimony of a Justice Higgins of

[31] Historically, Australia has been a country of many strikes, and of many laws banning strikes. The statute books of the states are the most blatant: the NSW Industrial Disputes Act of 1908 is one example. In Commonwealth law since the beginning of 'Conciliation and Arbitration' in 1904, strikes have been, 'broadly speaking', illegal for the parties covered by a current award (i.e. almost everyone in an 'industry'). The Fair Work Building Industry Inspectorate currently announces on its website that 'strikes are only lawful if protected industrial action for a proposed industrial agreement has been authorised by the Fair Work Commission'.

the *Harvester Case* versus rugby players meeting in Bateman's Hotel in the same year to found a League to better their recompense. The contradictions of the two spheres produce the contradictions of Australian society.

This contrast has sometimes resulted in direct confrontation, with the victory sometimes swinging one way or the other: 'early closing' laws ultimately retreating, but Darwin's Chinatown ultimately destroyed (Christie 1995).

This contrast has sometimes produced a living contradiction, perhaps most saliently in pre-1960s Australia; a dry Canberra versus a wet Queanbeyan; a ludicrous literary censorship that was lackadaisically enforced; a Darwin 'a free and easy town where everybody mixed with everybody' and 'where social classes and racial communities were strictly segregated' (Christie 1995); a severe White Australia policy that was yet in some ways a 'legal fiction' (Baker 1966);[32] an Australia that, for all its prohibitions, was 'tolerant' in a 'raffish' way.

Sometimes the two coexisted side by side, almost complementing one another: plenty of bushrangers, but no lynch mobs;[33] an antagonism towards police, but a 'surprising amount of deference to persons in authority by subordinates' (MacKenzie 1961);[34] strikes endemic but, with some exceptions, orderly (Walker 1986).

The incongruities of twentieth-century Australia might be seen as the manifestation of the simultaneous strength of societal technology and fraternity. Yet in the twenty-first century societal technology appears to be eclipsing fraternity. Union memberships wilt while their bureaucracies flourish and fester; political parties decline into recruitment agencies for political careerists; the sense of guild shrivels in the workplace while 'management' is rampant. The popular and graphic emblem of Australian fraternity has long been beer drinking: in 2013 half as much beer was drunk per head as forty years before.

3.6 The Underlying Causes

The retreat or advance of the spheres of life prompts the fundamental question: what is the source of their being abnormally large or small?

Most accounts of their shrunkenness or overgrowth have drawn on just two types of explanation: 'cultural–historical' or 'economic–environmental'.

[32] A total of 17,000 Chinese were admitted to Australia during the 1920s. A greater number, however, left.

[33] 'Kangaroo court' is not of Australian origin, but Texan (Richards 2015).

[34] The Eureka Stockade? One future Conservative prime minister of Great Britain was 'aghast' at the 'submissiveness' he sometimes encountered on the goldfields (Gascoyne-Cecil 1935, p. 19). 'The legend of the independent, free-thinking Australian mind has long puzzled . . . observers, who saw on every hand evidence of spineless timidity in the face of authority' (Penton 1943, p. 11). See the same in Crawford (1952, p. 46) and Robinson (1985, p. 16).

Cultural–historical explanations invoke culture as the immediate determining factor, with culture in turn explained by reference to some 'founding' history. The idiosyncratic institutional origins of Australia obviously invite various cultural–historical explanations of exceptionalism, and Hartz's is an illustration. Another variant of this sort of explanation would invoke the ethnic composition of the founding immigration, and the Australian illustration would be the recurrent, if not universally shared, hunch that heavy Irish immigration shaped Australian distinctiveness.[35] Another use of cultural–historical explanations consists of invoking the experiences a society did *not* have. Australia had no war of independence; no occupation; no war at all fought purely on Australia's account; and is the neighbour of no United States or Brazil.

In contrast, economic–environmental explanations suppose that economic motivations, when conjoined with material constraints, are decisive. The leading illustration of the 'economic–environmental' explanation of Australian singularity is 'the Bush', the Outback, the Back of Beyond; that enormous quantity of low and risky value land, studded by (a critical detail) outcrops of land made precious by their minerals. It is this 'outback' of drought, flood, and fire that makes the country Australia and not New Zealand: it is the outback that makes for the Australian way.

The wide brown land is the terrain of Russel Ward, but also Hancock's 'public utility state', where great distances make collective action more rewarding—possibly even rational; particularly in the natural monopolies of transport and communication. But other arguments might be woven out of Australia's physical endowment. Distance means area, and Australia's land is bountiful relative to her small population; more 'arable land' or 'agricultural land' per head than obvious comparators.[36] The large quantity of land will obviously make rents per acre low, but may also make rent per capita large.[37] And such high rents per capita will have the appearance of a mound of wealth that may be apportioned as one pleases, without an unwelcome diminution in its size.[38] An economy of vertical supply curves is congenial to a collectivist

[35] Ward gave an accent to Irishness, and explained South Australia's own individuality by its relative lack of Irish. Hirst, by contrast, asserts the essential Englishness of Australia (2014, p. 128). The unusually large presence of Irish is a fact (MacDonagh 1986), but divining the implications of this fact is perplexed by the fractures in 'Irishness', and the divergence of the reality of Irishness from its stereotypes (see Eggleston 1953b, p. 7). One reflective consideration of the question seems to avoid making a conclusion (O'Farrell 1986).

[36] It estimated that there is 23,222 m^2 of 'arable land' per head in Australia vs 5220 m^2 in the USA, 8,700 m^2 in Argentina, and 1,168 m^2 NZ (*CIA World Fact Book*). The World Bank's estimates of the broader category of 'agricultural land' seem generous, but taken at face value they imply 172,400 m^2 of agricultural land per head in Australia; 12,900 m^2 in the USA; 2,480 m^2 in New Zealand; and 34,600 m^2 in Argentina.

[37] If the demand for land is elastic then a larger supply of land will increase rents per capita.

[38] 'The Selection Acts were on the face of it a recipe for spreading the wealth and their operation has been compared to a gold rush. An alternative construction of the Selection Acts was that they were an attempt to compensate by legislation for an artificial scarcity that had been purposefully

economic vision that is kindred to the sphere of fraternity. This vision is made vivid with regard to the mineral bounty of Australia. An illustration: within eight years of European settlement coal was found 'littering the beach' (Perry 1963, p. 58). At various times since, Australia has been the world's leading producer of tin and gold; it is currently the largest producer of aluminium oxide and bauxite; ranked second in iron ore, gold, and lead; third for manganese, uranium, and zinc, and in contention for third place in coal and nickel.[39]

Another salient material feature of Australia is her population, or lack of it. Australia is a small-scale society. It is just large enough to be prone to the 'illusion of completeness' (Davies 1985, p. 243) and a 'delusion of competence' (Clement Freud cited in Boyd 1972, p. 24), but small enough to suffer from the expatriatism, amateurism, gossiping and score-settling of a small one (MacKenzie 1961, p. 146). Most significantly of all, there exists social theory to argue that small societies facilitate collusion: economically, politically, and socially (Olson 1965). Australia seems a convincing illustration. Is Australia not the society of the tidy stitch-up, whether in the party room, the Trades Hall, the Chamber of Commerce, the University Council, or Council of Governments? Is it not a society in which the inner-ring prevails and beguiles? Tellingly, a popular ABC current affairs programme is called 'Insiders'. The most bought edition of one national newspaper is the annual 'Power Issue' that identifies for its readers the 'most powerful people in the country'. Visitors past and present have been struck by the rule of golden circles. 'Exclusive and clique ridden' judged one British observer at the time of Federation (Rowland 1903, p. 122). Even 110 years later, one American political scientist declared: 'the one thing that has overwhelmed me about Australia and its politics is how cosy everything is. Despite its vast physical expanse, the country's political elites seem remarkably inbred. Party cliques determine candidate selection in mysterious ways, highly reminiscent of tightly-held 19th century machine politics of the US' (Loomis 2013, p. 39). Australia is a classless society with a ruling class. It is a country where the elite chooses its own successors, but recruits them from across society.

fostered by the Crown in the first place. State land was notoriously expensive; the 'preposterously high' price (Therry 1863, p. 2523) of £1 an acre was the benchmark in Australia, compared to $US1.25 per acre of the US Land Act of 1820 (about 5s).

[39] 'At December 2012, Australia had the world's largest economic resources of gold, iron ore, lead, rutile, zircon, nickel, uranium and zinc'. GeoScience Australia, <http://www.ga.gov.au/scientific-topics/minerals/mineral-resources/aimr>. The same bounty does not extend to petroleum, but it remains the case that Russia and Norway are the only developed countries with larger 'conventional' oil reserves per capita than Australia.

3.7 The Inertial Society

It is easy to see that environmental–economic and cultural–historical explanations of Australian exceptionalism attach different weight to the contingencies of her history. In most environmental–economic explanations, the long-run destination is not altered by shocks along the journey. Yes, shocks have consequences, but their consequences are passing, and the more distant the shock the less consequent it is. The system, in other words, is 'stable'. The simplest cultural–historical explanations, by contrast, implicitly endorse a cosmology of an unstable system; whereby the more distant a shock is, the *more* important it is, with the original shock seemingly the most important of all. Thus, the cultural–historical theorist is tempted to trace everything back to a year zero, the motley infancy of European society in Australia. Corruption in the NSW police force? Remind the reader that the first constables were convicts. Corruption in public offices? Speak of the Rum Corps. Industrial disputation? Call to mind the 'work ban' applied by the Marines in the service of Governor Phillip. But such extended lines of descent are inevitably arguable.[40] And, in any case, they are not necessary for some cultural sway. For the cultural–historical theorist is entitled to invoke a 'stable' system of *two* (or more) possible long-run destinations, with the implication that a sufficiently large shock may alter which road is being travelled. The upshot of such multi-equilibrium system is that larger shocks—which, on account of being larger, are rarer and so probably older—are 'determining' the way recent shocks are not; and yet the year zero—the year history supposedly unloads its burden on posterity—need not be literally the first year in the society's annals. Society's trajectory could be altered at a later date in the crucible of some crisis. A cultural–historical theorist of exceptionalism could, for example, hold up the traumas of the 1890s as the furnace that melted the inherited norms of liberal Britain and hammered them into a new mould. It was in 1889 that the APA Building ('the Australian Building') was completed in Melbourne, and was perhaps for some months the tallest building in the world. But in the four subsequent years, Victoria's real gross domestic product (GDP) was to fall by 16 per cent.[41] The subsequent harrowing decade was, of course, the midwife of the Australian Labor Party (ALP), Australia's singular industrial relations system and, above all, the Federation of the Commonwealth of Australia.

'Stable' and 'unstable' do not exhaust the cosmologies of explanation: there is a third cosmology. This does not contend that shocks long ago are more important than recent ones; or that recent ones are more important than

[40] In fact, the NSW police force was completely re-established in 1862.

[41] Male suicides in Australia averaged 15.3 per 100,000 pa in 1881–85. They averaged 20.2 per 100,000 pa in 1901–05.

distant ones. The third possibility maintains that all shocks, recent and distant, are of equal potential importance.[42] The upshot of this third cosmology is that there is not one long destination, or no long-run destination, but many.

To give a simple illustration of this third cosmology: suppose that it would have been better (that is, less costly) to have established initial European settlement at Newcastle (Australia) rather Sydney. Nevertheless, once Sydney had become established, it may well have remained rational to persist with Sydney as the centre. Sydney became a 'rational custom' by virtue of being established. Yet if some shock did move the metropolitan centre to Newcastle (or Jervis Bay, etc.), that new fact on the ground would be the (new) rational custom. A very similar, if less hypothetical, example involves Canberra. Inclement, remote, and costly, its choice of location as a national capital may have been inferior to a locale that was mild, easily accessible, and cheap. But, once established, it was rational to stick with it.[43]

The point works the commonplace that, if a wrong fork in the road is taken, once taken it may still be rational to hasten further along it, rather than retrace the path. Decisions become 'fate full'. The choice of political borders, for example, has a finality and rationally so. The Victoria–NSW border along the Murray may have been an ill-starred choice. But having been adapted to, it is not worth changing it. But if it was changed, it may not be worth changing it back. The decision to detach the Northern Territory from South Australia may have the same property, or the Australian Capital Territory's acquisition of self-government.

This model of 'rational custom' is evidently one of an outlay that is 'sunk' and that cannot be recovered. Thus, the fuel spent in taking one fork in the road a certain distance is sunk, and cannot be recovered. But sunk costs are not the only source of 'rational custom'. Rational discouragements to revise a past decision also arise where, to pursue the travel analogy, the very act of reversing course is costly of fuel. These 'revision costs' obviously include any resources consumed in deciding to revise an earlier decision. And revision costs extend beyond such 'process costs' of revising an earlier decision, to include any opportunity costs of deciding to revise (for deciding to revise X may entail not making a decision to revise Y).

The joint upshot of sunk costs and process costs is that it may be rational to choose the customary action/event/location.[44] This notion of 'rational

[42] History as random walk: if $Y_{t+1} = Y_t + u_t$ then $Y_{t+1} = u_t + u_{t-1} + \ldots$
By contrast, if $Y_{t+1} = aY_t + u_t$ and $a > 1$ then the more distant the shock, the more important it is. If $Y_{t+1} = aY_t + u_t$ and $a < 1$,then the more distant the shock, the less important it is.

[43] Notoriously, it would have been better for NSW to adopt a 5 ft 3 in railway gauge in 1853. But once a certain length of track had been built, it was rational to persist with extending the gauge.

[44] It *may* be rational to choose the customary, but it need not be: it may eventually prove rational to no longer choose it. Thus, to pursue the analogy of the site of the capital; if, over the next two hundred years, the location of the population shifts to the north, the costs of using

custom' presses the significance of history, without invoking the 'culture' of the historical–cultural. It elevates 'fate' without insinuating 'destiny'. It suggests 'path dependency' without strictly entailing 'memory'. 'Inertial' is probably the best term for capturing the phenomenon at stake, especially when inertia is properly defined as resistance to a change in state of motion, rather than as a state of rest; the rational response to the wrong choice of a fork in the road may be to travel further down the path.

Might Australia be prone to be shaped by rational custom? Australia is a thicket of constitutions, Upper Houses, judicial review, tiers of government; all making for sunk costs and process costs. Above all, Australian Federation—that 'last kick of the old radical colonial politics' (Waterson 1970, p. 41)—made for sunk decisions that have imparted 'tremendous... inertia' to the national political system' (Parker 1969, p. 62), where decisions 'continue long after the original purpose has disappeared... rather like a fugue in music' (Sawer 1966, p. 106). A straightforward illustration is federal finance: the doom of states finances was spelt by clauses in the Constitution of 1901 prohibiting state taxes, notwithstanding the apparent trust in the Constitution's jerry-rigged evasions of that fate.[45] The only escape would be an extra-legal withdrawal from Federation, but at a prohibitively high cost. Another illustration may be in workplace relations: it is tempting to think that the decision to allow the Commonwealth to legislate for compulsory arbitration—admitted to the draft constitution on the third attempt, at the meretricious entreaty of H. B. Higgins, and by a margin of twenty-two to nineteen following the gratuitous defection of Western Australia—was deeply fateful.[46] Intended for itinerant shearers and seaman who, by the nature of their trade, traversed states, Section 51 (xxxv) exploded in consequence, sustained by the strength of precedent in the constitutional decisions that forced its path; its retraction has rarely seemed worth the cost,[47] and efforts to rationalize it seem only to strengthen it.

Canberra as a capital may become so great that it does become rational to shift. There is a 'tipping point' latent.

[45] 'When the decision was made for a uniform customs tariff and inter-state free trade, the independence of the states was doomed' (Giblin 1949, p. 90). Giblin should have added the fact that the decision to vest 'excise' exclusively in the federal government prevented the states from taxing consumption. It might be retorted the US constitution has a very similar provision, yet in all but four American states sales are taxed. It was repeated High Court decisions which have defined 'excise' so as to remove consumption quite out of the reach of the states' taxation.

[46] The surprise affirmative of Western Australia later prompted La Nauze (1972, p. 208) to reflect that this provision was 'momentous for the social and political life of Australia... [and was] inserted by the group then least concerned with the problems and tensions of industrial society'.

[47] If not impossible. How could it come to pass that the sacred writ of the Engineers Case ever be altered? Only through the unlikely appointment of a majority judges who will be as insouciant about precedent as Isaac Isaacs was about the Griffith court.

To the extent that a role is awarded to rational custom, a different light shines on the significance of Australian exceptionalism. Economic–environmental explanations, by emphasizing adaptation to enduring physical realties, tend to be optimistic. By contrast, cultural–historical explanations—by invoking the non-rationality of origins—tend to be pessimistic. Rational custom, by acknowledging the burnt bridges of human existence, tends to an acquiescence without approval, and awaits the twist of chance.

3.8 The Law and the Word

The concept of rational custom provides a rational, if cheerless, explanation of the tendency of Australia to endure with the 'same old, same old'. But an entirely contrary foundation of this endurance may be advanced.

The various ways in which human beings respond to the other-worldly may be organized around the antithesis between the nomistic and the antinomian. This distinction is essentially between obedience and disobedience, and is captured in many familiar contrasts: the pharisaical versus the prophetical; 'superstition' versus 'enthusiasm'; mystique versus charisma; the Law and the Word.

Australia very much takes its religion in the first style. From these deserts, have any prophets come? Its culture positively suffocates the antinomian impulse. Thus the desiccation of nineteenth-century Methodism amidst the 'connexional principle'. Thus the fact that no religion, it has been observed, has ever been founded in Australia; the possibility appears to wither at the point of germination. Alfred Deakin, in retreat after loss of office in 1904, became fervently engaged with Islam (Gabay 1992). His cherished son-in-law entreated him to leave politics and lead a new church. Deakin wavered. And returned to politics to pass the Excise Tariff Act.[48]

Australia makes an obvious contrast to the USA, where the antinomian has had a more vigorous life—the latter a country born in the failure of mystique of monarchy; a country of revolutions, wars, revivals, and crazes. Characteristically, it was from the west coast of the USA there arrived in Australia revolutionary and (literally) incendiary socialism in the form of 'Wobbly propheticism' (Winters 1985, p. 126), to confront the bureaucracies of the unions and the Labor Party. From these examples it is evident that the nomistic and the antinomian are more than just responses to the other-worldly, and may have relevance for the questions of this book. The relevance would be

[48] Surveys have indicated that Australians commonly nominate Ned Kelly as their national hero, an undoubtedly charismatic figure (McIntyre 1992). But does the selection of Kelly indicate the strength of the charismatic in Australian life, or its degeneracy?

that the antinomian both drives, and is driven by, ideas; ideas strong and possibly noble; ideas necessarily crude, indistinct, and unreal. The nomistic, by contrast, chloroforms ideas, and places them under glass. One implication for Australian exceptionalism of the strength of the nomistic and the weakness of the antinomian is the weakness of unbound ideals in Australia and the strength of *idées fixe*. £1 an acre, a 7s per day wage, the 2½ inch wide wool comb, the four pillars of banking; it is in observing such formulas that much energy of Australian society has been poured.

References

Adams, F. 1892. *Australian Essays*. Melbourne: William Inglis.

Adams, F. 1893. *The Australians: a Social Sketch*. London: T. Fisher Unwin.

Anderson, H. 2002. 'The wild colonial Jack Donahue', *Journal of Australian Colonial History*, vol. 4, no. 1, pp. 57–80.

Baker, S. J. 1966. *The Australian Language*. Sydney: Currawong.

Barber, B. 1986. 'Louis Hartz', *Political Theory*, vol. 14, no. 3, pp. 355–8.

Belcher, M. 1999. 'Demographic influences in children and family in New South Wales 1820–1841', *Journal of Australian Colonial History*, vol. 1, no. 2, pp. 1–29.

Bolton, G. 1973. 'Louis Hartz', *Australian Economic History Review*, vol. 13, no. 2, pp. 168–76.

Boyd, R. 1972. *The Great Great Australian Dream*. Sydney: Pergamon Press.

Brooks, D. 2001. *Bobos in Paradise: The New Upper Class and How They Got There*. New York: Simon & Schuster.

Brûlé, T. 2015. 'Nanny state rules making Australia "world's dumbest nation"', *Sydney Morning Herald*, 28 May, p. 4.

Chesterman, R. N. 2013. *Queensland Health Payroll System Commission of Inquiry Report*, <http://www.healthpayrollinquiry.qld.gov.au/?a=207203> (accessed 20 November 2015).

Christie, M. F. 1995. 'The end of Darwin's Chinatown', *Northern Perspective*, vol. 18, no. 2, pp. 45–52.

Clarke, G. 1965. 'Urban Australia' in A. F. Davies and S. Encel (eds.) *Australian Society: a Sociological Introduction*. Melbourne: Cheshire.

Collins, H. 1985. 'Political ideology in Australia: the distinctiveness of a Benthamite society', *Daedalus*, vol. 114, no. 1, pp. 147–69.

Crawford, R. M. 1952. *Australia*. London: Hutchinson.

Daun, A. 1996. *Swedish Mentality*. Pennsylvania: Pennsylvania University Press.

Davies, A. F. 1958. *Australian Democracy*. Melbourne: Longmans Green & Co.

Davies, A. F. 1985. 'Small country blues: advantages and disadvantages of living in a small country like Australia', *Meanjin*, vol. 44, no. 2, pp. 243–52.

Davison, G. 2012. 'Rethinking the Australian Legend', *Australian Historical Studies*, vol. 43, no. 3, pp. 429–51.

Dilke, C. 1890. *Problems of Greater Britain*, 2 vols. London: Macmillan.

Dyster, B. 2007. 'Bungling a courthouse: a story of convict workplace reform', *Journal of the Royal Australian Historical Society*, vol. 93, no. 1, pp. 1–21.

Edwards, P. G. (ed.). 1979. *Australia through American Eyes, 1935–1945: Observations by American Diplomats*. St Lucia, Qld: University of Queensland Press.

Eggleston, F. W. 1953a. *Reflections of an Australian Liberal*. Melbourne: FW Cheshire.

Eggleston, F. W. 1953b. 'The Australian nation' in G. Caiger (ed.), *The Australian Way of Life*. London: Heinemann.

Encel, S. 1970. *Equality and Authority: A Study of Class, Status and Power in Australia*. Melbourne: Cheshire.

Fox, K. 2015. *Australian Legal Dynasties: The Stephens and the Streets*, <http://adb.anu.edu.au/essay/10/text30750> (accessed 20 November 2015).

Fraser, J. F. 1910. *Australia: The Making of a Nation*. London: Cassell.

Gabay, A. L. 1992. *The Mystic Life of Alfred Deakin*. Victoria: Cambridge University Press.

Gascoyne-Cecil, R. 1935. *Lord Robert Cecil's Gold Fields Diary: With Introduction and Notes by Ernest Scott*. Melbourne: Melbourne University Press.

Giblin, L. F. 1949. 'Financial aspects of the constitution' in G. Sawer (ed.), *Federalism in Australia*. Melbourne: Cheshire.

Grant, P. M. 1975. 'Henry Bournes Higgins, Victorian liberal, 1851–1901', MA thesis, University of Melbourne.

Hagan, J. and Turner, K. 2007. 'The Italian influence on political change in the Murrumbidgee NSW, 1941–2007', *Journal of the Royal Australian Historical Society*, vol. 93, no. 2, pp. 171–82.

Hancock, W. K. 1930. *Australia*. London: Ernest Benn.

Harris, A. [1847] 1953. *Settlers and Convicts*. Melbourne: Melbourne University Press.

Hartwell, R. M. 1955. 'The pastoral ascendency: 1820–50' in G. Greenwood (ed.), *Australia: A Social and Political History*. New York: Praeger.

Hartz, L. 1964. *The Founding of New Societies*. New York: Harcourt Brace Jovanovich.

Hirst, J. 1973. *Adelaide and the Country, 1870–1917: Their Social and Political Relationship*. Melbourne: Melbourne University Press.

Hirst, J. 1996. 'Russel Ward: the life and the work', *Australian Historical Studies*, vol. 27, no. 107, pp. 356–8.

Hirst, J. 2009a. *Building a Free Australia: Places of Democracy*. Canberra: Australian Heritage Council.

Hirst, J. 2009b. *Sense and Nonsense in Australian History*. Melbourne: Black.

Hirst, J. 2014. *Australian History in Seven Questions*. Melbourne: Black.

Horne, D. 1964. *The Lucky Country: Australia in the Sixties*. Melbourne: Penguin.

Jessop, G. 2009. 'Victoria's unique approach to road safety: a history of government regulation', *Australian Journal of Politics and History*, vol. 35, no. 2, pp. 190–200.

Kercher, B. 1996. *Debt, Seduction, and Other Disasters: The Birth of Civil Law in Convict New South Wales*. Sydney: Federation Press.

Kiddle, M. 1961. *Men of Yesterday: A Social History of the Western District of Victoria, 1834–1890*. Melbourne: Melbourne University Press.

La Nauze, J. A. 1972. *The Making of the Australian Constitution*. Melbourne: Melbourne University Press.

Lawson, R. 1980. 'Towards demythologizing the Australian Legend: Turner's frontier thesis and the Australian experience', *Journal of Social History*, vol. 13, no. 4, pp. 577–87.

Loomis, B. 2013. 'The politics of cosy relationships in the nation's chamber of secrets', *Australian Financial Review*, 21 June, p. 39.

McCarty, J. W. 1973. 'Australia as a region of recent settlement in the nineteenth century', *Australian Economic History Review*, vol. 13, no. 2, pp. 148–67.

MacDonagh, O. 1986. 'The Irish in Australia: a general view' in O. MacDonagh and W. Mandle (eds.), *Ireland and Irish-Australia: Studies in Cultural and Political History*. London: Croom Helm.

McIntyre, A. 1992. 'Ned Kelly as folk hero' in J. Carroll (ed.), *Intruders in the Bush: The Australian Quest for Identity*. Melbourne: Oxford University Press.

MacKenzie, J. 1961. *Australian Paradox*. Melbourne: FW Cheshire.

Martin, A. W. 1973. 'Australia and the Hartz "fragment" thesis', *Australian Economic History Review*, vol. 13, no. 2, pp. 131–47.

Martineau, J. 1869. *Letters from Australia*. London: Longmans Green.

Melville, H. [1851] 1972. *Moby-Dick*. Harmondsworth: Penguin.

Merritt, J. 1986. *The Making of the AWU*. Melbourne: Oxford University Press.

Merritt, J. 2008. 'Shearers, mountain stockmen and the Australian legend', *Journal of Australian Colonial History*, vol. 10, no. 2, pp. 59–72.

Métin, A. [1901] 1977. *Socialism without Doctrine*, trans. R. Ward. Chippendale, NSW: Alternative Publishing Co-operative.

O'Farrell, P. 1986. 'Writing the history of Irish Australia' in O. MacDonagh and W. F. Mandle (eds.), *Ireland and Irish-Australia: Studies in Cultural and Political History*. London: Croom Helm.

O'Farrell, P. 1993. *The Irish in Australia*. Sydney: New South Wales University Press.

Olson, M. 1965. *The Logic of Collective Action: Public Goods and the Theory of Groups*, Cambridge, Mass.: Harvard University Press.

O'Malley, R. 2013. *Mateship and Moneymaking: Australian Shearing: The Clash of Union Solidarity with the Spirit of Enterprise, 1895–1995*. Katoomba, NSW: Xlibris.

Palmer, N. 1931. *Henry Bournes Higgins: A Memoir*. London: Harrap.

Parker, R. 1969. 'Federalism: Australian brand' in H. Mayer (ed.), *Australian Politics: A Second Reader*. Melbourne: FW Cheshire.

Parnaby, J. E. 1967. 'The composition of the Victorian Parliament 1857–1861', in *Historical Studies: Selected Articles, Second Series*, comp. M. Beever and F. B. Smith. Melbourne: Melbourne University Press.

Partridge, P. H. 1973. *Society, Schools and Progress in Australia*. Sydney: Pergamon Press.

Peltzman, S. 1975. 'The effects of automobile safety regulation', *Journal of Political Economy*, vol. 83, no. 4, pp. 677–726.

Penton, B. 1943. *Advance Australia: Where?* London: Cassell.

Perry, T. M. 1963. *Australia's First Frontier: The Spread of Settlement in New South Wales, 1788–1829*. Melbourne: Melbourne University Press.

Pike, D. 1957. *Paradise of Dissent: South Australia 1829–1857*. London: Longmans Green & Co.

Pike, D. 1962. 'The small holders place in the Australian tradition', *Tasmanian Historical Research Association Papers*, vol. 10, pp. 28–33.

Quinlan, M. 1998. 'Regulating labour in a colonial context: maritime legislation in the Australian colonies 1788–1850', *Australian Historical Studies*, vol. 29, no. 111, pp. 303–24.

Richards, K. 2015. *The Story of Australian English*. Sydney: New South Publishing.

Robinson, P. 1985. *The Hatch and Brood of Time: A Study of the First Generation of Native-Born White Australians 1788–1828*. Melbourne: Oxford University Press.

Roe, M. 1963. *Philip Gidley King*. Melbourne: Oxford University Press.

Roe, M. 1965. *Quest for Authority in Eastern Australia, 1835–1851*. Melbourne: Melbourne University Press.

Rosecrance, R. 1964. 'The Radical Culture of Australia' in L. Hartz (ed.), *Founding of New Societies*. New York: Harcourt Brace Jovanovich.

Rowland, P. F. 1903. *The New Nation: A Sketch of the Social, Political and Economic Conditions and Prospects of the Australian Commonwealth*. London: Smith, Elder.

Sawer, G. 1952. 'The record of judicial review' in G. Sawer (ed.), *Federalism: An Australian Jubilee Study*. Melbourne: FW Cheshire.

Sawer, G. 1966. 'The constitution and its politics' in H. Mayer (ed.), *Australian Politics: A Reader*. Melbourne: Cheshire.

Serle, G. 1967. 'The Victorian Legislative Council, 1856–1950' in *Historical Studies: Selected Articles, First Series*, comp. J. J. Eastwood and F. B. Smith. Melbourne: Melbourne University Press.

Smith, B. 2010. 'Legend and reality: the genius of Russel Ward', *Journal of Australian Colonial History*, vol. 12, pp. 171–90.

Spate, O. H. K. 1968. *Australia*. Melbourne: Benn.

Stein, S. J. and Stein, B. H. 1970. *The Colonial Heritage of Latin America: Essays on Economic Dependence in Perspective*. New York: Oxford University Press.

Taylor, T. G. 1945. *Australia: A Study of Warm Environments and their Effect on British Settlement*. London: Methuen.

Therry, R. 1863. *Reminiscences of Thirty Years' Residence in New South Wales and Victoria*. London: Sampson Low, Son, and Co.

Trollope, A. 1873. *Australia and New Zealand*. Melbourne: G. Robertson.

Twopeny, R. E. N. [1883] 1973. *Town Life in Australia*. Victoria: Penguin.

Walker, R. B. 1986. 'Violence in industrial conflicts in New South Wales in the nineteenth century', *Australian Historical Studies*, vol. 22, no. 86, pp. 54–70.

Ward, R. 1954. *Man Makes History: World History from the Earliest Times to the Renaissance*. Sydney: Shakespeare Head.

Ward, R. 1958. *The Australian Legend*. Melbourne: Oxford University Press.

Ward, R. 1965. *Australia*. London: Ure Smith.

Ward, R. 1976. 'The Australian legend re-visited', *Australian Historical Studies*, vol. 18, no. 71, pp. 171–90.

Waterson, D. B. 1970. 'The Federation movement', *Journal of History (Victorian Historical Association)*, vol. 1, no. 4, pp. 35–44.

Winters, D. E. 1985. *The Soul of the Wobblies: the I.W.W., Religion, and American Culture in the Progressive Era, 1905–1917*. Westport, Conn.: Greenwood Press.

4

Utilitarianism contra Sectarianism

The Official and the Unauthorized Civic Religion of Australia

Greg Melleuish and Stephen A. Chavura

4.1 The Myth of Australia as Secular

One of the great myths of Australian political, social, and cultural development is the belief that Australia is an almost uniquely secular country which has always been guided by secular principles. Australians are understood to be worldly, materialist, and primarily concerned with the things of this world. Hence the term 'utilitarianism' becomes code for a set of these worldly materialist values which were considered to be the failings of an immigrant society composed largely of people from the lower orders of society. According to this view, Australia was 'born modern' (Kociumbas 1992, ix),[1] with 'modernity' including 'secular'. But what exactly is meant by 'secular'? Does it mean the complete absence of religion? Does it mean a social and cultural order devoted to a 'this world' view of the cosmos? Or is it simply more code for the supposedly materialist predilections of Australians?

The idea that utilitarianism is the supposed public philosophy of Australia found its fullest expression in an essay by Hugh Collins (1985, p. 148), in which he claims 'that the mental universe of Australian politics is essentially Benthamite'. It must be said that his case is weak. Indeed, there is a mass of

[1] A huge literature has since emerged which resituates Christianity, particularly Protestant Christianity, at the centre of Australian civil society and order from colonial times to the mid-twentieth century. A brilliant and recent study is Gladwin (2015). A popular but very thoughtful one is Williams (2015).

evidence against it. Henry Parkes, many times premier of New South Wales (NSW) from the 1870s to the 1890s, of Chartist roots, is claimed as an exemplar, but any sustained reading of what Parkes wrote indicates a strong adherence to an ideal of Britishness rooted in the seventeenth-century Puritan Commonwealth. Worse still, Collins is able to place Alfred Deakin, the dominant political figure of the first decade of the Commonwealth of Australia, within the Benthamite tradition, but only at the cost of making no mention of Deakin's debt to British philosophical idealism.

It can be argued that this portrayal of Australia as utilitarian owes much to those who were critical of what they saw as its failings. In particular, religious professionals and those with intellectual pretensions—and the two have often overlapped—have enjoyed themselves by denouncing the shortcomings of other Australians. The most notorious case was historian Manning Clark, son of a Church of England minister, who devoted six volumes of his *History of Australia* to decrying the faults and weaknesses of the bourgeois British in Australia. But he was only part of a long tradition in Australia of criticizing its materialist failings, that stretches back to W. C. Wentworth, John Woolley, J. D. Lang, and Henry Parkes. Although there may be some truth that a settler society such as Australia is prone to the pursuit of 'filthy lucre', one should look carefully at those who denounce it as being so, and the agenda which they are pushing. For example, advocates of liberal education in Australia have long identified their enemy as utilitarianism in order to justify their own particular programmes, especially with regard to university education, although what they mean by liberal education is a moveable feast (Melleuish 2015b).

The idea that Australia is somehow uniquely secular, the product of a modern, post-religious dispensation, is an illusion, brought on by an inadequate understanding of what religion, and the religious condition, means, together with a dash of wishful thinking. Australia is not necessarily all that far removed from the sorts of developments which occurred across societies of European derivation following the Reformation. Like them, the primary function of government has moved from a preoccupation with military matters to providing services for the civilian population; in nineteenth-century Australia this meant, above all else, building railways and schools. A key feature of the end of the confessional state has been the recognition of religious pluralism which, as shall be argued, raised all sorts of problems once the state involved itself seriously in education. This first came to a head during the French Revolution when the French state took control of the French Church, stripped it of its assets, and proceeded to make both welfare and education into matters controlled by the state. Jews and Protestants were also given legal equality. The immediate consequences were chaos and an enormous rift between church and state (McLeod 2000). Western countries generally faced the problem of renegotiating the place of religion in a modern pluralist society. They resolved it in different ways. Just as every member of the Anglosphere has a political system which has a family resemblance to the others but is distinctive, so the place of religion has come to differ in each such country (Monsma and Soper 2008).

Whereas Britain officially remained a Christian country with an established church, even as it accommodated non-conformists, Catholics, and many indifferent members of the Church of England, America became a country based on a secular constitution and a strong tradition of voluntarism and self-help which was effectively Christianized in the first half of the nineteenth century. The absence of a church establishment meant that nineteenth-century America was, in religious terms, a dynamic place where new religions emerged, from Mormonism to Seventh-day Adventism to Christian Science (Albanese 2007). In America, unlike France, Christianity and democracy were not merely reconciled but also self-supporting (Hatch 1989), which may be one reason why America has resisted secularization more than most other Western countries.

The Australian experience in terms of dealing with the reality of religious pluralism is distinctive, but not unique. Clerics, intellectuals, and politicians have, for different reasons, sought to emphasize that Australia was born, and remained, modern, secular, and utilitarian. However, this has not been the case. Religion has played an important role in Australia. As shall be argued, the religious history of Australia, and the history of Australia generally, makes perfect sense in the context of a culture which proclaimed itself as proudly British, and hence Protestant, while containing a large Irish Catholic minority which made a lie of its pretensions. As with Britain, one of the key factors of Australian history since the First World War has been the decline of Protestantism (Green 2009), which has also meant the decline of Britishness.

4.2 Religion in Australia

The place of religion in Australian history is complex. But then people came to Australia in an odd mix of circumstances, as convicted criminals at one extreme, to those seeking their luck in the goldfields at the other. None of these circumstances led to the renunciation of religion, although it did mean the role of religion was shaped by the types of people who came to the various colonies. At one extreme this meant the reformation of criminals, and, at the other, the beliefs and practices of young men who had travelled halfway around the world in search of their fortune. On top of all of this was the effective campaign by evangelicals, especially in NSW and South Australia, to separate the Church from state endowment. There were many reasons why such a society would achieve a reputation for irreligion.

Most importantly, Australia proved the perfect laboratory for aspirations for Church–State separation, aspirations that could not be decried as 'revolutionary' in a new, pluralist society with no long-standing tradition of Church establishment (Chavura and Tregenza 2015). At various points of time, close to 50 per cent of the population may have been adherents of the Church of England; but there has also always been a significant Catholic population, for a long time largely Irish in ethnicity, of above 20 per cent of the population. The rest were largely various forms of Protestant non-conformists, including adherents of the Presbyterian Church, which is the national Church of Scotland. What is worth noting is that, unlike America, Australia has not created any new religions, nor has its public religiosity been characterized by the more dynamic evangelical churches which prospered in the USA. Australian churches have largely been mainstream. The basic divide has been between the 75 per cent to 80 per cent who identified as Protestant and the 25 per cent who were Catholic. For Protestants, the key factor on any issue was the attitude of the adherents of the Church of England.

The basic issue facing Australian societies was that of managing religious pluralism in a society in which one church, the Church of England, was for a long time dominant. This was not just a religious matter, as religion was connected to ethnicity, in particular the vexed issue of the relationship between Great Britain and Ireland. Religion and race were entwined and difficult to disentangle. A primary concern was to ensure that religious difference did not turn into religious conflict, thereby creating a social order riven by violent, even murderous, activities, such as came to be the case in Ireland. In this regard one must say that Australians were remarkably successful; hatred there was, and suspicion, but bloody and violent confrontation was relatively rare. When confrontation did happen, there could be an almost farcical element to it, as the case of members of the Catholic Social Studies Movement and readers of Protestant Publications's the *Rock* clashing over an attempt to 'rescue' a nun from a convent (Duncan 2001, p. 123); or the Revd C. T. Forscutt being chased from the Domain when he argued that Irish Catholics should not be allowed to teach in NSW public schools (Melleuish 2015a, p. 64).

Despite claims that Australia was born 'modern', and hence without any real commitment to religious belief, there can be no doubt that, for a long time, an extremely high proportion of Australians claimed adherence to a religion. In fact, between 1947 and 1954 the proportion of those claiming no religious belief or who refused to answer the religious question in the census declined from 11.45 per cent to 9.96 per cent (Clark 1958, p. 285). It was only in the 1960s, in line with other Anglo countries, excluding America, that religious adherence began to decline seriously (Brown 2012). Religion mattered in Australia, and this can be seen in the fact that most Australian prime ministers of that period had a religious connection, such connections ranged from the Catholicism of Scullin and Lyons to the Anglicanism of William Morris Hughes to the more exotic religiosity of Alfred Deakin (Williams 2013). L. F. Fitzhardinge describes Hughes as 'deeply religious, with a profound belief in the after-life and the all-pervasiveness of God of which he seldom spoke except to a few old friends' (1979, pp. xvi–xvii).

Deakin is the most interesting and, perhaps, paradoxical of these figures. Reading his contributions to the Federation debates one does not find a man seeking to create a religious or Christian country. Although he voted in favour of the recognition of the deity in the preamble, he is not an outspoken advocate of the need to put God into the constitution; almost paradoxically that role falls to the Irish Catholic Patrick Glynn, future free trade member of the Commonwealth parliament and Liberal minister. Rather we find someone soaked in the traditions of British common law and constitutional theory. At times, one would think that one is reading Edmund Burke. But there also survives fervent prayers recorded in Deakin's private diary during this time (Gabay 1992, ch. 4). It is as if there was a disjunction between one sphere of Deakin's life and another.

Or was there? This all depends on how one understands the connection between political/legal ideas and Protestantism in the ideals of Britishness which underpinned much of the public culture of colonial and federated Australia. Henry Parkes (1867, p. 3) could speak of 'British subjects—of a Protestant nation, recollect, and subjects of a Protestant Crown'. A British country was a country which took its British inheritance for granted, and this most certainly can be seen in the Federation debates. That inheritance included Protestantism, but it was a Protestantism which could be simply taken for granted. In a way, Protestantism, common law, and an empirical approach to political matters were all just different elements of a complex culture. They were all part of what Marshall Hodgson (1993, ch. 8) has called 'cultural patterning'. Hence Deakin's strange religious explorations fitted in easily with his British political ideals. They were just two sides of his 'Britishness'.

4.3 Australia and the Secular

'Secularism' in Australian history can be viewed in two ways. One is that it was an expression of British cultural patterning and, hence, an element of the Protestant religious ideal. British Protestantism, especially within the Church of England, had evolved so that a certain 'this worldliness' was central to its religious outlook. It has been argued (Nemo 2006, ch. 6) that Latin

Christianity has always been more sympathetic to the realm of the 'this worldly' than both other religions and other forms of Christianity, especially Orthodox Christianity. If this is the case, then British Protestantism took this sympathy for things secular to a new level, with an emphasis on natural religion and an appreciation of utilitarianism, such as is found in the works of William Paley ([1785] 2002, bk 6.10). Christianity for Protestants was not only world-affirming, but affirming the world was inconceivable without Christianity. Rev. Professor John Woolley (1862, pp. 88–9) of Sydney University could speak of the 'real connexion between the secular and the sacred', that they are 'not independent': 'The churchman shall hear the voice of God in civil institutions... the citizen shall glorify the divine source of earthly virtue... ' Likewise, Alfred Deakin (n.d.) could write privately, 'Without God and without immortality there can be no true or efficient morality from generation to generation, no task for the race, and no goal for it to attain.'

The other way of considering secularism, and this does not contradict the first, is that it was a means to manage religious pluralism, of attempting to ensure that differences of dogma could be accommodated within a common Christian culture. It needs to be appreciated that the Australian colonies, as settler societies, were decidedly unsettled, as they were composed of people who had to come to terms with living in a society of strangers. Moreover, at various stages, such as in Victoria in the 1850s and NSW in the 1870s, there was a large influx of new people who had to be accommodated into the existing social order and for whom infrastructure needed to be provided. The remarkable thing is that this process occurred without much in the way of conflict and violence, except in the case of the extraordinary hatred at times directed towards the Chinese who came to Australia. The Chinese were considered to be outside the tent; everyone from the British Isles, plus small minorities from other parts of Europe, including the not insignificant Lutheran community, were inside. Parkes (1890, p. 222) spoke for nearly everyone in the Federation debates in demanding an immigration policy appropriate 'for a people modelled on the type of the British nation; and it is on that ground, and on that ground alone, that I have opposed the introduction of the Chinese'. Therefore the issue became one of managing diversity, not on the basis of ethnicity, but on religion. Religion was understood to be an essential, even necessary, element of society. It was the basis of morality and hence public order. Religion, declared Patrick Glynn, a South Australian delegate to the Federation conventions, 'pervades all the relations of our civil life. It is felt in the forms of our courts of justice, in the language of our Statutes, in the oath that binds the sovereign to the observance of our liberties... ' (Glynn 1897, p. 1185).

What this means is that the idea of creating a purely secular society, one from which religion had been banished, at least from the public sphere, was only ever the fantasy of a small minority of the population. Certainly there was a small and active group of 'infidels' or secularists, including E. W. Cole and H. K. Rusden in the 1860s and 1870s in Melbourne (Gregory 1973, pp. 107–12), and many of the *Bulletin* school in the 1890s had a rather jaundiced view of religion and the clergy (Docker 1991, p. 39). But, then, the 1890s and early twentieth century was a highpoint of Protestant political activity in Australia, with such issues as Sunday observance and local option regarding hotels high on the political agenda (Bollen 1972).

4.4 Religion, the State, and Education

From one perspective, the real issue in nineteenth-century Australia was the need to Christianize the population, to ensure that they did not slip beyond the grip of whatever church, or chapel, to which they were connected. Anyone who visits country towns in inland Australia can see how successful that operation was; almost all towns have churches of a variety of denominations. The churches were built and people attended them. Australia was not a de-Christianized society, and religion continued to play an important role in its social and cultural life. For example, clergymen played a significant role in the intellectual life of nineteenth-century NSW, as naturalists, political thinkers, and newspaper editors (Gladwin 2015; Williams 2015). The first work of philosophy published in Australia was a series of lectures delivered by the Rev. Barzillai Quaife (1872), who also tutored the young George Reid, the future NSW premier and Australian prime minister. Philosophy in Australia long continued to have strong links to religion (Franklin 2003).

State support for religion and for religious schools was followed by the development of state schools. John Gascoigne (2002, p. 30) has argued that the withdrawal of state funding for the churches, and the state supplanting the Church in education can be seen as an indication of the workings of the Enlightenment in Australia. To an extent this is true, but it can also be seen as a belated recognition within European culture of the futility of attempting to impose religious uniformity and homogeneity. Most of the other world civilizations had not attempted to impose religious unity; for example, the Ottoman Empire had developed the millet system (Finer 1997, pp. 1196–7), under which particular Christian and Jewish religious communities ran their own affairs according to their own laws with the proviso that Islam was dominant, as a way of dealing with the multiplicity of religious groups within its borders. The growing power of the state and its desire to control education was a solution to a problem. If the citizens of an increasingly democratic country were to be educated to a satisfactory level then this could not be achieved unless there were means to ensure that certain standards were met.

The establishment of universal primary education was a massive undertaking, comparable only to the building of the network of railway lines. The number of schoolteachers employed by the government in NSW increased from 370 in 1858 to 1,825 in 1878 (Golder 2005, pp. 197–9). This was an issue requiring a practical approach, but practical did not mean a radicalism grounded in secularism and utilitarianism. The states' approaches to the issue of religion in education varied. Victoria was the most radically secular in that it seemingly excluded religious instruction from its schools. But, then, Victoria was also the centre of radical secularism amongst the Australian colonies, which probably owes a lot to the type of person attracted to Victoria by the gold rushes. In Victoria, clergymen, 'along with judges, felons and traitors', were prohibited from being members of parliament (Gregory 1973, pp. 148–51). In a bizarre development, in what today would be described as 'political correctness', religious phrases were removed from the readers used in state primary schools in the 1870s (Austin 1961, pp. 230–1). But this did not mean that Victorians were necessarily laicists. Indeed, the question of religion and the Bible in schools was not a 'settled' issue such as protectionism. For example, Alfred Deakin (Parliament of Victoria 1898, pp. 1–8) would petition parliament in 1898 for the introduction of general religious instruction within normal school hours; and battles to either introduce or remove Bible readings from school lessons would continue up to the First World War. J. S. Gregory (1973, p. 217) shows that there was a greater blurring of the division in the first half of the twentieth century in Victoria, including the introduction of the following, 'I love my God and my Country', in a state school pledge as late as 1940. Certainly this concern for the secular purity of state schools did not prevent nineteenth-century Melbourne from having a reputation as a dour place which imposed a rigid Sabbatarianism—except for a short time in the 1890s—including the need for omnibus drivers to walk their vehicles past churches during Divine Service on a Sunday (Moore 2009, p. 3). In fact, a fairly strict Sabbatarianism remained in force in most of Australia until the 1960s.

There is a paradox here. It confirms that secular schooling was not meant to lead to the creation of a secular society. It confirms rather a particular view of the role of religion in society and its relationship to the wider culture; one which accepted that Australia was essentially a Christian, and predominately Protestant, country (hence Sabbatarianism) while recognizing that enforcing a particular religion was not the role of the state. It makes perfect sense if one accepts that the culture of the Australian colonies was British, and hence Protestant.

Public schooling in NSW was not as exclusive of religion as Victoria but was still, at its core, secular. Its chief architect, William Wilkins (1865, p. 6), has provided us with a well-reasoned rationale for ensuring that: 'The proper function of the primary school is to teach the elements of secular knowledge.'

To do so, Wilkins (1865, p. 7) develops both a theory of the state and a definition of religion. It is a very democratic theory of the state as 'the embodiment of the will of the *whole* people', which can only be 'entrusted to such objects only as are of universal benefit, so that *all* may *alike* participate in the advantages arising from public expenditure'. It must have a 'civil character' and it 'cannot rightly interfere with matters of opinion which do not directly affect the obedience of citizens to the law'. Wilkins defines religion to mean the 'attitude of the soul toward the Divine Ruler of the Universe'.

On this basis Wilkins develops two arguments. The first is that it is infringement of freedom of opinion and the civil nature of public education for the state to subsidize the teaching of the religion of particular denominations. If the state was required 'to provide the special religious teaching of each denomination, and to establish separate schools for that purpose':

> The resources derived from *all* would be applied to the purposes of a portion of the citizens; equal rights would not be afforded to all; schools would cease to be civil institutions; and the State would become the agent for the promotion and repression of opinion among its subjects. (Wilkins 1865, p. 3)

The second argument is that the schoolmaster should have nothing to do with the teaching of dogmatic theology because a 'religious education for children does not of necessity imply any acquaintance with dogmatic theology' (Wilkins 1865, p. 4). Wilkins was quite hostile to teaching dogma, and such things as catechisms, to primary school students, arguing that it involved them in simply learning words which they could not properly understand. His crucial argument is that it is possible to divide religion into a number of elements, of which dogma, or doctrine, is but one; the common element can be taught to all schoolchildren, doctrines peculiar to particular denominations can be left to those denominations.

It is a wonderfully elegant solution to a problem, if you were a cultural Protestant who could countenance your children reading the Bible in the King James Version without priestly supervision. However, there were other motives at work in support of a state-based education system. In NSW, the introduction of state secular schooling occurred in two stages, both involving Henry Parkes. The 1866 Act established state schools but kept funding for denominational schools. The 1880 Act abolished state funding for denominational schools. Introducing his Public Schools Bill in 1866, Henry Parkes (1876, p. 235) referred also to the fact 'that education thus carried on is unnecessarily expensive', the quality of the education, and the need to reach all students, as well as the fact 'that the present method is calculated to engender jealousies and uncharitable feelings among the different sections of society'. State funding of denominational schools was doomed because it was expensive and inefficient, it was difficult to ensure quality control, and there was a need to reach children in every part of the colony. It might be argued that such considerations involve a utilitarian mentality, but it would be truer to say that this concern with efficiency and economy was part of the civic element of Britishness and fitted easily with the country's Protestantism.

It is ironic that the other reason given by Parkes in 1866 for a government system of schools was to prove to be the opposite of what happened when, ultimately, governments decided to no longer fund denominational schools. The Catholic Church rejected the basis on which this model of schooling was based. The consequence was to 'engender jealousies and uncharitable feelings among the different sections of society'. From the viewpoint of the various British Protestant denominations, the idea of a state-run and funded education system was acceptable. Even the Church of England, which had been originally hostile to such an arrangement, accepted it. It can be argued that this was because the Church of England accepted the version of the nature of religion, and its relationship to the wider emerging British–Australian culture which Wilkins had explicated. Whereas the status of the 'secular' in Victorian education legislation was (probably deliberately) ambiguous, the 1880 Public Instruction Act in NSW explicitly stated that 'the words "secular instruction" shall be held to include general religious teaching as distinguished from dogmatical or polemical theology'. To be a good citizen one did not have to jettison one's Protestant religion; one's religious identity and one's civic identity were just two sides of the same coin.

4.5 Being Protestant, Being British

One can get a sense of how religious and civic life reinforced each other amongst British Protestant Australians in a recent study of members of the Enmore Tabernacle of the Church of Christ in the late nineteenth and early twentieth century (Hayward and Nutt 2014). The Church of Christ was a small Protestant denomination in Australia, and appealed largely to what might be described as the lower middle class. This group was composed of businessmen, politicians, and educationalists, of whom the best known was Reginald Marcus Clarke, the department store owner. Members combined a strong commitment to their Church with an equally strong engagement with the civic culture of which they were part. The group included two men, D. R. Hall and John Hindle, who were, at various times, Labor politicians.

For such individuals, their Protestant religion and their engagement with the secular world were mutually reinforcing. Referring to John Bardsley, another member of the congregation, G. T. Waldron wrote that 'Bro. Bardsley's life proves that a man can be a keen and successful businessman, and also an earnest and consistent Christian' (Hayward and Nutt 2014, p. 66). However, by the 1920s, one of this group, the Rev C. T. Forscutt, had become a somewhat ferocious cultural warrior, going into bat for the Protestant religion, the British Empire, and Australian democracy against what he saw as the twin evils of Irish Catholicism and bolshevism (Melleuish, 2015a). By this time Britishness was on the retreat.

Why was Catholicism seen to be the enemy? One of things which Forscutt attacked was the Catholic school system. The problem was that the introduction of a public school system had led to the creation of a separate and distinct Catholic school system; Protestants and Catholics were, by and large, socialized in quite distinct educational environments. This had occurred because the Catholic Church had refused to accept the sorts of ideas about religion which Wilkins had expressed so forcefully. It could not accept that there was an easy divide between religion and dogma. There was also the scandal of the Bible used as a textbook by students without the supervision of clergy (Polding cited in Legislative Council of New South Wales 1844, p. 49). The Catholic Church did not accept what was essentially the Protestant view of religion and theology. In part this reflected a Catholic hostility to the liberalism of the age, which was taken for granted to be part of the British Protestant identity. In 1864 Pope Pius IX issued the Syllabus of Errors, an attack on those liberal principles. In part it also reflected an Irish hostility to what they saw as their English oppressors back in Ireland.

There clearly was a fundamental divide between the attitudes and outlook of the Protestant British and the Catholic Irish. Advocates of public education, such as Parkes and Wilkins, had hoped that it would create a common culture but, in reality, it helped to entrench differences in that culture. To press the idea of Australia being 98 per cent 'British', as W. K. Hancock does in *Australia* (1930, p. 53), was illusionary. And at the heart of this division was education; more than anything else it kept the festering sore of sectarianism raw. Catholics resented the fact that they did not receive any support from the state for the education of their children. In fact, Catholic education could not have survived without the existence of the various teaching orders, and this meant Catholic women. It was tough, but a heroic achievement. There were hopes that Labor state governments would do something in this matter, but those hopes never led anywhere. When Labor gained power in NSW in 1910, the education minister was a Scottish Presbyterian, as was the head of the Education Department (Kildea 2002, chs 3 and 4).

Could it have been otherwise? The answer would have to be no. It could only have worked if the Irish Catholics had been willing to accept the British Protestant worldview, including its theological presuppositions, acquiesce in the universality of liberal principles, and accept its understanding of the place of religion in a wider secular world. Catholics were happy to live in, and participate in, a democratic society, but to accept the 'British ideology' was simply a bridge too far. This refusal was to have quite significant implications for the history of twentieth-century Australia.

The ascendancy of the ideal of Britishness in Australian political culture, and culture more generally, can be seen in the Federation debates of the 1890s. It is quite clear that a dominant theme of the debates was the desire to keep as close to the model of the British constitution as possible, and consequently to ensure that the constitution could evolve and adapt as circumstances changed. The constitutional debates were largely carried out in a discourse that came out of English common law and had profoundly Burkean elements (Chavura and Melleuish 2015).

This Britishness is equally illustrated by the attitude taken by the delegates on the issue of religion in the Constitution. This primarily revolved around two proposals: the inclusion of a reference to God in the preamble, and some guarantee of religious freedom. Both eventually were adopted, but their success did not mean that the Australian Constitution affirmed the ideal of Australia as a 'Christian country'. Most of the drive to have God included in the Constitution came from Protestant groups, particularly of the evangelical variety, and the 1890s represents a high point for such groups in this country in terms of activism on issues such as preventing gambling and excessive alcohol consumption, not to mention votes for women and Sabbatarianism. Such groups did believe that Australia was a Christian country. The primary opposition to having God in the preamble came from the minute Seventh-day Adventists who, having their Sabbath on a Saturday, feared that the preamble's inclusion could be used to impose strict Sunday observance (Ely 1976, ch. 6). They found their effective champion in Henry Bournes Higgins.

What Australia emerged with was God in the preamble and Section 116, which prevented the federal government from being able to enforce any religious observance on the people of Australia. It was a neat compromise. Parliament also came to be opened by prayers. Officially Australia was not a Christian country, but it was a free British society in which religion could flourish. The debates also contain this statement of the situation by Edmund Barton, who opposed putting God into the preamble:

> The whole mode of government, the whole province of the State, is secular. The whole business that is transacted by any community—however deeply Christian, unless it has an established church, unless religion is interwoven expressly and professedly with all its actions—is secular business as distinguished from religious business. The whole duty is to render unto Caesar the things that are Caesar's, and unto God the things that are God's. (Barton 1897, p. 1187)

Yet the irony of the situation is that, as Alan Atkinson (2014, pp. 296–8) has argued, and which was acknowledged at the time in the debates (National

Australasian Convention Debates 1898, p. 1739), there may have been no federated Australia if it had not been for Protestant activists in the wider Australian community, and their strong support for Federation. With the closeness of the vote in the key state of NSW, where Federation was rejected first time around, it may well have been the enthusiasm of these Protestant activists for Federation which enabled the vote to succeed in that state.

Part of the high point of Protestant political and social activity in Australia during this period was the creation of the Australian Labor Party, although it was generally recognized, in NSW at least, that Protestants supported the Free Trade Liberals. Catholics had tended to support the Protectionist Party, which made sense, as the doctrine of free trade had very strong roots in a particular form of Protestant theology (Melleuish 2014a). The ideological situation of the 1890s was quite confused; the Free Traders dabbled for a time with introducing a land tax, and George Reid's abolition of most tariffs in NSW, combined with his introduction of income tax, benefited the working classes. Only with Reid's anti-socialism campaign of 1906 did the ideological divisions assume a degree of clarity. The early Labor Party attracted many strong Protestants, including two members of the Churches of Christ, but over time it shed many of these people, including future Liberal Prime Minister, Sir Joseph Cook (Linder 1997–98). At the same time, the old Protectionist Party began to disintegrate.

Judith Brett (2002) has argued that when fusion between the Free Trade and Protectionist Liberals came in 1909, the reason many Protectionists joined with the Free Traders had nothing to do with ideology but much to do with conscience. The Labor Party asserted the supremacy of party once a decision had been made. For many Protestants this was inconsistent with the role of conscience, which is why so many of them, such as Cook, left the party in the 1890s. It is worth emphasizing that it was Protestants whom Labor shed, from the 1890s through to the conscription battles of 1917. It was not just a matter of conscience; being Protestant meant being pro-empire and pro-British, which did not bode well with increasing radical socialist opposition towards the war within the labour movement (Linder 1997–98). This is not to say that Labor politicians of Catholic origin could not be pro-British and pro-empire, as in the case of John Curtin (Curran 2011), but it is also interesting that Curtin was buried by a Presbyterian minister (Williams 2013, p. 107).

But perhaps it is the enigma of Sir Robert Menzies who best illustrates the coming fate of the liberal–British–Protestant connection in the second half of the twentieth century. Menzies is reputed not to have been a particularly religious man in terms of such things as churchgoing. But of all the prime ministers of Australia he was the one whose speeches owe the most to the Bible. Menzies was a master of the spoken word and he used his mastery to support liberal ideals and the Britishness of the British Empire. He drank the heady elixir of Englishness and came to embody it in Australia as an Anglophile Scot.

Menzies was very reassuring as an icon of British Protestantism in Australia, but somehow there was a certain lack of passion, unlike that shown by Billy Hughes. A good comparison might be with Margaret Thatcher, who has been characterized as the last great voice of non-conformity in British politics (Filby 2015). Mrs Thatcher breathed fire, but it came at a time when what she stood for no longer resonated with many people in Britain, which may explain why she encountered so much opposition. For Menzies, Britishness did not mean non-conformist zeal but rather something very Humean, an avoidance of the excess characterized by both superstition and enthusiasm. It was not devoid of belief but it was belief constrained by moderation (Menzies 1958). It was a style founded on restraint. The big problem was that style could come to dominate belief and passion. There was a certain puritanism about Menzies, just as there was of Thatcher. But it can be argued that it was this very British characteristic which was slowly dying during the course of the twentieth century. He was the last great politician to exemplify the cultural Protestant embrace of the secular. He (Menzies n.d., p. 1) was pleased to be asked to deliver a speech entitled 'The Christian Citizen in a New Era' because such a topic 'starts off by reminding us that... you cannot separate what is sacred from what is secular; and... you cannot above all things have a Christianity which begins only on Sunday morning and ends on Sunday night'.

4.6 The End of Protestant Australia

In his seminal study, *The Passing of Protestant Britain*, S. J. D. Green (2009) treats secularization in England in terms of the fate of Protestantism, including its powerful puritan element. It makes sense to consider the Australian experience in similar terms, and to see the decline of the Australian Protestant churches in terms of the decline of British Australian culture, especially since the 1960s. Of course there were other factors at work, including a new more comfortable and secure world which came into being in both Britain and Australia in the 1950s, and also the reality that it was women who ceased to play the religious role that they had previously played (Brown 2012, ch. 6).

Nevertheless, it is no coincidence that the decline of Protestantism in Australia occurred in tandem with the decline of Britishness which, of course, is related to the end of empire. In an 'age of comfort' (Melleuish 2014b), and with the loss of the élan which went with being part of an empire on which the sun never set, Protestantism made less cultural sense than it once did. In 1930 W. K. Hancock could still write of 'Independent Australian Britons' even if he made no mention of the Protestantism of those Britons; his generation, also the generation of Menzies and H. V. Evatt, Labor leader in the 1950s, was the last of that particular type of Australian. It was Manning Clark, another 'independent Australian Briton' but born some twenty years later, who spent much of his life attempting to consign such people to the dustbin of history.

The decline of Protestantism in Australia, the process of 'secularization', happened alongside a change in the relationship between religion and the broader public culture. As Protestantism was increasingly separated from the culture with which it had danced for so long, it no longer felt itself to be part of it, and came to take an adversarial role towards it. To be a Christian increasingly meant being part of a counterculture, and one's role was to bear witness to the failings of the mainstream (Chilton 2014). It was as if Protestants were back in the times of Perpetua, the second-century martyr.

As Green argues in relation to Britain, the role and place of Catholicism in Australia has to be considered quite separately to that of Protestantism. For one thing, Catholicism was never intimately linked to Britishness and always stood at one remove from the dominant culture of Australia. In this sense there was an 'Ascendancy', a hegemonic culture for a long time in Australia of which Catholicism was not part. Part of this was because of the latter's connection with Ireland. This meant that the fate of Catholicism has been somewhat different to that of Protestantism. While Catholicism has been affected by the 'age of comfort', it has not had to deal with the adverse effects of the decline of Britishness and empire.

This has meant that while Protestants have had to contend with the decline of both Britishness as a social and political ideal and Protestantism as a living faith in the form of puritanism, Catholics have retained an intellectual vigour which has helped to maintain a faith in themselves and their mission. This can be seen by comparing Robert Menzies with the Catholic intellectual and political activist, B. A. Santamaria. Menzies, with his Burkean faith in Britishness and its ideals of liberty and decency, was an avuncular figure in whom one could see embodied the ideals of British reasonableness. Santamaria, on the other hand, could be considered as the embodiment of unreasonableness; he most certainly would have been considered with disdain by David Hume. Santamaria (1997) went into politics armed with a philosophy based on quite clear principles. He may have tended towards fanaticism, but then so did the Protestant activists of the early twentieth century. The point remains that Catholics formed the backbone of the fight against communism in Australia because their intellectual formation provided them with a set of coherent principles. With the waning of empire, Protestant Britishness declined into either secularism or incoherence. There is a certain irony in the fact that, since 1990, the heirs of the Free Trade Party, once the natural home of Protestantism, are generally Catholic leaders, especially in NSW.

In recent years there has been a tendency to downgrade Manning Clark as a historian, especially on the right. Strangely enough, Clark may have had more insight than is normally appreciated. It may well be the case that British Protestantism has slowly dissolved into the Kingdom of Nothingness, as Clark instinctively seemed to understand (Clark 1978, ch. 12). But what he did not seem to understand was that the same was true for the heirs of the secular Enlightenment in Australia. There was little point in execrating Sir Robert Menzies if all one did was to replace him with a somewhat pale imitation in the shape of Gough Whitlam. And no amount of Carlylian excess could turn Whitlam into a secular saint.

The irony is that Clark, the descendant of Samuel Marsden and advocate of secular progressive political change, had a funeral in a Catholic church. He had resolved his own religious dilemma. He was one of the last embodiments of the 'Independent Australian Briton'. But his personal struggle perhaps reflected a wider issue in Australian culture and society. The fate of Australian culture, once its cultural patterning based on British Protestantism was no more, became uncertain. Nationalism has attempted to fill the void with an amount of success; at the same time, the reality of ethnic diversity, if not multiculturalism, needs to be embraced. But the old nexus of religion, politics, and culture has been effectively broken. To where this will lead remains undetermined.

References

Albanese, C. L. 2007. *A Republic of Mind and Spirit: A Cultural History of American, Metaphysical Religion*. New Haven, CT: Yale University Press.

Atkinson, A. 2014. *The Europeans in Australia*, vol. 3: *Nation*. Sydney: UNSW Press.

Austin, A. G. 1961. *Australian Education 1788–1900: Church, State and Public Education in Colonial Australia*. Melbourne: Pitman.

Barton, E. 1897. *Official Report of the National Australasian Convention Debates, Adelaide 1897*. Adelaide: Government Printer.

Bollen, J. D. 1972. *Protestantism and Social Reform in New South Wales 1890–1910*. Melbourne: Melbourne University Press.

Brett, J. 2002. 'Class, religion and the foundation of the Australian party system: a revisionist interpretation', *Australian Journal of Political Science*, vol. 31, no. 1, pp. 39–56.

Brown, C. G. 2012. *Religion and the Demographic Revolution: Women and Secularisation in Canada, Ireland, UK and USA*. Woodbridge: Boydell Press.

Chavura, S. A. and Melleuish, G. 2015. 'Conservative instinct in Australian political thought: the Federation debates, 1890–1898', *Australian Journal of Political Science*, vol. 50, no. 3, pp. 513–28.

Chavura, S. A. and Tregenza, I. 2015. 'A political history of the secular in Australia 1788–1945' in T. Stanley (ed.), *Religion after Secularization in Australia*. London: Palgrave Macmillan.

Chilton, H. 2015. 'Evangelicals and the end of Christian Australia: nation and religion in the public square 1959–1979', PhD thesis, University of Sydney.

Clark, C. 1958. *Australian Hopes and Fears*. London: Hollis & Carter.

Clark, C. M. H. 1978. *A History of Australia*, vol. 4: *The Earth Abideth Forever*. Melbourne: Melbourne University Press.

Collins, H. 1985. 'Political ideology in Australia: the distinctiveness of a Benthamite society' in S. R. Graubard (ed.), *Australia: The Dædalus Symposium*. Sydney: Angus & Robertson.

Curran, J. 2011. *Curtin's Empire*. Cambridge: Cambridge University Press.

Deakin, A. n.d. Untitled typescript, in *Papers of Alfred Deakin*, National Library of Australia, Box 18, Folder 3A, MS 1540/5/200, p. 1.

Docker, J. 1991. *The Nervous Nineties: Australian Cultural Life in the 1890s*. Melbourne: Oxford University Press.

Duncan, B. 2001. *Crusade or Conspiracy? Catholics and the Anti-Communist Struggle in Australia*. Sydney: UNSW Press.

Ely, R. 1976. *Unto God and Caesar: Religious Issues in the Emerging Commonwealth 1891–1906*. Melbourne: Melbourne University Press.

Filby, E. 2015. *God and Mrs Thatcher: The Battle for Britain's Soul*. London: Biteback.

Finer, S. E. 1997. *The History of Government*, vol. 3: *Empires, Monarchies and the Modern State*. Oxford: Oxford University Press.

Fitzhardinge, L. F. 1979. *William Morris Hughes: A Political Biography*, vol. 2: *The Little Digger 1914–1952*. Sydney: Angus & Robertson.

Franklin, J. 2003. *Corrupting the Youth: A History of Philosophy in Australia*. Sydney: Macleay Press.

Gabay, A. 1992. *The Mystic Life of Alfred Deakin*. Cambridge: Cambridge University Press.

Gascoigne, J. 2002. *The Enlightenment and the Origins of European Australia*. Cambridge: Cambridge University Press.

Gladwin, M. 2015. *Anglican Clergy in Australia, 1788–1850*. Suffolk: Boydell and Brewer.

Glynn, P. 1897. *Official Report of the National Australasian Convention Debates, Adelaide 1897*. Adelaide: Government Printer.

Golder, H. 2005. *Politics, Patronage and Public Works: The Administration of New South Wales*, vol. 1: *1842–1900*. Sydney: UNSW Press.

Green, S. G. D. 2009. *The Passing of Protestant England: Secularisation and Social Change c. 1920–1960*. Cambridge: Cambridge University Press.

Gregory, J. S. 1973. *Church and State: Changing Government Policies towards Religion in Australia: With Particular Reference to Victoria since Separation*. Melbourne: Cassell.

Hancock, W. K. 1930. *Australia*. London: Ernest Benn.

Hatch, N. O. 1989. *The Democratization of American Christianity*. New Haven, CT: Yale University Press.

Hayward, H. and Nutt, D. 2014. *Enmore Incorporated: Pioneers of Churches of Christ in New South Wales*. Sydney: Freshhope.

Hodgson, M. 1993. *Rethinking World History: Essays on Europe, Islam and World History*. Cambridge: Cambridge University Press.

Kildea, J. 2002. *Tearing the Fabric: Sectarianism in Australia: 1910–1925*. Sydney: Citadel Books.

Kociumbas, J. 1992. *The Oxford History of Australia*, vol. 2: *1770–1860 Possessions*. Oxford: Oxford University Press.

Legislative Council of New South Wales. 1844. *Report from the Select Committee on Education*. Sydney: Legislative Council of New South Wales.

Linder, R. D. 1997–98. 'The Methodist love affair with the Australian Labor Party, 1891–1929', *Lucas: An Evangelical History Review*, vols 23 and 24, pp. 35–61.

McLeod, H. 2000. *Secularization in Western Europe, 1848–1914*. London: Macmillan.

Melleuish, G. 2014a. 'A secular Australia? Ideas, politics and the search for moral order in nineteenth and early twentieth century Australia', *Journal of Religious History*, vol. 38, no. 3, pp. 1–15.

Melleuish, G. 2014b. 'Living in an age of comfort: understanding religion in the twenty-first century', *Telos*, no. 166, pp. 9–24.

Melleuish, G. 2015a. 'Anzac and Protestant sectarianism: the case of the Revd. C. T. Forscutt', *St Mark's Review*, no. 31, pp. 58–68.

Melleuish, G. 2015b. 'Democracy, utilitarianism and the ideal of liberal education in Australia', *Knowledge Cultures*, vol. 3, no. 3, pp. 123–43.

Menzies, R. G. 1958. *Speech is of Time*. London: Cassell.

Menzies, R. G. n.d. 'The Christian citizen in a new era', *Papers of Sir Robert Menzies*, National Library of Australia, Box 253, Folder 13, p. 1.

Monsma, S. V. and Soper, J. C. 2008. *The Challenge of Pluralism: Church and State in Five Democracies*. Lanham, MD: Rowman & Littlefield.

Moore, L. J. 2009. 'Never on a Sunday: a study of Sunday observance and Sunday public musical entertainments in theatres in Melbourne, 1890–1895', MPhil thesis, Australian Catholic University.

National Australasian Convention Debates. 1898. *Official Report of the National Australasian Convention Debates (Third Session): Melbourne 1898*. Victoria: National Australasian Convention Debates.

Nemo, P. 2006. *What is the West*? Pittsburgh, PA: Duquesne University Press.

Paley, W. [1785] 2002. *Principles of Moral and Political Philosophy*, Bk 6.10. Indianapolis: Liberty Fund.

Parkes, H. 1867. 'Proceedings of the NSW Legislative Assembly', *Sydney Morning Herald*, 18 July, p. 3.

Parkes, H. 1876. *Speeches on Various Occasions connected with the Public Affairs of New South Wales*. Melbourne: George Robertson.

Parkes, H. 1890. *Official Record of the Proceedings and Debates of the Australasian Federation Conference, 1890*. Sydney: Charles Potter, Government Printer.

Parliament of Victoria. 1898. 'Scripture instruction in state schools', *Parliamentary Debates*, 5 October, Melbourne.

Quaife, B. 1872. *The Intellectual Sciences: Outline Lectures*. Sydney: Gibbs, Shallard & Co.

Santamaria, B. A. 1997. *Santamaria: A Memoir*. Melbourne: Oxford University Press.

Wilkins, W. 1865. *National Education: An Exposition of the National System of New South Wales*. Sydney: Alexander W. Douglas.

Williams, R. 2013. *In God They Trust? The Religious Beliefs of Australia's Prime Ministers 1901–2013*. Australia: Bible Society.

Williams, R. 2015. *Post-God Nation? How Religion Fell off the Radar in Australia—and What Might be Done to Get it Back On*. Sydney: ABC Books.

Woolley, J. 1862. 'The office of Christian associations towards the state and the church, delivered before the Young Men's Christian Association, Wednesday, June 13th, 1855', in *Lectures Delivered in Australia*. London: Macmillan.

Legislation

An Act to Make More Adequate Provision for Public Education (NSW) 1880.

5

Tocqueville, Hancock, and the Sense of History

Henry Ergas

If Alexis de Tocqueville's *Democracy in America* can claim a special place in shaping America's vision of itself, so Hancock's *Australia* has long been a point of reference in Australian political thought. 'All the works of stature since 1930', Manning Clark said of Hancock's book, 'stem in part from the tree he grew' (Clark 1968, p. 332); while Neville Meaney, in his retrospective assessment of Hancock's 'remarkable achievement', described the book as '... the greatest work in the canon of Australian historical scholarship', with the 'mark of its greatness [being] that most subsequent Australian historians have been engaged, either directly or indirectly, in elaborating or refuting the themes which Hancock laid out in *Australia*' (Meaney 1985, p. 10).

But while *Democracy in America* remains omnipresent in American intellectual life, informing not merely scholarly discussion but also that country's always vigorous battle of ideas, *Australia*'s presence is a faint shadow, with an impact confined largely to academia and, even there, more often cited than read. It is unlikely an American student could complete a liberal arts degree without absorbing at least some chapters of Tocqueville's great work; Hancock's, by contrast, languishes, rarely touched, in university libraries. Tocqueville's work has been continuously in print since it first appeared; Hancock's was last republished in 1966. And while there has been a great revival of interest in Tocqueville over the last two generations, the generous reviews that greeted *Australia*'s last republication did not herald new life but a decline into the ranks of antiquarianism.

No doubt, that contrast is partly due to the works' respective merits. Tocqueville's sweep is vast, tackling questions whose global salience is at least as great today as it was in 1835 (see, for instance, Atanassow and Boyd 2013). And every student of society is enriched by reading and rereading

Tocqueville, not merely because of the beauty of his prose and the brilliance of his answers but also by the intricacy and subtlety of his reasoning. Hancock's scope is narrower and his methods are weaker. But, even so, Hancock's work is still dazzling, both in its form and in its content; and the mere fact that so many of its phrases and images have become integral to the rhetoric of Australian political debate highlights its continuing relevance.

The differing fate of *Democracy in America* on the one hand, and *Australia* on the other, therefore invites explanation. Obviously, that explanation must be informed by the works themselves; but a book's reception also depends on its broader context, and especially so for books immersed in the fundamental debates about a country's past and future. Comparing these works and exploring their fates is the goal of this chapter. Its aim is twofold: to explore and clarify the relationship between these canonical works, taking account of the fact that Hancock was greatly influenced by Tocqueville; and, on that basis, to examine some of the factors that might account for their contrasting fortunes.

Having considered a range of such factors, it suggests that two are especially important. The first is that, unlike the United States, Australia lacks a foundation myth that shapes political culture and political controversy. As a result, works that go to the origins and nature of the 'Australian Settlement' are less likely to be used as points of reference in the public debate, with that being all the more the case as immigration ensures so large a share of the population has little connection to, and knowledge of, the Australian past.

Second, even to the extent to which historical references do play a role, Hancock's *Australia*—with its strong critique of the 'Australian Settlement', and of the priority given to the pursuit of 'fairness'—will not sit easily with the mood of the present times. Rather, the dominant tendency is to rehabilitate that 'settlement' and, with it, at least some elements of the radical-nationalist view of Australian history. In contrast, in the United States, the intellectual debate between left and right is far more evenly matched, with *Democracy in America* serving as an authority on which both sides may draw.

5.1 Lives and Settings

In considering *Democracy in America* and *Australia*, it is useful to start by considering the seemingly very different backgrounds of the authors. After all, while Hancock was the grandson of a brick-maker and the son of a country clergyman, Tocqueville was an aristocrat, who counted as a great-grandparent Malesherbes, the great and liberal-minded administrator who, having acted as counsel for the defence of Louis XVI, was guillotined in 1794; and, as a cousin by marriage, Chateaubriand, one of the first and finest writers of French romanticism. Adding to the differences, while Tocqueville was intimately involved in the turbulent political life of post-revolutionary France, Hancock was always an academic, albeit one with many links to the administrative and political elites guiding the British Empire as it evolved into the Commonwealth of Nations.

Stark as those contrasts are, there are, however, also important similarities. Both considered their subject from the perspective of an outsider—Tocqueville as a visitor to what was then an exotic land, Hancock as an expatriate briefly and unhappily repatriated to Australia between lengthy periods in the UK. Both were very young: Tocqueville was 30 when the first volume of *Democracy in America* appeared; when *Australia* was published, Hancock was 32. Both intended their works to address and help form opinion on the crucial issues of the day. Both had an underlying commitment to liberalism, albeit (to adopt Oakeshott's fine phrase) not as 'a creed or a doctrine but a disposition', and with some hesitations, notably about its applicability in non-European societies (on Tocqueville and the colonies see Pitts 2005, pp. 165–239; on Hancock, see Low 2001, pp. 58–83 and Dubow and Marks 2001, pp. 149–79). And both were members of generations that faced anguishing doubts in the wake of traumatic events.

It is always true that, as Karl Mannheim put it, 'age separates in an existential way due to the temporality of experience', defining generations, each with its own shared beliefs, values, habits, and attitudes (Mannheim 1952, p. 288). But a vast literature suggests generational effects were especially strong for the intellectual cohorts who came to maturity after the upheavals of the French Revolution, on the one hand, and the First World War on the other (Wohl 1979; Spitzer 1987). It is worth spending a few moments on each of those generations in turn.

Tocqueville was only slightly younger than the group commonly referred to as 'the generation of 1820', which included such distinguished figures as Adolphe Thiers, Jules Michelet, Victor Hugo, and Honoré de Balzac; and his trajectory intersected with theirs, as did the formation of his world view. His generation, it might fairly be said, was one of the first to have a consciousness of itself as a generation: a consciousness most clearly expressed by Alfred de Musset in his 1836 autobiographical novel, *La Confession d'un Enfant du Siècle.* His contemporaries did not have first-hand memories of the Revolution, Musset wrote, but they reached adolescence in the midst of a 'world in ruins'. Left, after the collapse of the Revolution and then of the empire, with no clear path from the horrors their parents had lived through to the future they desired, they were gripped by what Musset famously described as the *mal de siècle,* a despair at being cast on 'a troubled sea filled with wreckage... where one cannot know whether at each step, one treads on living matter or dead refuse'.

Yet theirs was a generation that set itself great tasks. 'It is up to us', wrote Balzac, 'children of the century and of liberty, to speed the dawning of happiness among nations, to make the security of thrones coincide with the freedom of peoples' (Balzac 1936, p. 18): to reconcile, in other words, progress and order. Imbued with a conviction in their own abilities—a conviction underpinned by having succeeded in Restoration France's rigorous 'concours' (competitive examinations which served to reward the highest-achieving students and select among applicants for the professions and for literary and scientific honours)—the generation's leading intellectuals grappled with what the post-revolutionary, post-imperial society was to be, and how it was to operate. It was not a mere recipe for good government that they sought; it was to replace the shattered remains they had inherited with an entirely new synthesis, as is evident in the efforts of Henri de Saint-Simon, Victor Cousin, and Auguste Comte to formulate a general doctrine that could serve as the ideological cement of a new social order.

If the ambitions of the 'lost generation' of 1914 were more limited, the trauma it experienced was not. The loss of life during the First World War touched deep, reaching Hancock, too, in 1918 with the news that his older brother, Jim, had been 'obliterated at Pozieres'. He was, Neville Meaney tells us, 'haunted at night by dreams of his brother' and 'humiliated and guilt-ridden when his parents refused to allow him to enlist' (Meaney 1985, p. 12). The global turmoil of 1917–20 and the widespread criticism of the peace treaty signed at Versailles in 1919 bred disappointment and frustration; it was difficult not to believe that 'the apocalypse had only been postponed and that any restoration of the post-war era would only be temporary' (Wohl 1979, pp. 225–6).

For Hancock, the sense of fragility would have been made especially acute by his first encounter with Italy in 1922–23. As he wrote three decades later:

> I was an assiduous reader of Mussolini's speeches. They were forceful vivid speeches and they outraged my deepest political convictions. I believed that this man with his words, this man's thugs with their revolvers and clubs and castor oil were befouling and destroying values which I had cared for ever since my Melbourne days. (Hancock 1954, p. 92)

But all that was aggravated by the materialism, complacency, and parochialism he found on his return to Australia. From 1919 to 1925 the country had experienced an economic boom, reflected in the rhetoric of 'Australia Unlimited'; but, taken as a whole, the first post-war decade did little more than restore average incomes to their level in 1913 (Schedvin 1970, pp. 48–9).

Some of Hancock's older colleagues, such as Frederic Eggleston and Edward Shann, viewed the slowing of growth as symptomatic of the structurally flawed policies—including the entrenchment of industrial arbitration and the ever higher levels of tariff protection—pursued by governments that were incapable of resisting 'opportunistic state action' and were vulnerable to 'corrupt bargains' with private interests (Osmond 1985, pp. 152, 155; Shann 1930; Eggleston 1932; Melleuish 1995). For others, notably the more radical circle of Nettie and Vance Palmer that Hancock had befriended in his Melbourne University days, the roots of the malaise were even more profound, with 'delayed development, false starts and unfulfilled talents' marking 'a scurvy period, when Australians seem content to accept second-rateness, were deferentially inactive in most aspects of public and cultural life and shut themselves off as best they could from the world and modern thought' (Serle [1973] 2014, pp. 90, 151). But regardless of the precise diagnosis, it seemed undeniable that the aspirations of 'a glorious nation with no sordid past' had become 'a hollow mockery of departed hopes' (Walker 1976, p. 8).

In that sense, both *Democracy in America* and *Australia* are attempts to find bearings in a world of heightened uncertainty about the future of social order. Tocqueville was especially clear in that respect. 'I admit that I saw in America more than America', he wrote; in crossing the Atlantic 'it was the shape of democracy itself which I sought, its inclination, character, prejudices and passions; I wanted to understand it so as at least to know what we have to fear or to hope therefrom' (*Democracy in America* (henceforth *DA*), intro.[1]). Confronted with what Jacques Barzun has called the dominant problem of the Romantic era—the need 'to create a new world on the ruins of the old' (Barzun 1961, p. 14)—Tocqueville looked to America from the perspective of a man who, as he wrote in 1837 to his English translator and friend, Henry Reeve, had 'only one passion, the love of liberty and of human dignity' (Kaledin 2011, p. 3).

5.2 The New Regime

In examining America, Tocqueville well knew that 'democracy' would appear to his readership as anything but a self-evident good; on the contrary, 'even the first steps on the road to such an order' seemed likely to 'end in civil war, continual instability, reactionary regression and constant fear of revolutionary uprising' (Offe 2005, p. 12). At least until the fall of Napoleon, the term itself mainly referred to an antique form of government, famously disparaged by antiquity's great philosophers; once the Restoration era began in 1814, with its decision not to revert to the *ancien régime*, 'democracy' came to mean the acceptance of some degree of 'levelling' (on the history of the concept, see

[1] The translations from Tocqueville are largely drawn from the Goldhammer translation (Tocqueville 2004), checked against the Nolla historical-critical edition (Tocqueville 2009).

Dunn 2005; on the criticisms of Athenian democracy, see Ober 1998). For Tocqueville, however, 'democracy' was both a process for selecting governments and, even more importantly, a condition of society characterized by an irresistible tendency to 'equality' (Manent 1982).

Before the Revolution, society was viewed as a hierarchical organism whose specialized limbs, each with a recognized collective identity, performed the various functions essential for the well-being of the whole. In that hierarchy of estates, 'everyone knew his proper place, enjoyed the appropriate rights and duties and obeyed his superiors, receiving obedience from his inferiors in his turn: all in the last resort obeyed the monarch, through whom human society was slotted in with the divine' (Crone 2003, p. 99). Each person, Tocqueville wrote, could therefore see 'a man above himself whose patronage is necessary to him, and below himself another man whose co-operation he may claim' (*DA*, II.2.ii). But democracy cast that hierarchy aside, making the servant 'not a different man from the master', and so also dissolving their bonds of mutual obligation (*DA*, II.3.v).

Tocqueville saw much in this new world that 'saddens and chills' him; he was 'tempted to regret the state of society which has ceased to be' (*DA*, II.4.viii). As Harvey Mansfield put it, Tocqueville was, like his great admirer Leo Strauss, a 'friend but not an *enthusiast*' of democracy (Mancini 2006, p. 210). That is not to suggest he ignored its merits; on the contrary, as he explained in a letter to a friend soon after the first volume of *Democracy in America* appeared:

> To those for whom the word democracy is synonymous with destruction, anarchy, spoliation, and murder, I have tried to show that under a democratic government the fortunes and the rights of society may be respected, liberty preserved, and religion honoured. (Adcock 2014, p. 34)

Nor was he any less deeply committed to the cause of equality, writing, a few years before his death, that 'a more equal distribution of goods and rights in this world is the greatest aim that those who conduct human affairs can have in view' (Kaledin 2011, p. 147).

But he was also highly conscious of the risks. At the heart of those risks was the potentially noxious brew of resentment and isolation to which the new society could give rise.

The resentment came from the fact that democracy instilled in the minds of men an 'ardent, insatiable, eternal, invincible' (*DA*, II.2.v) hankering for equality that rendered inequalities of any sort increasingly intolerable and readily degenerated into a 'delirium' (*DA*, II.2.ix). That frenzy created an unavoidable sense of frustration, as the 'constant tension that exists between the instincts to which equality gives rise and the means it provides for their satisfaction torments and tires the soul' (*DA*, II.2.xiii). And the frustration was rendered all the more acute by a heightened sense of envy, because the 'equality that allows each citizen to entertain vast hopes...spurs them on', with the result that 'they struggle, they tire, they grow bitter' (*DA*, I.2.v).

At the same time, democratic societies, by making material achievement open to all, engendered a 'passion for well-being' that could displace every other pursuit (*DA*, II.1.v). With the bonds between people reduced to monetary form, individuals were increasingly isolated from one another, leading to an impoverishment of the social imagination and a pervasive social indifference. In an aristocratic society, individuals identified with others in their estate by the fact of similarity; and they were bound to particular people above and beneath them by ties of obligation (Manent 1982, pp. 74–5). In democracy, on the other hand, individuals merely shared an abstract sense of commonality with the broader mass, to whom they owed little and from whom they might expect even less. The desire to protect what one had, in a society in which 'all the citizens are constantly on the move and in a permanent state of transformation' (*DA*, II.3.xxi), could then fuel a fear of anarchy and disorder, inducing a compulsive grasping for order and a growing intolerance of difference.

The immediate result would be:

> An innumerable multitude of men, alike and equal, constantly circling around in pursuit of the petty and banal pleasures with which they glut their souls. Each one of them, withdrawn into himself, is almost unaware of the fate of the rest...they are near enough but he does not notice them. He touches them but feels nothing.
> (*DA*, II.4.vi)

But as the victims withdrew into 'a multitude of small private circles', these 'highly dangerous instincts' democracy unleashed posed even greater risks (*DA*, II.3.xiii).[2]

To begin, while a 'manly and legitimate passion for equality' elevates inferiors to the rank of superiors and so reconciles equality with liberty, there is also a 'depraved taste for equality', in which superiors are reduced to the level of inferiors (*DA*, I.1.iii). This 'depraved taste for equality' did not merely debase society; it also, and somewhat paradoxically, favoured a bargain in which individuals were ready to accept a master so long as that master subjected everyone equally.

In turn, that bargain was facilitated by an inherent trend to political and administrative centralization. Myriad forces were at work (Elster 2009, pp. 147–9).

[2] Tocqueville's French, 'instincts fort dangereux', better conveys a sense of foreboding than the English translation.

The economic forces were the clearest. Industry 'exposes [men] to great and sudden alternations of abundance and misery...and can also compromise the health and even the life of those who profit from or engage in it' (*DA*, II.4.v). As a result, 'the industrial class needs to be regulated, supervised, and restrained more than other classes, and it is natural for the prerogatives of government to grow along with it' (*DA*, II.4.v). At the same time:

> As a nation becomes more industrial, it feels a proportionately greater need for roads, canals, ports and other works of a semi-public nature.... The obvious tendency for all sovereigns nowadays is to assume sole responsibility for undertakings of this kind, thereby constricting the independence of the populations they rule more and more each day. (*DA*, II.4.v)

But there was a social dynamic too. Fully exposed to the vagaries of fortune, each individual would, from time to time, inevitably 'feel the need of outside help'; but he could not 'expect to receive it from any of [his equals] because they are all powerless and cold hearted' (*DA*, II.4.iii). He therefore 'naturally turns his attention to the one immense being that alone stands out amid the universal abasement' (*DA*, II.4.iii), that is, the state.

Finally, a turn to the state was consistent with the nature of reasoning in democratic societies. In such societies, individuals were neither tied to, nor identified with, concrete others but with the intangible notion of a political entity; it was therefore easy for them to conceive of relying on a remote and abstract structure, such as the state, to protect and enhance their needs.

All that could prove fatal to democracy. Equality bred conformism, partly because each individual could not readily disassociate himself from a 'public opinion' he helped to create, but mainly because isolation and the ever-present fear of rejection crushed all resistance, '[pervading] the souls even of those whose interest might inspire them to resist it' and '[altering] their judgment even as it subjugates their will' (*DA*, II.3.v). The result, as J. S. Mill put it in pursuing his reflections on *Democracy in America*, was that, because each man '[is] so lost in the crowd, that though he depends more and more on opinion, he is apt to depend less and less on well-grounded opinion', the quality of decision-making would deteriorate, and the willingness to stand alone against error with it (Kaledin 2011, p. 232).

Far from being self-correcting, opinions, no matter how flawed they might be, could therefore become self-perpetuating and remain dominant long after their fallacies were obvious.

'When an opinion takes hold in a democratic nation and establishes itself in a majority of minds, it becomes self-sustaining and can perpetuate itself without effort, because nobody will attack it', Tocqueville wrote (*DA*, II.3.xxi), anticipating much current research (Kuran 1997). Indeed, under the weight of conformism, even ideas in which no one any longer believed could persist, blocking innovation:

> No one combats the doomed belief openly. No forces gather to make war on it. Its proponents quietly abandon it one by one, until only a minority still clings to it. In this situation, its reign persists. Since its enemies continue to hold their peace or to communicate their thoughts only in secret, it is a long time before they can be sure that a great revolution has taken place, and, being in doubt, they make no move. They watch and keep silent. The majority no longer believes, but it appears still to believe, and this hollow ghost of public opinion is enough to chill the blood of would-be innovators and reduce them to respectful silence. (*DA*, II.3.xxi)

From the combination of conformism and centralization, it was but a small step to a new despotism, based not on brute coercion but on 'an immense tutelary power' that is 'absolute, meticulous, regular, provident and mild' (*DA*, II.4.vi). Driven by the principle of utility, rather than by respect for independence, it 'assumes sole responsibility for securing [its citizens'] pleasure and watching their fate' (*DA*, II.4.vi). As it matured, democracy could therefore degenerate, not into mob rule, as its traditional critics feared, but into a historically unprecedented bureaucratic state that, instead of fostering independent, morally alert individuals, transformed its citizens into easily managed sheep.

5.3 Democracy in Australia

That these themes would resonate with Hancock, as he confronted the Australia of the late 1920s, is unsurprising. Virtually from the moment of its initial publication, *Democracy in America* had echoed loudly in the controversies about the colonies' future. Barely a year after its second volume appeared in 1840, Herman Merivale, then Drummond Professor of Political Economy at Oxford and, from 1848, the powerful permanent under-secretary of the Colonial Office during the colonies' transition to responsible government, relied heavily on Tocqueville in his *Lectures on Colonization and Colonies* (Merivale 2010), which were required reading for the colonies' administrative and political elites (Beasley 2005, pp. 20–43). Tocqueville's concerns about democracy also figured prominently in the rambunctious debate about the New South Wales Constitution Bill in 1853, in which William Charles Wentworth, pointing to Tocqueville's unquestioned authority, emphasized that even an observer 'so deeply... imbued with democratic prejudices' as Tocqueville was obliged to concede that American democracy was a 'degrading' tyranny (Clark 2000, pp. 15–17). And the Tocquevillian strains were equally evident in New South Wales Governor William Thomas Denison, with his keen awareness of the 'essentially democratic spirit' animating the 'large mass of the colony' (Beasley 2005, pp. 69–75).

It is true that by the time of the Federation conventions, Tocqueville's role in Australian debates had been somewhat eclipsed by James Bryce's more legally oriented *American Commonwealth*.[3] But, as Hancock noted, while Bryce claimed that Tocqueville's 'brilliant generalisations [about America] were, generally speaking, out of date', they were not 'out of date for Australia'. On the contrary, said Hancock, 'Australians could attempt no more useful exercise than to read through *Democracy in America*, asking themselves: Is this true of Australia?' (Hancock 1930, p. 269). Indeed, Manning Clark tells us that when he received the commission to write *Australia*, Hancock:

> turned away temporarily from one of his earliest intellectual loves—reading the Italians from Dante, through Petrarch, Boccaccio and Machiavelli, and renewed his acquaintance with a man who had lived through his experience in reverse. He read again *Democracy in America* by Alexis de Tocqueville, who had gone as an aristocrat of some twenty-six years from the over-ripe salons of Restoration Paris, to tour the vulgar, egalitarian, democratic but magnificently alive, New World America and had come back to tell his class and his country that the future lay with equality of conditions, with democracy, with industry, with America and Russia rather than with the aristocratic remnants of the Old World. (Clark 1968, p. 331)

Yet even more than direct parallels to *Democracy in America*, what shines through in Hancock are similarities in the processes at work. Nowhere is that clearer than in the argument, which is at the heart of Hancock's book, that Australia's failings as a society arise because unbridled passions push what may be worthy aspirations to excess—thereby, much as in Aristotle, transforming virtues into vices. For example, the distinctly Australian 'sentiment of justice, the claim of right, the conception of equality' (Hancock 1930, p. 75) were not harmful in themselves, any more than the ideal of wages that are 'fair and reasonable' (Hancock 1930, p. 282). But while 'Australians are generally matter of fact people who distrust fine phrases and understand hard realities', 'in politics they have been incurably romantic', and, 'even when they have ceased to believe in impossibilities... continue to pursue them' (Hancock 1930, p. 277).

Equality was therefore taken too far: 'Properly anxious that everybody should run a fair race', Australian democracy is 'improperly resentful if anybody runs a fast race. Indeed, it dislikes altogether the idea of a race, for in a race victory is to the strong' (Hancock 1930, p. 183). The result was not merely

[3] Although the founders of the Federation 'occasionally cited the classic works of political philosophy and analysis, such as those of John Locke, James Harrington, Thomas Hobbes, Jeremy Bentham, Montesquieu, Tocqueville and John Stuart Mill', 'the most significant influences were the writings of James Madison, James Bryce, Edward Freeman, A. V. Dicey and John Burgess' (Aroney 2009, pp. 72–3).

to narrow opportunities—making Australia 'a country merciful to the average' (Hancock 1930, p. 304)—but to pursue policies to the point where they 'yield diminishing returns, until at last, they may become a positive danger to the national purpose which has called them into effect' (Hancock 1930, p. 128).

Moreover, while it was understandable that the harshness of Australia's geography and the disabilities it imposed on settlers would induce them to expect help from colonial governments, assistance had morphed into a perceived right to treat the state 'as a vast public utility'. That state's duty 'to provide the greatest happiness to the greatest number' meant that 'every economic difficulty is generalized as a political issue' (Hancock 1930, pp. 72, 277); but by demanding the political system adopt ends for which it inevitably lacked the means, 'Australian idealism has put too many of its eggs into the political basket', ensuring that 'government being constantly overstrained, is constantly discredited' (Hancock 1930, p. 277).

Echoing Tocqueville's remarks about the impatience and restlessness that characterize democratic societies, as they 'chase after' a degree of equality that 'invariably . . . eludes their grasp', Hancock identified 'perpetual exasperation' as 'the dominant note in [Australians'] public life . . . because they perpetually pursue a quarry they can never run to earth' (Hancock 1930, p. 276). And, just as Tocqueville thought the frustration with public life induced a 'love of public peace' which is 'often the only political passion [democratic peoples'] retain' and that 'becomes more active and powerful as all the others fade and die', so Hancock argued the 'perpetual exasperation' Australian democracy caused induced Australia's inward turn—the temptation to seek respite in a 'hermit's solitude'—which was a sign of the country's weakness, for 'it is only the weak who fear a stir in the shipping. The strong feel no need to close their ports' (Hancock 1930, p. 287).

However, the longer-term threat—'the warning [that] comes from the old countries'—was that 'if democracy is essentially mediocre it will become decrepit and be thrust aside' (Hancock 1930, p. 288); but the 'easy-going good nature and intellectual laziness' of Australians bred indifference to that warning. And it was even more difficult for it to be addressed given the predominance of what Hancock had earlier referred to as the 'mass production of tastes', 'mass production of ideas', and 'mass production of minds', that together created a 'respectable, comfortable, intolerant mediocrity' in which public opinion itself was just 'massed mediocrity' (Davidson 2010, p. 104).

5.4 The Points of Contrast

It is therefore easy to see the fundamental point of convergence between Hancock and Tocqueville: it lies in the tendency of democracy to transform equality from a virtue into an uncontrolled passion, unleashing a force all the more demonic as the traditional mechanisms that once legitimated social distinctions and social deference disappeared. The resulting excess was antithetical to the spirit of moderation that, at least since Montesquieu, had been at the heart of political liberalism (Jaume 1997, pp. 544–51). And as only the state could pursue the impossible degree of equality that was being sought, the outcome was a centralization of power which threatened democracy itself.

But the convergence between the two works masks very significant differences. To begin with, though Tocqueville and Hancock share the dialectic that converts virtue into vice, their methodologies are certainly not the same.

Tocqueville's analysis built on two broad intellectual foundations. The first, which applied at the level of societies as a whole, was Montesquieu's insight that societies have an underlying coherence that links the nature of a government with the crucial mores, norms, and passions it evokes and on which its operation relies. Drawing on others—including Sismondi, Guizot, and the Whig historian Henry Hallam (1777–1859) who, writing immediately before him, renewed the application of Montesquieu's approach to social and legal development—Tocqueville used that approach in framing the contrast between aristocracy and democracy.

The second, which Tocqueville derived from Pascal (with whom he lived 'a little every day' (Jaume 2013, p. 158), along with Rousseau and Montesquieu), is that of the inherent limits on human understanding, which, by its nature, combines a degree of insight (and hence of intentionality) with an inability to fully grasp the ultimate consequences of beliefs and actions. In Pascal, and more broadly in Jansenism, this limit corresponds to the 'hidden God', whose masked presence means all human affairs contain an element of mystery and of indeterminacy, always yielding an outcome which is the result of human conduct but not of human design. Combined with the then new idea of self-interest, and the focus on explanations that—by separating the concept of 'consciousness' from that of 'conscience'—took beliefs and motives into account, the notion that intentional action led to results which were unintended, and which could shape future results, was at the heart of advances in social thinking in the eighteenth century, setting the methodological context in which Tocqueville wrote (Sheehan and Wahrman 2015).

The distinctiveness of Tocqueville's analysis arises from the way in which he combines Montesquieu's macroscopic perspective with an examination, from the individual standpoint, of intended and unintended consequences. In looking at outcomes, Tocqueville seeks both to reconcile them to what Montesquieu would recognize as the core 'principle' or 'virtue' of the social system, and to explain them in terms of the processes by which individuals come to act as they do. Tocqueville is, in other words, never satisfied with merely observing and recounting social behaviour; rather, he invariably tries to explain why it occurs, under what conditions it might persist, and how the forces it generates could alter it and set off new, unanticipated, processes.

In that sense, although they are unashamedly anachronistic (and not especially illuminating in terms of the history of ideas), the efforts of Jon Elster and his collaborators to cast Tocqueville as a practitioner, *avant la lettre*, of Mertonian middle-range social theory serve a useful purpose (Elster 2007, 2009; Hedström and Swedberg 1998). By demonstrating that many of Tocqueville's explanations can be framed in terms of 'social mechanisms' that link preferences, beliefs, choices, and outcomes, they highlight those explanations' enduring explanatory power—a power evident in the ubiquity in contemporary social science of 'Tocqueville effects' and 'Tocqueville hypotheses'.[4] And that power gives Tocqueville's analysis a depth Hancock does not achieve.

To say that is not to imply that *Australia* does not provide behavioural explanations; it does, but they are often brittle. It may be, for example, that, as Hancock suggests, the settlers, struggling with an environment that was far removed from their experience and punishingly harsh, looked to government; but why did that remain the case once a largely urban population had achieved very high incomes? As for Hancock's generalizations, such as the description of Australians as political romantics, they frequently ring true, but they are characterizations, not explanations.

There is, in other words, a difference of method and even of stance. Tocqueville, unlike his good friend, J. S. Mill, saw little value in grand theoretical systems, such as Comte's positivism, that sought to transform the study of society into a 'science'; but he did believe it was crucial to illuminate the mechanisms (or what would now be referred to as the 'feedback loops') that connect actions and intentions, on the one hand, and social outcomes on the other. Moreover, he sought to discern in what he saw not merely human conduct but also the working out of forces that were 'providential'—with the term connoting both the possibility of a higher power and of a force that was irresistible.

In contrast, as Hancock later told Neville Meaney, 'conceptual frameworks bore me'. Even with respect to *Australia* itself, he said, 'it was people of which my friends were types and places which interested me', much more than any abstract generalizations. Despite the palpable influence on his thought of Croce and Collingwood, Hancock's 'historical style', Meaney concluded, 'was that of a conversationalist', with a focus, which became increasingly marked over the years, not on 'abstract and generalised structures but [on]

[4] Examples of propositions attributed to Tocqueville and frequently tested in the social science literature include the claims that revolutions are more likely when incomes are rising, rather than falling, as prosperity breeds ever rising expectations; that the transition to democracy is more fraught with risks than democracy itself; and that the autocratic regimes that face the greatest risks are not those that are most repressive but those whose repression is half-hearted.

the palpable and the particular, about individual people, places and problems' (Meaney 1985, p. 11), more like a witness giving evidence about what happened than 'as a judge delivering a verdict from which there is no appeal' (Roe 1978, p. 131).

5.5 Democracy under God

There is, however, a further difference, between *Democracy in America* and *Australia* which is both substantive and methodological. Having set out the main forces at work in Australian democracy, Hancock has relatively little to say about limiting principles: that is, about factors that explain why tendencies go as far as they do, but not further. Indeed, reading *Australia,* one would expect every process to be pushed to extremes. In effect, Hancock emphasized that:

> The tendencies of the age have always worked rapidly in Australia, for they have worked over a smooth surface where the past has left no historic obstacles to divert them or to dam them back. (Hancock 1930, p. 126)

Tocqueville too was well aware of the risks that the absence of inherited obstacles created in new societies, and he graphically depicted the future to which those societies might tend; but he also identified factors that could hinder, if they were unlikely to entirely suppress, democracy's inherent pathologies.

Some of those factors were institutional: the 'schools of democracy' he saw in the proliferation of voluntary associations, in town hall meetings, in the prevalence of jury trials. But no counterweight was of greater importance than 'mores', a term by which he meant not only the

> habits of the heart, but also . . . the various notions that men possess, . . . the diverse opinions that are current among them, and . . . the whole range of ideas that shape habits of mind. Thus I use the word to refer to the whole moral and intellectual state of a people' (*DA*, I.2.ix).

Indeed, so crucial were mores to Tocqueville that he considered demonstrating their significance his 'principal goal'. (*DA*, I.2.ix) And central to mores was religion.

It would be fair to say that Tocqueville's discussion of religion in *Democracy in America* is far removed from the religious reality of the Jacksonian era. Although he was touring America in the midst of the political fallout from the Second Great Awakening, he 'hardly seemed to take notice'; and while he claimed religion had been kept out of politics, vehement evangelical Christian crusades were underway which led opponents to complain about the 'Christian party in politics' (Heclo et al. 2007, p. 19, and, on the Second Great

Awakening, usually dated as covering the period from 1800 to 1830, see McLoughlin 1978, pp. 98–140). But perhaps more than anywhere else, his aim here was less to describe than to instruct—and it is easy to understand why his readers, still smarting from the trauma of the French Revolution, would have been especially concerned about the role of religion in the 'new world' Tocqueville had explored.

After the Constituent Assembly's law of 12 July 1790, enacting the Civil Constitution of the Clergy (which required the clergy to be elected, and forced clergymen to swear an oath of allegiance to the revolutionary regime), few issues were more divisive in France than the relationship between the Catholic Church and the French state (Perreau-Saussine 2012, pp. 69–80). The growth of ultramontanism—associated with the writings of Joseph de Maistre—ensured this remained so despite Napoleon's concordat with the Vatican and the Restoration.

Little wonder, then, that Tocqueville considered 'the organisation and establishment of democracy in Christian lands' as the 'great problem of our time' (Heclo et al. 2007, p. 6). And although he had lost his faith in his youth, his 'highest aim in entering political life', he declared in a letter to his brother, 'was to play some part in reconciling the spirit of freedom with the spirit of religion, and the clergy with the new social order' (Perreau-Saussine 2012, p. 74).

Set against that background, Tocqueville advanced three crucial contentions in *Democracy in America*. First, far from being weakened, the separation of Church and State strengthened the churches, as it distanced them from the vicissitudes and always dubious fortunes of politics, giving them the aura of permanence. Second, in a democracy, individuals, instead of turning away from religion, had an even greater thirst for it, as it filled the vacuum left by the disappearance of other forms of legitimate authority and assuaged the materialism and *anomie* democracy engendered, while meeting those needs in a manner consistent with democracy's promotion of abstract, impersonal reasoning. Third and last, religion, without ever intending to do so, made democracy sustainable, by imposing structure and constraints on the chaos of choice individuals faced in democratic societies and transforming mere self-interest into 'self-interest properly understood', a complex phrase by which Tocqueville meant self-interest viewed in the light of reason.

In short, 'religion keeps the Americans within certain limits and moderates their passion for innovation', so providing ballast to democratic society; for 'how could society escape destruction if, when political ties are relaxed, moral ties are not tightened?' (Kaledin 2011, p. 307).

It would be easy to view Tocqueville's argument as crudely functionalist—as the claim that since 'the main business of religions is to purify, control, and restrain that excessive and exclusive taste for well-being which men acquire in times of equality' (*DA*, I.1.v), religion prospers *because* it is socially useful. That would, however, be entirely incorrect. After all, democracy did not need religion: on the contrary, Tocqueville regarded it as an irresistible—indeed, 'providential'—force. Nor did religion need democracy: rather, Tocqueville saw the search for faith as man's most enduring feature, and—much as he disagreed with de Maistre's ultramontanism—he had no difficulty in repeating de Maistre's contention that man needs beliefs and craves dogmas.

Instead, if religion flourished, it was not because it served democracy but because democracy served it, creating propitious conditions for spiritual development; and, placed in those conditions, religion thrived not by helping democracy but by helping man—as Hugh Heclo puts it, for Tocqueville, 'The value of religion is not just that it is useful to democracy; it is useful to democratic man because it teaches truths about the human condition' (Heclo et al. 2007, p. 17). Moreover, as democracy relies so heavily on self-interest, which religion helps inform and transform, it serves democratic man all the more. And by strengthening the family, religion creates the environment in which democracy's 'softening' of mores can be transmitted from generation to generation.[5]

In short, in Tocqueville's account, democracy might not erect impermeable bulwarks against its own worst vices but it did cultivate stout defences of practices, institutions, and beliefs. Indeed, the fundamental—and perhaps most important—question about democracy was whether those defences could hold over time, or whether, as democracy matured, growing apathy would make them succumb to the new form of despotism discussed in section 5.2.

In contrast, Hancock does not pay much attention to forces that might blunt or discipline the excesses of Australian democracy. That omission is all the more striking because Tocqueville's list of institutions protecting democracy should have seemed directly relevant. Voluntary associations, for example, had proliferated from colonial times onwards (Davison 1978, p. 98),[6] and, as of the end of the nineteenth century, there was a strong movement in favour of activist local government and town planning (Larcombe 1976). Even more important was religion, which had long been a vigorous protagonist both in daily life and in the political and social controversies of the day, with its role becoming more pronounced with the sectarian conflict that followed the conscription referendums and the divisions over

[5] On the crucial role of the family and more broadly of the laity in early nineteenth-century French liberal Catholicism, a theme which echoes loudly in *Democracy in America* and is interwoven with Tocqueville's discussion of religion, see Harrison 2014.

[6] The widespread formation of returned soldiers' leagues during and after the First World War made associations an even more powerful force in social and political life (Crotty 2010, pp. 170–1).

Irish independence.[7] But although Hancock was close to his father, and attached significance to faith, religion simply does not figure in *Australia* (Davison 1978, pp. 504–5).[8]

However, by far the greatest omission, in terms of possible mitigating factors, was the middle class. Hancock shared the superficial disdain for suburbia of his friends from Melbourne University days, including Vance and Nettie Palmer, and Esmonde Higgins, Nettie's communist brother; as David Walker has noted, 'it is reasonable to suggest that Hancock's parties of initiative and parties of resistance, which has proved so persistent a notion, is a variation upon the theme of the two Australias that was central to the Palmers' criticism of 1920s Australia; 'the one creative, original and truly Australian, the other sterile, derivative and suburban' (Walker 1976, p. 205).[9] But the result of looking down on the middle class was to blind Hancock to what Allan Martin rightly described as the 'firm bourgeois reality' of late nineteenth-century Australia, from which 'stemmed on the one hand a liberalism which shaded into, and sometimes interpenetrated, the more readily defined radicalism of Labor, and on the other, a conservativism which always acted as a moderating political influence' (Martin 2007, p. 69; on the conservative tradition, see also Melleuish 2014).

It was not only the conservative tradition Hancock overlooked—a tradition that, Martin went on to say, 'was powerful not because it rested on big capital or social privilege, but because it drew its real strength from those urban groups which had spearheaded the main 19th century drive for democracy'; he missed, even more importantly, the currents of thought that 'firm bourgeois reality' had spawned. Going from the drive for self-improvement of mid-nineteenth-century 'moral enlightenment'—a faith, Michael Roe wrote, that 'reflected, in exaggerated strength, liberal principles' and which 'urged that everyone could, indeed must, become good, wise, prosperous, and responsible' (Roe 1965, p. 6)—to early twentieth-century vitalism (Rowse 1978, pp. 35–77; Roe 1984), these movements' impact went far beyond the realm of ideas.

Rather, their emphasis on the role that expertise had to play in devising 'a new art of statecraft for a new nation' (Osmond 1985, p. 53) provided the intellectual impetus for what was probably the most distinctive and enduring feature of Australia's governance: 'the long-established pattern,

[7] On the role of the churches in social reform, see Bollen 1972; on religion in Australian life generally, see Carey 1996.

[8] Much like Tocqueville, Hancock seems to have been somewhat distant from organized religion in his thirties, but never turned against it, and returned to it later in life. His interest in religious thought, with particular reference to his biography of Jan Smuts, is explored in Tsokhas 2001.

[9] The notion of parties of initiative and resistance has a long history in Australian political culture, and was made explicit by William Pember Reeves in 1894: see Sinclair 1965, p. 207.

carried further, perhaps, than in any other advanced society, of institutionalizing the resolution of conflicts over the allocation of values' (that is, of scarce resources), thereby removing 'important allocative decisions from a process of ad hoc bargaining or trials of strength . . . [and transferring them] to a system of adjudication based on committees, boards, tribunals, agencies, autonomous corporations and so on' (Parker 1965, pp. 88–9; see also Encel 1962 and Hughes 1980, pp. 263–89). In areas that ranged from industrial relations to tariff protection, the effect of thus distancing key decisions from party politics was to stabilize and dull the destructive political forces Hancock described, while nonetheless entrenching many of the harmful policies they had put in place. At the same time, the sheer size and reach of the decision-making apparatus this pattern gave birth to (going from the Tariff Board to the Commonwealth Grants Commission), shaped and helped perpetuate a powerful 'official family' that populated its structures, often with a marked moderate and ameliorist slant.[10]

Hancock therefore tended to underestimate the sociological and structural levees that protect Australian democracy, albeit at the cost of giving its institutions a greater degree of insulation from change than would have been desirable. The system of industrial arbitration and conciliation is a case in point. Formed mainly under the influence of a heady brew of late nineteenth-century 'middle-class' ideologies—spanning from Catholic social doctrine to the cult of expert decision-making and of the judicial paradigm that was common to the New Liberalism, the movement for 'national efficiency', and Fabianism—it not only institutionalized conflict but also defined roles and careers that were often powerful and lucrative, strengthening the commitment to the system of all those it involved. Hancock was well aware of the kind of trade unionists that system bred, with their 'pettifogging skill in the handling of court business' (Hancock 1930, p. 218); but he was less mindful of the solid phalanx of employers' advocates and judicial officials to whom it provided not only gainful employment but also high prestige, and who, together with their union counterparts, formed a 'club' that communicated frequently, socialized, and developed a shared view of the world.[11] If the 'perpetual bickering' in the 'Labour movement . . . between the practical men and the idealists' was won by the former, who were 'conservative and empirical in

[10] There is, in this respect, much truth in the view that: 'Federal political (and financial) dominance, combined with a powerful bureaucracy working geographically apart from the mainstream of Australian economic and social experience, may have introduced a much stronger element of public sector independence in Australian governing processes', compared to overseas (Butlin, Barnard, and Pincus 1982, p. 115).

[11] The 'industrial relations club' at the height of its influence is well (albeit entirely uncritically) portrayed in d'Alpuget 1977.

the familiar British fashion' (Hancock 1930, p. 202), it was also because the industrial relations system gave them so much to preserve.

Hancock's tendency to downplay the degree to which Australian institutions both brought the 'swarms of petty appetites' he denounced under some degree of control and, in the process, entrenched them, then carries over into his view of the country's future. Tocqueville's fear—and the root of his pessimism—was that because liberty 'is most formidable when it is a novelty' (*DA*, II.2.iii), American democracy might wither as it matured. In contrast, Hancock believed Australia's problems were signs of immaturity: of a people who, never having been 'compelled to shoulder the responsibilities and withstand the pressures which are part of the life of older peoples', had 'followed the line of least resistance' and so had 'not yet come of age' (Hancock 1930, p. 284). In thus coming of age, he optimistically believed, it would grow out of its teething difficulties, laying sounder bases for the nation's flourishing. In reality, of course, the opposite happened, as Australian democracy's institutional superstructure gave the policies he acutely criticized a permanence that persisted long after they had 'become a positive danger to the national purpose which . . . called them into existence' (Hancock 1930, p. 128).

5.6 The Contrasting Fates

But *Australia*'s lacunae, however serious they may be, can hardly explain the contrast between its fortunes and those of *Democracy in America*.

There was, after all, a time, not so long ago, when *Australia* was everywhere: when it shone as bright in Australian intellectual life as the star of *Democracy in America* did in American political and cultural debates. Indeed, documenting its pervasiveness—which ranged from the leading, fashionably left-leaning, sociology textbook of the 1970s (Encel 1970) to the quote at the front of Sidney Baker's remarkable compendium of the Australian idiom (Baker 1966)—was an important aspect of several perceptive critiques (Connell 1968; Osmond 1972; Walker 1976, pp. 204–6). Compared to the peaks of authority *Australia* then enjoyed, its subsequent decline in Australian political culture has the suddenness and scale of an extinction, made all the more startling by the fact that—whatever its limitations—no superior rival has emerged.

It would, of course, be an exaggeration to say *Australia* has entirely disappeared; it is, for example, extensively discussed, and its importance emphasized, both in a recent collection of essays by a well-known Australian sociologist (who also considers, albeit mainly in passing, Hancock's relationship to Tocqueville) (Beilharz 2015) and in a review essay by one of Australia's leading historians (Macintyre 2001, pp. 33–57), as well as in several studies of

Australian intellectual history by Greg Melleuish (see, for example, Melleuish 1995, 2014). It is also frequently cited in *The Oxford Companion to Australian History*, although it only receives three references in the more recent second volume of *The Cambridge History of Australia*.

There is, nonetheless, a sharp contrast between the book's lingering presence in what are clearly academic publications and the earlier prominence of Hancock's terms and tropes: for example, in the important collections of essays on Australia produced, both in 1963, by Peter Coleman and A. L. McLeod, and even more so in 'mass market' works such as Brian Penton's *Advance Australia Where?* (Penton 1943), which was much influenced by *Australia*, as well as in Donald Horne's *The Lucky Country*, which Penton had influenced in turn. The contrast is even sharper when the residual traces of *Australia* are compared to the 'Tocqueville industry' that is still going from strength to strength.

In part, *Australia*'s fate could be the result of its point of view merging into the intellectual background to the point of becoming a component of the 'common knowledge' that is simply taken for granted. Even thirty-five years ago, Ronald Conway, in describing Hancock as 'the father of modern Australia watchers', suggested that those who followed him had 'won easy royalties by merely filching his insights' (Conway 1980, p. 3); equally, according to a more recent assessment by Stuart Macintyre, *Australia* 'has entered so pervasively into the subliminal memory of historians that they unconsciously repeat its phrases and take its conclusions as their starting-point' (Macintyre 2001 p. 38).

But while there may well be some truth to those statements, they seem difficult to reconcile with the tendency of intellectuals—and even more so of academics—to cite authorities, sometimes to excess. Additionally, if the cause of *Australia*'s diminishing prominence is that it has merged into common knowledge, some explanation would be needed of why *Democracy in America* has not.

Rather, two factors seem more important in explaining the contrast. To begin with, while the American foundation myths have enduring power in shaping national debates, the more diffuse character of the Australian experience is such that 'among the Australian people only faint memories now remain of the origins of their polity' (Hirst 2008, p. 142). It also seems reasonable to suppose those memories have become increasingly faint as the polity's origins recede in time and as Australia has become more and more a society of migrants, who have little connection to, or knowledge of, the structural roots of the society in which they live. Again, the lack of any tradition comparable to 'Americanism' that would frame immigrants' understanding of their country of settlement makes historical memory all the more tenuous.

The result is that history plays little serious role in the policy debate, much less in the wider battle of ideas—bringing to mind Hancock's comment that while Tocqueville believed there was in America an 'instinctive distaste for the past', 'in Australia, defiance of "the truculent, narcotic and despotic past" has always been one of the most popular themes of forward-looking democracy'[12] (Hancock 1930, p. 270). It is unsurprising that, under those circumstances, canonical works such as Hancock's *Australia* would fade from prominence as the decades passed.

But that is not to say the policy debate is entirely amnesiac. There has always been a clash between a radical-nationalist view of Australian history—characterized by 'an obsession with the creative role of the Labor movement and a denial of the contributions [to Australia's progress] of the middle classes, the churches, the universities and non-radical reformist and liberal movements (Coleman 1962, p. 6)—and one which sees the impact of Labor as both more limited and, especially, more negative (Shaw 1962). While *Australia*, with its (misplaced) emphasis on Labor as the 'party of initiative', somewhat straddles that divide, it is undeniably critical of the policies Labor most enthusiastically endorsed, and nowhere more so than of the cult of 'fairness'.

That makes *Australia* profoundly inconvenient from the standpoint of that broad swathe of Australian public intellectuals for whom 'fairness' is a defining value. Little wonder then that Andrew Leigh, a Labor parliamentarian and former professor at the Australian National University, in approvingly quoting Hancock's summary of the Australian ethos as involving 'the sentiment of justice, the claim of right, the conception of equality', singularly fails to quote the concluding part of Hancock's sentence, which points to 'the appeal to government as the instrument of self-realisation' and so opens the way to Hancock's discussion of the damage the quest for fairness causes (Leigh 2013, p. 30). And little wonder, too, that the left-wing economic historian, Kosmas Tsokhas, who has described *Australia* as 'the most insightful and substantial study of Australian history and society *published before the 1960s*' (Tsokhas 2010, p. 262; emphasis added), defines its relevance to current debates in terms of what he claims is its recognition of 'prior Aboriginal ownership', the 'destruction of native forests by pastoralists and farmers', 'the important role of public investment and state enterprise in economic development', and 'a trend towards a cultural feeling and psychological awareness of national difference and separateness from Britain' (Tsokhas 2010, p. 262)—as if Hancock, rather than being a stern critic of the radical view of Australia's development, had somehow endorsed it. The result is a use of *Australia* which

[12] Hancock is citing a famous lecture by poet Bernard O'Dowd, which helped shape Australian cultural nationalism. However, in the lecture, O'Dowd spoke of the past as 'narcotizing', not 'narcotic' (O'Dowd 1909).

bears little relation, if any, to its substantive content and which can only survive if that content is ignored.

To that extent, the declining prominence of *Australia* reflects the renewed acceptance of the radical-leftist view of Australian history. Perhaps the most salient feature of that view is that instead of celebrating what Paul Kelly, echoing Hancock's 'three pillars' of the Australian Settlement (protection, state socialism, and the White Australia Policy), famously but prematurely described as the end of the Australian Settlement, it glorifies the continuing validity of the Settlement's underlying goals. Especially striking, in this respect, is the appearance of significant works that cast important elements of that settlement in favourable terms, with the relatively benign view of land reform, income redistribution, and protectionism set out in a recent, as of yet unchallenged, economic history of Australia (McLean 2013) contrasting sharply with that presented in the economic histories of an earlier generation of the Settlement's Hancock-influenced critics (such as Butlin, Barnard, and Pincus 1982, and Duncan and Fogarty 1984).

The American situation is entirely different. The debate about the American prospect remains extraordinarily vigorous; and fuelling that vigour is the far more even matching of rival intellectual camps that share a commitment to scholarly rigour while diverging markedly in their intellectual premises. From the date of its first publication, *Democracy in America* has been a point of reference and a critical resource for both sides of that debate. Just as both the 'disenchanted classical liberals' (such as William Graham Sumner and A. Lawrence Lowell) and the Wilsonian progressives drew on Tocqueville in debating the nature and impact of the administrative state (see Adcock 2014, pp. 173–234), so today both the disciples of Leo Strauss and their adversaries do so in considering the fragility of freedom (Mitchell 1995; Mansfield and Winthrop 2000; Mancini 2006, pp. 202–15).

There is no counterpart to those debates in Australia, bringing to mind Hancock's insight that any country which, because of an 'instinctive distaste for the past' (Hancock 1930, p. 270), seeks to always live in the present, is inevitably 'threatened with submergence by the more stupid ideas, credulities and quarrels of the day before yesterday' (Hancock 1930, p. 287).

Hancock's failure is, therefore, in many respects, his success. It is not his work's flaws that have condemned it; it is the endurance of the characteristics it insightfully observed. Just as *Democracy in America* is still the book of a great democracy that 'often disappointed' but 'never discouraged', 'marches indefatigably on towards the immense grandeur... at the end of the long road that mankind has yet to travel' (*DA*, II.1.viii), so *Australia* remains that of a nation that has not yet grasped the contours and limits of 'a destiny beyond prediction' (Hancock 1930, p. 314).

References

Adcock, R. 2014. *Liberalism and the Emergence of American Political Science*. Oxford and New York: Oxford University Press.

Aroney, N. 2009. *The Constitution of a Federal Commonwealth: The Making and Meaning of the Australian Constitution*. Cambridge: Cambridge University Press.

Atanassow, E. and Boyd, R. (eds.). 2013. *Tocqueville and the Frontiers of Democracy*. Cambridge: Cambridge University Press.

Baker, S. J. 1966. *The Australian Language*. Sydney: Currawong Publishing Co.

Balzac, H. de. 1936. *Sténie: ou, Les Erreurs Philosophiques*. Paris: G. Courville.

Barzun, J. 1961. *Classic, Romantic and Modern*. Boston, MA: Little, Brown.

Beasley, E. 2005. *Mid-Victorian Imperialists: British Gentlemen and the Empire of the Mind*. London: Routledge.

Beilharz, P. 2015. *Thinking the Antipodes: Australian Essays*. Melbourne: Monash University Publishing.

Bollen, J. D. 1972. *Protestantism and Social Reform in New South Wales*. Melbourne: Melbourne University Press.

Bryce, J. 1888. *The American Commonwealth*. Indianapolis, IN: Liberty Fund.

Butlin, N., Barnard, A., and Pincus, J. J. 1982. *Government and Capitalism: Public and Private Choice in Twentieth Century Australia*. Sydney: George Allen & Unwin.

Carey, H. M. 1996. *Believing in Australia*. Sydney: Allen & Unwin.

Clark, C. M. H. 1968. 'Hancock's Australia and Australian historiography: a note', *Australian Historical Studies*, vol. 13, no. 51., pp. 329–32.

Clark, C. M. H. 2000. *The Ideal of Alexis de Tocqueville*. Melbourne: Melbourne University Publishing.

Coleman, P. 1962. 'Introduction: the new Australia' in P. Coleman (ed.), *Australian Civilization: A Symposium*. Melbourne: FW Cheshire.

Connell, R. W. 1968. 'Images of Australia', *Quadrant*, vol. 12, no. 2., pp. 9–19.

Conway, R. 1980. 'The Australia watchers: fifty years since Hancock', *Quadrant*, vol. 24, no. 4., pp. 3–12.

Crone, P. 2003. *Pre-Industrial Societies: Anatomy of the Pre-Modern World*. Oxford: Oneworld Publications.

Crotty, M. 2010. 'The Returned Sailors' and Soldiers' Imperial League of Australia, 1916–46' in M. Crotty and M. Larsson (eds.), *Anzac Legacies: Australians and the Aftermath of War*. Melbourne: Australian Scholarly Publishing.

D'Alpuget, B. 1977. *Mediator: A Biography of Sir Richard Kirby*. Melbourne: Melbourne University Press.

Davidson, J. 2010. *A Three-Cornered Life: The Historian W.K. Hancock*. Sydney: University of New South Wales Press.

Davison, G. 1978. *The Rise and Fall of Marvellous Melbourne*. Carlton, Victoria: Melbourne University Press.

Davison, G. et al. (eds.). 1998. *The Oxford Companion to Australian History*. Melbourne: Oxford University Press.

Dubow, S. and Marks, S. 2001. 'Patriotism of place and race: Hancock on South Africa' in D. A. Low (ed.), *Keith Hancock: The Legacies of a Historian*. Melbourne: Melbourne University Press.

Duncan, T. and Fogarty, J. 1984. *Australia and Argentina: On Parallel Paths*. Melbourne: Melbourne University Press.

Dunn, J. 2005. *Setting the People Free: The Story of Democracy*. London: Atlantic Books.

Eggleston, F. W. 1932. *State Socialism in Victoria*. London: P.S. King and Son.

Elster, J. 2007. *Explaining Social Behavior*. Cambridge: Cambridge University Press.

Elster, J. 2009. *Alexis de Tocqueville: The First Social Scientist*. Cambridge: Cambridge University Press.

Encel, S. 1962. 'Power' in P. Coleman (ed.), *Australian Civilization: A Symposium*. Melbourne: FW Cheshire.

Encel, S. 1970. *Equality and Authority: A Study of Class, Status and Power in Australia*. London: Tavistock Publications.

Hancock, W. K. 1930. *Australia*. London: Ernest Benn.

Hancock, W. K. 1954. *Country and Calling*. London: Faber & Faber.

Harrison, C. E. 2014. *Romantic Catholics: France's Postrevolutionary Generation in Search of a Modern Faith*. New York: Cornell University Press.

Heclo, H., Bane, M., Kazin, M., and Wolfe, A. 2007. *Christianity and American Democracy*. Cambridge, MA: Harvard University Press.

Hedström, P. and Swedberg, R. 1998. *Social Mechanisms: An Analytical Approach to the Social Sciences*. Cambridge: Cambridge University Press.

Hirst, J. 2008. 'Empire, state, nation' in D. M. Schreuder and S. Ward (eds.), *Australia's Empire*. New York: Oxford University Press.

Hughes, C. 1980. 'Government action and the judicial model' in A. Tay and E. Kamenka, *Law-Making in Australia*. Sydney: E. Arnold.

Jaume, L. 1997. *L'Individu Effacé, ou le Paradoxe du Libéralisme Français*. Paris: Fayard.

Jaume, L. 2013. *Tocqueville, the Aristocratic Sources of Liberty*. Princeton: Princeton University Press.

Kaledin, A. 2011. *Tocqueville and His America: A Darker Horizon*, New Haven: Yale University Press.

Kuran, T. 1997. *Private Truths, Public Lies: The Social Consequences of Preference Falsification*. Cambridge, MA: Harvard University Press.

Larcombe, F. A. 1976. *The Stabilization of Local Government in New South Wales, 1858–1906*. Sydney: Sydney University Press.

Leigh, A. 2013. *Battlers and Billionaires: The Story of Inequality in Australia*. Melbourne: Black Inc.

Low, D. A. 2001. '*Imperium et Libertas* and Hancock's *Problems of Nationality*' in D. Low (ed.), *Keith Hancock: The Legacies of a historian*. Melbourne: Melbourne University Press.

Macintyre, S. 2001. 'Full of hits and misses: a reappraisal of Hancock's *Australia*' in D. Low (ed.), *Keith Hancock: The Legacies of a Historian*. Melbourne: Melbourne University Press.

McLean, I. W. 2013. *Why Australia Prospered: The Shifting Sources of Economic Growth*. Princeton: Princeton University Press.

McLeod, A. L. (ed.). 1963. *The Pattern of Australian Culture*. Ithaca: Cornell University Press.

McLoughlin, W. G. 1978. *Revivals, Awakenings, and Reform*. Chicago: Chicago University Press.

Mancini, M. 2006. *Alexis de Tocqueville and American Intellectuals*. Lanham, MD: Rowman & Littlefield.

Manent, P. 1982. *Tocqueville et la Nature de la Démocratie*. Paris: Gallimard.

Mannheim, K. 1952. *Essays on the Sociology of Knowledge*. London: Routledge & Kegan Paul.

Mansfield, H. and Winthrop, D. 2000. 'Introduction' in A. de Tocqueville, *Democracy in America*, trans. and ed. by H. C. Mansfield and D. Winthrop. Chicago: Chicago University Press.

Martin, A. W. 2007. *The "Whig" View of Australian History and Other Essays*, J. Nethercote (ed.). Melbourne: Melbourne University Publishing.

Meaney, N. K. 1985.'Reflections on Hancock's "Australia": following an interview with Sir Keith Hancock on 13 January 1985', *Australian Historical Bulletin*, no. 43, pp. 8–13.

Melleuish, G. 1995. *Cultural Liberalism in Australia: A Study in Intellectual and Cultural History*. Cambridge: Cambridge University Press.

Melleuish, G. 2014. *Despotic State or Free Individual: Two Traditions of Democracy in Australia*. Melbourne: Australian Scholarly Press.

Merivale, H. 2010. *Lectures on Colonization and Colonies, Delivered before the University of Oxford in 1839, 1840, and 1841*. Cambridge: Cambridge University Press.

Mitchell, J. 1995. *The Fragility of Freedom: Tocqueville on Religion, Democracy and the American Future*. Chicago: Chicago University Press.

Musset, A. de. 1836. *La Confession d'un enfant du siècle* [The Confession of a Child of the Century], <http://www.gutenberg.org/files/3942/3942-h/3942-h.htm> (accessed 20 November 2015).

Ober, J. 1998. *Political Dissent in Democratic Athens: Intellectual Critics of Popular Rule*. Princeton: Princeton University Press.

O'Dowd, B. 1909. *Poetry Militant: an Australian Plea for the Poetry of Purpose*. Melbourne: T. C. Lothian.

Offe, C. 2005. *Reflections on America: Tocqueville*. USA: Weber and Adorno; London: Polity.

Osmond, W. G. 1972. *The Dilemma of an Australian Sociology*. Melbourne: Arena Publications.

Osmond, W. G. 1985. *Frederic Eggleston: An Intellectual in Australian Politics*. Sydney: Allen & Unwin.

Parker, R. S. 1965. 'Power in Australia', *Journal of Sociology*, vol. 1, no. 2, pp. 88–9.

Penton, B. 1943. *Advance Australia: Where?* London: Cassell and Company Limited.

Perreau-Saussine, E. 2012. *Catholicism and Democracy: An Essay in the History of Political Thought*. Princeton: Princeton University Press.

Pitts, J. 2005. *A Turn to Empire: The Rise of Imperial Liberalism in Britain and France*. Princeton: Princeton University Press.

Roe, M. 1965. *The Quest for Authority in Eastern Australia, 1835–1851*. Melbourne: Melbourne University Press.

Roe, M. 1978. 'The subject and the subjective: Hancock's autobiography', *Meanjin*, vol. 37, no. 1, pp. 129–32.

Roe, M. 1984. *Nine Australian Progressives: Vitalism in Bourgeois Social Thought 1890–1960*. St Lucia: University of Queensland Press Scholar's Library.

Rowse, T. 1978. *Australian Liberalism and National Character*. Melbourne: Kibble Books.

Schedvin, C. B. 1970. *Australia and the Great Depression: A Study of Economic Development and Policies in the 1920s and 1930s*. Sydney: Sydney University Press.

Serle, G. [1973] 2014. *From Deserts the Prophets Come: The Creative Spirit in Australia 1788–1972*. Melbourne: Monash University Publishing.

Shann, E. 1930. *An Economic History of Australia*. Cambridge: Cambridge University Press.

Shaw, A. G. L. 1962. 'The old tradition' in P. Coleman (ed.), *Australian Civilization: A Symposium*. Melbourne: FW Cheshire.

Sheehan, J. and Wahrman, D. 2015. *Invisible Hands: Self-Organization and the Eighteenth Century*. Chicago: University of Chicago Press.

Sinclair, K. 1965. *William Pember Reeves: New Zealand Fabian*. Oxford: Clarendon Press.

Spitzer, A. B. 1987. *The French Generation of 1820*. Princeton: Princeton University Press.

Tocqueville, A. de. [1835] 2004. *Democracy in America*, trans. A. Goldhammer. New York: Library of America.

Tocqueville, A. de. [1835 and 1840] 2009. *Democracy in America: Historical-Critical Edition of De la démocratie en Amérique*, 4 vols, ed. E. Nolla, trans. J. T. Schleifer. Indiana: Liberty Fund, Indiana, <http://oll.libertyfund.org/titles/2284> (accessed 20 November 2015).

Tsokhas, K. 2001. 'A search for transcendence: philosophical and religious dialogues in W.K. Hancock's biography of J. C. Smuts', *The Round Table: The Commonwealth Journal of International Affairs*, vol. 90, no. 358, pp. 67–88.

Tsokhas, K. 2010. Review of "A Three-Cornered Life: The Historian W. K. Hancock" by Jim Davidson, UNSW Press, Sydney, NSW', *Journal of Australian Political Economy*, vol. 68., pp. 261–6.

Walker, D. 1976. *Dream and Disillusion: A Search for Australian Cultural Identity*. Canberra: Australian National University Press.

Wohl, R. 1979. *The Generation of 1914*. Cambridge, MA: Harvard University Press.

6

Australia's 'Talent for Bureaucracy' and the Atrophy of Federalism

J. R. Nethercote

This chapter has its origins in a call prior to Australia's general election of 2013 for a national discussion about her Federation, a call that arose from the view that there was much scope for improvement in the workings of Australia's Federation. But this call for such a national discussion immediately, and instinctively, gave rise to a question as to whether it is even possible to have a real debate about federalism in Australia.

The chapter argues that informed discussion of federalism is frustrated on two grounds. First, the intellectual fabric of the country, whether in law, history, political science, or economics, turns a blind eye to its federal character and the pervasive federalism in the ordinary life of Australia. A major reason for this deficiency lies in the continuing influence of British ways on Australian thinking. Second, federalism in Australia is weakened by the force of bureaucracy, and the bureaucratic habit, in Australia's governance. Governance of Australia's Federation is too much a case study in Australia's 'talent for bureaucracy'.

6.1 Federalist in Spite of Itself

Australia is one of the oldest federations in the world. Moreover, much of the country works on federal principles, in the sense that many country-wide organizations are state-based; national bodies are composed, often on the basis of equality, of delegates nominated by state branches.

The idea that membership should be represented according to numbers is much less frequently in evidence. Indeed, an important illustration of this point for many years was the Australian Labor Party. Although it stands for one-person:one-value, until the late 1960s Labor's supreme ruling body, the appropriately named Federal Conference, was composed of six delegates from each of its six state branches. These were the notorious '36 faceless men' whom Sir Robert Menzies mercilessly attacked during the 1963 federal election.

The Labor Party thus organized itself on the same basis as the Senate, rather than of the House of Representatives, notwithstanding all its rhetoric about democracy. During the past half-century representation on the basis of state equality has been qualified in the Labor Party, but the party remains far from a country-wide structure on a purely population basis.

That so many Australian organizations follow the federal principle makes it all the more surprising that federal sentiment in Australia is, except in sport, so inconspicuous. It is latent, even residual; rarely overt. Some reasons may be found in the major intellectual traditions in which those with interests in government are usually trained in Australia.

A conspicuous example is the law. When the Constitution of Australia was composed, a number of the leading figures versed themselves very thoroughly in federal government. Andrew Inglis Clark, who prepared the first draft, had a lengthy sojourn in the USA studying the workings of the American Federation and having discussions with various people deeply experienced in its politics, government, and the courts. This federal background was manifest not only in the first parliaments but, more significantly, in the personnel of the High Court in its original manifestation: Sir Samuel Griffith, Sir Edmund Barton, and Richard O'Connor.

That the federal sentiment was under pressure from an early stage may be found in the six referendums which the Fisher Labor government put to the people during its 1910–13 term of office. These referendums, which were all about enlargement of Commonwealth powers in matters such as monopolies, trade and commerce, corporations, and industry, held in April 1911 and again in May 1913 (at the same time as the general election of that year) failed, but only just. On each occasion they secured the support of three out of six states (Queensland, South Australia, Western Australia); the percentage of formal votes in favour on every question exceeded 49 per cent.

The Great War certainly seems to have stimulated national sentiment. This national sentiment was reflected in the *Engineers' case* of 1920, the case which brought great fame and not a little fortune to the young Robert Menzies. For present purposes, the significance of Engineers' lies in its consequences for judicial interpretation of the federal relationship, but it also immediately had a pronounced centralizing effect on industrial relations. With the three founding justices now gone from the Court, a new national spirit took over, and it had a marked centralist tone. The major spokesman was

Sir Isaac Isaacs, with reinforcement from H. B. Higgins, both alumni of the Constitutional Conventions, former attorneys-general of the Commonwealth (in the second Deakin and Watson Labor governments respectively), and, by 1920, fifteen-year veterans of the Court.

Prior to *Engineers'* the Constitution was viewed as a compact among the states and the Commonwealth, and cases were settled in a manner which sought to respect the various jurisdictions. This approach, however, became somewhat tangled, and that allowed Menzies to argue successfully that the Court should take a fresh look. This provided the opportunity for Isaacs and Higgins, both clearly more centralist than federalist, to introduce a doctrine based on conventional methods of statutory construction. This approach thereafter allowed Commonwealth powers to take full effect, leaving only residual powers for the state governments.

As it happens, this centralist view of the Constitution was given much support politically after the 1922 election, at which the Nationalist Party, led by William Morris Hughes, lost its majority in the House of Representatives. In the Coalition government which succeeded the Hughes government, the two leading figures were veterans of the Great War, S. M. Bruce and Dr Earle Page, neither of whom had been members of the Constitutional Conventions, nor of any state parliament. Bruce had strong connections with Melbourne but had mainly lived in Britain; Page, a founding member of the Country Party, had links with rural Australia rather than the city. It was, indeed, a new generation and not one directly involved in the design of the Federation.

Engineers' has been the lodestone of constitutional interpretation ever since. Judicial interpretation has been a major avenue for enhancement of Commonwealth powers and the progressive shift of the states from autonomy to agency.

The path has been similar in history. So far as Australia itself is concerned, the big theme is the ascendancy of the Commonwealth. Augmentation of the Commonwealth role is invariably portrayed as an indisputable and laudable sign of progress. Expansion of the Commonwealth role at home is matched by Australia's assertion of itself internationally. Intersection of the two, and exploitation of its international role to advance Commonwealth interests at home, has been much admired. Few reservations were expressed as the Commonwealth increasingly utilized the so-called external affairs power in the Constitution, section 51 (xxix), as a constitutional head of power for aggrandisement in, for example, the *Tasmanian Dams case*, the case in 1983 in which plans of the government of Tasmania to dam the Franklin River in south-west Tasmania were stopped. The counsel of Sir Harry Gibbs, a justice of the High Court from 1971 until 1981, and Chief Justice from then until his compulsory retirement in 1987, that the nation might just as well delete 'External affairs' and insert 'Anything' was not by any means a jest; the 'external affairs' power can now be activated by invoking any international instrument to which Australia is a signatory, whatever its subject matter and even if its application is exclusively domestic.

6.2 *Fédéralisme sans Doctrines*

Political science, like the law, eventually succumbed to the siren call of the Mother Country. The yardstick in the study of Australian government and politics became Westminster; though Walter Bagehot's *The English Constitution* (1867) periodically figured in reading lists, *The Federalist Papers* hardly appeared at all.

Two important texts of the post-Second World War period were overtly cast in a British mould; both authors had studied in Britain, one at Oxford, the other at the London School of Economics. L. F. Crisp's *The Parliamentary Government of the Commonwealth of Australia* (1949) (*Australian National Government* after 1965) and Gordon Greenwood's *The Future of Federalism* (1946) both favoured a unitary state and, in Crisp's case, a unicameral parliament. Crisp's book was exceedingly influential, over the years seeing off most likely rivals; even now, three decades after Crisp's death, it cannot be said to have been replaced. It is indicative of its approach that it contained nothing about the workings of federalism or Commonwealth–state relations; this was more defensible under the original title than that adopted in 1965, a major reason for which was to respond to complaints about the length of the first title by library cataloguers.

Greenwood's book might have had a greater influence had there been more interest in federal doctrine and practice, notwithstanding the fact that its basic argument was centralist; as it was, there was little such interest. A second edition was published in 1976 by which time, for three decades, Greenwood's scholarly interest had been firmly focused on 'Australia in world affairs', as evinced by his long editorship of books of that name.

A large and insightful volume, *The Government of the Australian States*, edited by S. R. Davis and published in 1960, could not really be said to have made the mainstream of political science in Australia, although it did make reading lists for specialist essays. At present the state best served in parliamentary, governmental, and political matters is New South Wales (NSW), as a consequence of sesquicentenary initiatives and some splendid publishing by Federation Press. But this is too recent to compete with an enormous concentration on the Commonwealth (which itself seems to be in decline, having lost ground to such fields as environmental politics).

Thus, Australia, inasmuch as it is studied, is studied very much as if it were a unitary state.

What interest there has been in federalism was in the past largely a practical or technical matter. Accordingly, Geoffrey Sawer's *Modern Federalism* (1969) had a fair readership and ran to several editions. But *The Federal Principle: A Journey Through Time in Quest of Meaning* (1978), a major study of federal theory by S. R. Davis, the professor of politics at Monash University for a quarter century, struggled for a readership in Australia itself, although it seems to have done reasonably well in other federal countries.

In shaping the Australian Federation, economists have been the main force, apart from the lawyers, who, in this matter, have something of a home-ground (High Court) advantage. In the raising, management, and allocation of government revenues in the Federation, their influence has been felt in many highly related fields, from taxation policy to distribution of the revenue, especially after the Commonwealth cornered the income tax during the Second World War.

Their influence has moved in two directions. As allocation of revenues to the states and territories became increasingly significant, economists, both through budget agencies and the Commonwealth Grants Commission, had a major role in devising the formulae and, later, the models for how the monies should be dispersed among states and territories.

Others, by contrast, have a more abstract view of the economy and are hostile to unnatural barriers to trade or the free movement of goods and services, capital and labour. For some of them, federalism may simply be a means for imposing artificial restrictions upon the workings of the economy. In this view, federalism is seen as something of a successor to feudalism so far as economic development and progress is concerned, imposing local impediments to the workings of markets.

Where there should have been some conspicuous unity between political scientists and economists concerns the very large disjunction between responsibility for raising government revenue and its subsequent public expenditure, usually referred to as vertical fiscal imbalance. Commonwealth pre-eminence in revenue collection, including the goods and services tax, and the allocation of monies to states and territories using equalization methodologies, effectively curtails self-government within the Federation and renders a good deal of rhetoric about enhancing accountability little more than cant.

This *tour d'horizon* largely concerns the undergraduate field. It is at that level that minds are largely shaped, but it is not the whole story. In university circles, the strongest interest in federalism has been at the postgraduate/research level, usually among economists or lawyers. These endeavours have had some impact, particularly in informing discussions among officials, discussions which sometimes involve academics and other observers. But, with the possible exception of the Federalism Research Centre at the Australian National University, struck down nearly two decades ago by Commonwealth fiat, their contribution has not been sufficiently sustained.[1]

If this analysis is accepted, even if only in broad terms, it can be seen that a national debate about federalism in Australia would only be possible in fairly bland terms. It provides some insight into why discussion of many questions of public policy is generally superficial.

But what is required is some appraisal of what ideas shape the workings of the Federation and, in particular, what are the implications, consequences, and costs of the prevailing equalization creed that all Australians, wherever they reside, are entitled to the same level of services. This is the point at which to move to Australia's 'talent for bureaucracy' and see what guidance it provides regarding the way federalism is practised in Australia.

6.3 The Talent for Bureaucracy

There are some notable aphorisms about the character of governance in Australia. A visitor from France in the nineteenth century contributed the observation about 'socialisme sans doctrine'. Sir Keith Hancock in 1930 informed readers that Australians view the state as a 'vast public utility'.

There is an illuminating but largely forgotten insight by Alan Davies, the Melbourne political scientist, in the opening paragraph of *Australian Democracy*:

> The characteristic talent of Australians [he wrote] is not for improvisation, nor even for republican manners; it is for bureaucracy. We take a somewhat hesitant pride in this, since it runs counter not only to the archaic and cherished image of ourselves as an ungovernable, if not actually lawless, people; but, more importantly, because we have been trained in the modern period to see our politics in terms of a liberalism which accords to bureaucracy only a small and rather shady place. Being a good bureaucrat is, we feel, a bit like being a good forger.
>
> (Davies 1958, p. 3)

By way of context, he added:

> The pervasiveness of bureaucracy is a feature of most industrial societies, and its spread, which has been slow and steady, has its roots not only in developing technology, but also—and especially in its political application—in the modern demand for security and equality. (Davies 1958, p. 3)

[1] The Australian National University has lately established an Australian Centre for Federalism. Very academic in disposition, available information about the Centre does little to suggest that it plans to be a forum for research about the workings of federalism in Australia or for thinking and debate about federal doctrine and philosophy.

In a telling passage he contended that:

> Australian appetites have merely been in a general way larger and coarser than the average, and much more concentratedly political. It is on the supply, rather than the demand, side that Australia has really scored: in particular by the construction in [the twentieth century] of a national government machine, which, thoroughly professional at the core, is nevertheless neither invidiously recruited, nor authoritarian in outlook, but even able, in an odd way, to draw nourishment from its envelope of representative democracy. (Davies 1958, p. 3)

Davies has by no means been the only scholar to detect these tendencies in Australian society. The historian, John Hirst, said a decade ago, that, when he addresses new students from abroad about Australian society, there is one thing he tells them that they should keep secret from Australians whom they meet:

> I tell them that Australians are a very obedient people. I advise them to keep this secret because Australians imagine themselves to be the opposite of obedient. They think of themselves as anti-authority. They love a larrikin. Their most revered national hero is a criminal outlaw, the bushranger Ned Kelly. Their unofficial national anthem honours an unemployed vagrant who commits suicide rather than be taken by the police troopers for stealing a sheep. (Hirst 2004, p. 113)

The appeal of bureaucracy to government (elected and career officials alike) may be found in a range of properties, summed up by Max Weber as 'Precision, speed, unambiguity, knowledge of the files, continuity, discretion, unity, strict subordination, reduction of friction and of material and personal costs...' (Weber 1948, p. 214).

There are two other properties of bureaucracy of considerable significance for this chapter: bureaucracy is inextricably associated with uniformity and standardization.

But before passing on from Weber, there is another passage of direct relevance:

> Bureaucratic organization has usually come into power on the basis of *a levelling of economic and social differences*. This levelling has been at least relative, and has concerned the significance of social and economic differences for the assumption of administrative functions.
>
> Bureaucracy inevitably accompanies modern mass democracy in contrast to the democratic self-government of small homogenous units.
>
> This results from the characteristic principle of bureaucracy: the abstract regularity of the execution of authority, which is a result of the demand for 'equality before the law' in the personal and functional sense—hence, of the horror of 'privilege', and the principled rejection of doing business 'from case to case'.
>
> (Weber 1948, p. 224; emphasis added)

6.4 Adjectival Federalism

And now back to federalism. Over the years there have been a number of adjectives applied to federalism in Australia. These include cooperative federalism, coordinate federalism, and pragmatic federalism. In each case the adjective plays a particular role—it may be an aspiration as to how the Federation might work better than it actually does; or it might be an attempt to describe the nature of a particular Federation; 'cooperative' is often used in the former situation whilst 'pragmatic' is employed in the latter. 'Pragmatic' is not an especially useful word for it mainly features in relation to a Federation which works but where observers have difficulty in describing how and, more particularly, why. It is a reminder of a well-known quip about federalism in Canada, namely that it works well enough in practice but unfortunately not in theory.

Sometimes there is talk of coercive federalism. This terminology is usually employed in political rhetoric in situations where it is considered that the central or federal government, in Australia's case, the Commonwealth, is unduly authoritarian in its relations with component governments of the Federation.

Coercive federalism, however, comes closest to what might be regarded as the most accurate descriptor of federalism in Australia, namely, bureaucratic federalism. Federalism in Australia has never actually been so described. There is a book entitled *Administrative Federalism*, a collection of documents on intergovernmental relations in Australia, but that name does not capture the essential character of federalism in Australia nor, indeed, the extent to which the practice of federalism is so much at odds with the goals and ideals of federalism.

Those goals and ideals have a long lineage. They are partly about self-government, autonomy, and the right of communities of varying sizes and composition to settle their own affairs, particularly domestic and internal affairs, as far as is possible. A second quality of federalism is a derivative, namely the opportunity for variety and diversity: communities have not only the right but, more importantly, the possibility of making their own decisions about a broad range of social, industrial, commercial, educational, and cultural activities. At a broader level, federalism is valued as a counter to concentration of power, a major feature of a unitary state even if only potentially rather than actually. Federalism is, also, seen as a mechanism for combining the advantages of size for, say, purposes of defence and security, without losing the advantages of locality and community in day-to-day living.

All these propositions have been contested on various grounds. Some people do not accept the idea of federalism at all. A. V. Dicey, who understood that federalism represented a desire for 'union but not unity', thought federalism simply meant 'weak government, legalism and conservatism'. Dicey saw these as deficiencies but there are others who see them as strengths in the federal idea.

Others criticize federalism on the pragmatic basis that few federations achieve the stated goals (locality; community; diversity; variety; experimentation). Failure to realize aspirations is a general criticism which may be made about many forms of government, so it begs the question of whether there is anything special about the attributed failings of federalism.

The crucial point about federalism in Australia is the pervasiveness of doctrines of equality and equalization, combined with a preference for the use of the word 'national', often a cover for 'central', and the decline of the word 'federal'. Although rarely recognized, realization of 'equality' in practice takes the form of standardization, homogenization, and even uniformity. It is the antithesis of diversity, variety, and choice. The quest for equality is at the expense of federalism.

6.5 Federation as a Bureaucracy: *Reform of the Federation Green Paper* (2015)

In 2015, the Liberal-National government published a document entitled *Reform of the Federation Green Paper*. It powerfully illustrates the struggle which federalism in Australia has to escape from the overlay of bureaucracy and the bureaucratic ethos.

It has been composed, appropriately enough, by an anonymous task force based in the Commonwealth Department of the Prime Minister and Cabinet. It has an obligatory expert panel of advisers composed of former state premiers and ministers, and academics and advocates of various kinds. The central mission purportedly derives from the:

> need to make sure our federal structure is working. Our Federation is not, as some argue, a relic from the past, broken beyond repair and ill-suited to the times.... A major part of the problem is that over time, the Commonwealth has become, for various reasons, increasingly involved in matters which have traditionally been the responsibility of the States and Territories.
>
> (Department of the Prime Minister and Cabinet 2015, p. 106)

As a consequence, the Abbott government is:

> committed to a White Paper on the Reform of the Federation. The White Paper will seek to clarify roles and responsibilities to ensure that, as far as possible, the States and Territories are sovereign in their own sphere. (ibid., p. 106)

The objectives are to 'reduce and end, as far as possible, the waste, duplication and second guessing between different levels of government'; 'achieve a more efficient and effective Federation, and in so doing, improve national productivity'; and to 'make interacting with government simpler for citizens' (ibid., p. 107).

Australian government is not seen as an arrangement of polities on a federal basis but essentially as a holistic, hierarchical administrative system for the provision and funding of services. It is the operation of this system which preoccupies the paper.

In so doing, it evokes some of the usual criticisms of federalism such as overlap and duplication. This is a hardy perennial in any discussion of federalism, but evidence and illustration has proven much harder to come by. By contrast, there will certainly be transaction costs in the working of a Federation and these will not only be financial; these, unfortunately, are rarely identified or considered.

From the beginning, the green paper is ambivalent about federalism. It opines, in the first paragraph, that 'Australia's Federation has worked well since 1901.' It enquires, shortly afterwards, if 'our Federation [is] still fit for purpose?' (ibid., p. 1). It later concludes that 'while the Federation is mostly working well, it is not working as well as it could, and this is contributing to a lack of confidence and trust in our system of government to deliver better services' (ibid., p. 2).

It is, however, unable, or at least unwilling, to speak of 'federalism' itself as a philosophy or a method of government. It prefers instead to speak of 'Federation' as '*the* system of national governance' (emphasis added). It is as if 'Federation' is simply a name for what is otherwise a single structure of government, albeit tiered. The green paper's preoccupation is with the 'pressure on all governments' budgets' and the need 'to secure Australia's future as a high wage and internationally competitive economy' (ibid., p. 2), that is to say, public finance and expenditure rather than federal governance.

The paper asks but does not answer clearly: 'what is the problem we are trying to solve?' It records that, according to one survey, more than 80 per cent of Australians think the performance of the Federation could be improved, but it confesses that 'what is not as clear is whether that problem is with the model of federalism, a perception of being "over governed", or something more concrete' (ibid., p. 4).

The paper conceives improvement in bureaucratic terms:

> Reform of the Federation will be worthwhile if it improves the incentives to deliver better services, enhances the accountability of all governments to Australians for taxes being well spent, drives productivity improvements and economic growth, and improves the way governments work together. (ibid., p. 10)

Except for those very familiar with Australian federalism, no one reading the paper would realize the pervasive significance of 'equalization' in the way the Federation works, especially its role in addressing what is described as vertical fiscal imbalance and in the practice of horizontal fiscal equalization. It is not even expressly mentioned in a statement by the Council of Australian Governments, issued in April 2015. This statement declares that any reallocation of responsibilities between the governments of the Federation should, inter alia, aim to '*be fair*: all Australians should be able to receive, choose and access high quality services, regardless of personal circumstances, location or socio-economic background'.

'Fairness', which appears conceptually to embrace equality, may be an inherent value in any government but it will usually come with costs. The consequences of a commitment to provision of high-quality services 'regardless of location' will certainly be considerable. It will have an impact on delivery of services, driving economic growth, even upon questions of accountability and the durability of programmes. But these are considerations which the green paper ignores.

6.6 Retrieving Federalism from Bureaucracy

Revival and revitalization—one might almost say restoration—of federalism in Australia calls for some hard thinking on several fronts. One such front is the weaknesses in terms of self-government and autonomy deriving from centralized revenue-raising. This weakness is aggravated when subsequent allocation of revenue to states and territories has an abstract basis in equalization methodologies and practices. The crucial link in responsible government between revenue-raising and public expenditure is thereby both lost and confused.

A second front antipathetic to true federalism is the persistent quest for public policy on a national basis, be it in education, health, housing, transport, or any other field. It is easy to support a move away from process stipulations in Commonwealth–state agreements but this really misses the point. The bureaucratic instinct continues to assert itself in the view that the test of compliance should be located in standards, results, and/or, most vacuous of all, 'outcomes'. The goal should be state autonomy and hence accountability. And accountability should be the business principally of state authorities and state electorates, not the Commonwealth auditor-general with augmented powers.

Most of all, ideas of equality, fairness, and, certainly, equalization, a technocratic virus, call for definition and clarity in their application in a federal context. These words have a beguiling simplicity but they have been the cloak for much standardization, homogenization, and uniformity.

The crucial task, in revival of Australia's Federation, thus lies in releasing it from the bureaucratic constraints which have increasingly enveloped it in the decades after the Second World War.

References

Bagehot, W. 1867. *The English Constitution*. London: Chapman Hall.

Crisp, L. F. 1949. *The Parliamentary Government of the Commonwealth of Australia*. London: Longman.

Crisp, L. F. 1965. *Australian National Government*. Melbourne: Longman Cheshire.

Davies, A. F. 1958. *Australian Democracy*. Melbourne: Longmans Green and Co.

Davis, S. R. (ed.). 1960. *The Government of the Australian States*. Melbourne: Longmans.

Davis, S. R. 1978. *The Federal Principle: A Journey through Time in Quest of Meaning*. Berkeley, CA: University of California Press.

Department of the Prime Minister and Cabinet. 2015. *Reform of the Federation Green Paper*. Canberra: Department of the Prime Minister and Cabinet.

Greenwood, G. 1946. *The Future of Federalism*. Melbourne: Melbourne University Press.

Hancock, W. K. 1930. *Australia*. London: Benn.

Hirst, J. 2004. *The Distinctiveness of Australian Democracy*, Papers on Parliament No. 42. Canberra: Parliament of Australia.

Weber, M. 1948. *From Max Weber: Essays in Sociology*. H. H. Gerth & C. Wright Mills (eds.), London: Routledge & Kegan Paul.

7

Australia's Industrial Relations Singularity

Phil Lewis

Australia's enduring approach to industrial relations is judged by both its champions and its critics as being unique. For most of the twentieth century, Australia's system of wage determination and industrial relations had only one or two counterparts in the industrialized world. (Singapore and, until 1992, New Zealand were very similar to the Australian system.) While Australia's system was considerably relaxed between the 1980s and early 2000s, it was significantly reregulated by Labor governments after 2007, with little attempt to reverse this by the incoming Liberal and National Party (LNP) government in 2013. Thus, Australia's unusual system still largely prevails.

While praise is heaped on Australia's centralized system by its supporters for the alleged superior outcomes, particularly with respect to 'fairness', its opponents point to its impediments to economic efficiency. While most (or at least many) economists argue that the Australian industrial relations system is an historical vestige in a modern free market, service-based economy, support for it is still very much entrenched in the Australian psyche and attempts at reform have, at times, meant political suicide for those attempting to change it.

The intention of this chapter is to provide a sketch of the current system, how Australia got where it is, how Australia compares with other countries, and the implications of the current system with respect to the most important issues facing the labour market.

7.1 Origins

Australia's industrial relations system had its origins in the pre-Federation colonies, in the midst of a number of bitter industrial disputes in the 1890s (Mitchell

1989). Most notable were the maritime dispute of 1890, which was particularly violent and involved the military in New South Wales (NSW) and Victoria and spread to New Zealand (Le Rossignol and Stewart 1910); and the shearers' strike of 1891, which is credited with leading to the formation of the Australian Labor Party (Sykes 1964). The unease among organized labour, employers, politicians, and the public led to calls for an 'independent arbitrator' to avoid bitter confrontation between employers and workers. This led to the proliferation during Federation years in all the states, and New Zealand, of Arbitration and Industrial Courts with the power to determine wages and conditions.

The key legislation, though not quite the first, was by the Commonwealth. In the face of the insistent coaxing of H. B. Higgins, the 1898 Melbourne constitutional convention had resolved, by a narrow margin, to include in Section 51 of the Constitution of the Commonwealth of Australia this article:

> (xxxv.) Conciliation and arbitration for the prevention and settlement of industrial disputes extending beyond the limits of any one State.

Sanctioned by this provision, in 1904 the new Commonwealth parliament passed the Conciliation and Arbitration Act 1904, supported in varying degrees by all three governments of that year, Labor, Protectionist, and Free Trade. The chief objects of the Act were stated on its commencing page as:

i. To prevent lock-outs and strikes in relation to industrial disputes;
ii. To constitute a Commonwealth Court of Conciliation and Arbitration having jurisdiction for the prevention and settlement of industrial disputes;
iii. To provide for the exercise of the jurisdiction of the Court by conciliation with a view to amicable agreement between the parties;
iv. In default of amicable agreement between the parties, to provide for the exercise of the jurisdiction of the Court by equitable award;
v. To enable States to refer industrial disputes to the Court, and to permit the working of the Court and of State Industrial Authorities in aid of each other;
vi. To facilitate and encourage the organization of representative bodies of employers and of employees and the submission of industrial disputes to the Court by organizations, and to permit representative bodies of employers and of employees to be declared organizations for the purposes of this Act;
vii. To provide for the making and enforcement of industrial agreements between employers and employees in relation to industrial disputes.

(Commonwealth of Australia 1904)

Thus the Commonwealth Court of Conciliation and Arbitration was created to settle disputes between employees, unions, and employers. When it ruled to settle a dispute, the decision was known as an 'award'. But, critically, awards contain a whole set of employment conditions, including minimum rates of pay.

Minimum wage rates are usually traced to the now famous (or infamous?) Harvester Case of 1907. The case was symptomatic of the insular nature of the Australian economy at the time, where a key objective of government policy was protection. Firms were seen to have to be protected from competition from imports through the tariff and workers to be protected from competition from cheap imported (mostly Asian) labour through the White Australia Policy. The Harvester Case related to agricultural machinery manufacturer, the Sunshine Harvester Company. Agriculture was a major industry in Australia at the time, and with growth of the industry came increased demand for agricultural machinery and large profits for manufacturers of farm machinery. As part of Labor government policy for workers to share in the benefits of tariff protection, the Excise Tariff Act 1906 imposed a tax on employers who did not pay a wage that was 'fair and reasonable', which Section 40 of the Act ordained would be determined by the Court of Conciliation and Arbitration.

Under the presiding judge, Mr Justice Higgins, the Court was charged with establishing this minimum wage. The hearing took place in Melbourne between October 1907 and November 1907. Higgins heard evidence from employees of Sunshine Harvester, and received estimates of the total weekly outlays of nine households of unskilled working men, ranging from £1 18s to £3 13s and 7d. On 8 November 1907 Higgins judged that the Sunshine Harvester Company was obliged to pay its employees a wage that met 'the normal needs of an average employee, regarded as a human being in a civilised community', regardless of profitability or 'capacity to pay'. He deemed this wage to amount to 7s per day (or £2 2s per week); precisely the minimum daily wage that unions had incessantly sought for unskilled workers since the mid-1890s (Macarthy 1970, p. 6). Higgins' wage decision became the basis of the universal practice of state and Commonwealth Courts of Arbitration declaring a 'basic wage' and, with the passage of decades, a whole set of other conditions of work as part of any 'award'.

While (most) economists argue that prices (in this case wages) are better determined by supply and demand, the principle of Court-determined wages and conditions specifically denied this proposition. In defining a 'fair and reasonable wage', Higgins ruled:

> The provision for 'fair and reasonable' remuneration is obviously designed for the benefit of the employees in the industry; and it must be meant to secure to them something which they cannot get by the ordinary system of individual bargaining with employers...

> The standard of 'fair and reasonable' must therefore be something else, and I cannot think of any other standard appropriate than the normal needs of an average employee, regarded as a human being in a civilised community.
>
> (CCA 1907, p. 34)

Thus, enshrined in this process was the principle that the labour market, left to its own devices, could not be relied on to deliver desirable outcomes and, indeed, would deliver undesirable outcomes. Therefore, it was necessary for government (or their appointed judiciary) to impose what they regarded as desirable. Strangely, to some at least, this view still holds sway among many in Australia today, probably best manifest in the 2007 election where the defining issue was the LNP Coalition's attempt to deregulate the labour market.

The Harvester judgement was made under the Excise Act of 1906, not the Conciliation and Arbitration Act of 1904. Higgins' judgement was resisted by Sunshine Harvester, and, in 1908, the High Court declared the use of the Excise Act to set a wage unconstitutional (High Court of Australia 1908). For all that, the 'Harvester Judgement' is often thought of as a defining point for the Australian awards system, and, certainly, the repudiation of 'capacity to pay' established by Higgins became the basis of the setting of the minimum wage, and, indeed, the authority for setting wages above the minimum.

In addition to the 'basic' (i.e. minimum) wage, in 1919 'penalty rates' for work during 'unsocial' hours was introduced by the Court for work on Sundays:

> The [extra rate for Sunday work] is given because of the grievance of losing Sunday itself—the day for family and social and religious reunion, the day on which one's friends are free, the day that is the most valuable for rest and amenity under our social habits...
>
> The norm of work should be six week days and Sundays free, the departure from the norm should be two time-and-a half rates, which is equivalent to one double rate. (CCCA 1919)

In 1947 penalty rates were extended to Saturdays, 'the great day of recreation... on which competitive sports and various forms of organised social activities and public entertainment are held' (CCCA 1947), and in subsequent awards a myriad of other penalty rates for working 'unsocial hours' were introduced.

But, contrary to common myth, Arbitration and Conciliation—which was the legal basis for tribunal-determined wage rates—had, in origin, nothing to do with setting 'decent' living standards, but everything to do with settling industrial disputes.

Whether the Act succeeded in 'preventing and settling' industrial disputes is arguable, on both empirical and a priori grounds. In terms of frequency of disputes, one international comparison of the 1940s found disputes in Australia three times as frequent as in the UK, five times as frequent as in the USA, and ten times as frequent as in Canada (Higgins 1951). It could also be argued that compulsory arbitration has impeded the development of good industrial relations because the parties have come to believe that disputes will ultimately be arbitrated however they conduct themselves.

Certainly, the Act greatly increased the legal standing and prerogative of 'registered' unions, and the number of unions and union membership, which tripled to over 365,000 between 1901 and 1911 (ACTU 2015). Compulsory arbitration played a major part in the expansion of unionism, because it provided a number of benefits to registered unions. These included corporate identity, preference for union members, and a monopoly of coverage in certain designated industries. Most importantly for unions, the system now gave them a guaranteed role in industrial relations. Arbitration guaranteed the existence of registered unions, because employees could only be represented by a registered union in the case of a dispute, and it was only necessary for one party to activate the arbitration process by reference to a tribunal. This procedure effectively obliged employers to recognize unions. It seems obvious that many unions were formed because of the benefits which the arbitration system gave them.

In 1930 the power of unions was significantly increased by the Scullin Labor government (Sykes 1964). The original Act contained a clause prohibiting strikes and lockouts, with fines and penalties, including imprisonment, for breaches of these provisions. These provisions were also included in states' legislation. The 1930 amendments abolished prohibition of strikes and lockouts and replaced them with much weaker employer rights to include 'bans' clauses in awards, for breaches of which employers could seek court injunctions and contempt-of-court fines for ignoring these injunctions.[1] However, bans became a very common form of union action in exercising bargaining power (Sykes 1964).

The Menzies government, beginning in 1951, introduced a process of statutory amendment to the Act whereby the Arbitration Court could issue mandatory orders to comply with an award, with penalties (including imprisonment) for non-compliance by unions and individuals. The Arbitration Commission still needed to approve an anti-ban clause in the award.

In 1969, however, the viability of these penalties was sorely tested by the case of Clarrie O'Shea (1906–1988), the Victorian state secretary of the tram workers union and a leading member of pro-China Communist Party, CPA (ML). He was jailed for contempt of the Industrial Court when he disobeyed a court order that his union pay fines, under the penal sections of the Act. His jailing resulted in unprecedented strike action in several states, including a general strike in Victoria. The matter was 'solved', intriguingly, with an anonymous benefactor paying the union's fines.

[1] In 1936 the High Court ruled that anti-strike provisions could be included in awards.

Although the penal laws were not repealed, they were never used again and so unions effectively now had the whip hand over employers and the Commission.

To summarize the system of compulsory arbitration:

- In the classic system, arbitration always began with a 'dispute' between firms and unions. This did not need to be an actual strike.
- Either party could unilaterally invoke arbitration on the basis of a dispute. Thus arbitration was 'compulsory' rather than by mutual agreement.
- Only 'registered' unions could appear before the Court.
- Registration was not a right, but a privilege granted by the Court, and a privilege that could be refused if there already existed another union to which workers could 'conveniently belong'.
- Employers also had corresponding 'registered' employer associations which had the privilege of appearing before the Court.
- The Arbitration Court (or Industrial Court) would make an award over wages, conditions, and eligibility for employment.
- Courts (often) had the power to require 'preference' for the employment of unionists over non-unionists.
- The award had the legal status of legislation binding employers. It was in no way 'a contract' between employer and employee; it was not even a contract of a compulsory kind.
- The award was subject to no appeal beyond the Full Bench of the Arbitration Court (or Commission).
- The composition of the Court (Commission) was decided wholly by government. Employers and unions had no formal role, or rights, in the making of appointments.
- The Courts generally were not enforcers of the awards. They were not 'policemen' of the system. Menzies founded the Industrial Court in 1956, but it proved fairly feeble.

It should be noted that the conditions and rates of pay of some 'awards' were, in fact, reached, not through arbitration process, but through bargaining between unions and employers. The role of industrial tribunals was simply to ratify these bargains. Such awards became known as 'sweetheart' or 'consent' awards. With these exceptions, wage determination was highly centralized. When a tribunal made a decision it affected all firms and workers in the occupation or industry covered by that award. In the early 1980s, compulsory arbitration was the dominant form of wage determination. Among other things, awards generally contain clauses covering not only ordinary pay rates and 'penalty' rates, but also:

- meal breaks;
- leave of various types—including recreation, sick, and long service;
- loading and allowances;
- special rates for dangerous or piecework;
- employment, grievance, and termination procedures;
- career structures;
- superannuation.

By the 1980s, many (most) awards had become very complex and detailed. For instance, the Metal, Engineering and Associated Industries Award 1998 had over 300 classifications, each with different rates of pay and conditions of work (AIRC 1998).

7.2 The System Crashes

The industrial relations system appeared to be working to many people's satisfaction, particularly unions and big business, until the system was severely tested and its inherent problems exposed in the face of international crisis.

The events of the mid to late 1970s presented a massive challenge to the Australian economy, based as it was on protecting itself from the ill-winds of international competition and the vagaries of a free-market economy. The shock to many developed economies, including Australia, known as the 'oil shock(s)', demanded far-reaching changes in economic management, including falls in real wages. However, what eventuated was a series of wage explosions which spread, due to the centralized system, throughout the Australian economy, largely due to the industrial muscle of unions under the leadership of the then Australian Council of Trade Unions (ACTU) president, Bob Hawke. Inflation reached over 17 per cent in 1975 and the unemployment rate rose from 2 per cent to over 6 per cent. A further wages explosion in 1978–1980, again under Bob Hawke's leadership, this time impacted most on unemployment, which rose to over 10 per cent.

It is generally recognized that Australia's previous regime of centralized wage bargaining and one of its major planks—indexation of wage rises to changes in the consumer price index (CPI)—was a major reason for the perpetuation of inflation in the 1970s and early 1980s.

7.3 The First Attempt at Change: Hawke and Keating

Somewhat ironically it was Bob Hawke, the Labor prime minister from 1983 to 1991, who, in 1983, used the system of compulsory arbitration, with the agreement of the ACTU, to reduce wages growth, under the 'Prices and Incomes Accord'. This was done by the Australian Industrial Relations Commission (AIRC) only partially indexing award wages to the CPI, contrary to its previous practice of automatically increasing award wages by the full percentage rise in the CPI.[2] Lewis and Kirby (1987) modelled the impact of the Accord and found that real wages fell by 10 per cent below what would otherwise have been, increasing employment growth by 8 per cent. In the period 1983 to 1990, the unemployment rate fell from 10 per cent to 6 per cent and inflation fell from 11 per cent to 1 per cent (Lewis and Spiers 1990).

In the period 1983–87, periodic adjustments were made to all award wages ('National Wage Decisions'), in that every award wage was increased by the same percentage or (sometimes) the same dollar amount. But in 1987 the Commission ruled that the wage increases granted would not automatically be applied to every award. Instead, firms and employees would have to justify them through what was termed the 'structural efficiency principle'. Other wage decisions of a similar nature followed and, finally, in its 1991 decision, the AIRC encouraged workers and their employers to bargain directly with each other at the enterprise level. This introduction of 'enterprise bargaining' was perhaps the most significant change to industrial relations in Australia's history.

It has to be noted, however, that only registered unions could bargain. Also, unlike common law contracts, enterprise agreements bound all employees to whom they applied, including those not employed at the time of a vote on the agreement, those who did not vote at all, and those who voted against approval of the agreement. Awards continued to apply and formed a 'floor' to wages and conditions which could be agreed on.

But 'enterprise bargaining', within these boundaries, was given a further stimulus by the 1993 Industrial Relations Act, and by 2006 one half of all employees in the federal jurisdiction were covered by an enterprise agreement. In some states more dramatic changes occurred. In Western Australia and Victoria legislation permitted workplace agreements which were completely outside the award system.

The introduction of enterprise bargaining was accompanied by union amalgamation sponsored by the ACTU. This was rationalized as increasing 'functional flexibility', which had been seriously hampered by strict limits on how firms could allocate work according to, among other things, the 'trade', level of seniority, or to which union a worker belonged. The idea was that this inflexibility would be reduced by individual craft-based unions being merged. The result was a frenzy of union amalgamation, so that, between 1987 and

[2] In a cosmetic change, the Australian Conciliation and Arbitration Commission had been re-established in 1988 as the Australian Industrial Relations Commission.

1996, the total number of unions decreased from 316 to 132 (Griffin 2002). The original unions were reluctant to relinquish their titles, however, and the resultant mega-unions usually had extremely long names. For instance, one amalgamation resulted in the Communications, Electrical, Electronic, Energy, Information, Postal, Plumbing and Allied Services Union. (Although its official name remains very long, it is now commonly known as the CEPU.)

7.4 A Renewed Attempt at Change: The Howard/Reith Reforms

Under Prime Minister John Howard, the LNP government from 1996 to 2007 attempted to further progress the reforms of Hawke/Keating. The major features of industrial relations reform was to make individual contracts, known as Australian Workplace Agreements (AWAs), the main form of the setting of wages and conditions. AWAs were actually introduced in 1996 but by 2005 less than 5 per cent of employees were on AWAs. These AWAs were still subject to judicial review to determine as to whether they satisfied a 'no disadvantage' test. In 2005 the government announced substantial amendments made to the Workplace Relations Act 1996 by the Workplace Relations Amendment (WorkChoices) Act 2005. Perhaps surprisingly for a document proposing reduced regulation, the legislation was 758 pages long. The bulk of the new WorkChoices regimen commenced on 27 March 2006.

A major feature of WorkChoices was the replacement of the federal basis of award tribunals with the creation of a unitary workplace relations system, based on the 'corporations power' of the Commonwealth government instead of the industrial relations powers of Section 51 of the Constitution, on which the system had rested for a century. Under these powers all employers that are deemed in law to be 'corporations' (generally any businesses that have Ltd in their titles) were subject to the system devised by WorkChoices.

Other features included:

- Increasing the capacity of employers, employees and unions to be parties to a collective agreement. For instance, employers and employees were only required to 'lodge' the agreement with the new Workplace Authority, rather than be scrutinized and certified by the AIRC.
- Limiting the role of awards, such as reducing the 'number of allowable' matters in awards.
- Modernizing the role of the AIRC from a one of enforcement to one of facilitator.
- The establishment of the Australian Fair Pay Commission (AFPC) to replace the AIRC for the purpose of setting minimum wages and conditions.

- Unfair dismissal protection removed for workplaces of 100 or fewer workers or for 'operational reasons'.
- AWAs no longer subject to the 'no disadvantage test' and allowed to override other types of agreement.
- Secret ballots before industrial action that is 'protected'(i.e immune from civil liability).
- Union rights of entry prohibited from agreements.

Finally, under the 'Australian Fair Pay and Conditions Standard', the Commonwealth legislated five 'minimum conditions' that employers were required to observe, including a minimum rate of pay, maximum ordinary hours of work, annual leave, personal leave, and parental leave.

Existing awards were *not* abolished, but the intention was that the federal award system would wither away, as new awards could not be arbitrated. The only way in which a 'new' award could be made was as a result of the award rationalization process, largely subject to ministerial direction, rather than as a decision of an independent arbitral body. Awards were to provide only residual protections, as the emphasis was firmly on the making of individual and collective agreements between employers and employees, with no approval mechanisms and no comparison to otherwise applicable award conditions. Once an agreement was lodged, the award that would have otherwise applied to the relevant employee was no longer applicable to that employee. Nor could an employee ever return to coverage by that award. The one obligation of the employer was to ensure that it provided the five minimum 'Australian Fair Pay and Conditions Standard' conditions.

Of the 1.13 million employed under registered agreements between March 2006 to June 2007, 399,000 thousand, or 35 per cent, were on AWAs. Thirty-two per cent of these were in Retail, Accommodation and Food Services (DEWR 2010). Thus the 1997 emphasis on AWAs being most prevalent among mainly professional workers changed in the 2005 legislation to those in low-skilled, low-paid employment.

It can be argued that the WorkChoices reforms were not radical or a major departure from the path of reform begun by Hawke and Keating (Lewis 2008). Reforms were based on the premise that improving the well-being of Australians, including the ability of government to provide for the least fortunate, relies on economic growth which can only be achieved through improving competitiveness and productivity. Labour market regulation prevents businesses from organizing labour and capital in different ways in order to achieve competitiveness and productivity. This is now largely recognized, to varying degrees, by most academics, commentators, and politicians. However, the vested interests in regulation managed to halt (and reverse) much of the progress which had taken place since 1983.

Unfortunately, and somewhat unusually, for John Howard, the industrial relations proposals lacked the thoroughness and preparedness that had gone into reforms such as the Goods and Services Tax and welfare. The need for industrial relations reform was taken as an act of faith with little reasoned analysis of the benefits to the economy, such as more jobs, higher productivity, or lower unemployment. Perhaps most telling was the obvious discomfort displayed by the prime minister when quizzed in the media about whether anyone would be worse off under his proposals. Regulation of markets always benefits some parties, to the detriment of others. The onus is on those supporting deregulation to demonstrate the benefits of deregulation to the economy as a whole.

The lack of reasoned argument and detail made Howard a perfect target for Labor, the ACTU, and much of the media. Perhaps not surprisingly, WorkChoices was vigorously attacked by the unions. They and Labor had obviously struck a chord with the general public, if we are to believe opinion polls, and the ACTU put massive resources into a campaign against WorkChoices. Workplace industrial relations was shaping up as the defining issue in the upcoming federal election in 2007.

In the face of almost daily adverse reports of unpopular impacts of WorkChoices, the government announced a new 'fairness test' to apply to all new AWAs after 7 May 2007 under the Workplace Relations Amendment (A Stronger Safety Net) Act 2007. The fairness test required the newly strengthened Workplace Authority, previously the Employment Advocate, to vet all agreements and to be satisfied that employees get fair compensation for modifying or removing protected award conditions such as leave loadings, penalty rates, overtime payments, and breaks. The fact that every agreement had to be vetted, rather than giving employees the right to choose to have an agreement vetted, may seem to have been somewhat of an overreaction to the criticism of WorkChoices. The 'fairness test' applied only to employees earning less than $75,000 per year and related only to the conditions that would be covered by the award (if any) relevant to that job. As the federal election was taking place, there was a huge backlog of AWAs which had been rejected outright or had been sent back to employers for amendment. Given the complexity and cost to employers of AWAs, employers virtually gave up using them.

7.5 The Rudd Reset

In its approach to regulation it was important for Labor and the new Labor leader, Kevin Rudd, to come up with an alternative which would wind back WorkChoices, without giving the impression that the Labor Party was simply a puppet of the union movement, and return Australian industrial relations to a largely discredited inflexible system. Rudd also wished to present himself as an economic manager and a friend of business.

The original Labor response to WorkChoices came in the form of Fair Work Australia, which implemented Labor's proposals in 2008 onwards. The main points were:

- AWAs abolished, with existing AWAs to be phased out by 2012.
- Individuals earning over $100,000 (up from $75,000) can negotiate employment contracts without reference to awards.
- National Labour Standards—the new name for the old Australian Fair Pay and Conditions Standard of Work Choices, expanded from six to ten, prescribed by legislation:
  - (i) a maximum standard working week of 38 hours for full-time employees, plus 'reasonable' additional hours;
  - (ii) a right to request flexible working arrangements;
  - (iii) parental and adoption leave of 12 months (unpaid), with a right to request an additional 12 months;
  - (iv) four weeks paid annual leave each year (pro rata);
  - (v) ten days paid personal/carer's leave each year (pro rata), two days paid compassionate leave for each permissible occasion, and two days unpaid carer's leave for each permissible occasion;
  - (vi) community service leave for jury service or activities dealing with certain emergencies or natural disasters. This leave is unpaid except for jury service;
  - (vii) long service leave;
  - (viii) public holidays and the entitlement to be paid for ordinary hours on those days;
  - (ix) notice of termination and redundancy pay;
  - (x) the right for new employees to receive the Fair Work Information Statement;
- No pattern bargaining (identical bargains with two or more employers).
- Restrictions of union officials' right of entry to workplaces limited to requiring 24-hours notice.
- Unfair dismissal claims can be made after twelve months' employment in firms with fewer than fifteen employees and after six months in firms with fifteen or more employees.

Also included in the Rudd measures were abolishing the AFPC, Office of the Employment Advocate, Office of Workplace Services, and the Industrial Relations Commission, and bringing their functions together under a new 'one-stop-shop', Fair Work Australia. Wages are now determined by Fair Work

Commission (FWC)-approved agreements or awards determined by the FWC. Over 100 awards remain, covering about 20 per cent of employees. All enterprise bargains require the approval of the FWC, and the FWC can 'order' bargaining which could be construed as compulsory arbitration in a different guise.

Despite the claims of the government that the FWC was to be an independent arbiter, the FWC was (and still is) heavily loaded in favour of organized labour. This was made obvious by the appointment, by then industrial relations minister, Julia Gillard, of five commissioners, out of a total of six, with union backgrounds.

The Rudd government changes represented a significant reregulation of the labour market compared to the Howard days. Indeed, in most respects the labour market had become more regulated than it had been under the Hawke/Keating reforms.

A case which exemplifies the absurdity of the current system of 'bargaining' is that of Toyota's automotive manufacturing enterprises in Australia. In 2013 Toyota sought to make changes to an enterprise agreement with its 3,000 employees at the Altona plant in south-west Melbourne to offset a proposed pay rise. Under the agreement, due to expire in March 2015, neither Toyota nor the unions could make any further claims in relation to wages or other terms and conditions before 2015. Among the proposed changes was a reduction in the minimum Christmas shutdown period from twenty-one days to eight days, and, instead of employees being required to be available to work a maximum twenty hours overtime each month, they were to be available to work a minimum of twenty hours overtime each month. Toyota also wanted to do away with certain payments including 'respiratory' allowances, 'dirty money' allowances, and 'new competency skill' payment.

Toyota planned to put the new deal to a ballot of all employees which, given the chronic unprofitability of Toyota Australia and the mortal state of car manufacturing in Australia, was almost certain to be passed. The Australian Manufacturing Workers Union (AMWU) opposed the changes and sought to stop the ballot. Justice Mordy Bromberg ruled that the variations sought by Toyota were 'significant' and that Toyota was trying to make additional claims. He ruled that in doing so, Toyota breached the workplace agreement and contravened the Fair Work Act. Justice Bromberg said the only way new wages and conditions can be introduced is if both parties choose to do so. However, the 'parties' clearly only included the AMWU and did not include the Toyota workers. Justice Bromberg ruled that the ballot of employees could not go ahead.

The decision put further pressure on Toyota continuing to operate. In 2014 Toyota announced its decision to cease operations as the sole remaining vehicle manufacturer in Australia, with the loss of over 2,500 jobs.

7.6 The Effects of Labour Market Regulation

There is now acceptance by many that the freeing up of the labour market had been a major factor in the success of the Australian economy, particularly for small business. Nevertheless, important inflexibilities remain and have been strengthened since 2007, particularly minimum wages and penalty rates, which mainly apply to the services sector: the biggest employer of part-time and casual workers. Also, the difficulty (or inability) of adapting workplace agreements to changing circumstances, as in the Toyota case, seriously affect an economy's ability to adjust to change.

Setting minimum award wages for the various occupations and industries, and imposing the same minimums on all firms within an industry, it is argued, severely impedes the efficient adjustment of firms necessary for a well-functioning market economy. Further, most awards set down the hours during which standard hourly rates of pay apply and the premium (or penalty) that has to be paid for hours outside this. These penalties may constrain firms, particularly where demand reaches peaks outside standard hours. Extending the range of hours over which standard pay rates apply and, more generally, abolishing limits on working arrangements again leads to greater flexibility. Imposing blanket conditions across firms impedes functional flexibility.

Enterprise and individual bargaining are often objected to by those more concerned with equity rather than efficiency. It is argued that these act to protect workers in weak bargaining positions, who are likely to be lower-paid workers. The evidence shows that the relative pay of low-paid workers is higher in Australia than in most industrialized countries (Lewis 2006). Increased labour market flexibility would be expected to cause a decline in the relative pay of low-paid workers. Critics of individual contracts extend the argument that the ability of individuals to bargain for wages and conditions is far less than for workers as a whole.

Awards now essentially have relevance for a (relatively large) minority of the workforce who are not able to bargain for better pay and conditions. However, although the award system only applies to about 20 per cent of the workforce, its impacts are important. It has been argued that it affects the most disadvantaged in the labour market through increasing unemployment (Lewis 2005), has adverse impacts on Australia's service sector (Lewis 2014), and raises wages of many workers by providing a 'floor' for wage bargaining in many non-award agreements (Lewis 1997).

Compliance costs, such as unfair dismissal payouts, have a disproportionate impact on small businesses because, as a percentage of wages, compliance costs are higher for small businesses. Mean compliance costs, as a percentage of turnovers of the smallest firms, have been calculated at more than six times that of the largest firms and more than twice that of the medium-sized firms

(Cabalu et al. 1996). Lewis et al. (2015) estimate that the compliance costs of regulation to small businesses in Australia are significant—about $10 billion per year for the economy (two thirds of 1 per cent of annual gross domestic product (GDP)) as a whole, and result in inefficiency for business and the economy. It is very clear that small businesses regard taking on a new employee as a costly and high-risk activity, and will avoid doing so until there is no alternative.

Although there are many issues arising from labour market regulation, much of the focus recently has been on minimum wages and penalty rates.

7.7 How Do Other Countries Do Things?

The main theme that emerges from section 7.5's commentary on Australia's industrial relations and the brief overview of comparator countries in this section is that no other significant comparator country has tribunal-determined wages to the extent that Australia does. Also, no significant country has such extensively legislated national standards. For instance, long service leave is a legislated entitlement in Australia and nowhere else. In this section a number of comparator countries are examined to provide a contrast with Australia and illustrate its uniqueness.

7.7.1 *United Kingdom*

The UK used to be famous (notorious) for the strength of its union movement, and much of the militant attitudes of (some) unionists in Australia drew comparisons with the considerable industrial disruptions characteristic of the UK up to the early 1980s. However, the UK has undergone considerable changes in industrial relations since then. Most obvious is the decline in union density, which reached a peak of 56 per cent in 1979, coinciding with the election of the Thatcher government, but now stands at 25 per cent (DBIS 2015a).

In the UK, pay and conditions are largely negotiated at the company or plant level in the private sector, and through sector-level agreements in the public sector. There are no national agreements across sectors in the UK and this has not been a feature of the UK system, except for some experimentation with prices and incomes policy in the 1970s. However, although there are no formal mechanisms for the coordination of wage bargaining in the UK, in practice agreements in certain companies and sectors often act as informal benchmarks for agreements in other areas. Collective agreements are voluntary and are not enforceable but collective agreements are normally incorporated into individual contracts of employment that are legally enforceable.

Collective bargaining in the UK became far more decentralized during the 1970s and 1980s. In this period, many companies in the private sector left sectoral agreements and, in the public sector, collective bargaining also became more decentralized. In 1970, collective bargaining covered 70 per cent of the workforce (Marchington, Waddington, and Timming 2011), but by 2013 only 27 per cent of workers had their pay determined by collective agreements, with 70 per cent of workplaces having pay set by management (DBIS 2015b).

There is little government intervention in wage and employment negotiations or arbitration. But the government does have an important role as the major employer in the economy, with the public sector accounting for 25 per cent of total employment. A national minimum wage first came into force in the UK on 1 April 1999, and covers almost all workers above compulsory school-leaving age. The rates of pay are based on the recommendations of the Low Pay Commission (LPC), an independent body that recommends increases in the national minimum wage. The LPC board consists of nine members—three trade union representatives, three employers, and three labour market experts. A different minimum wage rate applies to different groups of workers, according to age. These groups are divided as those aged 22 and above, 18 to 21, and 16 to 17. The main rate for workers aged 21 and over is currently (in 2015) set at £6.70 an hour. The development rate for 18–20 year olds is £5.30 an hour, and the development rate for 16–17 year olds is £3.87 an hour.

7.7.2 New Zealand

New Zealand had an industrial relations system which was the nearest equivalent to Australia's compulsory arbitration and wage fixing, with the same degree of state intervention and regulation. This had its origins in the Industrial Conciliation and Arbitration Act 1894, designed mainly to prevent strikes but also to encourage the organization of labour and working conditions in a period of high unemployment and fears of workers having to undertake 'sweatshop' labour (Le Rossignol and Stewart 1910). The Act remained the basis of New Zealand industrial relations law until the 1980s.

As in Australia, labour market reform occurred under a Labour government that enacted legislation to move New Zealand away from its highly centralized system. The most significant was the Employment Relations Act of 1987, which aimed to make bargaining the dominant form of determining wages and conditions, and reduce the role of the state and abolish awards. A series of legislation throughout the 1990s continued the trend to deregulation. According to Rasmussen and Lamm (2005), the transformation in New Zealand industrial relations was profound. Now decentralized bargaining is the norm, and with declining union density (under 17 per cent in 2104), 'direct employer–employee bargaining became the norm and individual employment contracts covered the majority of employees' (Rasmussen and Lamm 2005, p. 484).

However, the government plays an important role in determining a range of minimum pay and conditions. There are over twenty conditions, or 'rights' as they are called, covering such things as leave, minimum wages, health and safety, and union membership. Employees cannot be asked to agree to less than the minimum rights.

Minimum wages in New Zealand are governed by the Minimum Wage Act, which specifies that all employees aged 16 years or more must be paid the statutory minimum wage. The statutory minimum wage applies to all types of jobs and employees, including home workers, casual, temporary, and part-time employees. The statutory minimum wage does not apply to those undertaking recognized industry training, and doing at least sixty 'credits' per year; such persons are paid the training rate/youth rate. Labour inspectors may grant an exemption from minimum wages to a person with a recognized disability that significantly slows his or her work and makes him or her incapable of earning the minimum wage (MBIENZ 2015).

The 2015 rates are set at $NZ 8.20 for a person between 16 and 17 (youth rate and training rate), and $NZ 10.25 for persons aged 18 and over (MBIENZ 2015).

7.7.3 USA

The culture of the USA is largely associated with individualism and its commitment to the free market, and this is reflected in its industrial relations system. There is a much greater emphasis in the USA on individual effort, ambition, and ability while bargaining, and differences between employees and employers are best settled on a one-on-one basis. Collective action is largely regarded as only resorted to when individual response resolution has been expended (Katz and Colvin 2011). There is a three-tier structure of industrial relations in the USA. Local unions deal with the daily interaction with employers at the workplace level. Typically, these local unions are affiliated with a national union, while labour federations act as umbrella organizations for national unions and provide overall direction for the labour movement, as well as services like training and government lobbying.

In 2014, only 11 per cent of workers were union members (down from 22 per cent in 1985), and only 6 per cent in the private sector (Unionstats 2015). The reasons for the decline in union density are similar to those observed in Europe and Australia. Employers have also learned that using positive human resource management practices such as installing formal grievance systems, comprehensive benefit plans, and worker involvement programmes, have reduced the demand for services which have been typically offered by unions. Finally, in the past several decades the federal and most states governments have increasingly provided for the protection of workers' rights by passing a variety of legislative actions relating to civil rights, occupational health and safety, disability, and minimum wages (Katz and Colvin 2011).

Federal minimum wages are established under the Fair Labor Standards Act, and affect all full-time and part-time workers in the private sector and in federal, state, and local governments. Covered non-exempt workers were entitled to a minimum wage of no less than $7.25 per hour in 2015, with an overtime pay rate of 1.5 for work hours in excess of forty for a given week. Exceptions may apply to certain full-time students, student learners, apprentices, and workers with disabilities, where lower wages may be paid under special certificates issued by the Department of Labor. Some workers are exempt from minimum wage coverage, including commissioned sales employees, computer professionals, drivers, farm workers, salesmen, and those employed in firms that have a turnover of less than $500,000 per year (USDOL 2015).[3]

7.7.4 *Japan*

The industrial relations system in Japan has its origins in the post-war US occupation (ILO 2015). The Trade Union Law introduced in 1945 guarantees the rights of unions to organize and take industrial action. The Labour Standards Law of 1947 prescribes minimum wages and conditions of work. The Labour Relations Law of 1946 sets out procedures for reconciliation and arbitration.

The Japanese IR system is characterized by collective bargaining at the individual enterprise level with a generally non-confrontational attitude by both employers and workers. The reasons for this have been associated with the tradition of lifelong, or at least long-term, association most workers have with enterprises. Many managers will have worked their way up from positions of the people with whom they are negotiating. Also, relatively long periods of economic stability have meant that workers and firms have shared in economic prosperity (Suzuki 2010). But in the wake of the Global Financial Crisis, which impacted greatly on Japan's otherwise highly stable economy, the industrial landscape has changed somewhat. There has been a rise in the number of workers now employed in what would have been regarded in non-traditional arrangements such casual employment (Suzuki 2010).

[3] Many states also have minimum wage laws. Where an employee is subject to both state and federal minimum wage laws, the employee is entitled to receive the higher of the two rates.

In Japan, the term 'minimum wage' refers to the national weighted average amount per hour of the various minima applying across the country. There are two kinds of minimum wage: the regional—applied to all employees in a region regardless of difference of industries—and the specific—applied to workers in specific industries. In 2015 the minimum wage was ¥780 ($A8.58) per hour.

7.7.5 *France*

The French industrial relations system, like much of its economy, is characterized by significant government intervention. The government sets minimum wages, can extend national collective agreements to firms and employees, and can force negotiations on employers and employees on a number of employment issues. Perhaps the most famous example of recent government intervention was the introduction by the socialist government in 2000 of the maximum 35-hour week. However, by 2014 the Organisation for Economic Co-operation and Development (OECD) reported that French workers worked an average of 39.5 hours a week, just under the Eurozone average of 40.9 hours a week (OECD 2015).

Trade union density is low by international standards, 8 per cent (OECD 2015), but unions are notoriously militant. French unions are quite different from those in other countries mentioned in this section in that they are highly political and characterized by division and conflict. France has five trade union 'confederations' recognized as nationally representative for bargaining purposes. The rights to bargain on behalf of workers are not dependent on any actual union presence within firms. In addition to these five unions there are numerous other sector-specific unions.

The French system of statutory national minimum wage was introduced in 1970 ('salaire minimum interprofessionnel de croissance' or SMIC) and is pegged to consumer prices. It may also be raised by decree of the Council of Ministers, through the application of a review procedure. The SMIC is an hourly rate of pay, but since 1972 it has been complemented by a minimum monthly pay level for all employees whose working hours are at least equal to the statutory working week. In addition, it is the traditional role of collective agreements at industry level to fix minimum rates of pay for each occupational category.

In 2015 the minimum rate for those 18 years of age or older, or with at least six months of 'professional practice', was €9.61. Minimum wages for employees under 17 years old and between 17 and 18 years old with less than six months' professional practice receive, respectively, 80 per cent and 90 per cent of the adult rate (Wage Indicator Foundation 2015).

7.8 The Impact of Minimum Wages and Penalty Rates: The Balance Sheet

Table 7.1 shows the minimum wage and average hourly earnings for Australia and selected countries. In summary, New Zealand, France, and Australia have relatively high minimum wages compared to the USA, Canada and Japan. Of the countries chosen, the USA has the lowest minimum wage and it has been argued that this is the reason it has better employment outcomes (see, for instance, Burtless 2002). Burtless points out that the US experience is different to that of most of the OECD, and attributes this to regulations in both the product and labour markets.

There is overwhelming evidence that employment is negatively related to wages. People are unemployed because, given the minimum wage, firms cannot find profitable activities for them to be employed to do. Lower wages make activities which were previously unprofitable now profitable. For some, the wage at which they can carry out profitable work might be very low. Since Australia has long had a minimum wage we cannot tell what the market wage would be if there were no minimum. However, it can be deduced from the characteristics of the unemployed, particularly the long-term unemployed—namely that they are low skilled—that their market wage would be low (Lewis 2005).

Nevertheless, the experience in the USA has been that:

> Job opportunities for less qualified workers can be found in low-wage retailing, cleaning and landscape services, agriculture, manual labour, and informal child care. With relatively little training, less educated job seekers can find work as home health aides for the elderly and disabled... (Burtless 2002, p. 122)

While Burtless's observations may be correct, they would no doubt send into apoplexy many Australians who would prefer to see people out of work rather than in low-paid jobs—this is a part of Australian culture which has proved to be quite pervasive judging by the continued aversion to reducing minimum

Table 7.1 Minimum Wages Relative to Median Wages of Full-Time Workers, 2003 and 2013, per cent

Country	2003	2013
Australia	58.3	54.0
Canada	40.0	44.1
France	58.0	62.8
Japan	33.1	39.0
New Zealand	53.1	59.5
United Kingdom	42.6	46.9
United States	33.9	37.4

Source: OECD (2015).

wages and penalty rates. This ethos goes back to Justice Higgins who, in the 1909 Broken Hill Case, pronounced:

> If a man cannot maintain his enterprise without cutting down wages which are proper to be paid to his employees—at all events, the wages which are essential for their living—it would be better he should abandon the enterprise.
>
> (CCA 1909, p.32)

The effects of minimum wages are well-known (Lewis 1997). Those who manage to get a job are better off: workers producing value-added just above the minimum wage will be substituted for those producing value-added below the minimum wage. Those made unemployed are worse off. Minimum wages redistribute jobs and income away from the worst off, and towards the not so badly off.

On top of the minimum wage specified in awards for work in 'normal' hours, penalty rates also apply. They vary between awards, but in order to make international comparisons the penalty rates applying in retail are considered here. In Australia, for permanent employees, an additional 100 per cent on Sundays and an additional 150 per cent on public holidays applies, making pay rates 200 per cent and 250 per cent, respectively, of the standard wage rate. For casuals, an additional 75 per cent on Sundays and an additional 150 per cent on public holidays applies, making pay rates approximately 160 per cent and 220 per cent, respectively, of the standard casual loaded wage rate for these employees (FWC 2014).

In the UK minimum wages are not greater on weekends or public holidays, but for work on designated rest days employees receive a day off in lieu. In the USA, there are no federal general statutory provisions. In a small number of states a loading of 50 per cent applies on Sunday, for example, in Rhode Island and Kentucky. Canadian employees receive a 50 per cent loading on Sundays. In New Zealand there is no statutory loading for Sunday work but this is negotiable by the employer and employee and stated in the employment contract or collective agreement. For work on public holidays a loading of 50 per cent applies and a day off in lieu. In Japan rest days are negotiable and work on these days attracts a loading of no less than 25 per cent and no more than 50 per cent (PC 2011).

Clearly, penalty rates are much more prevalent and higher in Australia than in other countries, and would be expected to have much bigger negative effects on employees, businesses, and consumers (Lewis 2015).

7.9 Conclusion

What the chapter shows is that there is considerable variation in industrial relations systems, with all of the countries having varying degrees of decentralized determination of wages and conditions and different degrees of government enforcement of minimum rates of pay and worker 'rights'. However, Australia is clearly unique in that no significant comparator country has wages determined by tribunals to the extent that Australia does; and no significant country has such extensively legislated national standards.

While Australia was, in many ways, a leader in pursuing labour market reform in the 1980s, it has now gone into reverse and is falling behind other countries (Fraser 2015). The current government has shown little stomach for tackling these trends to reregulation of the labour market. It looks, therefore, as if Australia's industrial relations will become increasingly irrelevant at best, or a severe brake on economic growth at worst, in a service-based economy which requires increased labour market flexibility.

References

ACTU (Australian Council of Trade Unions). 2015. *History of Unions*, <http://www.actu.org.au/about-the-actu/history> (accessed 20 November 2015).

AIRC (Australian Industrial Relations Commission). 1998. AP789529CRV: Metal, Engineering and Associated Industries Award 1998, <http://www.airc.gov.au/consolidated_Awards/AP/AP789529/asframe.html> (accessed 20 November 2015).

Burtless, G. 2002. 'How can supply side policies reduce unemployment?', *Australian Journal of Labour Economics*, vol. 5, no. 2, pp. 115–42.

Cabalu, H., Doss, N., and Dawkins, P. 1996. 'Employers' compliance costs', Discussion Paper 96/10, Centre for Labour Market Research, Curtin University of Technology, Perth.

DBIS (Department of Business and Innovation Skills). 2015a. 'Trade union membership 2014', *Statistical Bulletin*, <https://www.gov.uk/government/collections/trade-union-statistics> (accessed 20 November 2015).

DBIS. 2015b. *The National Minimum Wage*, <https://www.gov.uk/government/news/new-national-minimum-wage-rates-announced> (accessed 20 November 2015).

DEWR (Department of Employment and Workplace Relations). 2010. *Agreement Making in Australia under the Workplace Relations Act, 2007 to 2009*, <https://docs.employment.gov.au/documents/agreement-making-australia-under-workplace-relations-act-2007-2009-0> (accessed 20 November 2015).

Fraser, J. 2015. 'Australia's log-term challenges', Economic Society of Australia Conference of Economists, Brisbane, 7 July, <http://www.treasury.gov.au/PublicationsAndMedia/Speeches/2015/Australias-longerterm-economic-challenges> (accessed 20 November 2015).

FWC (Fair Work Commission). 2014. *General Retail Industry Award 2010*, <https://www.fwc.gov.au/documents/documents/modern_awards/award/ma000004/default.htm> (accessed 20 November 2015).

Griffin, G. 2002. *Union Mergers in Australia: Top-Down Strategic Restructuring.* Melbourne: National Key Centre in Industrial Relations, Monash University.

Higgins, B. 1951. 'Wage-fixing by compulsory arbitration: the lessons of Australia', *Social Research*, vol. 18, no. 1, pp. 335–69.

Higgins, H. 1907. *Ex parte HV McKay (Harvester Case)*, Commonwealth Arbitration Reports vol. 2.

ILO (International Labor Organisation). 2015. *National Labour Law Profile: Japan*, <http://www.ilo.org/ifpdial/information-resources/national-labour-law-profiles/WCMS_158904/lang–en/index.htm> (accessed 20 November 2015).

Katz, H. and Colvin, A. 2011. 'Employment relations in the United States' in J. Bamber, R. Lansbury, and N. Wailes (eds.), *International and Comparative Employment Relations: Globalisation and Change.* Crows Nest, NSW: Allen & Unwin.

Le Rossignol, J. and Stewart, W. 1910. 'Compulsory arbitration in New Zealand', *Quarterly Journal of Economics*, vol. 24, no. 4, pp. 660–712.

Lewis, P. 1997. 'The economics of the minimum wage', *Australian Economic Review*, vol. 30, no. 2, pp. 204–7.

Lewis, P. 2005. 'Low pay or no pay?' *Policy*, vol. 21, no. 3, pp. 14–20.

Lewis, P. 2006. 'Minimum Wages and Employment', Research Report 1/06 Melbourne: Australian Fair Pay Commission.

Lewis, P. 2008. 'Industrial relations and the labour market' in C. Aulich and R. Wettenhall (eds.), *Howard's Fourth Term.* Sydney: New South Wales University Press.

Lewis, P. 2014. 'Paying the penalty? The high price of penalty rates in Australian restaurants', *Agenda: A Journal of Policy Analysis and Reform*, vol. 21 no. 1, pp. 5–23.

Lewis, P. 2015. 'Technological and structural change in Australia's labour market' in Committee for the Economic Development of Australia, *Australia's Future Workforce.* Melbourne.

Lewis, P. and Kirby, M. G. 1987. 'The impact of incomes policy on aggregate wage determination in Australia', *Economic Record*, vol. 63, no. 181, pp. 156–62.

Lewis, P. and Spiers, D. J. 1990. 'Six years of the Accord: an assessment', *Journal of Industrial Relations*, vol. 32, no. 1, pp. 53–68.

Lewis, P., Richardson, A., and Corliss, M. 2015. 'Compliance costs of regulation for small business', *Journal of Business Systems, Governance & Ethics*, vol. 9, no. 2.

Macarthy, P. G. 1970. 'The living wage in Australia: the role of government', *Labour History*, no. 18, pp. 3–18.

Marchington, M., Waddington, J., and Timming, A. 2011. 'Employment relations in Britain' in J. Bamber, R. Lansbury, and N. Wailes (eds.), *International and Comparative Employment Relations: Globalisation and Change.* Crows Nest, NSW: Allen & Unwin.

MBIENZ (Ministry of Business, Innovation and Employment, New Zealand). 2015. *Labour Information*, <http://employment.govt.nz/> (accessed 20 November 2015).

Mitchell, S. 1989. 'State systems of conciliation and arbitration: the legal origins of the Australian model' in S. Macintyre and R. Mitchell (eds.), *Foundations of Arbitration: The Origins and Effects of State Compulsory Arbitration, 1890–1914.* Melbourne: Oxford University Press.

OECD (Organisation for Economic Co-operation and Development). 2015. *OECD StatExtracts*, <http://stats.oecd.org/INdex.aspx?DataSetCode=MIN2AVE> (accessed 20 November 2015).

PC (Productivity Commission). 2010. 'Economic structure and performance of the Australian retail industry', Productivity Commission Inquiry Report no. 56, 4 November 2011.

Rasmussen, E. and Lamm, F. 2005. 'From collectivism to individualism in New Zealand employment relations', proceedings of the 19th conference, Association of Industrial Relations Academics of Australia and New Zealand, Sydney.

Suzuki, H. 2010. 'Employment relations in Japan: recent changes under global competition and recession', *Journal of Industrial Relations and Labor*, vol. 52, no. 3, pp. 387–401.

Sykes, E. 1964. 'Labor arbitration in Australia', *American Journal of Comparative Law*, vol. 13, no. 2, pp. 216–48.

Unionstats. 2015. *Union Membership and Coverage Database from the CPS*, <http://www.unionstats.com> (accessed 20 November 2015).

USDOL (United States Department of Labor). 2015. *'Wages'*, <http://www.dol.gov/dol/topic/wages/minimumwage.htm> (accessed 20 November 2015).

Wage Indicator Foundation (2015), *Minimum Wages in France*, <http://www.wageindicator.org/main/salary/minimum-wage/france> (accessed 20 November 2015).

Legislation

Commonwealth of Australia. 1904. *Commonwealth Conciliation and Arbitration Act No. 13 of 1904 relating to Conciliation and Arbitration for the Prevention and Settlement of Industrial Disputes extending beyond the Limits of any one State.*

Cases

CCCA (Commonwealth Court of Conciliation and Arbitration) 1907, *Excise Tariff Application- McKay, H.V. ex parte, (1907)*, AR 1, pp.1–34.

CCCA 1909. *Barrier Branch of the Almagamated Miners Association of Broken Hill vs the Broken Hill Propriety Co. Ltd (1909)*, AR 3, pp. 1–77.

CCCA 1919. *Federated Gas Employees Industrial Union v Geelong Gas Company and Others (1919)*, AR 13, pp. 468–9.

CCCA 1947. *The Metal Trades Award re Rheem Manufacturing—Judgement re Rates of Pay for Work Performed on Saturdays and Sundays*, AR 609, pp. 609–23.

High Court of Australia, 1908, *R v Barger*, 6 CLR 41.

8

Australia's Electoral Idiosyncrasies

William O. Coleman

In many countries it is contrary to law for prisoners to vote. In Australia it is, for a wide range of offenders, compulsory. This is one unlooked-for upshot of a distinct electoral Australian idiosyncrasy; unlike any other developed country, it is obligatory to vote.[1] But this idiosyncrasy is merely the most conspicuous of several singularities respecting Australia's electoral politics. Others include the universal use of 'preferential voting' (PV) in single-member seats,[2] the early introduction and enduring use of a variant of proportional representation (PR), an Electoral Commission of a power quite unmatched elsewhere, and the persistence of a distinct and national-level Country Party of considerable political significance.

These peculiar institutions are a settled and unquestioned part of the Australian political framework. Most, indeed, provide the occasion for national self-congratulation. They seem to constitute proof of the nation's attachment to democracy, a commitment epitomized, it is proudly held, by Australia's adoption of the secret ballot before any other polity.[3]

This chapter surveys the origins of these particularities, and weighs what they actually signal about the nature of Australian society. It argues that they are not evidence of some special congruity of the Australian outlook to

[1] 'Compulsory voting' means here that all those eligible to enrol are required by law to enrol, and all enrolees are required by law to vote. In measuring the extent of compulsory voting it needs to be recognized that laws to compel voting are no longer enforced in Belgium or Greece. With the abandonment of compulsory voting by Chile in 2012, no Organisation for Economic Co-operation and Development (OECD) country apart from Australia can currently be said to have compulsory voting.

[2] 'Preferential voting' is the Australian usage for what is elsewhere variously known as the 'alternative vote', the 'instant run-off', and 'ranked voting'.

[3] Thus, it is claimed 'Australia and New Zealand share the honour of being the oldest continuous democracies' (Hughes and Costar 2006, p. 8).

democracy. It contends that, on the contrary, the Australian sense of democracy is undeveloped.

8.1 The Secret Ballot

Australia claims parentage of the secret ballot, and the world rightly concedes the claim by having it called for many years the 'Australian ballot' (Crook and Crook 2011). It was in 1856 that Victoria, Tasmania, and South Australia almost simultaneously introduced provisions for the modern secret ballot.

This inauguration of *secret* ballot voting was not, of course, the first use of ballot voting in the modern world. The USA had commonly adopted ballot voting in the wake of the American Revolution.[4] This 'American ballot' was not secret, as, typically, voters presented themselves to the polling officer with a ballot that had been produced and supplied by the candidate they favoured, and which was of a distinctive appearance. This did not necessarily prevent the revelation of the voter's vote when they wished to conceal it, and it accommodated the revelation of the voter's vote when they wished to disclose it. Thus, if American ballot voting afforded some impediment to the intimidation of voters, it was little bar to their bribery, and bribery was endemic. Nevertheless, one variant of ballot voting effectively secured secrecy a few years before the Australian schema. In 1851 Massachusetts required that ballots be placed in envelopes of uniform appearance before being submitted to electoral officers, and the scheme was judged in the event to serve secrecy 'very well' (Brunet 1952).

Yet what today is universally recognized as a secret ballot only arrived as the gift to posterity of the Legislative Council of Victoria of 1856. After a debate of 'extreme crudity', the dubiously democratic Council resolved to introduce a secret ballot. But at this point the Council found that it 'had not the faintest idea' (Scott 1920, p. 11) of how such a ballot would actually be effected. The vague talk in the chamber of 'urns', 'marbles', and 'peas' indicates how unapparent to these law-makers were the procedures that we take for granted. But opportunely one of the Council's members, Henry Chapman, drafted an elaborate but lucid statement of the procedures of secret ballot voting that would be recognized today. The one deviation from the familiar was that the legislation required voters to cross out the names of the candidates they did not want, rather than cross the name of the candidate they favoured. It was South Australia's 1858 revision of its own initial secret ballot legislation that, at the instigation of the colony's Returning Officer, William Boothby, required

[4] New York state in 1776, for example. 'By 1787–1788 nine states had substantially adopted the practice' of ballot voting (Ratcliffe 2013, p. 234).

each elector to place an X against the name of their preferred candidate, rather than crossing out the names of the others.[5]

What does this history mean for the significance of this Australian 'first'? The displacement by Australian ballot of the older 'American ballot' can be construed as merely the substitution of government-printed ballots for the private provision of ballots (Brent 2006). Yet this substitution is almost universally taken to be an obligatory accessory of a genuine election. Thus in the mid-1850s, Australia, a society in which there had been no election for any public position until just sixteen years before, appeared to suddenly overtake the USA in the vigour of its pursuit of democratic process. That, however, would be a very partial evaluation. For in the 1850s the USA was undergoing a democratic revolution which Australia was never to be part of: the election of judges. The 1849 constitution of the new state of California inaugurated the election of judges, and between that date and 1913 'every new state entering the Union embraced this scheme of selection, as did most of the previously settled states' (Hall 1984, p. 347). By contrast, the Australian colonies' entire engagement with this new front of democratization was limited to the Gold Fields Act of 1855, which decreed that the tribunals to decide mining disputes would be composed of nine persons elected by miners, along with the governor's single nominee. But even this fairly minor excursion into democratic judicial selection was 'swept away' just three years later by a new Act that replaced the courts with appointed wardens (Birrell 1997).

Indeed, while South Australia was perfecting the secret ballot, a 'judicial reign of terror' over her democratic legislature was being unleashed by the 'antics' of the Chief Justice, Benjamin Boothby. After entering public life through 'rabble-rousing' Chartist agitation, he had embarked on a legal career. In a complex exercise of patronage by the Colonial Secretary, he was offered an appointment to the Supreme Court of South Australia, which, in the face of unsatisfied creditors, he accepted (Taylor 2013). He arrived in Adelaide in 1853, accompanied by a close-knit family group that included his eldest son, William, who, it will be recalled, was to add the finishing touch to the secret ballot in 1858. Through 'a narrow, pedantic construction of the principles of imperial constitutional law' Benjamin Boothby attempted to limit the powers of the South Australian parliament (Castles 1969, p. 195). While he 'sat on the bench, invalidity was always on tap, and freely and frequently he declared the statutes of the local parliament to be repugnant, unconstitutional and void' (Hague 2005, p. 220), including not simply the Real Property Act—of Torrens System fame—but also, by implication, every Act passed by its conscientiously democratic legislature since 1857. The ire and enmity provoked by this

[5] New Zealand stuck with the procedure of crossing out unwanted candidates until 1990.

cyclops of judicial arrogance ultimately resolved in his 'amotion' (removal) in 1867. But the significance of the disaster lay in the absence of one response: it appears to have constituted no impulse to democratize the choice of judges, American style. Any such democratization of the choice of judges would, of course, have been perfectly alien to centuries of British tradition. Just as the secret ballot was.

The impression left by these events is that in the years of the ballot's birth Australia was much deeper steeped in government, and much less steeped in democracy, than was the USA. Australia's landscape in these years was studded with handsome and sometimes entirely redundant courthouses, 'palatial' government houses (the 'best of any British colony' (Trollope 1874, p. 246); 'incredible' (Martineau 1869, p. 22)), along with 'stupendous' house of parliament, with carefully maintained Hansards (at least in Queensland), and a ceaseless gush of parliamentary papers.[6] The machinery of government, if new cast, was elaborate and robust for a new society of fewer than a million inhabitants. And this is seen in the detailed crafting and effective dispatch of the secret ballot legislation.

Fortuitously for Australia's reputation for democracy, in the secret ballot 'government' and 'democracy' were complementary. But perhaps 'Benthamism' identifies the complementary agent better than 'government'. For while the secret ballot had engaged the interest of no significant theorist of democracy (Tocqueville ignores it; and Mill notoriously opposed it), Bentham was a strenuous advocate of it. Indeed, consonant with his 'method of details'—the method of technical trivia—Bentham wrote in remarkable detail on how a secret ballot would be actually implemented (Bentham 1819, section V, article V). It might be said that in the secret ballot Bentham's faith in operational detail bore fruit. The man who crafted the technology of the secret ballot, Henry Chapman, was a vehement Philosophic Radical, who, in the decade prior to his emigration to Australasia, had been a contributor to the *Westminster Review*, and was the active ally of John Roebuck, the House of Commons' most heated Utilitarian, and the 'intimate friend' of John Stuart Mill. Indeed, Chapman apparently wrote to Mill to report the good news of the secret ballot provision of Victoria's Electoral Act, only to have Mill inform him he no longer supported such a ballot (Neale 1967).

But in Chapman's advocacy of the 'secret ballot' there was an irony that was fully shared by Bentham. Both Chapman and Bentham unhesitatingly took the already extant ballot of the USA to amount to a secret ballot. 'In the State of New York', wrote Bentham, 'the members of the House of Representatives are, all of them, elected by secret suffrage. It was, declaredly, as a measure of

[6] In the three years 1843 to 1845, the tryo Legislative Council of News South Wales produced 1,730 pages of committee reports and other matter.

experiment, that in 1777 secresy [sic] was in this case appointed in the first instance: by the experience of forty-two years it stands confirmed' (Bentham 1819, p. 4). Chapman shared Bentham's judgement of the effective 'secresy' of the American ballot, and could invoke some relatively direct experience for his judgement. From 1823 to 1833, he lived in Quebec, championed responsible government in Canada, visited New York and Philadelphia, and rejoiced in Andrew Jackson's 'immense triumph of the people' in 1828 over their enemies, who 'fell before the mighty influence of the *ballot-box*'(Chapman 1835a, p. 12). Chapman here is *not* deploying the term 'ballot-box' merely as a symbol of democracy; he is specifically referring to the concrete feature of US voting—the ballot—that he believed made for democracy. To Chapman, the question of the merit of the American ballot, and its replication in Great Britain, was the question of all others, which distinguished the ultra-Liberal from the Whig. His own answer was absolute, and in *Fallacies of the House of Commons on the Ballot in America* he defended the American ballot from its English detractors:

> Lord Stanley . . . merely tells us that in his opinion the Ballot in America is no protection against bribery, and does not promote secrecy. I have seen, perhaps, ten times as much of America and Americans as Lord Stanley, I have mixed with the people, and I assert Lord Stanley's opinion is erroneous, and his statements incorrect. (Chapman 1835b, p. 15)

Stanley could conjecture, said Chapman, how, under ballot arrangements then prevailing in the USA, a 'landlord' might be able to observe how someone voted. But:

> Pray my Lord Stanley, can you not perceive that a law might be so framed so as to prevent the said landlord, from being within hearing or seeing distance?
> (Chapman 1835b, p. 15)

Here we see the crux of Chapman's position on the ballot. The American 'secresy' ballot had done its mighty work across the Atlantic. It required only a Benthamite penchant for technical detail to perfect it in Britain and her dominions.

8.2 Proportional Representation

Any claim for Australia to have pioneered PR would be more precarious than that regarding the secret ballot. History customarily awards the Swiss canton of Ticino with the first use of PR, in 1890. But Adelaide Municipal Council can place a serious claim for the deliberate, if minute and passing, exercise of PR in 1840. And the state of Tasmania introduced, in 1896, a sophisticated version for its legislature—the Hare–Clark—a version of which has been used since 1949 to elect Australia's powerful Senate.[7]

In moving from the secret ballot to PR we move from a Benthamite acclamation of the majority to a Millian wince at the multitudes.

An account may begin with Thomas Rowland Hill, the devisor of another revolutionary 'bit of paper' of the Victorian age—the postage stamp.[8] In 1839, while he was composing his proposals for postal reform, Hill was also formulating electoral schemes for South Australia, in his capacity as the secretary of its Colonization Commission. His scheme was, in fact, borrowed directly from his father, Thomas Wright Hill (1763–1851). Raised in a strict Dissenting household, Hill senior had taught Sunday School as a youth in Joseph Priestley's chapel in Birmingham, and was married in the city two weeks after a raging 'Church and King' mob had destroyed Priestley's 'meeting house', along with his residence and library. Hill's electoral scheme does not impute any superiority in judgement to the mass.

Hill's 'Scheme for Conducting Elections' began with the contention that the 'national assembly should be a reflex [i.e. a reproduction, as if in a mirror] . . . of the nation itself', and must include minorities, since 'in the minority the most intelligent part of the nation is often found' (Hill 1860, p. 86). Specifically, he proposed a scheme of a multi-member electorate, where any collection of voters of a minimum number were free to constitute themselves into a 'quorum' that would return one member to represent them. It was Thomas, the third of his five sons—all destined for noteworthy careers in public administration—who actualized the scheme in Adelaide in 1840.

Hill's scheme of election would very possibly have perished but for finding its evangelist in Thomas Hare. The general context of Hare's sense of mission was his disappointment at the outcome of the Great Reform Act. 'The system since 1832', complained Hare, 'vastly increases the number of electors who are subject to moral or mental degradation, or both, and at the same time, with few exceptions, fills the representative assembly with an inferior class men . . . a legion of other spirits more vile than those which were cast out' (1873, pp. 88–90). Hare's scheme is, then, at bottom, an expression of a Millian repugnance at the great throng of base natures and superficial minds.

Hare's individualist ('elitist'?) position was shared by Helen Spence (1825–1910), Australia's earliest and most indefatigable advocate of PR. One may concede a significance to the fact that her father had been town clerk at the much remembered essay of PR in Adelaide Municipality in 1840; and that

[7] Perhaps only the second chambers of the USA and Italy have more power than Australia's Senate.

[8] In a prompt adoption of Hill's proposal, New South Wales (NSW) issued the world's first prepaid (if unadhesive) postage stamps.

her good friend, Caroline Emily Clark, was a niece of Thomas Rowland Hill. But her principles in the decade she embarked on her cause were also consonant with the individualist underpinning of Hare's case. She derided the radical Berry government in Victoria, opposed paying salaries to members of parliament, and, like Hare, was against the secret ballot. Her 1861 *Plea for Pure Democracy: Mr. Hare's Reform Bill Applied to South Australia* presented Hare's scheme as 'a means of ensuring representation of minorities by men of virtue, learning and intelligence' (Eade 1976). Consistent with this posture, the only immediate attraction in Australia to PR was shown by the (appointed) Upper House of NSW.[9] The Lower House—newly elected on universal male suffrage—rebuffed the Upper House's attempt to introduce the discordant notes of a minority into the chorus of the majority.

The man of 'virtue, learning and intelligence' who actually brought PR to Australia was Andrew Inglis Clark (1848–1907). Clark was also, like Hill and Spence, of a Dissenting background. In 1874 he complained in a journal of ideas he edited that the 'representation of minorities is... totally unknown in Tasmania' (Clark 1874a, p. 71). In a later issue he declared the need for parliaments to be a 'reflex of opinion'—an obvious echo of Hill—and advocates Hare's scheme (Clark 1874b, p. 249). But such thoughts seem to have then lain dormant for two decades until quickened by American Progressivism, with which Clark keenly sympathized. In 1890, he visited the USA, 'saw much of the leading "progressives"... and for the rest of his life maintained a correspondence with these leaders of advanced liberal thought', especially Oliver Wendell Holmes (Reynolds 1958, p. 62). Clark was forging these ties just as PR was beginning to chime with Progressive schemes of electoral reform that targeted the political machines that throve on mass franchises. Thus, in 1896, John R. Commons, also raised in a Dissenting household, declared in his book, *Proportional Representation*, that 'The decay of representative bodies has come about through universal suffrage' (Commons 1896, p. 318). In 1896, Clark, after repeated attempts, finally secured the establishment of the Hare system as the method for electing the Tasmanian Legislative Assembly. Sadly, its introduction revealed that not all minorities are elevated: a disgraced politician managed to scrape a quota by exploiting the patriotic flurry of the Boer War, and the scheme was temporarily abandoned in dismay. But it was soon revived, and has remained in place ever since.

PR in Australia presents this puzzle: how could an electoral scheme of such an anti-majoritarian timbre ever take root in such a collectivist culture? Culture, it seems, was less important than chance: since it was chance that threw up circumstances that conferred on one party an at least passing advantage

[9] See Sir Roger Therry's *Reminiscences* (1863) for one forceful advocacy of PR as a remedy for democracy.

from the introduction of PR. In the approach to the 1949 election, the Labor government had a massive majority in the Senate owing to previous victories under a voting scheme that amounted to a 'winner takes (nearly) all' system (see Lijphart 1997). But the government was doubtful of its popular support, and suspected that, under the existing system, the 1949 election would produce an anti-Labor majority in the Senate. A PR system would also do this, seemingly. But a twist lay in the fact that senators were elected for six years, with half of the Senate up for election every three years. It was guessed that the massive Labor preponderance in the 1946 Senate cohort would overbalance any modest anti-Labor majority that PR would produce in the 1949 cohort, with the upshot being the preservation of an overall Labor majority. And so it was that PR came to Australia's powerful second chamber. This occurred at the nadir of minority parties in Australia; as one later commentator noted, 'the debate on that legislation was remarkable for not one parliamentarian of the day recognised the potential of the new arrangements in attracting smaller parties... our majority parties in 1948 surrendered much more than they recognised—that is the prospect of controlling the Senate when they controlled the Treasury Benches' (Reid 1972, p. 20). Since 1963 such a control has occurred in only three years. The sudden importunate embrace of PR has had 'a profound influence on Australian government' (Reid 1972, p. 21).

Chance, surprise, and paradox seem to be masters of the passage of PR in Australian political experience. It is hard to see Tasmania introducing PR without Inglis Clark; and it is hard to see the Senate embracing it without the Tasmanian precedent. It is plain to see a high-minded wish to preserve the minority voice ultimately ending in the partisan manoeuvre of a mass party to secure its majority, but producing no majority; and, eventually, having elected to the Senate, in 2013, an Australian Motoring Enthusiasts Party candidate on the basis of 0.12 per cent of the total first-preference vote. It is a great distance from Dr Priestley's Sunday School to the Australian Motoring Enthusiasts Party, but the journey seems to have been travelled.

8.3 Preferential Voting

The Australian Commonwealth, and all mainland states, either permit or require PV for their Lower Houses of parliament.[10] Outside Australia, PV is only infrequently found beyond the level of local government. It is not unique to Australia, and has been episodically instituted elsewhere; thus, in

[10] The law governing preference voting has been strictly upheld; in 1996 a self-described 'anarcho-Stalinist' was jailed for three weeks for urging the public to vote 'contrary' to the preferencing stipulations of the Commonwealth Electoral Act.

the period 1915–31 it prevailed in Alabama under the aegis of the Temperance Union and the Ku Klux Klan. But in Australia it began earlier and has endured longer than anywhere else. It is an unchallenged piece of the institutional furniture, assimilated into the Australian way of doing things, and successfully proselytized to neighbouring countries in a dependent relation to Australia.[11]

It was in 1893 in Queensland, a ready forge of electoral contrivances, that a form of PV—'contingent voting'—first appeared. It was presented by the government as a more convenient form of the double ballot that had established itself in Europe: any candidate who came neither first nor second in first preferences would be deemed to have lost, and their votes would be allocated between the top two candidates, according to preferences indicated on the ballots. It has been explained by some historians as a response by the anti-Labor parties to the Labor menace. Indeed, the Labor leader opposed by the government had won his own seat with less than 50 per cent of the vote; but in parliamentary debates he seemed not very aware of any threat in the legislation. He dismissed contingent voting as 'tinkering' and opposed it only on the grounds that it would increase informal votes.[12] In the event, Labor had no cause to be exercised;[13] the result of not a single seat in the subsequent election was decided by the new voting system. In fact, in the approximately one thousand Queensland electoral contests over the subsequent fifty years, only twelve were decided by preferences. This irrelevance may be part of the explanation of the system's pervasive and perennial endurance.

The example of Queensland was not immediately imitated at the federal level upon federation in 1901. The political triangle of Protection, Free Trade, and Labor would seem a fertile field for preferencing, and the Protectionist's Deakin and Labor's Watson did consider the advantage of swapping preferences through PV (Reilly 2004, p. 84). But the formation of a two-party system by 1914 appeared to make PV irrelevant. It was the sudden emergence of a third party at the close of the First World War that incited the establishment of PV nationally. The emergence of the Country Party split the anti-Labor vote between itself and the Nationalist Party, and minority Labor victories were in prospect. The Nationalist Party passed the 1918 Commonwealth Electoral Act instituting PV in the House of Representatives.

Thus, whereas the secret ballot and PR can claim, at least in part, some foundation in ideas and ideals, PV is squarely the child of political advantage—in spite of the fact that the democratic credentials of PV are plainer to see.[14]

[11] Thus in 1995 Fiji adapted PV with considerable assistance from the AEC, and with arguably injurious results (Fraenkel 2010; Rydon 2001).

[12] Several members of the government voted against the measure.

[13] The Labor leader, Thomas Glassey, did, in the event, lose his own seat. But he faced only one other candidate.

[14] In a three-candidate field, no Condorcet loser can ever win under PV.

But these partisan origins make PV's endurance puzzling. If it benefited the anti-Labor coalition at the expense of Labor, at least until the emergence of the Greens, why has Labor tolerated the system? Perhaps its endurance rests on it not, in fact, seriously offending or favouring any political interest. Political scientists have repeatedly shown that only a small percentage of election results are changed by preferences (Reilly 2004, p. 86). And alterations in the actual winner of government on account of preferences are surprisingly few, and highly anomalous in their direction. (In the 1961 election, Communist Party preferences saved the anti-Labor government.) But there is some empirical evidence that, without changing the party that wins the majority of seats, PV increases the number of seats won by the party that loses (Johnston and Forrest 2009). To put it another way, PV may have the effect of reducing the number of marginal seats.[15] In this possibility we may have a clue to its endurance: here is a scheme that appeals to all established political parties; here is a scheme that leaves unchanged the award of the great prize, victory, while introducing a consolation prize to the loser.

8.4 Compulsory Voting

This is the most conspicuous of Australia's quirks.[16] Yet Australia is neither the first nor the only country to compel voting. Sorting through the rags of psephological history reveals that Georgia experimented with it as long ago as 1776. And contemporary advocates of compulsory voting can compile a list of about two dozen countries that currently ordain it. But of all the numerous excursions into compulsory voting, it is in Australia that the method persisted. And it has done so with broad support; polls for several decades have indicated about 70 per cent of the public at large favours compulsory voting. Labor strongly supports it; and, despite all formal evidence that compulsion is to Labor's advantage (Jackman 1999; Chong et al. 2006), the anti-Labor government of 2004–7 that controlled both Houses made no move to abolish it, notwithstanding goading from some its senior members.

Compulsory voting began as an attempt to use law to defeat geography. Its pioneering introduction in Queensland in 1914 is usually interpreted as a defensive manoeuvre by the anti-Labor government in the face of a prospective Labor victory in an approaching state election. But its advocates were specifically rural: a pastoralist and three members of the Farmers'

[15] PV would, for example, reduce the number of marginal seats if the typically distributed party (the Greens?) are stronger in seats where the party that their preferences favour (Labor) is also stronger.

[16] Voting is compulsory at state and federal levels. NSW, Victoria, and Queensland also require voting in local government elections.

Parliamentary Union (Atkin 1969). Travelling in rural seats to polling booths could be arduous, and potential voters would demand various forms of assistance from candidates. And, as political scientists stress, political engagement is typically weaker in the hinterland than in the city. It is not surprising that the National Party remains in favour of compulsory voting; and psephological studies predict it would be significantly damaged without it (Jackman 1999; Chong et al. 2006). In any case, Labor in 1914 was diffident about the new law, and its unconcern proved justified; Labor romped home in the election of 22 May 1915. Federal Labor smartly adopted compulsory voting for its 'General Platform', and legislated to compel voting in constitutional referendums.

But it was not under Labor that compulsory voting in federal elections was instituted. It was brought about in 1924 under a Nationalist-Country party government, by means of a Private Members' Bill, which was passed after a brief debate in which only back-benchers spoke (Gow 1971). This truly furtive introduction of compulsory voting at the national level makes its motivation harder to gauge than if the legislation was both resisted and championed. But the very fact of its bipartisan support speaks clearly enough. Compulsory voting will appeal to slumping political parties, as much as 'compulsory buying' will appeal to slumping businesses. And both of the larger parties had slumped in the preceding election: Labor votes fell from 811,244 in 1919 to 665,145 in 1922; the Nationalist Party from 860,519 in 1919 to 553,920 in 1922. Parties were henceforth relieved of 'getting out the vote', and even the Liberal Party (or at least its organizational structure) remains in favour of compulsory voting. A further common interest in both major parties with regard to compulsory voting arises from the possibility of it reducing the size of the typical swing, and the consequent reduced uncertainty about the haul of seats: this will occur if each party has a certain bloc of voters who, whenever disappointed with 'their' party, will not vote at all if allowed to not vote, but will never switch to the other party if forced to vote. (For empirical evidence see Andrews, Fry, and Jakee 2005.)

And yet it would be wrong to depict compulsory voting merely as an expedient response to post-war circumstances. In 1905, Prime Minister Deakin, with the crushing defeat of his Protectionist Party in 1906 perhaps already apparent, avowed compulsory voting would serve 'as a great safety valve' for Protectionists and Labor (Reid and Forrest 1989). By 1914 the legislatures of the Commonwealth and all states but NSW had considered compulsory voting bills. Indeed, there had been numerous enactments of compulsion across the world (John and DeBats 2014), reflecting a mood rather than any partisan calculation. The mood was Progressivism. Thus, a classic Progressivist politician such as Franklin Knight Lane—appointed by Theodore Roosevelt to the Interstate Commerce Commission and Woodrow Wilson as

Secretary of Interior—advocated compulsory voting. The rightful emphasis on the Progressivist attraction to compulsory voting provides a hypothesis as to why Australia introduced it and stuck with it: Progressivism never ended in Australia. The 'up and doing' spirit; the belief that a 'common good' was making its claims upon all at every point of life; and, above all, the 'triumph of centralizing national consciousness over regional, state, and local identities' (Milkis and Mileur 1999)—these phenomena are characteristic of both American Progressivism and Australian 'Deakinism'. But they had more stick in Australia, and did not readily wilt in the aftermath of the First World War. In Australia there was no debunking version of the war; no retreat from the world; no spurning of the League of Nations; no halt to the expansion of the central state; and prominent Progressivist figures—such as George Swinburne, Tom Bavin, G. S. Beeby, and Herbert Brookes (a 'devoted follower' of Alfred Deakin, and stalwart of a Nationalist Party committed to compulsory voting)—all continued to wend their way through the post-war world. The fresh political talent, S. M. Bruce, seemed in quite their mould.[17]

This continuity of 'Australian Progressivism' is seen in the minister responsible for the introduction of compulsory voting, George Foster Pearce, whose quarter-century-long ministerial career began with defence in 1908, and ended with external affairs in 1937. His parliamentary activity also included the advocacy of voting machines, and the launching of the Council for Scientific and Industrial Research, in which he maintained an 'unflagged interest'. In 1909 Pearce had overseen the introduction of compulsory military training: 'Compulsory education, compulsory arbitration, compulsory military service he had long believed were compatible with and, indeed, essential to, democracy.'[18] And so compulsory voting.

Such a reliance on ideological stance to explain compulsory voting does beg the question of how an unideological public could be reconciled to such an impingement of their prerogatives.

One explanation would be that 'compulsory voting' isn't actually compulsory. Free and easy Australia has never been reconciled with compulsory civic virtue. So the fine for not voting is, at the federal level, less than the price of a

[17] Clearly there was some shift in outlook in post-war Australia. Thus, Labor discarded a heavily Progressivist mantle for a socialism of its own conception, and an obdurate Higgins could only resign from the Arbitration Court after it had been reshaped by its former partisans. 'The belief in human perfectibility died a glorious death in Alfred Deakin', sighed Eggleston (quoted in Osmond 1985, p. 51). Yet the pages of his *Reflections* reveal how Eggleston kept the faith in the old creed, both in specific articles (e.g. irrigation) and the general (e.g. the 'scientific approach' to social problems). Tellingly, despite his complete frustration in dealing with a system of lawyer-determined wage rates, Eggleston vaunts H. B. Higgins for establishing as imperative a 'logical criteria' for determining wage rates (Eggleston 1953, p. 63).

[18] 'Government could produce a near perfect electoral roll, and it could complete the job by engineering a near perfect turnout. Government could do anything—even make apathetic men and women into citizens' (Hirst 2002, p. 323).

packet of cigarettes. And how many absentees pay the fine? Sunday newspapers entertain their readers with reports of the ludicrous excuses of absentees accepted by electoral commissions. Indeed, how many citizens are enrolled? Alternatively, an entirely different explanation would be that compulsory voting has become an almost pleasant ritual into which Australians have been successfully habituated.

Perhaps these explanations of the public's complaisance miss something. Church attendance was once compulsory in Australia, following the letter of English laws from Elizabethan times. Compelling church attendance could only ever be effectively pursued in an essentially religious society, and was soon abandoned. Australians are commonly described as unreligious, but they have a faith in the political. Perhaps they trail to the booth on account of that faith.

8.5 The National Party

The enduring strength of a rural-based party in Australia—the National Party—has been rightly judged 'unique' (Costar and Woodward 1985, p. 2). Other developed countries have had rural-based parties, but none continued to prosper into the second post-war generation. In the 1920s 'farmers' parties' burgeoned in Norway, Sweden, Denmark, and Finland, but in the post 1945 period all discarded their rural identity, adopted Centre Party monikers, and, in some cases, underwent total ideological metamorphoses. In 1920s Canada, a United Farmers Party reigned in some provinces, and the Progressive Party had some successes at the federal level. But these elements ultimately subsumed themselves within the Conservative Party, the Liberal Party, or the New Democratic Party. In New Zealand a small Country Party existed from 1925 to 1935 before disappearing.

But Australia's National Party endures. It and its earlier incarnations (the Country Party, and the National Country Party) have provided one of Australia's prime ministers, and seven of her sixteen deputy prime ministers. The party has, in the past, secured the premiership of Australia's most industrialized state; has ruled in its own right in the fastest-growing state; and on occasion has won more seats than the Liberal Party in the largest state. Its share of the vote has fallen significantly since the 1980s. But in spite of the massive contraction of the relative importance of primary industries (from about 25 per cent of gross domestic product in the years of the party's origin to only 2.5 per cent in 2013/14) one tenth of MPs elected to the 2013 House of Representatives caucused with the National Party.

This persistence belies no loss of identity. Bitter electoral contests with the Liberal Party continue at the national, state, and local level; in the hung parliament of 2010 one National MP sat on the cross-benches rather than join in coalition with the Liberal Party; National Party MPs have, in recent years, served in Labor Cabinets;[19] and three times over the past century there have originated, from the National Party, MPs that have either secured Labor minority governments, or felled anti-Labor ones.[20]

The singularity of this endurance is highlighted by the fact that organized rural-specific politics came late to Australia: when American prairies were aflame with populism, there was no organized rural-specific party in the sunburnt country. In the September 1914 federal election the two parties—the Australian Labor Party and the Commonwealth Liberal Party—together won 98 per cent of the vote, with both easily spanning the rural–urban divide. At the state level, NSW beyond the Great Dividing Range was a near continuous expanse of Labor seats (twenty-seven of its forty-six seats were from outside Sydney), with the Commonwealth Liberal Party reaching beyond Sydney, up and down the long rural coast.

It was the upheaval of world war that split anti-Labor forces. The first 'Country' member of the federal parliament was elected on 14 December 1918. The general election of December 1919 returned to the federal parliament seven 'Country Party' parliamentarians, almost depriving the government of a majority. The new politics were even more starkly evinced in 1922, when the Country Party entered into government with five of the eleven ministries, including the Treasury.

How did it come to pass that, since 1918, there have been two anti-Labor parties when there had been only one before?

It might be construed as the correction, or overcorrection, of the lopsided political economy of both parties before the First World War. The Deakinite political economy of the pre-war era had been essentially an urban transaction. The expansion of the apparatus of state was inevitably focused on the metropolis: the successful Kyabram movement of 1902 to overthrow the Deakinite Premier of Victoria, Alexander Peacock, originated from the bush. The 'Harvester Judgement' of 1907 amounted, of course, to a tax on the purchase of agricultural implements. These pre-existing rural–urban tensions were inflamed by the First World War through the high prices of foodstuffs paid by cities, and by the price maxima subsequently imposed on the sellers of foodstuffs. The war revealed to rural producers so many policy devices that could powerfully harm—or powerfully benefit—them, and rural producers strived to win command of these new tools.

[19] South Australia, Karlene Maywald 2004–10.

[20] William McWilliams in 1929; Alexander Wilson in 1941; Rob Oakeshott and Tony Windsor in 2010.

Yet there is another explanation why, from 1918, there were two anti-Labor parties when there had been only one before. And that is that there had not been one before. Until they fused in 1909 the anti-Labor parties had been two: Protectionist and Free Trade. The cause of Protectionism was not exclusively urban; it had knitted together certain urban and rural interests. But, a victim of its own success, once Protection had become the established policy of the country, and no longer furnished a shibboleth to sort the Gileadite from the Ephraimite, its urban seats defected to Labor, and the rural ones to the new Commonwealth Liberal Party. What the Country Party was reopening, then, was not some papered-over split between bush and city, but the difference in outlook between Protectionist and Free Trader. Consider the ten seats held by official Protectionists in 1906 and not subsequently won by Labor; 'anti-Labor Protectionist' seats. If we exclude two won by Protectionist candidates of 1906 who contested the 1922 election under Nationalist colours we are left with eight: of these, six were won by Country Party.[21] Further to the same conclusion, all the leaders of the Country Party from 1921 to 1990 represented seats that in the initial Federation election of 1901 were won by Protectionists.[22] The identification of the Country Party with the old Protectionist Party shorn of its urban wing is underlined by the fact that the accession of the Country Party to the Cabinet did not, contrary to the obvious interest of export-orientated farmers, provide a counterweight to the pre-existing 'principle' of protection to manufactures (Reitsma 1960, p. 21). The two ardent Free Traders of the new party were exiled to the backbench, while, from 1923, rural producers were given ex officio representation on the Tariff Board, joining the representatives of manufacturers and importers.

The adherence of the new Country Party to protection suggests that the interpretation of the Country Party as promoting the interests of agriculture is superficial. The adherence of the Country Party to protection suggests its underlying position is better approximated as 'Property but not Market'. In the days of its origin this formula served well foodstuff-producing agriculture, faced with Labor's aspiration to abolish freehold title and city-based consumers' demand for cheap food. But 'Property but not the Market' is a formula of far broader application than the encounter of farmer and townsman. Property but not the Market is a formula deployed in numerous other circumstances with distinct success. It was the economic creed of Catholic Christian Democracy, including its representative in Australia after the Second World War, the Democratic Labor Party (DLP). The DLP and the Country Party were a good fit, and in Western Australia the two parties ultimately amalgamated.

[21] Cowper, Gippsland, Richmond, Riverina, Bendigo, and Swan.

[22] Cowper, Barker, Darling Downs, Indi, Richmond, and New England. Queensland, a redoubt of the Country Party from the late 1930s, returned no Free Trade members in the 1901 parliament.

A still closer parallel to the Country Party's successful deployment of Property but not Market was in Ireland's Fianna Fáil. Founded about the same time as the Country Party, Fianna Fáil was 'essentially a rural phenomenon' defending the rural periphery against the urban centre; a voice for 'small farmers and petty bourgeoisie' against pastoralists; offering protectionism and cultural conservatism, and enduring in the face of the de-ruralization of Ireland (Dunphy 1995, p. 16). The triangle of Labour, Fianna Fáil, and Fine Gael that dominated Ireland for many years could be seen mirrored in the Labor, Country, and Liberal Parties of Australia, but with the greater urbanization of Australia so enlarging Labor that in Australia 'Fianna Fáil' and 'Fine Gael' were forced into a defensive coalition. It might be argued that the formula of 'Fianna Fáil' was so strong it disturbed even Labor. The mysterious figure of Jack Lang—the Big Fella, of Labor but perhaps essentially alien to it—may form a counterpart to De Valera—the Long Fellow—and another testimony to the potency of the formula.

8.6 The Australian Electoral Commission

The Australian Electoral Commission has been described as 'a rarity' (Brent 2009, p. 407) with regard to its independence, scope, and power.

The Australian Electoral Commission has many roles in the electoral system. It is a keeper of the mysteries—only it actually understands how Senate seats are decided. It is keeper of the faith—with active education programmes at home, and missionary activities abroad. Above all, it alone decides the boundaries of the seats in the House of Representatives. The Commonwealth Electoral Act affords the legislature no right to annul the Commission's decisions, and ordains its decisions 'shall not be challenged, appealed against, reviewed, quashed, set aside or called in question in any court or tribunal on any ground' (Commonwealth Electoral Act, section 77).

The Australian Electoral Commission began in a more humble way in 1902, as an ordinary branch of the Department of Home Affairs, with its methods modelled on the electoral practice of South Australia that dated back to 1853. The key innovation in that year was the transferal of the responsibility for enrolment and the good conduct of elections from magistrates to 'returning officers'; salaried clerks of the public service. The greater significance was the appointment of William Boothby, who, from 1856 to 1903:

> superintended every parliamentary election in South Australia, drafted every Electoral Act, gave unshakeable evidence to every relevant inquiry and was the first of the federal electoral commissioners to complete his rolls and electorates for the Commonwealth. (Castles 1969, p. 196)

Boothby has been judged 'a landmark in the development of electoral administration, not only in Australia, but in some ways the world'. His example and authority were such that he was the inevitable appointment as returning officer for the first election of the new Commonwealth, in 1901. In the following year, legislation created a salaried and full-time Chief Electoral Officer, a position 'not to be found outside Australia' (Brent 2009, p. 414). It instituted a Napoleonic bureaucracy by creating for every electorate a Divisional Returning Officer (DRO), subject to the direction of the Electoral Office. This institution of the DRO has been judged 'unique' (Brent 2009, p. 405).

The Commission was busy, formulating seventy-six redistributions between 1901 and 2004. But until 1984, if either House disapproved or negated the proposal, the Commission could be directed to make a fresh proposal; and such was the case in 1912, 1936, and 1968. In 1984 the Australian Electoral Commission was instituted as an 'independent statutory authority', a favourite creation of Australian law-making. It was to be governed by three persons, who once appointed were not removable, and its redistributions were no longer subject to the approval or disapproval of the parliament.

The independence of the Australian Electoral Commission is without parallel, but has an obvious justification. As one American observer puts it:

> In Australia an allegation that a redistribution plan for seats in the House of Representatives in any state or territory was 'a political product from start to finish' is almost unimaginable. (Engstrom 2005, p. 8)

Unimaginable, yes; but untrue? 'Rational actor' models give no license to the supposition that parties draw boundaries with more partisanship than independent commissioners. On the contrary, the value that a political party places on the predictability of the number of seats it wins encourages it to corral votes in 'safe seats' thereby creating buffers that will withstand ill winds, but at a cost to its average harvest of seats (see Crain and Tollison 1990). But such an a priori analysis ignores many considerations. A more empirical method might be more telling. Consider the state where electoral commissions had their genesis, South Australia. After a long experience of gerrymanders, that state has gone to a greater length than any other by having its constitution ordain that its electoral commissioners will ensure 'as far as practicable' that the party that wins more than 50 per cent of the vote will win government (Constitution Act, part v, division 2, section 83). The most recent elections, in 2014, were conducted under that provision. But the party that won 53 per cent of the two-party preferred vote won only twenty-two of the forty-seven seats.

8.7 The Myth of Democracy

Australia's electoral idiosyncrasies are often portrayed as a proof of a special Australian commitment to democracy. Australia is said, on their account, to be a 'pioneer' of democracy, and officials of other Western countries even, it has been said, take 'pilgrimages' to learn from Australia.[23] This chapter rejects this contention. With the possible exception of the emergence of the Country Party, none of these idiosyncrasies seem to breathe the spirit of democracy.

But what is democracy? 'Democracy' is understood here as the pre-eminent ideology of legitimation of the modern state, and, in consequence, amounts to a reconciliation of those domains that a successful state must reconcile: that of societal technology; that of fraternity; and that of autonomy (the sphere self-determined, and self-ended, activity).

As an anthem of the modern state, democracy must honour what societal technology esteems: the rationalistic, the systematic and the uniform. Here lies the special strength of Australian democracy. An electoral mechanism is an exemplar of 'social technology', and Australian democracy is second to none in the completeness and accuracy of its electoral rolls, the orderliness and efficiency of its polling days, and the sophistication of its many methods of voting and electing.[24]

As an anthem of the modern state, democracy must exemplify the aspiration to oneness and equality. This powerful sentiment is gratified by a wide franchise, as such a franchise confers an equality that is impossible to secure elsewhere in life. The strength of fraternity in Australia has, then, manifested itself in the encouragement of a wide franchise, even if, contrary to the myth-making of Australian democracy, Australia cannot be deemed the 'pioneer' of mass franchise.[25] Perhaps the aspiration to oneness and equality has been even better gratified by compulsory voting: this provides the supreme theatre of oneness, as all vote as one.

Finally, as an anthem of the modern state, democracy must respect the self-assertion of the sphere of autonomy.

[23] 'British electoral experts have made pilgrimages to both Canberra and Wellington' (Sawer 2001, p. vi).

[24] 'Australia has probably the most thorough provisions in the world for the maintenance of electoral rolls' (Wright 1980, p. 30).

[25] By 1828, a generation before the advent of manhood suffrage in NSW and Victoria, the 'principle of universal manhood suffrage (at least for whites)' had been formally established in eight US states (Ratcliffe 2013, p. 284). That the southern states of USA maintained de facto racial disqualification into the mid-twentieth century needs no comment. Queensland formally excluded Aboriginals from the franchise until 1965 (Wear 2005). South Australia was the first Australian state to enfranchise women, in 1895; Idaho was the first US state, in 1896.

What we recognize as real democracy is a harmonizing composition of these three arenas of life. But as each of these wax or wane, the resultant 'democracy' will take on a very different complexion. When autonomy is destroyed, fraternity and technology are still sufficient to produce the peculiar mummery of 'democracy' that the USSR was so devoted to: the bizarre spectacle of the elaborate and evidently sincere 'no-choice election':

> Elections are taken very seriously in the Soviet Union... enormous efforts are expended on the electoral process... the media and officials give extensive, ritualised coverage to the elections... There are painstakingly detailed rules and regulations about nominations... and electoral... commissions... that take immense care and attention to detail—down to the arrangements for fire protection for polling stations... the secrecy of the ballot is meticulously observed... ballots are not numbered or named... Elections are held on Sundays to ensure everyone has the chance to vote... The great emphasis on the participation in the election makes it an almost anti-social act to not vote.
>
> (Selections from Karklins 1986, p. 451; Jacobs 1970, p. 64; Hill 1976, p. 592)

And there was just one candidate on the ballot.

The moral is plain: the sphere of autonomy is essential to real democracy; real democracy amounts to one discharge of autonomy. But the sphere of autonomy is impoverished in Australia, and that impoverishment has stunted her democratic spirit. This is seen in the boredom Australians seem to display at the prospect of greater self-direction. Thus in 1978 the Australian Capital Territory (ACT) rejected self-government by an overwhelming margin; in 1998 the electors of the Northern Territory rejected statehood; and 'new state' movements in Australia have been feeble. In the constitutional referendum of 1999 Australians were not offered the possibility of directly electing a president. The election of police commissioners—let alone judges—is totally unheard of. Thirteen of seventy-six senators in 2016 held their seats without having been elected by the Australian public, as Senate seats may now be bequeathed—like so many rotten boroughs—on mid-term retirement.[26] In a 2014 survey (Lowy Institute 2014), only 39 per cent of Australians aged 18 to 29 years agreed to the proposition: 'Democracy is preferable to any other kind of government'.

The poverty of the democratic spirit in Australia is also manifested in the stunted conduct of her parliament, an institution that the plaudits of Australian democracy usually pass over. Yet parliamentary life is the heart of democracy. Japan conducted general elections during the Second World War,

[26] In 1977 section 15 of the Constitution was altered so that senators retiring mid-term would be replaced forthwith by a person of the same party. Most who supported this seemingly innocuous revision did not anticipate the consequent deal-making that would shuffle politicians in and out of Senate seats without the alarm and inconvenience of facing voters.

while Britain suspended them: which was the more democratic? It was a House of Commons unsanctioned by 'perennial' elections that on 8 May 1940 realized perhaps the most consequential expression of any democracy ever.

Australian parliaments are weak. They lack defences: houses of parliament have been abolished, in blank defiance of public opinion.[27] They lack scope of action: the executive may enter into treaties and appoint judges, without the approval or enquiry of any House of Parliament. And they lack inner life: Private Members' Bills are almost unknown, and 'in no other Westminster style polity has the speakership been so debased' (Hirst 2006, p. 21). Above all, 'the Pledge', perfected by Labor and imitated formally by the Country Party and informally by the Liberals, has virtually extinguished the prerogative of MPs to vote as each thinks best, leaving only a tiny sanctuary of choice consisting of matters of 'conscience'.[28] The consequent condensation of parliament into two blocs leaves it an arena of political diktat rather than of political exchange. This constraint of MPs' choice of vote is accompanied by a constraint on speech, with an accompanying debasement of parliamentary disputation. One manifestation of this debasement is the rarity—almost complete absence—of significant parliamentary eloquence from Australian history. A more serious upshot may be the strange and dubious ascendancy of newspapers in Australian political life, with each paper constituting an extra-parliamentary *Orateur*.[29]

Australian democracy smacks too much of the polling booth and not enough of the parliamentary chamber.

References

Andrews, L., Fry, T. R. L., and Jakee, K. 2005. 'Compulsory Voting: Some Analytics and a Test from Australia'. RMIT University: Melbourne.

Atkin, G. 1969. 'The introduction of compulsory voting in Queensland, 1914', *Armidale and District Historical Society Journal and Proceedings*, vol. 12, pp. 29–48.

Bentham, J. 1819. *Bentham's Radical Reform Bill: With Extracts from the Reasons*. London: E. Wilson.

[27] In 1917 a referendum to abolish the Legislative Council of Queensland was rejected by 179,105 votes to 116, 198. Nevertheless, in 1921 the Council was abolished.

[28] Australian political parties display 'a degree of party discipline unequalled by few of the world's parliamentary democracies' (Wildavsky 1961, p. 438).

[29] The entire distinction between newspaperman and politician could dissolve in Australia: thus Deakin and Pearson wrote many editorials for *The Age*. The editor of that newspaper, David Syme, not only 'converted' Deakin to protectionism, but ultimately secured the undertaking of George Reid, the Free Trade prime minister, that Syme would vet all appointments to a projected tariff comission (Turner 1911, p. 96).

Birrell, R. 1997. 'Guided democracy: the local courts after Eureka', *Royal Historical Society of Victoria Journal*, vol. 68, no. 1, pp. 37–52.

Brent, P. 2006. 'The Australian ballot: not the secret ballot', *Australian Journal of Political Science*, vol. 41, no. 1, pp. 39–50.

Brent, P. 2009. 'Stuck in a rut: the problem with Australia's electoral apparatus', *Australian Journal of Political Science*, vol. 44, no. 3, pp. 405–19.

Brunet, M. 1952. 'The secret ballot issue in Massachusetts politics from 1851 to 1853', *New England Quarterly*, vol. 23, no. 3, pp. 354–62.

Castles, A. C. 1969. 'Boothby, Benjamin (1803–1868)', in the *Australian Dictionary of Biography*, vol. 3. Melbourne: Melbourne University Press.

Chapman, H. S. 1835a. 'The American ballot box' in J. A. Roebuck (ed.), *Pamphlets for the People*, no. 5. London: Longley.

Chapman, H. S. 1835b. 'Fallacies of the House of Commons on the ballot in America' in J. A. Roebuck (ed.), *Pamphlets for the People*, no. 7. London: Longley.

Chong, D., Davidson, S., and Fry, T. 2006. 'It's an evil thing to oblige people to vote', *Policy*, vol. 21, no. 4, pp. 10–16.

Clark, A. I. 1874a. 'Our electoral districts', *Quadrilateral*, vol. 1, no. 4, pp. 71–7.

Clark, A. I. 1874b. 'Hare's system of representation', *Quadrilateral*, vol. 1, no. 11, pp. 249–51.

Commons, J. R. 1896. *Proportional Representation*. Boston: T. Y. Crowell & Co.

Costar, B. and Woodward, D. (eds.). 1985. *Country to National: Australian Rural Politics and Beyond*. Sydney: George Allen & Unwin.

Crain, W. M. and Tollison, R. D. (eds.). 1990. *Predicting Politics: Essays in Empirical Public Choice*. Ann Arbour, MI: University of Michigan Press.

Crook, M. and Crook, T. 2011. 'Reforming voting practices in a global age: the making and remaking of the modern secret ballot in Britain, France and the United States, c. 1600–1950', *Past and Present*, no. 212, pp. 199–237.

Dunphy, R. 1995. *The Making of Fianna Fáil Power in Ireland, 1923–1948*. Oxford: Clarendon Press.

Eade, S. 1976. 'Spence, Catherine Helen (1825–1910)', in the *Australian Dictionary of Biography*, vol. 12. Melbourne: Melbourne University Press.

Eggleston, F. W. 1953. *Reflections of an Australian Liberal*. Melbourne: FW Cheshire.

Engstrom, R. 2005. *Revising Constituency Boundaries in the United States and Australia: It Couldn't be More Different*, <http://apo.org.au/files/Resource/engstromaug05.pdf> (accessed 20 November 2015).

Fraenkel, J. 2010. 'The alternative vote in Fiji: electoral engineering or ballot rigging?', *Commonwealth and Comparative Politics*, vol. 39, no. 2, pp. 1–31.

Gow, N. 1971. 'The introduction of compulsory voting in the Australian Commonwealth', *Australian Journal of Political Science*, vol. 6, no. 2, pp. 201–10.

Hague, R. M. 2005. *Hague's History of the Law of South Australia, 1837–1867*. Adelaide: Barr Smith Press.

Hall, K. L. 1984. 'Progressive reform and the decline of democratic accountability: the popular election of Supreme Court judges, 1850–1920', *American Bar Foundation Research Journal*, vol. 9, no. 2, pp. 345–69.

Hare, T. 1873. *The Election of Representatives, Parliamentary and Municipal: A Treatise*. London: Longmans, Green, Reader & Dyer.

Hill, R. J. 1976. 'The CPSU in a Soviet election campaign', *Soviet Studies*, vol. 28, no. 4, pp. 590–8.

Hill, T. W. 1860. *Selections from the Papers of the Late Thomas Wright Hill*. London: J. W. Parker & Son.

Hirst, J. 2002. *Australia's Democracy: A Short History*. Crows Nest, NSW: Allen & Unwin.

Hirst, J. 2006. *Labor's Part in Australian History: A Lament*. Canberra: Pandanus.

Hughes, C. A. and Costar, B. (eds.). 2006. *Limiting Democracy: The Erosion of Electoral Rights in Australia*. Sydney: UNSW Press.

Jackman, S. 1999. 'Non-compulsory voting in Australia? what surveys can (and can't) tell us', *Electoral Studies*, vol. 18, pp. 29–48.

Jacobs, E. M. 1970. 'Soviet elections: what they are, and what they are not', *Soviet Studies*, vol. 22, no. 1, pp. 61–76.

John, S. and DeBats, D. A. 2014. 'Australia's adoption of compulsory voting: revising the narrative—not trailblazing, uncontested or democratic', *Australian Journal of Politics and History*, vol. 60, no. 1, pp. 1–27.

Johnston, R. and Forrest, J. 2009. 'Electoral disproportionality and bias under the alternative vote: elections to Australia's House of Representatives', *Australian Journal of Political Science*, vol. 44, no. 3, pp. 521–8.

Karklins, R. 1986. 'Soviet elections revisited: voter abstention in noncompetitive voting', *American Political Science Review*, vol. 80, no. 2, pp. 449–70.

Lijphart, A. 1997. 'Disproportionality under alternative voting: the crucial—and puzzling—case of the Australian Senate elections 1919–1946', *Acta Politica*, no. 32, pp. 9–24.

Lowy Institute. 2014. *2014 Lowy Institute Poll Confirms Australian's Ambivalence about Democracy*, <http://www.lowyinstitute.org/news-and-media/press-releases/2014-lowy-institute-poll-confirms-australians-ambivalence-about-democracy> (accessed 20 November 2015).

Martineau, J. 1869. *Letters from Australia*. London: Longmans Green.

Milkis, S. and Mileur, J. (eds.). 1999. *Progressivism and the New Democracy*. Amherst, MA: University of Massachusetts Press.

Neale, R. S. 1967. 'H. S. Chapman and the Victorian ballot', *Australian Historical Studies*, vol. 12, no. 48, pp. 508–21.

Osmond, W. G. 1985. *Frederic Eggleston: An Intellectual in Australian Politics*. Sydney: George Allen & Unwin.

Ratcliffe, D. 2013. 'The right to vote and the rise of democracy, 1787–1828', *Journal of the Early Republic*, vol. 33, no. 2, pp. 219–54.

Reid, G. S. 1972. *Parliament and the Bureaucracy in Australia*. Canberra: Australian Institute of Political Science.

Reid, G. S. and Forrest, M. 1989. *Australia's Commonwealth Parliament 1901–1988: Ten Perspectives*. Melbourne: Melbourne University Press.

Reilly, B. 2004. 'Preferential voting and its political consequences' in M. Sawer (ed.), 2001, *Elections: Full, Free and Fair*. Sydney: Federation Press.

Reitsma, A. J. 1960. *Trade Protection in Australia*. Brisbane: University of Queensland Press.

Reynolds, J. 1958. 'A. I. Clark's American sympathies and his influence on Australian federation', *Australian Law Journal*, vol. 32, p. 62.

Rydon, J. 2001. 'Fiji and the export of electoral systems', *Australian Parliamentary Review*, vol. 16, no. 1, pp. 44–8.

Sawer, M. (ed.). 2001. *Elections: Full, Free and Fair*. Sydney: Federation Press.

Scott, E. 1920. 'The history of the Victorian ballot', *Victorian Historical Magazine*, vol. 8, no. 1, pp. 1–13.

Taylor, G. 2013. 'The early life of Mr Justice Boothby', *Adelaide Law Review*, vol. 34, no. 1, pp. 167–201.

Therry, R. 1863. *Reminiscences of Thirty Years' Residence in New South Wales and Victoria*. London: Sampson Low, Son & Co.

Trollope, A. 1874. *Victoria and Tasmania*. London: Chapman & Hall.

Turner, H. G. 1911. *The First Decade of the Australian Commonwealth: A Chronicle of Contemporary Politics, 1901–1910*. Melbourne: Mason, Firth & McCutcheon.

Wear, R. 2005. '"Adventure, heterodoxy, knavery": Queensland's electoral experience', *Queensland Review*, vol. 2, no. 2, pp. 87–96.

Wildavsky, A. 1961. 'Party discipline under federalism: implications of Australian experience', *Social Research*, vol. 28, no. 4, pp. 437–58.

Wright, J. F. H. 1980. *Mirror of the Nation's Mind: Australia's Electoral Experiments*. Sydney: Hale & Iremonger.

9

Socialism in Six Colonies

The Aftermath

Jonathan Pincus

In 1890 the Australian colonies collectively operated by far the largest government-built, government-owned, and government-operated railway system in the world.[1] That year was marked by a severe economic downturn sparked by the Argentinian government's difficulties in meeting guarantees to the private railways that British capital had financed. Such capital had also financed railways in Australia, Canada, India, and in the USA. But only in Australia was government then a significant owner of railways—making all capital and operational decisions, with profit or loss assumed by the taxpayer. Other substantial government-owned or operated rail systems were in Germany, Canada, and little Belgium, the first the result of nationalization after the war with France in 1870, and further nationalizations in the 1880s. But for perspective, the USA and Great Britain, with scarcely any publicly owned lines, around the First World War accounted for over half of the world's railway capital and activity (Acworth 1920). In many countries with substantial private rail systems, governments provided assistance through rights of way, land grants, monopoly charters, tax concessions, cash subsidies, subscriptions to capital raising, and guarantees of interest and dividends; and often government reserved the power to regulate freight rates and fares or to demand repayment of assistance, if profits were deemed excessive. But in Australia governments *owned* and built them.

Australia, then, followed its own special way, and continued doing so: for although through the first half of the twentieth century other nations

[1] In 1891 Australia had over 15,000 km of track (Ergas and Pincus 2014, p. 228). The other large state railways were Canada's Intercolonial Railway, of about 1,100 km, and that of Prussia, which by 1886 had, largely by nationalisation, reached a length of 20,050 km (Bradford 1907, p. 69).

nationalized their rail systems, many were subsequently privatized; whereas in Australia, apart from dedicated mining lines, the rail systems remain publicly owned (but with some significant private freight operators).[2]

The Australian state-owned railways were large monopolies; until well into the twentieth century they employed more workers than any other enterprise; their main workshops were the largest establishments in secondary industry; and they dominated state budgets.[3] The railways' state ownership, monopoly status, and large size all helped shape their history as enterprises, and their wider influence on economic, social, and political life.

Whatever the initial balance between its costs and benefits, the state rail system that evolved became ever less efficient as it collided with the formation of strong labour and country parties. It offered those forces ample grounds for institutionalized rent seeking—indeed, the risks were already apparent in the 1890s.

What difference did the early advent in Australia of public ownership of rail have on the railways as enterprises? How did the experience in rail affect the ownership and operation of other public utilities and institutions more broadly? What effects did the railways have on Australia's economic and social life, and on politics?

The thesis of this chapter is that the institution of state-owned railways reverberated through the Australian economy and society of the twentieth century, most directly through the effects on the efficiency of the railways themselves and of transport modes generally, and indirectly through the initiation of independent statutory authorities; through the effect on attitudes and policies towards monopoly and competition, as socially beneficial arrangements; and via union and Australian Labor Party political influence.

9.1 Sowing

9.1.1 *Why Government Ownership?*

We begin with *aetiology*: how the Australian governments chose public ownership and operation of railways, and why they persisted with what the eminent economic historian, Noel Butlin (1959), called 'colonial socialism'.

In the late nineteenth century and beyond, Australia had an international reputation not only as a social laboratory, but also as having an economy that was heavily 'socialized', that is, replete with state-owned enterprises, and not merely those typically owned by local government. However, the agreed interpretation, especially after Albert Métin's book (Métin [1901]

[2] Pacific National since 2002; and QR National (now Aurizon) since 2010.

[3] For example, in 1923–24, for Australia as a whole, gross revenue from state railways and tramways, £45m, was more than double state taxation revenue, £20m. (ABS 1925, pp. 387–91.)

1977), was that Australia's was a case of 'socialism without doctrine'. It was pragmatism, not ideology, which led to state-financing, construction, and operation of railways. Nonetheless, there were lasting consequences of the choice of public over private ownership, some of them ideological.

It may well be that, due to convict origins and the exigencies of antipodean life, the Australian colonists looked to government more keenly than elsewhere in the empire. Regarding rail, however, Butlin remarked that 'except in South Australia... opinion was originally strongly opposed to government entry into railway building', and concluded that 'the failure of private enterprise was, in a sense, accidental' (the 'accident' being the gold rushes, drawing men and finance away from the private railways), and so the government of Victoria was forced into ownership 'somewhat against its will' (Butlin 1959, pp. 39–40, 840; Coghlan 1918).[4]

The colonial governments had no material superiority over private companies, or vice versa, in access to technical know-how, to high-level engineering and management skills, or to construction labour. The technology of constructing and operating railways was readily transferable, facilitated by the rapid development of an integrated international market in railway engineering skills and experienced personnel. The British engineers, so prominent in the history of Australian railways, were but a small sample of those who travelled the world planning, constructing, and operating major transport infrastructure, rail in particular; and Britain supplied much of the world's rolling stock and, to a lesser extent, rails. In construction, private railway companies would have employed day labour in Australia, just as did the governments.[5] As to incentives for efficiency, whatever the theoretical advantages of the profit motive over public service, they would have been attenuated by the guarantees that the counterfactual private railway companies would undoubtedly have been granted. What the colonial governments did have, however, was superior access to finance.

9.1.2 *The Significance of Loan Markets*

The public sector's advantage in the loan market was substantial initially and increased over time. In 1858, the nascent colony of Victoria floated on the London market a remarkable public loan of £8 million. So successful did the colonial governments become at loan raising that, over the next three

[4] Shortly after the discovery of diamonds and the granting of responsible government, the Cape Colony of South Africa nationalized the formerly private railways in the early 1870s, and embarked on a huge expansion.

[5] Chinese construction workers were employed in USA, but apparently not in Australia. In response to the arrival of large numbers of Chinese on and around the goldfields, Victoria placed an arrival tax on them in 1855, and so many landed in Robe in South Australia and walked to the fields.

decades, Australian securities 'absorbed almost three-quarters of the portfolio [non-equity] investment that passed through the formal British capital markets'; moreover, they gained de facto 'trustee' status (Davis and Gallman 2001, pp. 524, 759–60), so that they could borrow at appreciably lower interest rates than were paid by South Africa, Argentina, and Japan (Obstfeld and Taylor 2004, pp. 210–13).

The favourable and improving place in the financial market—compared with private borrowers and with most other governments—tilted the balance against future privatization—a possibility (along with the outsourcing of operations) variously discussed in the colonies during the latter part of the nineteenth century (Clark 1908, p. 404).

Clearly, instead of servicing public railway debt, the state's fiscal capacity could be used to meet guarantees made to private lines, as in many places, including Canada and Argentina.[6] Under either arrangement, losses could be passed to the taxpayer, thus likely reducing the interest rate demanded by lenders (and distorting the incentives facing various parties). The state, in addition to selling or renting land—as could a land-grant private line—could also capture land values (enhanced by the infrastructure investment) through export taxes and import tariffs, whose ultimate incidence would fall—however inefficiently—on the relatively abundant factor, land. And protective import tariffs were soon adopted in Victoria, as a means of retaining population after the gold rushes.

It was an Australian advantage in the financial markets, albeit shared, that the colonies were within the sphere of British law and custom, represented by the continuing presence of British governors.[7] The colonies' financial reputations were enhanced by their gathering and publication of reliable information about the railways and their wider economic and social situations. Moreover, there was a very active press. According to Frederic Eggleston (1932, p. 2), an astute observer and former Victorian railway minister, an important factor making for efficiency was that the colonial systems were 'never altogether outside the range of controversy', so 'its protagonists constantly had to prove their case and as difficult problems arose they were compelled to devise methods of solving them'.[8]

[6] However, in the Argentine at least, the very fact of foreign ownership weakened the railway companies politically, in times of crisis or labour conflict (Duncan 1937).

[7] It is a standard argument that the capacity of early modern governments to borrow from their own citizens was enhanced if the rule of law applied—which gave borrowers confidence in the transaction; and if the nation enjoyed relatively democratic institutions—so that the borrowers had regard for the welfare of the lenders (Macdonald 2006). The proposition put here is that the same conditions also made it easier for the Australian colonists to borrow in Britain.

[8] Although highly critical of state socialism with developmental objectives, Eggleston was a supporter of the 'Australian Settlement' of Alfred Deakin, and approved a reliance on statutory corporations for non-developmental purposes.

9.1.3 *The State as 'One Big Company'*

The outcome was that, for many decades, the rail systems were planned, constructed, and operated with reasonable degrees of technical efficiency, but fell well short of the economic ideal. In time, as we will recount, the system ran into large secular deficits under the influence of democratic politics and of industrial relations. Subsequently, in the twentieth century, the underlying railway finances deteriorated further, when motorized road (and, later, air) transport and travel became preferred alternatives for many users.

In Germany, after the nationalizations of the 1870s, the state treated its rail monopoly as a 'milch cow', rather in the way of a private monopolist (Acworth 1920). In Australia, in contrast, only for a relatively short period did their public owners aim at a 'commercial' rate of return after interest payments. Subsequently, the financial test was weakened, first through crediting to rail the enhancement they caused to land values (albeit in very imprecise ways, using traffic forecasts), and later by acceptance of the idea of the state as 'one big company' that should 'be able to balance its accounts' overall (NSW valuer-general in 1924, cited in Butlin, Barnard, and Pincus 1982, p. 264); or, as W. K. Hancock (1930) had it, as one great public utility. However, such a holistic approach proved unsustainable, once the railways placed intolerable burdens on the public purse during the 1930s Depression.

9.2 Reaping

9.2.1 *Railway Finances*

An outstanding characteristic of Australian railways was their sheer size. They absorbed the largest shares of public investment and borrowing: even in the 1920s, when there were other insistent claimants for funds, railways accounted for almost 30 per cent of public investment (down from 40 per cent in the previous decade: Butlin, Barnard, and Pincus 1982: 268); their annual income and expenditure flows dominated public budgets into the 1930s; and they became the largest single employer in the colonies and, for some decades, in the states.[9] Moreover, they posed the most pressing and persistent puzzle of reconciling democratic political control with the imperatives of their efficient and effective operation as enterprises. In all of these

[9] By the end of the 1890s there were over 10,000 railway employees in Victoria (Serle 1971, p. 26). In the 1920s employment in railway services (excluding employment in railway workshops and construction) averaged 63,000; or over 4 per cent of the Australian workforce (Keating 1973, p. 236). The annual reports of the states railway departments record 110,673 employees in the year 1928/29 (New South Wales 1929, p. 36; Victoria 1929, p. 58; Queensland 1929, p. 33; South Australia 1929, p. 8; Western Australia 1929, p. 77; Tasmania 1929, p. 19).

manifestations of size, the railways left legacies, some temporary, some permanent. Here we deal briefly with finances.

The railways accounted for more than 40 per cent of the interest on the public debt in 1931 (ABS 1932). New South Wales (NSW) Premier Jack Lang used to say, 'As goes the rail revenues, there goes the state budget' (quoted in O'Connor 2005, p. 34: see Table 9.1).

When a private enterprise makes persistent losses, its capital is written down through sale or bankruptcy. When a large state-owned enterprise makes persistent losses, then the deficits damage the public accounts, unless the government reneges on its obligations—as Argentina did repeatedly, but not Australia, despite Jack Lang's effort in 1932. In the 1890s, the colonies' railway interest bills were met, but caused severe fiscal stringency that may have worsened the depression (Boot 1998). Wage rates were cut in the Great Depression (but not as much as the general price level fell) and capital works virtually ceased. Concern about the foreign exchange demands for public debt

Table 9.1 Losses of State Railways, 1919/20–1938/9, As million £A and as per cent of states' revenues

	Commonwealth Year Book, £	Annual Reports, £	Commonwealth Year Book, %	Annual Reports, %
1919/20	1.83	2.12	5.8	6.7
1920/21	3.66	4.03	9.8	10.8
1921/22	2.10	2.45	5.6	6.6
1922/23	1.23	1.63	3.2	4.2
1923/24	1.20	1.73	2.9	4.2
1924/25	0.48	0.85	1.1	1.9
1925/26	2.70	3.13	5.9	6.8
1926/27	3.52	4.61	6.9	9.0
1927/28	4.74	4.94	8.7	9.1
1928/29	4.01	4.51	7.0	7.8
1929/30	7.58	7.96	13.0	13.7
1930/31	8.68	9.89	14.6	16.6
1931/32	4.70	6.93	8.4	12.4
1932/33	2.99	5.12	4.9	8.4
1933/34	2.65	4.52	4.5	7.6
1934/35	1.14	2.42	1.8	3.9
1935/36	1.11	2.23	1.7	3.3
1936/37	0.30	1.51	0.4	2.1
1937/38	–0.14	1.42	–0.2	1.9
1938/39	2.11	3.77	2.8	5.0
1919/20–1938/39	56.60	75.80	108.0	142.0

Notes: The *Commonwealth Year Book* measures differ from those of the *Annual Reports* largely on account of their disregarding the increased cost of servicing debt to British bond holders subsequent to the depreciation of the Australian pound in 1931. The measures of both the *Commonwealth Year Book* and the *Annual Reports* disregard the removal from railways' accounts of about £32 m of debt by the Qld Railways Capital Reduction Act of 1931 and the Tasmanian Railways Capital Reduction Act of 1936. Similarly, both disregard the £800,000 granted to NSW Railways by NSW Treasury each year throughout the 1930s. The combined effect of these is to underestimate losses by about £2m pa.

Sources: *Commonwealth Year Book* and *Annual Reports* of six railways (New South Wales 1929; Queensland 1929; South Australia 1929; Tasmania 1929; Victoria 1929; Western Australia 1929). State revenue is defined as the sum of state taxation, land revenue, Commonwealth grants, and 'other revenue' (Barnard 1982).

servicing was partly responsible for the 'trade diversion' strategy in the 1930s, of discrimination against imports from the USA and Japan.

The Second World War generated traffic for the railways, but maintenance was deferred. For the first time since very early days, in the 1950s railway revenue fell short of working expenses; by the mid-1970s, the gap was 20 per cent. Thereafter, railways lost market shares of both passenger and freight, and their finances deteriorated further (Butlin, Barnard, and Pincus 1982, p. 285).

By the early 1990s, railways losses were estimated at over $4 billion a year, and cumulatively amounted to about two-thirds of state enterprise debt (Industry Commission 1991). Under the National Competition Policy of the 1990s, most government rail enterprises have been divided into corporations that provide the travel and freight services, and those providing the rail infrastructure. The former were not expected to cover costs from revenues: as an indication, in 2006–07 the five large government urban transport enterprises—including trams and ferries—recovered 60.5 per cent of accounting cost. In the early 2000s, the rail infrastructure enterprises monitored by the Productivity Commission (PC) produced low or negative returns on the assets that they used (PC 2008).

9.2.2 *Competition Policy*

Australian railways were granted monopolies over rail services in their colony or state: apart from some relatively minor competition over Riverina trade, there were no 'competitive' or 'duplicate' lines. (Canadian railway history, in contrast, was mightily influenced by competition from its neighbour to the south; and, in the Canadian Pacific and Canadian National Railways, created a duopoly.) Consequently, in the later nineteenth and early twentieth century, Australian railways could not give rise to the private 'trusts' that became a potent political issue in the USA, sparking the creation of what has been called 'the regulatory state' in that country, one focus of which was the preservation of rivalrous competition. Arguably, the existence and experience of state railway monopolies contributed to the widespread ignorance or scepticism in Australia about the social value of competition—public monopolies were considered a very desirable form of industrial organization, and private cartels were not only permitted (until the 1970s) but also judicially lauded, as in the judgement of the 1912–13 Coal Vend Case.[10] The Deakinite package in the early years after Federation had an anti-competitive bias against low-priced

[10] 'Cut-throat competition is not now regarded by a large portion of mankind as necessarily beneficial to the public... The intention of the parties was to put the Newcastle coal trade on a satisfactory basis, which would enable them to pay adequate wages to their men and sell their coal at a price remunerative to themselves' (cited in French 1994, p. 94).

imports; against wage rates set in the market; and, compounded with racism, against low-wage immigration. Moreover, private businesses grew accustomed to look to government for many of their productive needs, rather than to other businesses.

The greatest long-term threat to the economic viability of railways was the increasing competition from new and improving forms of transport and travel, motor trucks, motorcars, and aeroplanes. Branch rail lines had been built on the assumption that it was unprofitable to cart produce other than wool more than about 20 km. When road transport became cheaper than rail for low-density traffic, it would have improved the financial results of rail to have closed a considerable number of lines. However, by the 1960s, very few had been closed, due to local lobbying (Hunter 1965, p. 94).

In the USA, the railways were singularly unsuccessful in resisting the building of highways parallel to their lines; in contrast, Argentina, with its now nationalized system, planned to build highways to feed rail or ports (Duncan 1937, p. 572). In Australia, the dual roles of the state governments clashed. As owner of the rural railways, the states vigorously restricted the competition of road transport (and, especially in Victoria, the railways slashed freight rates and improved their services).[11] But the states had the responsibility for the construction and maintenance of all but local roads. Politically, it was hard for the states to resist demands for more and better roads and bridges, in view of the increases in motor vehicle ownership; moreover, the states received some financial assistance from the Commonwealth, which for decades favoured 'main roads' connecting rural cities and towns. The compromise was that the highways and roads were built, but road transport, especially rural transport, was heavily regulated so as to protect the states' main assets.

The result was, as the American diplomat, Pierrepont Moffat, wrote in 1936 to Secretary of State Cordell Hull, 'no-one may use a truck (even when he owns one) to transport anything (even his own chattels) except to a railroad station—any paralleling of the railroad is prohibited except on payment of a prohibitive tax; one cannot hire a motor car for a pleasure trip into the interior without paying a sizable tax to compensate the railroads for the loss of revenue' (in Edwards 1979, p. 50): the details may be wrong, but the result—protection of the railways—was what mattered.

In Victoria, Robert Menzies as Minister of Railways extended the restriction on road competition from the urban areas to the rural (Motor Omnibus Acts of

[11] The Railway Acts prevented commissioners from price discrimination, and especially from increasing any fares or freight rates (Hunter 1965, pp. 94–5). Similar restrictions were common in countries where railways were privately owned.

the 1920s).[12] The board established under the Transport Regulation Act of 1933 refused to license car services that Reginald Ansett provided between Ballarat and two rural towns that were connected to Ballarat (Marlborough and Hamilton). In response, Ansett purchased a plane, and offered weekday services between Melbourne and Hamilton: 'It was not the first air competition for Victoria Railway's passenger traffic, but it was the first airline established purely to compete with the railways' (Lee 2009, p. 155).

9.2.3 *Spread of Government Ownership*

It is hard to be confident that the example of 'colonial socialism' in rail directly stimulated public ownership of other enterprises—where they were generally afforded, if not monopoly rights, then competitive advantages over private enterprises. However, there were indirect effects.

That governments had operated, reasonably satisfactorily, a public enterprise as large as a rail system; that colonial governments had achieved favourable access to capital markets largely on account of rail: both could have made for the further extension of the scope of public ownership. Indeed, during the second half of the nineteenth or the early twentieth century, many initially private utilities or infrastructure became publicly owned, including wharves, telegraph, and telephone; and many other utilities that could have been private were publicly owned from the start, including postal services, and reticulated urban water supply and sewerage. In at least one case, there was a complementarity between railways and another service that helps explain the public takeover—the telegraph was a communications tool used by the railways, and the telegraph lines needed a right of way, which the railways had. But in many other cases, the timing suggests that the existence or example of rail was not important—and, besides, public ownership of some kind was common in Britain and elsewhere for many of these utilities in the period.

Moreover, there were variations among the colonies and states: although Sydney trams were publicly owned, Melbourne's remained private. In addition, fiscal stringency (caused, to some significant extent, by railway finance) contributed to the later sale or closure of the 'petty socialist' enterprises of the 1910s—brick and lime works, quarries, timber mills, clothing factories—in direct competition with private enterprises; and the reiterated socialist objective of the New South Wales Labor Party to nationalize (with compensation) was abandoned in favour of government controls on gas price and profit,

[12] Much later Robert Menzies wrote that 'We have, for example, socialist railways and a socialist Post Office, mostly to our great advantage', and argued for the 'two airline' policy on the grounds that 'free for all' competition was inconsistent with the maintenance of 'the highest standards' of safety and service (1970, pp. 121, 138).

which freed the public budget for more popular spending, on transport, education, and health (Abbott 2014).

Two Victorian public enterprises owe their origins, to some extent, to the need to reduce dependence on strike-prone NSW for suitable coal: the State Electricity Commission of Victoria (SECV) in 1920 (Butlin, Barnard, and Pincus 1982, pp. 251–8); the Gas and Fuel Corporation in 1951 (Proudley 1987). Despite this common factor, it is reasonable to conclude, especially for SECV, that the Victorians' familiarity with statutory corporations also played a part.

Public ownership of rail affected economic policy and practice in other ways, especially through efforts to isolate the rail systems from political interference.

9.2.4 *Politics and Unions*

Because the railways were run in an integrated fashion, they gave rise to permanent government jobs, internal labour markets, and unionization (Seltzer 2014); and because railway employees were so many and because of their electoral distribution, they had significant political influence.

In the second half of the nineteenth century, three men—Duncan Gillies, James Patterson, and Thomas Bent—all held the position of commissioner and minister for the railways, and later became premiers of the colony of Victoria: 'the railway commissionership was much coveted by ambitious politicians' for the patronage to be dispensed, and the influence that the position gave them on the timing and location of construction of new lines' (Lee 2009, p. 81).

By the 1890s, patronage had mostly ended; but serious industrial relations troubles had started. It is telling that Edmund Gerald FitzGibbon, the able first chairman of the Melbourne Metropolitan Board of Works, reversed his support for the expansion of the board's own labour force in 1891 (rather than day labour or contracting out) for fear it would make the board unduly vulnerable to industrial disputes and union pressure. Equally striking is the Irvine government's 1903 Constitution Act that created a separate roll and parliamentary representation for public servants, and especially railway employees, in an effort to dilute their political influence. (Of the sixty-eight Legislative Assembly members, two were to be elected by railway officers.) This followed a bitter dispute between the Irvine government and the Enginemen's Association; and the ineffectiveness of earlier Victorian legislation restricting the political rights of government employees (Plehwe 1983). Eggleston (1932, p. 146), former minister for railways in Victoria, pointed out that 'Mere sale of the Victorian railways would not accomplish much. In all countries where railway organizations exist, their problems become political.'

Other famous railway strikes were in 1917—which started in NSW, spread to other states and industries, and involved over 100,000 men; 1946 in Western Australia (engine drivers); 1948 in Queensland workshops (for nine weeks); 1950 in Victoria (for fifty-five days). Of interest here are events in Queensland in the later 1920s. Premier William McCormack, formerly a senior office bearer in the Australian Workers Union, fought bitterly with the union over a variety of issues when he was Labor premier from 1925 to 1929. Railwaymen who had supported a strike at a sugar mill, by refusing to load 'black' cane, were dismissed. The strike soon collapsed, but the unions campaigned against McCormack in the election of May 1929, and his Labor government was defeated (Kennedy 1986).

The railways were intensively unionized; and the pursuit of the interests of railway workers led many into politics and parliament: from the Eveleigh workshops alone came twenty-five members of the NSW parliament, including three Labor premiers: James McGowan, William McKell (later Governor-General), and Joe Cahill (O'Connor 2005). But the most famous former railway employee as politician was Ben Chifley, Commonwealth treasurer and prime minister: Chifley, being an engine driver, was in the working-class 'elite'; he took a leading part in the 1917 strike.[13]

9.2.5 *Railway Commissions*

At first, all the colonies with responsible government placed the enterprises within a department of railways or public works.[14] Initial efforts to insulate railway management—associated with Ben Hey Martindale's recruitment in NSW—collapsed,[15] and in both NSW and Victoria the systems were run under ministers whose primary resource was patronage, albeit shared with department heads (see Wettenhall 1961, 1987).

Reaction to the extent and nature of political interference came first in Victoria, reflecting the size of the deficits, the excesses of sometime railway minister (and later premier) Thomas Bent, and the decreasing political pay-off from patronage. Franchising of the rail service to the private sector was considered but rejected.

[13] One of Australia's largest law firms, Slater and Gordon, was founded in 1935 by Bill Slater, who had been attorney general in several Labor governments, and later Australian minister to the Soviet Union. In 1923 he opened his own business in Unity Hall, the Australian Railways Union's building in Bourke Street, after the Victorian branch of the militant union offered him its legal work (Cannon 2002).

[14] This and the next sections draw heavily from Wettenhall (1961), Serle (1971), Lee (2009) and Ergas and Pincus (2014), and the *Australian Dictionary of Biography*.

[15] Martindale was from 1858 the chief commissioner of railways (amongst other posts) in NSW, holding considerable responsibility until he resigned in 1861, following vigorous criticism from members of the Legislative Assembly (Abbott 1974). In contrast, John Whitton from 1857 served as engineer-in-chief for thirty-five years (McMartin 1983).

In 1883 Victoria deviated from the British system of ministerial responsibility by creating the Railways Commission with a degree of autonomy from the minister, in an effort to shield the railways from political interference (Butlin 1964, pp. 352–7). It was proto-corporatization, but without the independent economic regulation of the twentieth century.

This system of corporate governance works best when the ministers confine the exercise of their ultimate power to matters of genuine importance; and when the commissioners are paragons of virtue, ability, responsibility, and application.

By international standards, the Victorian commission model was an important innovation, giving rise to Métin's famous 'socialism without doctrine'. The commission model was consistent with the spirit of the age, which stressed ministerial accountability to parliament and enhanced professionalization of the public service, sought through reforms of the 1880s in Victoria and NSW. The British administrative 'revolution in government' (Finer 1952; MacDonagh 1977) reverberated in the Australian colonies, both through the 'generation of the 1850s' (Serle 1971, pp. 316–17) and through the efforts of governors such as the enormously energetic Sir Hercules Robinson, governor of NSW.[16]

Wettenhall (1961, p. 83) regarded this innovation in public administration as all the more remarkable because it happened when Victorians were striving for democratic reforms. The other colonies (and New Zealand, albeit temporarily) soon copied the commission system: South Australia in 1887, NSW and Queensland in 1888, Western Australia in 1902, and Tasmania in 1910; and it 'provided the basic framework from which the various [public] corporate systems of Australia have developed' (Wettenhall 1961, p. 85). However, in NSW, Sir Henry Parkes insisted on separating the functions of operating completed lines from that of constructing new lines: all new proposals for railway or other works were to be referred to a Parliamentary Standing Committee on Public Works. Although parliamentary questions could be asked of the responsible minister, the railway commissioners could not be compelled to answer. Government control was reserved for use if there were serious excesses or failings on the part of the commissioners (Wettenhall 1961).

Over the subsequent decades, various attempts at improvement were made. The most important being; the Victorian 'recoup' arrangement, whereby the railways were compensated for the financial detriment imposed by explicit ministerial directives; the clarification of what was meant for the minister to have ultimate control, while still allowing autonomy to the commissioners; and the separation of railways accounts from the Consolidated Revenue Fund. And, as noted, the model became a template, adapted and used widely.[17]

[16] Robinson urged NSW governments to a more rapid rate of railway building (Nairn 1976).

[17] Parkin (2003) suggested that state policy development was retarded by existence of semi-autonomous public agencies.

9.2.6 *Political Economy*

State-owned enterprises are used in the pursuit of government objectives that can be obtained more easily or more fully than were the enterprise private. These include purposes in the interest of the citizens generally, like national defence, national identity or unity, and national or regional economic development. But, almost inevitably, state enterprises come to be used to advance or protect sectional interests: in short, rent seekers.

The colonial railways were large enterprises that were intimately connected to the everyday lives and livelihoods of citizens; arguably, more intimately and more widely connected than any other public or private enterprise. Moreover, because the railways loomed so large in the colonies' financial accounts, there was a wide public interest in the efficiency and economy with which the public enterprises operated.

Therefore, the railways and their operation would inevitably be matters of public and political attention, giving rise to much lobbying—and to a greater extent than would have been the case were the railways privately owned.

There was (and is) a tension between two desirable objectives—democratic control and efficiency, once representative and responsible government was granted (from the 1850s, with Western Australia receiving it in 1890). In theory and largely in practice, the ministry was collectively responsible for the actions of government; and a minister was individually responsible for actions on matters within the specific ministry, and responsible for outcomes, to the extent that causes and responsibilities could be assigned.

There have been two sources of difficulties of governance, regarding large infrastructure projects. The first is what economists call 'the agency problem'. A principal, in this case the minister or government, wishes to build and operate a railway system; only the engineers—the agents—have the required knowledge. As a consequence, for decisions about infrastructure generally, engineering has often been the dominant profession, and not only in Australia. Specifically, for well over a century, engineers made many of the major decisions about Australian railways, or, at least, had very significant influence, whether as senior departmental officers, or railway commissioners, or outside experts. Many of their decisions were splendid; some, however, put the dictates of engineering above those of economics.[18]

The second governance problem arises because the benefits and costs of the railways were large and unevenly distributed.

It is useful to distinguish three types of benefits (each with their concomitant interest groups): benefits that were distributed narrowly; those distributed

[18] Blainey (1966, p. 245) outlines how, although NSW, South Australia, and Victoria had originally plumped on a common ('Irish') gauge, they ended up with different gauges: it was all the fault of a new (Scottish) chief engineer in NSW.

widely; and an intermediate set. Two narrow groups gained most. First were those whom the railways employed (or bought materials or equipment from). Members and ministers were intensively lobbied for patronage jobs—the NSW railways became 'a kind of out-door relief establishment for those who cannot obtain work elsewhere' (Wettenhall 1961, p. 22); the same in other colonies.

The other 'narrow' interests were those of landholders nearest to where a line was built and operated, who put pressure on the decisions about whether, where, and when to construct and run lines. This reached a peak in Victoria during the lead-up to Duncan Gillies' 1884 'Octopus Bill' for the construction of about 1,500 km of lines: 'Backed by their local railway leagues, the training-grounds of so many politicians, the country members whose lines were in jeopardy rallied for the fray.' The commissioners reported favourably on most of the proposals and, in the event, parliament authorized even more lines (Serle 1971, p. 36).[19] 'Although Gillies referred all questions to the board for decision and conscientiously refrained from interference, he failed to protect the commissioners from the demands of other parliamentarians' (Beever 1972).

Intermediate, in terms of size and salience of interest, were classes of customers charged less—sometimes considerably less—than the cost of service, or less than comparable services elsewhere in the system.

There were also two diffused groups affected by the enterprise, the first being the broad mass of citizens with an interest in reaping the wider benefits that railways created through their stimulation of economic and social development generally; and the second being the taxpayers, who had an interest in the financial results of the enterprise that loomed so large in the public accounts. For both, the efficient and effective operation of the railway enterprise generally was imperative, and the appropriate capture of some of the benefits as railway revenue in Treasury financial accounts.

9.2.7 *Decline in Patronage*

The political 'dilemma' facing MPs and ministers was the result of the trade-off between, roughly, maximizing aggregate net benefits, versus the creation of benefits to narrow interests, of a kind that generated a palpable pay-off for the individual MP or minister. The terms of this trade-off changed over time.

In the second half of the nineteenth century, governments were formed around often-temporary coalitions: the party system did not then exist.[20] The

[19] The bill also mandated the end of the patronage system, so that its subsequent and not infrequent use was illegal.

[20] There were at least thirty-one changes in the political head of the department in charge of public works in NSW from 1856 through 1891 (Butlin 1964, p. 352).

patronage system allowed a member of parliament to offer individualized benefits to constituents and others, which was a feasible political arrangement when constituencies had relatively few, mostly immigrant, voters. As the population grew, and with the beneficial effects of the 1866 Public Schools Act in NSW and the 1872 Education Act in Victoria, the patronage system started to become a net burden on members of parliament, and was a source of damaging scandals: 'It was by voicing the *collective* demands of local pressure groups for railways, schools and other facilities, rather than supplying *individuals* with government billets, that the urban politician increasingly won support' (Serle 1971, p. 117). Also relevant were the 1883 reforms, somewhat along Northcote–Trevelyan lines, with an independent Public Service Board and a new system of classification. Closely associated was the notion of placing public decisions and public administration more generally on a 'scientific' basis—from eugenics to town and country planning—through their delegation to 'independent' experts and by successive refinement of the administrative machinery.

9.2.8 *Rule by Experts*

The commission system seems to exemplify a persistent strand of Australian exceptionalism: the heavy reliance on public guardians, purportedly disinterested and expert individuals; or, more commonly, commissions and committees of great number and variety, into whose hands the various parliaments have placed significant non-judicial power.

Whatever its weaknesses, the commission model reduced the pressure to seek efficiencies through the installation of private management, and the model, once well established, provided a template for structuring the provision of a wider range of services, from sewerage to electricity to a shipping line. In that sense, the Australian story seems consistent with the notion of 'path dependence' or self-reinforcing processes: organizations achieving early success (by accident or design) secure internal and external economies that make their eventual displacement costly.

What of the counterfactual, private railways? The broad structure of the system in each colony was relatively easy to determine. However, the exact location of lines and their extensions were more contested, and would have been under private ownership; and there would always have been political struggles over fare levels and structures. If, as in other countries, the private lines had been provided guarantees, then most likely (in the counterfactual) the Australian colonies and states would have felt a heavy fiscal burden, especially in economic downturns, and been subject to political pressures.

The chief railway commissioner in Victoria from 1883 to 1898 was Richard Speight, previously assistant general manager of the Midlands Railway (UK).

Under him, a series of deficits of over £200,000 was converted temporarily into a small surplus by 1885–86 (Lee 2009, p. 84). However, the huge losses at the end of the decade were 'a crucial feature of Victoria's history' (Serle 1971, p. 81). In 1892 Speight resigned, largely the result of severe criticism from David Syme in *The Age* newspaper. According to Butlin (1964, p. 357), this marked the end of the dominating role played by British experts.

Although Speight presided over extravagant spending on the Newport workshops, Flinders Street station, and the 'Outer Circle' in Melbourne's suburbs,[21] much of the responsibility for the financial woes lay with governments and ministers.[22] The doubling of the mileage of the system in the decade from 1882 was decided by government, including lines with no chance of returning revenue greater than cost within decades—there were diminishing returns to railway investment.[23]

The reign of Speight was a transitional period. What followed was not only, as reading Wettenhall (1961) could suggest, that the colonies and states learnt from experience about how to create better governance frameworks for railways. In addition, a decline in the pay-off from patronage, and other changes, meant that it was an attractive, even winning, political strategy to create a commission with wide autonomy, but with the minister retaining final responsibility for some areas (but expected to use this power sparingly, on 'important' matters).

An indication that the reforms to the commission system resulted in a satisfactory compromise is that Harold Clapp, an American, served as Victorian railway commissioner from 1920 to 1939. (His salary was £5,000 (Adam-Smith 1981), and said to be the highest in the country's public service.) On the other hand, in NSW between 1888 and 1932 (when the office of commissioner of transport was established), there were forty-four official inquiries into aspects of the railways, including thirteen Royal Commissions.[24]

9.3 The Reckoning

9.3.1 *Evaluation*

Ideally, we would like to tease out the effects of public ownership and operation, by contrasting them with private results elsewhere, or through a

[21] 'The theory of railway-led suburban growth met its nemesis in the Outer Circle Railway' (Serle 1971, p. 160).

[22] Speight made many improvements in the physical system from an engineering point of view: standardization of some equipment, and improvements in rolling stock and in signalling systems (which last, unfortunately, did not prevent the fourth in a series of serious accidents).

[23] In addition, there was the (often illegal) use of the railways as 'a kind of out-door relief establishment for those who cannot obtain work elsewhere' (Lee 2009, p. 83, quoting John Woods, sometime railways minister).

[24] South Australia, with its departmental system, had none (Zalums 1975).

counterfactual. However, there is a substantial complication in pursuing these comparative questions: it was not public sector involvement itself but the earlier arrival of and persistence with public sector ownership and operation of that differentiated Australian railways.

Many forms of assistance were provided to both private systems elsewhere and to the government systems in the Australian colonies and states. Moreover, as noted, many countries nationalized their railway systems (at least for many decades). And many other countries—including New Zealand—embarked on massive expansions of their railways in the latter decades of the nineteenth century and the early decades of the next. That is to say, other countries may have taken different paths or had different timing, but ended up in similar positions.

Consequently, it is difficult to assign to public ownership itself definite responsibility for the observed Australian outcomes, rather than to public sector intervention more generally. Therefore, instead of attempting a systematic comparative analysis, this chapter draws selectively from international experience.

First, the outcomes: the financial results of Australian railways were briefly discussed in section 9.2.1; here the purview is broader, on net social value.

It should be said that the only effort at quantifying the economic costs and benefits of an Australian railway system, Davidson (1982), concluded that the NSW system produced a net economic benefit overall, 1852 to 1972/73, with 'internal rates of return' no lower than 10 per cent for any of the subperiods examined, and higher than the rates of interest on the debt. Admirable as it is, Davidson's calculation did not account for all costs, including those arising from the regulation of competition from other modes. Moreover, it is very doubtful that a Davidson-like calculation would show a net benefit for the period after 1972. Nobody has attempted this kind of calculation for any other state, but some have offered qualitative judgements.

Noel Butlin (1964), although critical of the extent of branch line construction and rivalry over Riverina trade, judged that the branches paid off in the 1920s. For Victoria in the nineteenth century, Frost (2000) arrived at similar qualitative conclusions: the railways made a net positive contribution to the colony's economy. Boot (2000) demurred, citing the lax investment criteria that were applied by government, as well as the difficulties that Victoria had in meeting its debt obligations during the depression of the 1890s.

What difference did the public ownership make and, more narrowly, what difference was made by early reliance on it? Unfortunately, Davidson's calculation cannot tell us—in particular, it sheds little light on the gap between the best feasible outcome and the actual. Maybe private railways would have contributed more to economic and social welfare; maybe not. The most ambitious effort along these lines is Bogart (2010), comparing the cost-efficiency of the rail systems of different countries and different ownership arrangements, from the 1880s to 1912. His conclusions were that, although trends in cost inefficiency varied across countries, nationalization generally damaged efficiency, whereas greater state railway construction improved efficiency. For the period 1900 to 1912, of the eighteen countries (Russia, Norway, Sweden, The Netherlands, Belgium, France, Switzerland, Spain, Italy, Japan, US, Argentina, Britain, Germany, India, Canada, Austria, and Australia), Australia ranked sixth least cost inefficient.

Cost-efficiency, however, is not economic efficiency: a system that performed well, in terms of cost per tonne-kilometre, may have been providing services that generated more costs than benefits. This could be the case, for example, if there were too many branch lines, or poorly sited trunk lines.

Bogart's methodology is designed to allow like-with-like comparisons of unlike countries. In a direct pair-wise contrast, Acworth (1920) was acerbic: 'Will any one deny that, even handicapped as they are [in the capital market], the private railways of Texas are giving to the people of Texas a more ample, a more efficient, and a cheaper service than the Government of New South Wales gives to its citizens?'[25]

9.4 Conclusion

From the 1850s, Australian governments have been responsible for the financing, construction, and operation of railways—urban, suburban, and rural—with the exceptions being some lines dedicated to minerals carriage, and the outsourcing in recent decades of some 'above rail' operations. In other countries, extensive government railways were initiated later than the 1850s, often beginning with the nationalization of substantial private rail lines or networks.

This chapter discussed some causes and consequences of this Australian distinction—the early initiation of state railways. However, it is difficult to isolate what was due solely to precociousness in state ownership. For one thing, there was state ownership in all Australian colonies—no Australian counter-example existed. As to other countries, the extent and nature of state intervention itself make comparative inferences dubious: where there were privately owned railways, as in the USA, Canada, and Argentina, they mostly received financial and regulatory assistance from government, of a kind (and sometimes of a quantum) that the Australian state railways enjoyed.

[25] Acworth (1920, p. 24) related how 'a distinguished railway man' from America—presumably Clapp of Victorian railways—admitted 'I have the ton-mileage figures. I dare not publish them. If I did publish them, they would show a ton-mile rate so excessive as compared with other countries similarly situated, where the traffic is mainly in agricultural products carried long distances, that public opinion would enforce a sweeping reduction in rates and bankrupt the undertaking.'

One apparent difference related to land values. The revenues of private rail companies were boosted when the lines enhanced the value of land granted them by government. In Australia, the government railways had no land grants, except rights of way, and the government garnered some of this 'developmental dividend'; and that very fact early became an argument for subsidies to railways from general government revenues. For land-grant railways, the revenue gain was determined by the grants themselves; for state railways, some official made a forecast or guess. This may have encouraged lax capital and operating decisions.

Too much should not be made of this difference. Any land grants were, in some fashion, the result of speculations about the size and nature of the 'developmental dividend'; and government assistance was not confined to land grants—financial assistance to private lines was funded from general government revenues, themselves dependent to some extent on the same 'dividend'.

Therefore, the chapter has to be content with suggesting plausible and long-lasting consequences:

- An innovative form of governance—Railway Commissions—which was refined and adopted widely, and not only for rail- and tramways.
- The commission system reinforced a tendency of Australian parliaments to establish 'independent' or expert bodies, with considerable power to make decisions.
- The Australian public grew accustomed to government monopolies and more dubious about the benefits of competition between private enterprises.
- The state railways provided a strong impetus towards unionization, and the forging of solid links between unions and the ALP.
- For many decades, Lang's aphorism held true: 'As goes the rail revenues, there goes the state budget.'
- When motorized transport became more attractive, governments distorted modal choice through regulations designed to protect their largest asset, the railways.
- Rail assets continue to be used to provide services that make losses that cannot be easily justified on grounds of beneficial spillovers or their distributional incidence.

References

Abbott, G. J. 1974. 'Martindale, Ben Hay (1824–1904)' in *Australian Dictionary of Biography*, vol. 5. Melbourne: Melbourne University Press.

Abbott, M. 2014. 'The limits of socialism: the New South Wales Labor Party and the proposal to nationalise the gas industry', *Labour History*, no. 107, pp. 115–27.

ABS (Australian Bureau of Statistics). 1925. *Official Year Book of the Commonwealth of Australia*, no. 18. Melbourne: Government printer.

ABS. 1932. *Official Year Book of the Commonwealth of Australia*, no. 25. Melbourne: Government printer.

Acworth, W. M. 1920. *Historical Sketch of State Railway Ownership*. London: J. Murray.

Adam-Smith, P. 1981. 'Clapp, Sir Harold Winthrop (1875–1952)' in the *Australian Dictionary of Biography*, vol. 8. Melbourne: Melbourne University Press.

Barnard, A. 1982. *Government Financial Data, 1850 to 1982*, Source Papers in Economic History no. 12. Canberra: Australian National University.

Beever, M. 1972. 'Gillies, Duncan (1834–1903)' in the *Australian Dictionary of Biography*, vol. 4. Melbourne: Melbourne University Press.

Blainey, G. 1966. *The Tyranny of Distance: How Distance Shaped Australia's History*. Melbourne: Sun Press.

Bogart, D. 2010. 'A global perspective on railway inefficiency and the rise of state ownership, 1880–1912', *Explorations in Economic History*, vol. 47, no. 2, pp. 158–78.

Boot, H. M. 1998. 'Government and the colonial economies', *Australian Economic History Review*, vol. 38, no. 1, pp. 74–101.

Boot, H. M. 2000. 'Government and the colonial economies: a reply to Frost', *Australian Economic History Review*, vol. 40, no. 1, pp. 86–91.

Bradford, E. 1907. 'Prussian Railway Administration', *Annals of the American Academy of Political and Social Science*, vol. 29, no.1, pp. 66–78.

Butlin, N. G. 1959. 'Colonial socialism' in H. G. J. Aitken (ed.), *The State and Economic Growth*. New York: Social Science Research Council.

Butlin, N. G. 1964. *Investment in Australian Economic Development, 1861–1900*. Cambridge: Cambridge University Press.

Butlin, N. G., Barnard, A., and Pincus, J. J. 1982. *Government and Capitalism, Public and Private Choice in Twentieth Century Australia*. Sydney: Allen & Unwin.

Cannon, M. 1998. *That Disreputable Firm: The Inside Story of Slater & Gordon*. Melbourne: Melbourne University Press.

Clark, V. S. 1908. 'Australian economic problems. I. The railways', *Quarterly Journal of Economics*, vol. 22, no. 3, pp. 399–451.

Coghlan, T. A. 1918. *Labour and Industry in Australia: From the First Settlement in 1788 to the Establishment of the Commonwealth in 1901*. Melbourne: Macmillan of Australia.

Davidson, B. R. 1982. 'A benefit cost analysis of the New South Wales railway system', *Australian Economic History Review*, vol. 22, no. 2, pp. 127–50.

Davis, L. E. and Gallman, R. E. 2001. *Evolving Financial Markets and International Capital Flows: Britain, the Americas and Australia, 1865–1914*. Cambridge: Cambridge University Press.

Duncan, J. S. 1937. 'British railways in Argentina', *Political Science Quarterly*, vol. 52, no. 4, pp. 559–82.

Edwards, P. (ed.). 1979. *Australia through American Eyes, 1935–1945*. Brisbane: University of Queensland Press.

Eggleston, F. W. 1932. *State Socialism in Victoria*. London: PS King & Son.

Ergas, H. and Pincus, J. J. 2014. 'Infrastructure and colonial socialism' in S. Ville and G. Withers (eds.), *The Cambridge Economic History of Australia*. Cambridge, MA: Cambridge University Press.

Finer, S. E. 1952. *The Life and Times of Sir Edwin Chadwick*. London: Methuen.

French, R. S. 1994. 'Judicial approaches to economic analysis in Australia', *Review of Industrial Organization*, vol. 9, no. 5, pp. 547–68.

Frost, L. 2000. 'Government and the colonial economies: an alternative view', *Australian Economic History Review*, vol. 40, no. 1, pp. 71–85.

Hancock, W. K. 1930. *Australia*. London: Benn.

Hunter, A. (ed.). 1965. *The Economics of Australian Industry: Studies in Environment and Structure*. Melbourne: Melbourne University Press.

Industry Commission. 1991. *Rail Transport*, Report No. 13. Canberra: AGPS.

Keating, M. 1973. *The Australian Workforce, 1910–11 to 1960–61*. Canberra: Australian National University.

Kennedy, K. H. 1986. 'McCormack, William (1879–1947)' in the *Australian Dictionary of Biography*, vol. 10, Melbourne, Melbourne University Press.

Lee, R. S. 2009. *The Railways of Victoria 1854–2004*. Carlton, Victoria: Melbourne University Publishing.

MacDonagh, O. 1977. *Early Victorian Government, 1830–1870*. New York: Holmes & Meier.

Macdonald, J. 2006. *A Free Nation Deep in Debt*. Princeton, NJ: Princeton University Press.

McMartin, A. 1983. *Public Servants and Patronage: The Foundation and Rise of the New South Wales Public Service, 1786–1859*. Sydney: Sydney University Press.

Menzies, R. G. 1970. *The Measure of the Years*. Melbourne: Cassell.

Métin, A. [1901] 1977. *Socialism without Doctrine*, trans. R. Ward. Chippendale, NSW: Alternative Publishing Co-operative.

Nairn, B. 1976. 'Robinson, Sir Hercules George (1824–1897)' in the *Australian Dictionary of Biography*, vol. 6. Melbourne: Melbourne University Press.

New South Wales. 1929. *New South Wales Tramways: Report of the Commissioners*. Sydney: Government printer.

Obstfeld, M. and Taylor, A. M. 2004. *Global Capital Markets: Integration, Crisis and Growth*. Cambridge: Cambridge University Press.

O'Connor, P. G. 2005. *On Wooden Rails: Celebrating 150 Years of Work on the NSW Railways*. Sydney: Rail, Tram and Bus Union (NSW Branch).

Parkin, A. 2003. 'The states, federalism and political science: a fifty-year appraisal', *Australian Journal of Public Administration*, vol. 62, no. 2, pp. 101–12.

PC (Productivity Commission). 2008. 'Financial Performance of Government Trading Enterprises 2004–05 to 2006–07', Commission Research Paper, Canberra.

Plehwe, R. 1983. 'Political rights of Victorian public employees', *Australian Journal of Public Administration*, vol. 42, no. 3, pp. 362–75.

Proudley, R. 1987. *Circle of Influence: A History of the Gas Industry in Victoria*. Melbourne: Hargreen Publishing.

Queensland. 1929. *Queensland Railways: Report of the Commissioner for Railways for the Year Ended*. Brisbane: Government printer.

Seltzer, A. 2014. 'Labour, skills and migration' in S. Ville and G. Withers (eds.), *The Cambridge Economic History of Australia*. Cambridge, MA: Cambridge University Press.

Serle, G. 1971. *The Rush to be Rich: A History of the Colony of Victoria, 1883–1889*. Melbourne: Melbourne University Press.

South Australia. 1929. *Annual Report of the South Australian Railways*. Adelaide: Government printer.

Tasmania. 1929. *Report on the Working in the Government Railways*. Hobart: Government printer.

Victoria. 1929. *Report of the Victorian Railway Commissioners*. Melbourne: Government printer.

Western Australia. 1929. *Report on the Working of the Government Railways, Tramways and Electricity Supply*. Perth: Government printer.

Wettenhall, R. L. 1961. *Railway Management and Politics in Victoria, 1856–1906*. Canberra: Royal Institute of Public Administration.

Wettenhall, R. L. 1987. *Public Enterprise and National Development: Selected Essays*. Canberra: Royal Australian Institute of Public Administration (ACT Division).

Zalums, E. 1975. *A Bibliography of South Australian Royal Commissions, Select Committees of Parliament, and Boards of Inquiry, 1857–1970*. Adelaide, South Australia: The Flinders University.

10

We Must All Be Capitalists Now

The Strange Story of Compulsory Superannuation in Australia

Adam Creighton

Australians dwell on their nation's sporting triumphs, but few realize how much their country punches above its weight in funds management. With just 0.3 per cent of the world's population, Australia had almost 7 per cent of the pension assets in Organisation for Economic Co-operation and Development (OECD) countries in 2014, a bigger share than any country bar the UK and USA (OECD 2015). In stark contrast to arrangements in other developed nations, where, in return for higher taxation, governments typically provide a guaranteed retirement income linked to individuals' earnings, Australians' incomes in retirement increasingly depend on the skill with which they have grown their mandatory 'superannuation' savings in their working years. The reform linked the fortunes of ordinary people to national and global investment markets, supercharging both Australians' financial assets and the industry that manages them.

While eighteen of thirty-four OECD countries now have some form of mandatory private saving scheme, these typically complement government-funded, earnings-related schemes or provide 'defined benefits' to retirees, where pension providers bear the investment risk. Apart from Mexico and Chile, Australia is the only OECD nation where compulsory and privately managed defined contribution (DC) accounts, beyond a means-tested flat-rate pension, are the extent of government intervention in retirement incomes.[1]

[1] President G. W. Bush, a long-time supporter of individual private saving, failed to convince Congress in 2005 to divert a share of Americans' social security contributions into personal private savings accounts.

Embodying elements that appeal to both the right and left—individual responsibility and state paternalism—and emerging alongside growing fiscal and demographic pressures, Australian superannuation has come to be seen as a policy triumph. 'One of the finest examples of progressive social policy that a nation can introduce', declared Fiona Reynolds, head of the Australian Institute of Superannuation Trustees (St Anne 2012, p. xi). A former editor of the *Australian Financial Review*, David Love, wrote that compulsory superannuation was among 'the most sweeping and beneficial set of changes in financial policy, financial engineering, and social policy attempted in any democracy during the 20th century' (Love 2008, p.1). Mercer's 2014 Global Pension Index put Australia second, behind only Denmark, in a comparison of the 'sustainability', 'integrity', and 'adequacy' of twenty-five countries' retirement systems. Endorsed by the World Bank as early as 1994 (World Bank 1994), Australia's superannuation scheme is seen as a model for countries anxious to avoid the fiscal burdens associated with ageing populations and pay-as-you-go social security. Similar privately-managed DC systems were rolled out in Argentina, Bolivia, Colombia, Hungary, and Poland in the 1990s.

Despite this acclaim, the efficiency and fairness of superannuation have come under increasing scrutiny. This chapter explains the nature, impact, and origin of Australia's superannuation system and critically assesses it against its claimed benefits. It concludes reform of its defects has proceeded at glacial pace, in part because two powerful vested interests—the trade union movement and the financial services sector—form a united front against any changes that would threaten their influence or fees.

10.1 The 'Pillars' of Australia's Retirement-Income System

English-speaking countries share many institutional similarities owing to their common law British heritage. But retirement policy is emphatically not one of them. National retirement income systems are typically classified using the World Bank's 'pillar' framework (World Bank 1994). 'First pillars', funded from general taxation, are designed to alleviate poverty and are either means-tested or paid universally (regardless of means). 'Second pillars' mandate contributions to defined benefit (DB) or DC funds, which can be publicly or privately managed, and aim at replacing an individual's work–life income in retirement. This is where most of the international variation is observed. 'Third pillars' are tax concessions for voluntary saving specifically for retirement.

When it comes to retirement systems, among OECD nations, Australia has most in common with Chile and Mexico. These three countries stand out for having means-tested public pensions complemented by mandatory *privately* managed DC accounts.[2] By contrast, the USA, Canada, and UK operate publicly-funded DB schemes, structurally similar to those in Europe and Japan, while New Zealand and Ireland have no second pillar schemes to speak of. Some countries, such as Switzerland and Sweden, have public DB and privately-managed DC schemes operating in tandem.

While superannuation receives more publicity, Australia's first pillar 'age pension' is the backbone of its retirement income system. Introduced in 1909, it is available to men and women from age 65 regardless of employment history.[3] A generous and easily satisfied means test (the value of the principal residence is not included, and couples can have up to almost $1 million before they are ineligible for even a part-pension) has seen coverage balloon from around a third of retirees in 1910 to around 70 per cent or 2.4 million people in 2014, of which around 60 per cent receive the maximum fortnightly payment. Rates are periodically increased so couples receive around 42 per cent of male average weekly earnings and singles two-thirds of that amount.

While means-tested or 'targeted' basic pensions reduce the incentive to work and discourage saving, they do slash the fiscal cost of retirement provision. Thus in 2009 Australia's old-age pension amounted to 3.5 per cent of gross domestic product (GDP), compared to an average of 7.8 per cent of public expenditure on pensions across the OECD.[4] Only Iceland, Mexico, and Korea spent less. The pension makes up around 10 per cent of total federal government outlays compared to around a quarter or more in France, Germany, and Italy. But while Australia's public expenditure on retirement provision as a share of GDP is relatively meagre, the value of other concessions to pensioners is surpassed only in Japan, Denmark, Norway, and Sweden. Indeed, the value of such concessions in Australia –which include significant discounts on medication, local and state taxes, and public transport—are the world's largest as a share of expenditure on retirement provision. It is well known in Australia that retirees arrange their affairs to receive a part-pension in order to access such concessions.

The second pillar in Australia was only firmly laid in 1992 when it was legislated to compel all employers to divert a rising share of their employees' earnings—currently 9.5 per cent—into privately managed, individual accounts that could not be accessed until retirement. Thus superannuation coverage, once the preserve mainly of public servants and senior white-collar workers, jumped from about 40 per cent of the workforce in the 1970s to

[2] Denmark and Israel are almost in the same group, but their pillar one pensions are universal rather than means-tested.

[3] The eligibility age is scheduled to rise progressively to 67 years by 2023.

[4] Such comparisons do not include the value of compulsory private savings, which in Australia's case come to around 5% of GDP a year. Novak (2014) argues this practice understates the cost of compulsory saving and the size of government.

62 per cent in 1988 (ABS 2009). By 2007 94 per cent of employees were covered (91 per cent of the workforce—contributions are not compulsory for the self-employed). By 2015 superannuation assets, spread across more than 31 million individual accounts, had swelled to more than $2 trillion, equivalent to 125 per cent of Australia's GDP.

10.2 The History and Political Economy of 'Super'

Historical accident, political pragmatism, and Australia's unique industrial system have paved the way for and sustained superannuation rather than deliberate agitation by social reformers. Social security in the USA in 1935 and earnings-related state pensions in the UK in 1948, by contrast, arose from radical policy agendas, prompted by the devastation of the Great Depression, which envisaged a greater role for government. Despite multiple attempts to replicate such policies in Australia, public interference in retirement saving and provision was remarkably minimal until the 1980s.

While some government instrumentalities (such as railways) and some state governments had superannuation for their employees, the story of super really begins with the conservative Bruce-Page government's setting up of a Royal Commission in 1923 into prospects for an Australian equivalent of the UK's 1911 national insurance legislation. 'One of the main causes of industrial unrest is the ever-present dread which haunts the workers of the privation and suffering which will be brought upon his dependents in the event of sickness, unemployment and old-age', the prime minister said in 1925.[5] Unlike Britain's scheme, Bruce's subsequent 1928 legislation envisaged benefits payable in relation to old age as well as sickness and disability. But his bill failed under heavy opposition from Friendly Societies and the Labor Party, and his government was defeated in 1929 (for unrelated matters). Labor was adamant any additional government support would be payable by higher income earners through general taxation, not via contributions from workers themselves.

Conservative Australian interest in such schemes did not die with Bruce's government. President Roosevelt's New Deal included old-age social security, reinforcing the global trend towards contributory schemes. 'Experience in Great Britain and in other countries over many years has proved that much can be done towards solving the problems which confront the worker as a result of ill-health, unemployment and old age by the institution of a system

[5] <http://electionspeeches.moadoph.gov.au/speeches/1925-stanley-bruce> (accessed 20 November 2015).

of National Insurance', said conservative Prime Minister Joseph Lyons in 1937.[6] But the greater impetus was fiscal rather than ideological. Old-age pensions expenditures had been growing rapidly as the number of recipients and life expectancy increased. By 1930 pensions had come to absorb almost all the £11.1 million of federal direct taxation revenue; by 1935 they absorbed almost 34 per cent of all government revenue (Watts 1980).

Under heavy pressure from officials to make pension and health expenses contributory, the Lyons government in 1938 introduced, in the words of its Treasurer, 'one of the most far-reaching schemes of social reform that has been presented to the Federal Parliament' (Casey 1938, p. 793). It would oblige workers earning less than £7 a week (around half the working population at the time) to pay 3 shillings a week (2 shillings for women), or a little over 2 per cent of their wages, into a national insurance fund that would pay sickness benefits, medical benefits, and 'superannuation pensions'.[7] 'The only effective basis for ensuring the protection of the workers is on the principle of compulsory and contributory insurance', Treasurer Richard Casey said.

The legislation passed but was never implemented. Once again it met strong opposition from doctors, the Labor Party, and Friendly Societies,[8] fearful of being crowded out. An unprecedented letter-writing campaign against the proposal erupted across the east coast of Australia (Huf 2015; Coleman et al. 2006). By March 1939, with war approaching in Europe, the government postponed the scheme indefinitely.

'From 1937 the labour movement had campaigned against the contributory principle as an "impost on workers" rights and an abuse of the minimum wage', notes Huf. Labor's opposition to forcing the lower paid to fund expanded social benefits would fade, however. The new Curtin government imposed savage tax increases in 1943, justified by war expenses and to create a National Welfare Fund that would provide old age, sickness, maternity, and unemployment benefits. The number of low- to middle-income earners (on less than £500 a year) liable to pay income tax jumped by a factor of fifteen times over the four years by 1943. 'The crowning irony in hindsight... was the ALP's role in imposing far heavier taxation on far more low-income earners than any UAP [conservative] government would have believed possible or prudent', argues Watts (1980, p. 187). The Fund provided scope for contributory DB pensions to develop, but it ossified under subsequent governments into a mere accounting device and was abolished in 1985.

[6] <http://electionspeeches.moadoph.gov.au/speeches/1937-joseph-lyons> (accessed 20 November 2015).

[7] In terms of retirement incomes, the scheme amounted to an exemption of all insured persons of eligible age from the then considerable means testing of the ordinary age pension.

[8] Voluntary, civic organizations with missions to pool resources to help the needy.

For the thirty years after the war occupational superannuation plans (benefiting from long-standing tax concessions) grew rapidly among public sector and, more haphazardly, among private sector workers. Australia was the only major English-speaking country not to have an earnings-related contributory scheme during this period. Thwarted twice already, the conservative side of politics, represented by the newly created Liberal Party, in power from 1949 until 1972, gave up on the idea. The Whitlam Labor government set up a National Superannuation Committee of Inquiry in 1973, whose 1979 recommendations gave a third and final endorsement to an earnings-related public pension scheme. But by that time Labor had been voted out emphatically, and the conservative Fraser government ignored the endorsement.

Meanwhile trade unions, peeved that higher pensions remained the preserve of the higher paid, started agitating for superannuation for trade unionists. The Federated Storemen and Packers Union, inspired by earlier waterfront successes, won employer-paid superannuation for its members in 1979 (St Anne 2012, p. 12). By September 1985 superannuation had become a central objective of the Australian Council of Trade Unions (ACTU), the peak organizing body of the union movement. Australia's deteriorating economic conditions—inflation and unemployment were each near 9 per cent in the mid-1980s—had convinced the newly elected Hawke Labor government, and a more economically sophisticated union leadership, that limiting cash-in-hand pay rises would help control inflation (Love 2008, p. 92).

Compulsory superannuation emerged in a deal between a Labor government and Australia's trade union movement, which resulted in half of workers' 6 per cent pay rise in 1986 diverted into special retirement funds managed in trust by representatives of trade unions and employer associations. In that year, the government and the ACTU successfully convinced Australia's Conciliation and Arbitration Commission (CAC), an industrial tribunal, that such amounts should be diverted into industry superannuation funds. Employer groups appealed, but the High Court agreed superannuation was an 'industrial matter', foreshadowing its inclusion of hundreds of 'award' agreements that governed the pay and conditions across Australian enterprises and industry.[9] Australia's unusual and highly centralized industrial relations system was able to foster the spread of superannuation across vast swathes of the workforce without parliamentary involvement. It was the then-renamed Industrial Relations Commission's rejection of the ACTU–government claim for a further increase in superannuation in 1991 that prompted the Hawke government to legislate in 1992.

[9] The CAC decision covered only workers subject to federal, rather than state, awards.

The elevation of superannuation from obscurity to the forefront of national reform in the early 1980s was thanks largely to the efforts and collaboration of Bill Kelty and Paul Keating, secretary of the ACTU and federal Treasurer, respectively. Kelty and Keating, visionary, intelligent, persuasive men, wanted to leave their mark on Australia's industrial framework: 'Keating dominated the cabinet and Kelty dominated the unions; their alliance reinforced their individual power... they formed an enduring partnership which shaped Australia's economic path' (Kelly 2008, p. 281).

Superannuation was still controversial. 'We're back in power and the first thing we do is start taking money off workers for some bastard offspring of the institutions of capitalism', said one union sceptic (Love 2008, p. 91). Meanwhile the Liberal Opposition, while supportive of the freer trade and financial deregulatory agenda of the Hawke government, opposed introduction of universal superannuation. It opposed what it saw as a paternalist encroachment on people's earnings that handed significant power to union-dominated industry funds.

That two conservative governments had tried and failed to introduce a European-style publicly funded retirement income, while the Labor Party succeeded in instituting a privately managed one based on individual accounts is a great irony of Australian history. How could a party that once spurned contributory insurance have so heartily endorsed a new privatized version? Former Labor leaders, nursing an atavistic disdain for finance, would have loathed the implicit reduction in workers' take-home pay and implicit subsidy to the financial services sector. But the Labor Party of the 1980s had changed. Under new leadership it had dropped its socialist ideals, and, like its New Zealand counterpart, absorbed the teaching of free-market economics—a particularly urgent lesson given the exigencies of the 1980s. Labor was more comfortable with investors and appreciated the benefits that would flow to Australians from freer global trade and investment.

Superannuation was also a way to bolster the waning power of trade unions, the primary financial and organizational supporters of the Labor Party. The diminution of manufacturing in the economy, among other reasons, had seen trade union membership steadily dwindle from around 60 per cent in the 1950s. Thirty years later only 45 per cent of workers were members, and only 17 per cent (12 per cent in the private sector) in 2013. Industry superannuation funds, with half of their directors union-appointed and half chosen by employer associations, offered union officials opportunities for lucrative postings and platforms to influence the investment of hundreds of billions of dollars. The ten largest industry funds managed $233 billion in 2014. The potential for conflicts of interest of directors, given competing loyalties to unions, employers, and members, has underpinned calls for greater transparency (Staley 2010). Industry funds invest twice as much (16 per cent) of their assets in infrastructure and property, sectors with relatively unionized workforces, as retail funds.

10.3 Australia's Super System Today

10.3.1 *Accounts*

Australian employers are currently obliged to direct 9.5 per cent of employees' earnings up to $203,240 a year into an eligible superannuation fund of the employee's choice.[10] If an employee doesn't choose a fund, their employer will for them, guided in some cases by industrial agreements. Accounts are fully vested with the individual account holders (although courts can split accounts in case of divorce), may be consolidated with other accounts, and are bequeathed at death.

This arrangement is known in Australia as the Superannuation Guarantee (SG). It is effected via the Superannuation Guarantee Charge Act 1992, which imposes on employers who do not comply a tax that that exceeds the guarantee liability.[11] The SG is a minimum; state and federal public servants and university lecturers typically enjoy SG rates of 15 per cent or more, and most employers allow their staff to make extra contributions. In practice, the SG rate for most workers is 8.075 per cent because all contributions are taxed at flat rate of 15 per cent.

Over the year to June 2015 employers paid around $20 billion every three months into superannuation funds on their employees' behalf, equivalent to around 10.5 per cent of the national wage bill. While employers are formally obliged to make mandatory contributions (at least for staff earning more than $450 a month), in the long run the incidence of compulsory superannuation falls entirely on workers, reducing their 'take-home' pay. 'The increase in the employee's retirement income is achieved by reducing their standard of living before retirement', concluded the Rudd government's 2010 inquiry into the taxation system.

During 2015 individuals added a further $5 billion and $6 billion a quarter to their accounts. Generous tax concessions, which encourage workers to make contributions to superannuation from their pre-tax income, encourage contributions above the minimum rate. The total value of voluntary and SG contributions cannot exceed $30,000 annually for those under 49 years of age, and $35,000 for those 50 and over (designed to help tardy savers 'catch up' as

[10] Contribution rates are 10% and 6.5% in Chile and Mexico, respectively.

[11] In 2011 Roy Morgan, an Australian polling firm, challenged the validity of the Act, arguing that because its purpose was not to raise funds for general revenue it could not be sustained under the Commonwealth's taxation power. The High Court dismissed the case, arguing a law does not cease being a tax because raising revenue is secondary to its purpose.

they approach retirement). A maximum of $540,000 over three years can be contributed after tax. Concessional taxation necessitates such caps.

The superannuation savings of the vast majority of Australians, comprising around 29.7 million accounts and $1.26 trillion in early 2015, are held in one or more of almost 300 competing funds. These vary considerably in size, origin, and investment approach; but all are trusts, regulated by the Australian Prudential Regulation Authority (APRA). Under the Superannuation Industry Supervision Act 1993, trustees must manage the accumulations in the best interest of fund members, with the sole purpose of maximizing their ultimate retirement incomes. The trustees typically invest in domestic and foreign shares, bonds, cash, and property, on the advice of investment managers and asset consultants.

'Industry' funds, which have trustees drawn from trade unions and employer associations from a particular industry, managed around $437 billion across forty-four funds in 2015.[12] Almost 150 'retail' funds, which are for-profit and typically established by large financial institutions, managed $546 billion. Larger funds dominate—in 2014 the biggest industry and retail funds, respectively, were Australian Super ($64.9 billion) and AMP ($58.2 billion). A recent inquiry found around 80 per cent of these APRA-regulated superannuation funds held only around 20 per cent of assets. Public sector and corporate funds, which are not open to the general public, managed the balance of the APRA-regulated funds.

Industry and retail funds compete with each other and with what are known as 'self-managed superannuation funds' (SMSFs), which have grown rapidly to become the largest part of the market. As their name suggests, the members of a SMSF are also its trustees. Each such trust may have no more than four members. They appeal to older, wealthier, and financially astute Australians who want to personally oversee investment of their retirement savings. They report to the Australian Taxation Office rather than APRA; their total assets by 2015 had more than quadrupled over ten years to just under $600 billion spread across 550,000 accounts (each typically with husband and wife members). SMSF average balances of around $1 million dwarf averages of under $40,000 in industry and retail funds.

For Australians born before 1960 superannuation savings can be accessed at age 55, rising to age 60 for individuals born in 1964 and after.[13] In 2012, average superannuation balances at retirement were around $200,000 for men, around twice that of women. Withdrawals and earnings are tax free for

[12] In 2015 the government moved to ensure one-third of directors of all such public offer superannuation funds were 'independent', part of a push to apply the same governance standards to super funds as those that prevail for listed companies.

[13] Early access to maximum value of $10,000 is permitted in cases of severe financial hardship.

superannuants aged 60 and over, and they can be accessed as a lump sum, drawn down, annuitized, or some combination thereof. Scope to take superannuation benefits as lump sums has been subject to consistent criticism. But the Productivity Commission (PC) has found only 16 per cent of Australian superannuation benefits by value were taken as lump sums in 2012 and 'little evidence to suggest they were being squandered'. And the median size of lump sums was $20,000, reflecting an overwhelming preference for income streams among superannuants with sizeable savings (PC 2015).[14]

Most superannuation savings convert to account-based pension products, where retirees draw regular incomes from their accumulated savings. Assets attributable to DB members—who by definition receive an indexed income stream—have dwindled to only 11 per cent of super assets. To stop funds being used as tax shelters, the government stipulates annual minimum 'draw down' rates, rising from 4 per cent for under 65s to 14 per cent for retirees aged 95 and over. Superannuation monies bequeathed to non-dependents are taxed at a flat rate of 17 per cent, otherwise they are tax free. Around 31 per cent of all superannuation assets in 2014 were in account-based pensions—a share due to rise to 38 per cent by 2030 as the population ages—and of these around 95 per cent were in account-based pensions. Annuities, which would provide insurance against individuals outliving their savings, are not popular. Australia's annuity assets amount to about 0.3 per cent of annual GDP compared with 28.8 per cent in Japan, 15.4 per cent in the USA, and more than 40 per cent in some European countries.

10.3.2 *Taxation*

Australia is also distinguished by the unique, and unfortunate, way it taxes superannuation: contributions and earnings are taxed at 15 per cent while most benefits accessed after age 60 are tax free. No other OECD country follows this approach; instead, governments typically exempt contributions and earnings from tax, and later tax withdrawal of benefits at ordinary income tax rates. This is the better approach. It diminishes the incentive to take tax-concessional lump sums (as a means of avoiding the progressive taxation of income), provides a psychological benefit to up-front contributions, and maximizes the ultimate accumulation. 'There may [also] be social benefit from government sharing the investment risk of individual contributors under a DC scheme', argue Bateman et al. (2001).

[14] It found 90% of retirees with superannuation balances up to $10,000 took a lump sum, but only 10% of retirees with super assets between $200,000 and $300,000, and barely any thereafter.

The highly concessional taxation of Australian superannuation is of long standing. The 1915 law establishing federal income tax provided for full tax deductibility of employer contributions to superannuation, and exempted super funds from earnings taxation. If, on retirement, benefits were taken as lump sums, only 5 per cent of the sum was taxed at personal income tax rates.[15] But in 1988 this architecture was changed radically. Facing a difficult budget, the then Treasurer Paul Keating imposed a tax of 15 per cent on contributions and earnings, and lowered benefit taxes to zero for lump sums up to a moderate indexed amount. This dramatically improved the short-term position of the budget, but at significant long-term fiscal cost (given the ageing of the population).[16] While the taxation of benefits was removed and simplified by a subsequent government in 2006, this basic architecture remains.

10.3.3 *Investment Risk*

Another unusual, but not necessarily disadvantageous, aspect of Australian superannuation is the large weighting to more volatile assets. A recent Mercer survey of eleven major pension systems found in 2014 a 'higher exposure to equity investments in the Anglo-Saxon markets', especially in Australia where equities made up 50 per cent of assets, more than any other country, except for Hong Kong. Australia had 68 per cent of pension funds invested in 'growth' assets, again the highest, while the European countries with retirement systems most similar to Australia's, Denmark and the Netherlands, had less than 24 per cent (Mercer 2014). Cash and fixed interest investments were the biggest component of every OECD nation's pension funds, except the USA and Finland, but make up less than a third of total Australian pension fund assets (OECD 2014). Apart from a prohibition on leveraged investing, Australian superannuation trustees have no more than a fiduciary duty to manage investments prudently, which goes some way to explaining the contrast. Other jurisdictions often impose restrictions: Mexican pension funds need to invest at least 65 per cent in government bonds, while in Denmark at least 60 per cent of pension assets must be 'low risk'. Also, the relative rarity of DB schemes in Australia means trustees do not feel compelled to invest mainly in less volatile assets.[17]

[15] In 1983 a progressive and higher tax on lump sums (with a maximum rate of 30%) was introduced, dulling the incentive to take benefits as lump sums.

[16] One subsequent Labor leader told the author this change in tax may have been the biggest strategic tax blunder of this generation given the relative growth of funds in the pension phase.

[17] Australia's relatively small corporate bond market and a company tax system that provides refundable credits to shareholders also add to the appeal of equities.

The freedom afforded fund managers in Australia means funds may not be managed respectfully of members' attitudes to risk. Indeed, SMSFs are managed more conservatively than funds managed on behalf of members, suggesting individuals might prefer less risky portfolios. The latest, 2014, data show less than 25 per cent of SMSF funds were invested in shares (0.5 per cent were invested in foreign shares compared to 22 per cent for APRA-regulated funds), while 30 per cent in cash and term deposits. Certainly, real net returns in Australia have been more volatile than elsewhere. Australian funds topped the OECD's international league table in 2013, returning a real net return of 10.2 per cent, second only to the USA (11.7 per cent). But over the five years to 2013, the average annualized real return was 2.1 per cent, the fifth lowest among the twenty-seven OECD countries.

While individuals bear the investment risk in DC schemes in contrast to DB schemes, the political risks to retirement benefits are far greater in the latter. The lack of a clear link between contributions and ultimate benefits gives governments scope to alter the real value of benefits. In the 1960s and 1970s, during which time consumer prices rose around 300 per cent, the UK government failed to index a public DB scheme and has repeatedly watered down pension commitments since (Bozio et al. 2010). Recent travails of Greece provide a starker example. In 2012 a Greek on average earnings entering the workforce could expect to retire on a public pension equal to 110 per cent of his final salary, the highest replacement ratio in the world (Antolin et al. 2012). As of 2015 there seemed little prospect of this undertaking being fulfilled.

10.4 A Costly Remedy for a Manufactured Problem

> Once it becomes the recognized duty of the public to provide for the extreme needs of old age . . . irrespective of whether the individuals could and ought to have made provision themselves . . . it seems an obvious corollary to compel them to insure (or otherwise provide) against those common hazards of life. (Hayek [1960] 2006, p. 249)

Frederick Hayek's *Constitution of Liberty* provided a cogent case for compulsory saving, years before any such schemes existed. Hayek argued that, in a democracy, the bulk of people would recognize that they could vote themselves pensions (raised via economically damaging taxation), thereby systematically under-saving and shifting the burden of their future upkeep onto other taxpayers. Compulsorily saving would be an antidote, dramatically curbing the need for publicly-funded retirement pensions. So a measure that in appearance was paternalist could be, in reality, a hard-headed savings measure. But as superannuation has matured, its practical flaws have cast doubt on both the fiscal and paternalistic arguments that chiefly justify it.

10.4.1 *Misguided Savings*

In 2015 *The Australian*, a national right-of-centre broadsheet newspaper, editorialized in favour of compulsory superannuation 'as a way to improve public finances and keep taxes lower by reducing pressure on pensions'.[18] While this is the most popular supporting argument, the effect of superannuation is the exact opposite. In short, the forgone revenue as a result of the tax concessions for superannuation contributions and earnings dwarfs the savings in age pension outlays. Far from the Hayekian ideal of replacing the age pension, projections show 67 per cent of retired Australians would still be receiving it in 2053, down from 70 per cent in 2015—after what would be more than 60 years of compulsory saving!

'An increase in the superannuation guarantee would . . . have a net cost to government revenue even over the long term', said the 2010 tax inquiry, explaining that the resulting boost to private saving was more than offset by a fall in public sector saving. The forgone revenue of the two main tax concessions—a flat 15 per cent tax on earnings and contributions—amounted to $27.3 billion in the 2015 financial year according to Australia's Treasury, offset by superannuation tax of $6.2 billion.[19] The Australian Institute of Actuaries, in its submission to the tax inquiry, estimated this net cost to the federal government budget would rise from 1.1 per cent of GDP to more than 2 per cent over the next thirty-five years.

Naturally, this net budget cost induces extra savings that reduce the pension payments some Australians receive, but not, in aggregate, by enough to make the concessions worthwhile. 'This is primarily because the structure of the tax expenditure in superannuation results in most of it being directed to high income earners who are never likely to draw the Age Pension', the Institute said. Almost 60 per cent of the concessions by value accrue to income earners in the top income quintile according to the government's 2015 financial inquiry.[20] This is also the case because of the generosity of the age pension eligibility test, which means extra savings in superannuation have little impact on pension payments. In 2015 the government sought to tighten

[18] *The Australian*, 8 July 2015.

[19] Calculating forgone income is difficult because of alternative opportunities to minimize tax such as 'negative gearing' of property.

[20] Australia's income tax rates rise from 19% for earnings above $18,400 to 49% for income above $180,000, implying a significantly larger superannuation tax discount for taxpayers in the top tax bracket.

the eligibility criteria by reducing the level of financial assets at which the age pension would be entirely withdrawn.[21]

But it would be naive to think Hayek's ideal of a vanishing pension, thanks to compulsory saving, will ever become a reality. The actuarial value of the age pension—which is in effect a lifetime annuity, having guaranteed payments indexed to real wages—in 2015 was a little less than $500,000 and almost $700,000 for a couple.[22] These sums are broadly equivalent to the superannuation savings an average wage earner could accrue over forty years of work, assuming reasonable returns. To propose a change in the means test that, in effect, compels ordinary workers to amass their own pensions rather than, as now, have them paid mainly from taxation that falls mainly on higher income earners, would be politically courageous indeed.

10.4.2 *Excessive Overheads*

Superannuation is not costly only to government. It is also blighted by high investment and administration costs that drastically impede its efficiency. Whatever their other problems, publicly-managed schemes are relatively cheap to operate because collection, administration, and investment of contributions can occur through the pre-existing centralized machineries of the state. Privately-managed schemes do not benefit from the same economies of scale, and have greater incentives to obfuscate and multiply costs.

In their 2003 review, Drew and Stanford found an 'inefficient, low return and high cost' superannuation system wracked by 'severe principal-agent problems'. Since then, the total expense ratio has fallen gradually from 1.37 per cent to 1.12 per cent or around $20 billion in 2013, a ratio that remains around three times the median OECD average level. For instance, the average asset-weighted cost of US 401(k) plans was 71 basis points in 2006. The largest US fund, the Thrift Saving Plan, is managed for less than 5 basis points. The Grattan Institute argues fees have absorbed a quarter of gross fund earnings since 2004, and trimmed typical retirement balances by around 20 per cent (Minifie 2014). Facilitating lower fees is 'the largest single opportunity for microeconomic reform in the economy', it says. A 2014 government inquiry into the financial system found fees had fallen by less than half of what they should have given average fund size grew from $260 million to $3.3 billion over the decade to 2013.

Lack of member interest has limited competition. Surveys routinely show fewer than 5 per cent of people change funds in a given year for reasons other

[21] For a couple the sum would fall from around $1.1 million to $823,000 (a level still far above the average for retirees).

[22] The value is higher for women because they have longer life expectancies at retirement age.

than changing jobs.[23] Recent surveys show almost a third of Australians would rather be given $200 in cash than receive $2,000 in superannuation. Meanwhile, almost $20 billion in superannuation monies are 'lost', and almost a third of Australians had two or more superannuation accounts, according to Westpac's 2013 and 2014 'Lost Super' surveys.

Reflecting mainstream economic theory, there has been little evidence that funds charging higher fees have outperformed the market by a sufficient margin over a long period.[24] Yet around 80 per cent of Australian superannuation assets are managed actively, around double the share in other advanced countries. 'Asset consultants and funds managers vehemently oppose the use of passive management of equity', note Drew and Stanford (2003).

Concerned about the impact of fees, the government required, from 2013, contributions from employees who did not choose a fund to be paid into a new class of 'My Super' funds. These were meant to be 'no frills' funds making greater use of indexing to keep costs down. Since establishment, their expense ratios have fallen to 80 basis points, with projections showing further modest falls in coming years.

What has clearly been a boon for the financial services industry has also been a significant distortion of the economy. Morris (forthcoming) laments 'rent extraction by private sector managers on a massive scale' in Australia, pointing out that the share of the workforce involved in financial services has swelled to 3.7 per cent of Australia's workforce, more than Britain's 3.5 per cent, even though the latter is a global finance hub. 'The greatest gift Paul Keating ever gave was to the finance sector, which has made consistently super normal profits, in part on the back of ordinary people's savings', a former Liberal Party leader in the early 1990s told *The Australian* (10 May 2014).

10.4.3 *Insufficient Saving*

Next to fiscal probity, a wish to boost saving both at the individual and national level has become the main argument to justify superannuation. Here the policy has had more success, if still mixed. In common with other Anglophone countries, household saving ratios trended sharply downwards from the 1970s, falling in Australia from a peak of around 20 per cent in 1975 to zero in 2003, before jumping and levelling out around 10 per cent since the onset of the global financial crisis (Kirchner 2012). At the same time, Australian

[23] Around a fifth of workers still cannot choose their own superannuation fund because of industrial agreements.

[24] Economists such as William Sharpe and Eugene Fama have demonstrated the problems with so-called active fund management.

household debt ballooned from 50 per cent of disposable income in the early 1990s to 150 per cent. Nevertheless, most econometric studies conclude that superannuation has increased household saving. An oft-cited study estimates the economy-wide saving offset at just 38 cents in the dollar (Connolly and Kohler 2004). In 2011 the Treasury estimated national saving was 1.5 per cent of GDP higher than it would have been (Gruen and Soding 2011).

But boosting saving does not necessarily justify superannuation. In an open economy like Australia's, with access to global capital markets, domestic savings need not govern domestic investment. It may be argued that concerns about high current account deficits and falling savings rates were always misplaced (see Kirchner 2012). High current account deficits, a supposed result of 'too little' domestic saving, could in fact welcome signs of strong foreign demand to invest locally.

And lifting saving is not necessarily fair either. The fact that the legal liability of the 'guaranteed' superannuation contributions falls on employers obscures the incidence of compulsory superannuation. With an elastic supply of capital, the economics of the incidence is clear: the burden falls on employees, just as with a payroll tax paid by employers. Any extra saving therefore arises largely as a result of lower take-home pay for low- to middle-income earners, who cannot easily reduce other saving.

Notwithstanding the likely aggregate boost to overall saving, a popular belief in a 'savings gap' in retirement underpins calls to lift the SG rate further. In 2013 the supposed shortfall for the current working-age population was \$727 billion or \$67,000 per person, according to one widely quoted periodic study sponsored by the Financial Services Council. Yet such analyses typically ignore assets beyond superannuation, such as housing, equity in business, other financial assets, and expected bequests (Rothman 2011). It also neglects the fact that several categories of expenses are typically absent in retirement: including looking after children, commuting to work, and mortgage payments.

In fact, the combination of the age pension, the SG, and other assets are currently producing replacement rates between 50 per cent and 65 per cent, with the lower percentages applicable to higher income earners for whom the means-tested age pension is a smaller share of future income. These rates are already around in the middle range of those found in OECD countries, where, in 2011, typical replacement rates varied from 110 per cent in Greece to 30 per cent in Ireland (OECD 2014). But they are projected to rise to 80 per cent or more over the next twenty-five years.

'None of these replacement rates assume any contribution to spending in retirement from reverse mortgages or part time paid work', notes Rothman (2011, p. 21). It is revealing that potential income from the largest component of retirees' wealth—their principal residence—is entirely excluded even from the more realistic attempts to estimate preparedness for costs in retirement. Even if some people systematically under-save, a one-size-fits-all compulsory saving rate ignores the naturally wide variation in personal circumstances, work habits, and consumption preference throughout the population.

10.5 The Current Outlook

On departing politics in 1996, former Labor leader Paul Keating was adamant the SG rate should increase to 15 per cent, and furious that the subsequent Howard government capped it at 9 per cent. By then the Liberal Party had developed an ambivalent relationship with superannuation. As a tyro politician in 1995, Tony Abbott, a later Liberal Prime Minister, famously declared superannuation to be 'one of the biggest con jobs ever foisted by government on the Australian people'(Abbott 1995, p. 1574). But the system has become politically difficult to unwind: Labor has diligently fostered the illusion that superannuation contributions were a costless 'extra' rather than forgone wages, making superannuation popular among workers.[25] At the same time, the traditional donors and supporters of the Liberal Party—the financial services industry—began benefiting handsomely, extracting billions in fees in an environment where compulsion severely blunted price competition.

Perhaps uniquely, superannuation has united two of the most powerful, and traditionally opposed, vested interests in Australia—the trade union movement and the financial services sector—a fact that should ensure its continued expansion. A growing array of lobby groups has emerged, often funded indirectly by unions or fund managers, to advocate and stress the supposed national and personal benefits that flow from expanding and maintaining superannuation.[26]

It is no surprise, then, that the Rudd Labor government, in 2010, explicitly ignored the Treasury's advice not to lift the SG further (because of the added burden on lower-income earners' take-home pay and fiscal cost), and legislated a gradual increase to 12 per cent by 2019. Equally, the subsequent conservative Abbott government has only delayed the increase until 2025, and said little about superannuation fees.

Successive governments have only tinkered at the edges of superannuation since 1992. Government 'co-contributions', subsidies for low-income earners, and tax surcharges have come and gone; contribution limits have shifted

[25] This became especially blatant in 2010, when the Rudd Labor government consciously linked the projected revenues from a new mining tax with the legislated increase in the SG.

[26] The Association of Superannuation Funds, Industry Funds Network, the Financial Services Council, the Australian Institute of Superannuation Trustees, and the SMSF Association are among the more prominent.

while governance standards have been tweaked here and there. What might have been a significant change—introduction of fund choice for most employees in 2005—has failed in practice, given the tiny share of people who bother to choose.[27] This certainly is not for want of choice: in 2014 the 194 biggest APRA-regulated superannuation funds all together offered almost 44,000 different investment options.

Rather, the salient trends evident from the early 1990s have continued: the value of superannuation assets has grown faster than national economic output and SMSFs have outpaced the growth of other sectors as wealthier households escape the high costs of APRA-regulated funds. Retail and industry funds have continued their battle for market share, while corporate and DB funds have dwindled. At the same time, Australian households, especially those nearing retirement age, have become more vulnerable to outcomes in financial markets (whether they realize it or not).

This is likely to continue. The Labor Party is committed to increasing the SG and making the taxation of superannuation earnings more progressive. The Coalition plans to strip back the significant competitive advantages afforded to industry funds and reform their governance. Currently, where new employees do not nominate a superannuation fund (and the vast, uninterested, bulk do not), employers are obliged to direct their SG contributions to funds specified in one of the 122 awards. Almost 90 per cent of these were industry funds in 2014, which therefore enjoyed the lion's share of $9 billion in default superannuation contributions, according to a 2015 estimate by the Financial Services Council. In 2015 a bill to ensure a third of industry fund directors were 'independent' was introduced to parliament. While improving job prospects for professional directors and consultants, none of these changes is likely to reduce costs for members.[28]

10.6 Conclusion

While Australian retirement policy was at the vanguard of innovation at the beginning of the twentieth century, Australia had become a laggard by the early 1980s. Even New Zealand—which now has the simplest, least interventionist approach to retirement policy among OECD nations—operated a publicly-funded DB system from 1938 and a compulsory saving system in

[27] Until July 2005 employees could not choose into what fund their mandatory superannuation contributions were paid. Contributions were typically paid into funds specified in industrial agreements or selected by employers.

[28] Indeed, some academic evidence suggests 'independent' directors destroy corporate value because their own finances are not dependent on the performance of the company in question. See the work of Swan and Forsberg (2014).

1975, both later disbanded (Marriott 2009). But, since the 1980s, superannuation has become an entrenched component of Australian policy—part of a new 'Australian Settlement'.

Other countries should be wary to replicate it. Superannuation has distorted the economy in favour of financial services, artificially boosted the power of trade unions and employer groups, and enriched the fund management sector at the expense of ordinary workers, who inevitably pay little attention to their compulsory savings. It has achieved higher national and personal savings largely by reducing the standard of living of lower-income workers, who are not able to offset the effects of compulsion. The existing framework could be improved significantly by diverting all default contributions into a low-cost index fund, either managed by a public agency or contracted out by government tender. Anyone would be welcome to shift their savings to a (more expensive) provider.

Most egregiously, superannuation has largely failed its core justification: reducing significantly the share of older Australians in receipt of the age pension. So long as the principal residence, emotively called the 'family home' in Australia, is excluded from the eligibility test, this is unlikely to change. Because of this, all other taxes in the economy have had to be higher than they would otherwise have been, with all the economic damage that entails, even before the costs of complexity and administration are factored in.

Superannuation is the policy equivalent of using a sledge hammer to crack a nut, where the nut is a supposed tendency to 'under-save'. This popular justification is built on arbitrary and sweeping assumptions about what is desirable or necessary in retirement as a share of pre-retirement income. It crucially ignores the potential for retirees to draw on typically their biggest asset, their home. Never has there been a grass-roots political movement advocating forced saving to alleviate myopic behaviour. In fact, far from being irrational under-savers, Australian retirees have been adept at arranging their financial affairs to maximize their receipt of the age pension and associated financial concessions.

Even if a significant portion of people do systematically under-save, it is extreme paternalism to expect the government to try to correct such a habit. A means-tested age pension already provides a basic level of income that alleviates poverty. Beyond that, in a free-market economy individuals should be free to save as much or as little as they like. Indeed, the very existence of compulsory saving might discourage households from paying attention to their saving habits, believing that the government has worked out the optimal savings schedule for them.

Superannuation has also created powerful vested interests—with significant influence in both Australia's major political parties—that have popularized the false notion that superannuation contributions are a burden not on workers but on employers. If Australians had ever been asked explicitly whether they would like a portion of their wages compulsorily withheld in complex accounts until they retired, they almost certainly would have said no, as New Zealanders emphatically did in 1997, when given the chance in a referendum.[29]

References

Abbott, T. 1995. *Parliamentary Debates: House of Representatives*, vol. 204, Canberra: Commonwealth of Australia.

ABS (Australian Bureau of Statistics). 2009. *Australian Social Trends: Trends in Superannuation Coverage*, cat. no. 4102.0, Australian Bureau of Statistics, Canberra.

Antolin, P., Payett, S., and Yermo, J. 2012. 'Coverage of private pension systems: evidence and policy option', Working Paper on Finance, Insurance and Private Pensions, no. 20, Paris: OECD.

Bateman H., Kingston, G., and Piggott, J. 2001. *Forced Saving: Mandating Private Retirement Incomes*. Cambridge: Cambridge University Press.

Bozio, A., Crawford, A., and Tetlow, R. 2010. *The History of State Pensions in the UK: 1948 to 2010*, Institute of Fiscal Studies, <http://www.ifs.org.uk/publications/5000> (accessed 20 November 2015).

Casey, R. 1938. *Parliamentary Debates*, vol. 155, Canberra: Commonwealth of Australia.

Coleman, W., Cornish, S., and Hagger, A. 2006. *Giblin's Platoon: the Trials and Triumph of the Economist in Australian Public Life*. Canberra: ANU Epress.

Connolly, E. and Kohler, M. 2004. 'The impact of superannuation on household saving', Research Discussion Paper 2004-01, Sydney: Reserve Bank of Australia.

Drew, M. and Stanford, J. 2003. 'A review of Australia's compulsory superannuation scheme after a decade', Discussion Paper No. 322, School of Economics, University of Queensland, Brisbane.

Gruen, D. and Soding, L. 2011. 'Compulsory superannuation and national saving', *Treasury Economic Roundup*, no. 3, pp. 45–56.

Hayek, A. [1960] 2006. *The Constitution of Liberty*. London: Routledge Classics.

Huf, B. 2015. 'The experience of politics in the age of reform: comparisons in approaches to social policy history in Australia and the United States', *Australian–US Comparative and Transitional Labour History Conference Proceedings*, University of Sydney, 8–9 January.

Kelly, P. 2008. *The End of Certainty*. Sydney: Allen & Unwin.

Kirchner, S. 2012. 'Compulsory super at 20: "libertarian paternalism" without the libertarianism', CIS Policy Monograph 132, Sydney: Centre for Independent Studies.

[29] In 1997, 92% of New Zealanders rejected a proposal to introduce a Compulsory Retirement Saving Scheme where contributions up to 8% of earnings would have been paid into individual retirement funds.

Love, D. 2008. *Unfinished Business: Paul Keating's Interrupted Revolution*. Melbourne: Scribe.

Marriott, L. 2009. 'The politics of superannuation in Australasia: saving the New Zealand standard of living', *Australian Journal of Political Science*, vol. 44, no. 3, pp. 477–95.

Mercer. 2014. *Asset Allocation of Pension Funds around the World*. Sydney: Financial Services Council.

Minifie, J. 2014. *Super Sting: How to Stop Australians Paying Too Much for Super*. Melbourne: Grattan Institute.

Morris, N. Forthcoming. *Australian Superannuation: A Cautionary Tale*.

Novak, M. 2014. 'The Australia "low taxing country" myth', Occasional Paper, Melbourne: Institute of Public Affairs.

OECD (Organisation for Economic Co-operation and Development). 2014. *Pension Markets in Focus*, <http://www.oecd.org/daf/fin/private-pensions/Pension-Markets-in-Focus-2014.pdf> (accessed 20 November 2015).

OECD. 2015. *Pension Funds in Figures*, <http://www.oecd.org/finance/Pension-funds-pre-data-2015.pdf> (accessed 20 November 2015).

PC (Productivity Commission). 2015. 'Superannuation for post-retirement', Canberra: Commission Research Paper, Productivity Commission.

Rothman, G. 2011. 'Projecting the adequacy of Australian retirement incomes', paper presented at *UNSW Colloquium of Superannuation Researchers*, Sydney, 14 and 15 July.

St Anne, C. 2012. *A Super History*. Melbourne: Major Street Publishing.

Staley, L. 2010. 'Keeping super safe', Occasional Paper, Melbourne, Institute of Public Affairs.

Swan, P. and Forsberg, D. 2014. 'Does Board "Independence" Destroy Corporate Value?' *27th Australasian Finance and Banking Conference*, 16–18 December 2014. Sydney: University of New South Wales.

Watts, R. 1980. 'The origins of the Australian welfare state', *Historical Studies*, vol. 19, no. 75, pp. 175–98.

World Bank. 1994. 'Averting the old-age crisis: policies to protect the old and promote growth', Policy Research Report, Washington, DC: World Bank.

11

Australia's Economic Mores through the Lens of the Professional Sports Industry

Individual Rights or State Paternalism?

Richard Pomfret

Spectator sports play a major role in Australia and in many Australians' identities. Sports are sometimes dividing when a grand final takes place, but they can unify the nation when a cricket test series or America's Cup race features Australia, or when a mega-event like the Olympic Games is held in Australia. Around half of adult Australians are spectators at a sporting event during a year, and the Melbourne Cup is the race that stops the nation.[1] As elsewhere, sports have become a major industry, with billion-dollar TV contracts for the most popular winter team sports and over fifty Australian sports players earning over a million dollars a year (Table 11.1).

The sports industry highlights a paradox at the heart of Australian exceptionalism: the contrast between the self-perception of Australians as rugged individualists and the existence of an intrusive state. Sport is one of the few areas in Australian life where the tall poppy syndrome is muted, and sports stars, even in team events, are esteemed and idolized. At the same time, the sports industry is characterized by regulations on employees' rights to bargain or to choose their employer or workplace location that would be unacceptable, and even illegal, in the rest of the economy; in no other major sporting nation are such restrictions as extreme as in Australian domestic competitions,

[1] In 2010 43% of Australians over 15 were spectators at a live sporting event (ABS 2012). The most popular sports, measured by number of different individuals attending, were Australian Rules football, horseracing, rugby league, motor sports, soccer, cricket, rugby union, harness racing, tennis, and dog racing. From 1880 the Melbourne Cup repeatedly attracted crowds of 100,000; today it is watched by millions on TV, and is a public holiday in Victoria.

Table 11.1 Fifty Highest-Paid Australian Sports Stars, 2014, million $A

Name	Sport	Pay	Name	Sport	Pay
Andrew Bogut	Basketball	16.2	Matt Jones	Golf	2.31
Adam Scott	Golf	15.5	Mitchell Starc	Cricket	2.2
Jason Day	Golf	10.65	Geoff Ogilvy	Golf	2.17
Marcus Ambrose	Motor racing	5.68	Steven Bowditch	Golf	2.08
Tim Cahill	Soccer	5.5	Julian Wilson	Surfing	2.0
Grant Balfour	Baseball	5.18	Mark Bresciano	Soccer	2.0
Patrick (Patty) Mills	Basketball	4.61	Mark Webber	Motor racing	2.0
Shane Watson	Cricket	4.5	Craig Lowndes	Motor racing	2.0
Dante Exum	Basketball	4.34	Joel Parkinson	Surfing	1.8
Mitchell Johnson	Cricket	4.1	James Courtney	Motor racing	1.8
Michael Clarke	Cricket	4.0	George Bailey	Cricket	1.8
David Warner	Cricket	3.8	Aaron Finch	Cricket	1.8
John Senden	Golf	3.43	Stuart Appleby	Golf	1.77
Steve Smith	Cricket	3.1	Stephanie Gilmore	Surfing	1.75
Marc Leishman	Golf	3.07	James Whincup	Motor racing	1.6
Mile Jedinak	Soccer	3.0	Taj Burrow	Surfing	1.5
Brett Holman	Soccer	3.0	Josh Kerr	Surfing	1.5
James Faulkner	Cricket	2.8	Israel Folua	Rugby union	1.5
Mick Fanning	Surfing	2.7	Will Power	Motor racing	1.5
Aron Baynes	Basketball	2.7	Brett Lee	Cricket	1.5
Daniel Ricciardo	F1	2.6	Alex Leapai	Boxing	1.5
Ryan McGowan	Soccer	2.5	Gary Ablett	AFL	1.5
Cadel Evans	Cycling	2.5	Zac Purton	Horseracing	1.5
Brad Haddin	Cricket	2.5	David Hussey	Cricket	1.4
Glenn Maxwell	Cricket	2.5	Karrie Webb	Golf	1.28

Source: BRW rich list, <http://www.brw.com.au/p/business/brw_top_sports_earners_list_for_6VLF7mok4PMxzOxHAMb9KK> (accessed 18 July 2015).

or the exemption from laws and public policies so comprehensive. Despite large and growing revenues, the sports industry benefits from substantial public subsidies, which also appear to be more substantial than in other sectors of the economy and in other countries.

This chapter analyses the nature of the paradox, and looks at why intrusive regulations are accepted, or even welcomed, by producers and consumers; why subsidies are paid with little oversight or taxpayer protest; and why governments are such willing providers of support to the industry.

Section 11.1 describes the historical evolution of the major team sports in Australia. It relates how modern commercialized spectator sports began in the second half of the nineteenth century with the increased discretionary income of workers in the USA, UK, and Australia, and makes comparisons with the USA and UK. In all three countries, by 1900 the most popular events were team sports, organized into leagues, but with distinctive industry structures. Sections 11.2 and 11.3 outline how labour regulations and public policy have effectively reduced the cost of both labour and capital for professional sports teams in Australia relative to the rest of the world. Section 11.4 records how with innovations in transport and broadcasting, the revenues of the sports industry increased greatly over the twentieth century, and in the twenty-first century many sports are global. Labour restrictions have been modified by forces of globalization, but they operate to differing degrees in the major team sports of Australia; while soccer is completely integrated into global labour markets, the Australian Football League (AFL) is almost completely sheltered. At top levels, individual sports such as golf and tennis are entirely international, and the highest-earning Australian sports stars are in international sports such as golf, tennis, and Formula 1 car racing, or work overseas (Table 11.1). Overall, Australia remains distinctive in the way in which domestic competitions are regulated and in the willingness of Australian governments at all levels to provide financial and other assistance to the industry.

11.1 Historical Background

The popularization and commercialization of team sports was a direct consequence of the industrial revolution in the eighteenth century. By the middle of the 1800s, the benefits of economic growth were becoming more widely spread as industrial workers' wages allowed discretionary spending beyond food, shelter, and clothing. Factory workers and social reformers also succeeded in reducing working hours, first for children and then for adults. By the 1840s and 1850s, skilled workers in New Zealand and Australia had obtained a forty-hour week,[2] and similar changes would gradually be introduced in Western Europe and North America. For working-class men with leisure time, team sports became a popular pastime, both for playing and watching others play.

The great sports innovation in the 1860s and 1870s in the cities and industrial towns of Britain, North America, and Australia came from entrepreneurs who realized that by enclosing a ground they could charge entry fees that could be used to pay professional players and perhaps also to make a profit. People were paying to watch baseball in the USA in the 1860s, and the National League, formed in 1876, was the world's first professional sports league. In England and Australia cricket became a popular spectator sport, especially when representative teams from the two countries met in Test matches, starting in 1877, but even games between English county teams could attract 10,000 people. In English soccer, the FA Cup, established in

[2] Average hours worked per week were higher, but fell rapidly in Australia after 1870, from over fifty-five to under forty-five in 1913 (Huberman and Minns 2007; Shanahan and Wilson 2013). A couple of reasons for the larger crowds at late nineteenth-century sporting events in Australia were the lower average hours worked, and their faster reduction compared to the USA (from sixty-seven to fifty-eight) and UK (from fifty-seven to fifty-six).

1871, started as a competition among former pupils of private schools, but in the 1880s became dominated by teams from the industrial regions. Crowds of 10,000 could be attracted to soccer games between local rivals, and by the end of the decade the FA Cup Final attracted over 20,000 spectators; in 1888 twelve teams from the industrialized parts of England formed the Football League.

In Australia, attendance at sports contests was even bigger than in England. Cricket was the most popular summer sport, while in 1866 a crowd of 34,000 watched an Australian Rules football game between South Melbourne and Geelong (Vamplew, 1992, p. 437). The 1880 Melbourne Cup was watched by an estimated 100,000, and contests in other individual sports, such as rowing, could also attract large crowds (Ward 2009, p. 588). In the late nineteenth century, an international boxing circuit of top fighters developed in Britain, North America, and Australasia (Taylor 2013), and a world heavyweight champion has been recognized since the 1880s.

The evolution of the principal winter sports was different in the leading colonies of Victoria and New South Wales (NSW). As in the USA and UK, modern winter sports were often played as adjuncts to the major summer sports, and there was more disagreement over the appropriate rules, for example, for rugby or Association Football in England. In Melbourne during the gold rush of the 1850s, Australian Rules were devised as the best combination of both nascent English football codes, but failed to catch on in NSW, where spectators preferred rugby. In Sydney, a crowd of 52,000 saw NSW play New Zealand at rugby in 1907, just before the Australian split in favour of rugby league over rugby union.[3] With Australian Rules dominant in three of the large states, and rugby league in the other two (plus, later, Canberra), the Australian football situation lacked the dominance of a single code as in the USA, South Africa, or New Zealand, and was little influenced by the spread of soccer until the immigration of southern Europeans in the 1960s.

The most popular truly national sport, cricket, was imported from Britain, and remains the greatest cultural glue between Australia and Britain, even while language, entertainment, and other aspects of Australian life became Americanized. Yet the organization differed in the crucial respect that Australia did not share the class distinction that characterized English cricket until the 1960s. This is not to deny the existence of financial disputes between players and a hidebound board, which boiled over in 1912 when several top cricketers refused to tour England, and the weakened Australian team 'set records for poor performance on the field, and for alcohol consumption and disorderly

[3] In contrast to the situation in Britain, the origins of rugby league in Australia lay not in the issue of amateurism versus professionalism but in a conflict between well-to-do administrators and wage-earning players. So, as in cricket, Australian rugby became a commercial sport without conventions of 'gentlemen' and 'players', although disputes over money could flare up between players and administrators (Chesterton 2007).

behaviour off the field' (Ward 2009, p. 593). Nevertheless, this was a different order of magnitude from the situation in England, where amateurs were identified by their title (Lord, Sir, Mr, etc.) and professionals by their surname and initials, and an annual Gentlemen vs Players game between amateurs (the Gentlemen) and professionals (the Players) was played from 1819 until 1962, when the concept of amateurism was abolished.[4] In Australia, cricket was more obviously the people's sport, with placement in the national team usually on merit.[5]

The organization of major team sports changed little for most of the twentieth century, but the audience increased due to radio and TV. In the USA, after the broadcast of the 1921 Dempsey–Carpentier world heavyweight boxing championship and the spread of TV after 1945, radio and then TV became major revenue sources for sports leagues. In Australia, radio and TV helped to broaden audiences beyond the live spectators, but the commercial impact was delayed due to the dominant role of the public broadcaster. The most important competitive and structural changes occurred during the last quarter of the twentieth century, largely driven by increased TV revenues. Following media baron Kerry Packer's successful challenge of the traditional cricket organization by establishing 'World Series Cricket' in the 1977/78 Australian cricket season (Haigh 1993), Packer's monopoly of rugby league broadcasting rights was challenged by his rival, Rupert Murdoch, who, in the mid-1990s, established a Super League of disaffected and new clubs. Both of these challenges led to increased TV revenues for the sports concerned and higher wages for players.

In the 1980s and 1990s, spurred by reduced transport costs and national TV coverage, Australian Rules and rugby league both attempted to go national and hence came into head-to-head code competition. None of these changes led to a large expansion in the number of clubs, as the league structures were kept essentially unchanged except for the introduction of individual clubs (either by relocation or by expansion, as in the USA) in states not previously served by the code.

[4] The distinction between amateurs and professionals was less powerful in immigrant countries than in Europe. In the USA, the Knickerbocker Club's influence rapidly declined after the formation of the first professional baseball league in 1876, and Australian Rules football, although devised by graduates of English and Irish private schools and colleges, never distinguished between paid or unpaid players. Australia abided by the amateur requirement that persisted until the second half of the twentieth century in global events such as the Olympic Games and Grand Slam tennis tournaments.

[5] The major exception was exclusion of Aboriginals, despite the fact that, in 1868, the first Australian team to tour Britain had been an Aboriginal team. In 1869 Victoria's *Act to Provide for the Protection and Management of the Aboriginal Natives* made it a legal offence to remove any Aborigine from the colony of Victoria without the approval of the government minister, effectively curtailing their involvement in the game beyond the local level. This element of Australia's broader paternalistic and restrictive policy towards Aboriginals is ignored here.

Following the relocation of one club to Sydney in 1982, the Victorian Football League (VFL) (renamed the Australian Football League in 1990) expanded to Perth (two clubs), Adelaide (two clubs), and Brisbane (one club, merged with a Melbourne club), which brought the complement to sixteen by 1997. The national expansion effectively reduced the West Australian and South Australian leagues to second-tier events. Ruthless controls to ensure competitive equality (i.e. a draft and salary caps) ensured that newcomers could quickly become champions (Perth, Adelaide, Brisbane, and Sydney teams had all won the AFL by 2005). Meanwhile, rugby league established teams in Perth, Adelaide, Melbourne, and (unlike the AFL) in Auckland, but, amid internal divisions between the Australian Rugby League and the Super League, the Perth and Adelaide clubs folded. As rugby union went professional and established the Super 12 competition in 1996, rugby league failed to maintain any hold outside the original two rugby states (NSW and Queensland) plus Canberra and Melbourne. In little over a decade, the AFL appeared to have won the code competition, although rugby league remains popular in its heartlands of Sydney and Brisbane. This was achieved without sacrificing the closed cartel organization, largely because Australia's five big cities are so much bigger than the next largest towns that there is limited pressure for new entrants. The rugby union Super 12 (now Super Rugby) competition and the soccer A-League, founded in 2004, also adopted a closed cartel structure.

The Australian situation is interesting because, despite the four major football codes (AFL, rugby league, rugby union, and soccer) having differing characteristics and histories, all have taken on US-style structures. In the state-based competitions, the top league constituted a closed cartel of clubs who alone competed for the championship, and the cartel determined which clubs could join or would be ejected from the league. Yet despite the US-style closed cartel structure, in stark contrast to the promotion-relegation system of most British competitions and soccer worldwide, Australian sports in the twentieth century differed from the US model of private ownership and profit-maximizing behaviour. Most Australian clubs are membership-based with opaque accounts.

11.2 Sport Labour Markets

The basic economics of professional team sports is simple. A few dozen players perform in a closed stadium, and other necessary inputs are minimal. Much of the revenue is economic rent, as greater revenues do not generate increased output (supply is price inelastic). The size of the rents has substantially increased over the last half-century with improvements in TV technology. For example, the AFL generated revenues over $700 million in 2010 (Cook and Davies 2012, p. 64) that were boosted in 2011 by a five-year TV deal worth

$1,252 million; and in 2012 the National Rugby League (NRL) announced a $1,025 million TV deal. The rents are distributed to owners, administrators, players, and others, although some rents might be dissipated if clubs spend on providing better facilities for players or spectators. The distribution of rents will be changed in the players' favour if clubs bid up wages to attract better players, and clubs may collude to limit such 'arms races'. Greater rents have led to increased competition between league administrators, individual clubs, and players for a greater share, and have encouraged non-transparency with respect to the size and distribution of rents.[6]

Professional sport is a peculiar industry, with many inherent distortions of competitive markets that are addressed differently in different countries. Monopoly power is pervasive, due to the demand for an undisputed champion and to the need for a central body that organizes schedules, sets rules, and resolves on-field disputes. The universal desire to know which team is the best cannot be satisfied if there are several parallel leagues whose teams never meet. However, that does not mean that the league must necessarily be a closed cartel of clubs, as in the major professional sports leagues in Australia and North America. In European soccer, a system of promotion and relegation enables clubs to move in and out of the top league based on playing performance (Szymanski and Zimbalist 2005). At the same time, as clubs compete to be champions they need worthy opponents. In a closed cartel some clubs may be weaker, for example, due to a poorer catchment area; without threat of relegation from the league, there may be collusion to establish and maintain 'competitive balance'. Moreover, the quality of output in terms of individual games and interest in the league overall may be a function of the competitive balance. Hence, a case may be made for exemption from competition policy both due to the natural monopoly of national leagues and to the desirability of ensuring that affluent clubs do not dominate.

The regulatory environment in which major sports operate is unique to the sector, but varies considerably from country to country. In the closed cartels characterizing Australian professional team sports, leagues restrict entry of new clubs, engage in price-fixing, and impose restrictions on the labour market that are anti-competitive and would be illegal in other sectors. In Australia, competitive balance has been the most often cited reason for regulatory exemptions, although there is some dispute about exactly what competitive balance entails (Lenten 2009b) and about the impact of competitive balance on attendance.[7] The competitive balance argument is used to

[6] For example, AFL clubs' and league management's accounts are not publicly available, and players' wages are only known from rumours in the media.

[7] While some Australian authors have found a strong positive correlation between competitive balance and attendance (Borland and Lye 1992; Lenten 2009a), studies of other leagues have found less support, e.g. Donihue et al. (2007) on US baseball, and Czarnitzki and Stadtmann (2002) on

justify restrictions on the labour market such as payroll caps or the reverse-order draft. The degree to which such restraints on workers' rights (as well as on the application of occupational health and safety protection or the ability to seek legal redress for grievous bodily harm) are accepted by players and supported by public policy varies across countries. But acceptance of such restraints is especially strong in Australia and, in contrast to the USA, where competing leagues and players' strikes and owners' lockouts have been common, stable organizational structure and labour market tranquillity have been the norm in Australia.

Most professional leagues engage in some form of revenue distribution, and this is especially important when the league negotiates TV deals and then shares the revenue among the clubs. Hence, governing bodies carry with them authoritative power that has the capacity to seriously compromise the fortunes of any individual club. Sports leagues have successfully kept much of their decision-making outside the legal system, so that disadvantaged clubs are denied the redress that companies in other industries could seek.

The Australian sports leagues all employ forms of payroll or salary caps, and many have player draft systems. For example, in the AFL, a player draft exists which effectively permits the lowest-ranked clubs to have first pick of new entrant players and those out of contract, with some exemptions (e.g. a father–son connection to a club).[8] While some trade of players between clubs is permitted outside of the draft, this is effectively relegated to a barter system over player switches and draft pick trading. The rationale is to ensure competitive balance, and under this system only three teams have not contested the AFL Grand Final since 1997. However, there is little evidence that, when a few teams dominate, the popularity of team sports declines; evidence from European soccer leagues suggests otherwise.[9]

Both the player draft and the salary cap are restrictions on workers' bargaining rights, and Australian sporting leagues stand out in terms of forced labour mobility. While some government allocation of labour, such as teachers, has

German soccer. In the UK, some of the largest attendances for lower-ranked soccer clubs occur when meeting vastly superior opposition, i.e. the chance of an upset or the opportunity to see star players draw crowds. Teams in the English Premier League generally charge higher prices for home games against the strongest teams, indicating greater demand for such games as opposed to games between equally matched teams.

[8] For details of Australian draft systems see Booth (1997, 2004), Dabscheck (2004), and Cook and Davies (2012). Reverse-order drafts may create perverse incentives, with lower-ranked teams deliberately losing games ('tanking') to ensure a higher draft pick (Taylor and Trogdon 2002; Borland et al. 2009; Klugman 2012). Mehra and Zuercher (2006) offer a sceptical view of the competitive balance argument.

[9] Although over forty teams have competed in the English Premier League since its formation in 1992, just four clubs (all from London or Manchester) have won the title in all years but one; yet attendance and TV audiences are on the rise rather than in decline. Similarly, the Spanish Liga's dominance by two clubs (Real Madrid and Barcelona) and the German Bundesliga's by one club (Bayern Munich) have not dented their popularity.

traditionally taken place, in particular to more remote locations, these have generally been seen as temporary measures at early career stages or have been combined with financial compensation. Sports players arguably have as much right to choose their location of employment as any other worker in Australia and, although there may be a case for restricting movement between clubs within a season, the career-long restrictions are unparalleled, and reduce players' bargaining power over other considerations such as wages.

Capping each club's total wages represents a transfer of wealth from players to owners or other vested interests. Moreover, enforcement of such regulation is difficult (Davies 2011), as illustrated by the length of time over which Melbourne Storm breached the NRL salary gap in 2008 and 2009 before being punished. Furthermore, even if a payroll cap promotes competitive balance by ensuring that all clubs have a wage bill that is approximately equal, long-term market signals to players may be distorted, and there have been several cases of players moving from one football code to another; the signing by AFL expansion team Greater Western Sydney of former NRL player Israel Folau is an example of shifting code loyalty. Teams that are successful in attracting spectators could be argued to deserve to reinvest the rewards of their success just as firms in other industries do.

In sum, competitive balance has provided a basis for pervasive distortion of market forces, particularly in labour markets. Some elements are present in other countries, but the AFL is an extreme case:

> The Australian Football League (AFL) is one of the most regulated sporting leagues in the world, operating both a salary cap and draft system in its quest to create a more even competition. (Cook and Davies 2012)

The regulation is internal to the league, and is supported by non-application of public regulatory policies, such as competition policy. Football players earning hundreds of thousands of dollars a year for playing a game they love are not ready targets for sympathy, but they are earning less than the value of their marginal product, and this is primarily to the benefit of other rent-seekers, such as sports administrators.

Apart from the non-application of competition policy and labour laws, the AFL—and presumably other sports leagues—is exempted from large parts of Australian corporations law and has virtually tax-free status (Forbes 2014). The blurring of the sporting ethos and business practice, routinely displayed in much of the media, exacerbate the difficulty of applying a sensible regulatory regime to professional team sports and other sporting activities that have become big business.

More importantly, in terms of Exceptionalism, Australia's sporting labour markets are becoming increasingly idiosyncratic. In North American major sports, players have unionized and have gradually won increasing free agent status for senior players. Players' associations have been much weaker in Australia, apart from the isolated success of the rugby league players.[10] In the European Union (EU), sports labour markets were revolutionized by a successful legal case brought by the Belgian player, Marc Bosman, in 1995, in which the EU courts ruled that retain-and-transfer rules were an illegal restraint of trade; since then, with minor restrictions (e.g. for youths), players sign fixed-term contracts at the end of which they can move to any employer. The EU outcome is a labour market much like that in other industries, and with much higher wages for players (and their agents).

The workplace passivity of the Australian sports players is also reflected in their reluctance to seek legal redress for grievous bodily harm or equipment malfunction, and to ensure conformity with standard occupational health and safety conditions. Rugby league players have successfully sued for damages, but the cases are few, and have few parallels in other sports.[11] Clubs try at all costs to keep cases out of the civil courts or away from quasi-legal settings such as the Australian Sports Anti-Doping Authority, and the players and media acquiesce in this.[12]

There is no doubt that the peculiar nature of professional team sports justifies nuanced application of competition policy and other legislation. However, the distribution of the large rents involved in team sports turns on the interaction between the regulatory environment and market forces, and pursuit of a more or less active public policy affects the financial returns to different groups. In other countries, with increased recognition of the size of the rents, players have become more purposeful in securing their share, and governments have become more aware that the sports industry is big business. In the UK, for example, tax collection was lax in the twentieth century, with professional sports clubs in financial trouble often given extensive leeway, but in the twenty-first century the tax authority has become insistent on prompt payment of taxes and issues credible threats of bankruptcy to clubs that fall behind. In Australia this interaction between the regulatory environment and

[10] In 1990–91 players challenged the rugby league draft system in court, where it was ruled a restraint of trade, and subsequently the NRL has acknowledged that changes to the labour market need the approval of the players' association. The AFL Players' Association, in the mid-1990s, negotiated collective agreements with a minimum wage in return for a commitment that no player would seek redress through an industrial tribunal. Subsequent AFL agreements included statements that all parties accepted the need for the draft and salary caps, which forestalled any restraint of trade action under common law.

[11] A 1993 case established that liability for injury included the offending player's club, if, for example, players were not trained to play in a way that reduced the likelihood of injuring opponents. Yet it remains hard to prove negligence by players or club. In 2005 Jarrod McCracken succeeded in obtaining $97,000 damages from two Melbourne Storm players and their club (but not from the NRL), on the grounds that the spear tackle that paralyzed him was intended to cause injury.

[12] Following the revelation of widespread drug abuse by Essendon AFL club, *The Australian*, on 23 June 2014, ran an op-ed headlined 'Get Canberra out of Sport'. Davies (2012) deals with the legal issues in greater depth.

market forces has largely been one of complaisant governments permitting restrictive practices.

11.3 Government Subsidies for Professional Team Sports

Apart from wages, the other major expense for a professional team sports club is the stadium. In Australia, the four football codes and cricket have all benefited from state-subsidized construction, renovation, and expansion of their stadia. The new stadia in Brisbane, Adelaide, and Perth are the major projects since the turn of the century, when the Sydney Olympics included a new stadium, but there have also been many smaller publicly-funded projects, often benefiting individual clubs (Table 11.2).

It is not inevitable that sports stadia are state-funded. In the EU such subsidies are treated as industrial assistance to individual producers, and are illegal. This has not stopped clubs from building new stadia if they believe the benefits from the new facility will exceed the costs. In the USA, stadia were mostly privately built until the Second World War. In the 1950s, professional sports leagues used their ability to offer and transfer franchises to convince cities or states to subsidize state-of-the-art stadia in order to attract teams and to become or remain a 'major league city' (Siegfried and Zimbalist 2006; Coates 2007), but since 2000 public funding of stadia has been waning as taxpayers (e.g. in New York and in Los Angeles) voted down proposals for stadia funding. In Australia, although codes cannot easily threaten to move teams from a city if a stadium is not built, they have still been successful in pressuring states and cities to subsidize stadia. For the largest projects, interstate competition has had an 'arms race' effect, for example, stadium construction in Brisbane and Adelaide put pressure on Western Australia to build a bigger and better stadium in Perth.

The list in Table 11.2 is incomplete because funding for stadia, surprisingly in view of the state's involvement, is not transparent. The *133rd Report of the Public Works Committee to the South Australian Parliament* in September 2000 opened with the amazing statement: 'The Public Works Committee is unable to determine the extent and nature of any government financial support for the new grandstand at Football Park due to conflicting content of available information', and concluded with a comment on the concerns of this official watchdog on public spending:

> The Public Works Committee is concerned that government support for the grandstand has been provided through some mechanism deliberately devised to avoid scrutiny and accountability in relation to the expenditure of a significant sum of public monies.

Table 11.2 Selected Sports Stadium Projects in Australia, 2002–14

Stadium	Date	Financing (million $A)	Principal users
Suncorp, Brisbane	2002–3	280 + 12 state in 2006–7	NRL, RU, A-League
Sydney Cricket Ground	2006–7	25 federal	Cricket, AFL
Sydney Cricket Ground	2012–14	97.5 state, 50 federal, 50 SCG trust	Cricket, AFL
Melbourne Cricket Ground	2006–7	77 state, 15 federal	Cricket, AFL
Robina, Gold Coast	2006–8	130 state	NRL
Adelaide Oval	2007	25 state, 25 federal	Cricket
Penrith	2007	5 state	NRL
Energy Australia, Newcastle	2008–9	10 federal + state	NRL and A-League
AAMI (Football Park), Adelaide	2008–9	100 state	AFL
Skilled (Kardinia Park), Geelong	2008–9, 2012–	14 federal, 46 state, 1.5 city	AFL
Brookvale, Manly	pledged	6 state, 4 local	NRL
Rectangular Stadium	2010	267.5 state	A-League, NRL
Sydney Showground Stadium	2012	45 state, 12 AFL, 7 Royal Agricultural Society of NSW	AFL
Adelaide Oval	2014	535 state, 30 federal	Cricket, AFL, SANFL
Perth Rectangular Stadium	2014	95 state (stage 1)	A-League
Perth	proposed	690 state and federal	AFL, NRL, cricket and A-League

Notes: Few of these figures are known with any degree of accuracy. Governments are inconsistent in reporting what is included in the cost, and in some cases hiding the numbers. Press coverage varies, depending on whether the media is emphasizing the quality of stadia built in rival states or minimizing the perceived impact on taxpayers in their own.

Source: Wilson and Pomfret (2014, p. 79).

The subsidy appeared to be around $10 million.

Some of the projects listed in Table 11.2 can be identified with individual politicians who want to boast about the size of the funding but more often prefer to hide the taxpayers' bill.

The issue is not the popularity of the new stadia, which are clearly seen as vote-winners by politicians of all hues. The issue is how the stadia are paid for.[13] Revenue from live and TV spectators and from sponsors and advertisers should cover construction costs, as in the EU and increasingly in North

[13] State governments often defend sports spending on public health grounds, but that is more applicable to participatory sports than spectator sport, and spending on stadia and elite athletes dwarfs public spending on facilities for amateur sports. In the Queensland government's 2003/04 budget, for example, the combined cost of all amateur sports projects was less than 1 million dollars, while the state government was providing most of the funding for the $280 million Suncorp Stadium and a new stadium on the Gold Coast costing $130 million, for which the main tenants would be professional sporting teams (Wilson and Pomfret 2009; Pomfret and Wilson 2011).

America. If there are positive externalities then some public support may be justified, but the extent to which the state covers the cost (usually close to 100 per cent) is extreme.[14]

11.4 Australia in the Global Sporting Economy

Globalization of sport impacts on Australia's ability to persist with sporting Exceptionalism. Global individual sports in which Australians excel (e.g. golf, tennis, surfing, motor racing) cannot be subject to the restrictive practices described in Sections 11.3 and 11.2. In cricket, commercialization was driven by global TV coverage, reflected in the World Series episode described in Section 11.1,[15] and, more recently, in the rise of the Indian Premier League, where teams compete financially to hire the best players. In athletics, tennis, and rugby union, greater commercialization dates from the abandonment of 'amateur' status, which was also driven by increased revenues from TV coverage and globalization.

Australia has had periods of dominance in cricket, rugby union, and rugby league on the world stage. However, Australia has had no sports player among the world's top hundred earners in recent years. This can be explained by the current absence of very top players in golf and tennis, where international prizes are large but have a steep gradient (i.e. winners take much more than second place and so forth), and by the limited payrolls in Australian domestic team sport competitions, by North American or European standards. The impact of globalization is apparent in the distribution of the top earners in Table 11.1. In 2014 Australia's top earners played basketball or baseball in the USA or soccer overseas, or were on the international circuit for individual sports such as golf, surfing, tennis, cycling, or car racing. Australian cricketers were well paid for playing for the national team, but those on the rich list all had lucrative contracts with the Indian Premier League.

The four football codes offer an interesting comparison. The most popular, AFL, is essentially domestic and has the most regulated labour market, while soccer is totally global and has a relatively free labour market. The two rugby

[14] When the Adelaide Oval was rebuilt in 2014 at a cost of at least $565 million, the AFL's contribution was $5 million.

[15] World Series Cricket has influenced the rules, establishing the six-ball over as the global standard, rather than the eight-ball over that had been the Australian norm since the early twentieth century. The commercial angle to this decision was that six-ball overs offered more frequent breaks for advertising.

codes lie somewhere in between, with rugby union offering the most attractive conditions for top players due to the international opportunities, especially in the lightly regulated EU labour market. Despite their popularity in terms of spectators and TV rights, the four football codes' Australian teams provide only Ablett on the 2013 and 2014 list of the fifty top-paid sports stars, and Folua in 2014. Australia has several soccer players among its fifty highest-paid athletes, which may seem surprising given Australia's performance in the 2014 World Cup, but the point is that even playing in the second level in England or in weak leagues in the Middle East, Australian soccer players earn far more overseas than starting players or superstars in the A-League—or in the AFL, NRL, or Super XV Rugby.

Australia has long savoured international success in sports, especially cricket, but also Olympic athletes, and winners in sailing, golf, tennis, or cycling have become national heroes. In the late twentieth century, roughly in parallel with the increased commercialization and state support for team sports, Australian governments increased spending on attracting and hosting international sports events, and on promoting the success of Australian participants in such events. Expenditure on the 2000 Sydney Olympics dwarfed that on the 1956 Melbourne Olympics, which today looks like an event from another era. The failed bid for the 2022 FIFA World Cup was largely government-funded. States have spent considerable amounts, usually non-transparently hidden behind claims of commercial sensitivity, on hosting a range of more or less mega sports events.[16]

The Australian Institute of Sport (AIS) also provides publicly-funded training for elite athletes. The AIS was opened in 1981, in part in response to the perceived national shame of winning no gold medals at the 1976 Olympic Games, and has enjoyed strong bipartisan public support. Of the sixteen highest-paid sports stars in 2012 (i.e. those earning over 3 million dollars), half benefited from publicly subsidized training via the AIS.[17] Jolly (2013, p. 44) estimated an annual cost per athlete of $28,000 in 1999, which had risen to $50,000 by 2012, but suggestions that there should be repayment from any future income, as in the Higher Education Contribution Scheme, have been rejected by both major political parties.

[16] Wilson and Pomfret (2014) provide examples from South Australia. Unsuccessful bids such as South Australia's Commonwealth Games bids, or its part in Australia's 2022 World Cup bid, clearly wasted taxpayers' money. But successful bids can be even more costly, as in Adelaide's disastrous hosting of the Australian Le Mans motor-racing event. On the cost of hosting the Sydney Olympics, see Giesecke and Madden (2011).

[17] Two of the most successful AIS alumni, Andrew Bogut and Matthew Dellavedova, played in the 2015 National Basketball Association (NBA) Finals. They were likely to be the two highest-paid Australian sports stars of the year, and their success brought large revenues to two privately-owned US basketball teams, but it is difficult to see much return to Australia from such government spending.

In sum, public economic policy towards professional spectator sports in Australia has two main components. With respect to monopoly power and operation of labour markets, as well as occupational health and safety and other worker protection legislation, public policy has consisted of de facto exemption from ordinary law for professional sports leagues. This laissez-faire environment has been reinforced by the weakness of labour unions or other organizations to protect the interests of the players employed in the leagues. Furthermore, professional sports leagues are exempted from large parts of Australian corporations and tax law. Second, governments at all levels have spent large amounts of public money on facilities for professional sports teams. Other public spending on sports includes bidding for and hosting mega-events, from the Olympic Games down, and training elite athletes. None of these policies enjoys much support among sports economists, and the clear pattern in other democratic countries is of governments pulling back from treating the sports industry as a special case and from providing large subsidies for stadia or mega-events.

11.5 Conclusions

What is distinctive about the organization of the professional sports industry in Australia, and to what extent is it typical of Australian Exceptionalism?

A long-standing trait dating back to the industry's nineteenth-century origins is the idea of a 'fair go'. There has been no overt discrimination by class, and in the major domestic competitions no amateur/professional divide such as characterized English cricket or rugby for a century after these became popular spectator sports, although during that century there was serious discrimination against Aboriginals. (Australia did, of course, comply with international norms when competing in the Olympic Games, the Grand Slam tennis tournaments and rugby union, which were restricted to amateurs for much of the twentieth century.)

In professional team sports, many aspects of American professional sports industries were adopted (e.g. the closed cartel structure rather than the open access promotion/relegation system). However, private ownership was not embraced, and the teams remained members' clubs, although the ownership structure and accounting are often opaque.[18] There was also distrust of unregulated markets and, importantly, the impact of radio and TV on potential

[18] The AFL and its clubs have hundreds of thousands of members. However, for the purpose of the Corporations Act, the AFL's 'members' are no more than the 239 guarantors who each guarantee the league's debts to a maximum of ten cents! Individual clubs 'are likewise controlled by a small inner cabal' (Forbes 2014).

revenues was muted by the dominance of the public broadcaster, the ABC. Only in the final decades of the twentieth century did TV revenues and globalization of some sports lead to major commercially driven change.

Third, government policies, either by omission or commission, have privileged the industry, often in an egalitarian guise (competitive balance) or as a populist cause (funding stadia or mega-events, or training young athletes to win Olympic medals or test matches). Anti-competitive practices and suppression of workers' rights, which are illegal in other parts of the economy, have been tolerated in professional sports. It is a multi-million dollar industry that pays virtually no corporate taxes and benefits from large state subsidies. Unlike other regulated sectors, however, the major beneficiaries are not the workers in the industry, but rather an unelected and largely unaccountable group of administrators.[19]

Fourth, accounting of spending by clubs, leagues, and governments is non-transparent, despite the large amounts involved. Much of the spending is controlled by an interconnected clique of 'WOMBATS' (white old men in blazers and ties). The professional sports industry cannot be characterized as state paternalism, but the state acquiesces in a paternalistic structure that sharply inhibits the individual freedoms of the skilled workers in the domestic market.

These traits can be found in other countries with similar histories of professional sports, but comparison with North America and the UK reveals a far more regulated environment in Australia, especially in sports sheltered from global competition (e.g. AFL), with a smaller share of revenues accruing to players and considerable opaqueness about who receives the remainder of the revenues. Australian governments offer extensive financial support to professional sports, and although similar types of state support can be found in other countries, among democracies Australia appears to be an extreme case in the amount of government funding.[20] In North America and Europe, the twenty-first century has seen increasing public debate about state spending on professional sports (e.g. funding stadia or hosting mega-events) with popular grass-roots movements often forcing reversal of spending decisions; in Australia, such debates are practically absent.[21]

The sports industry reflects many traits of Australian Exceptionalism, especially the paradox of belief in the fair go and individual prowess coexisting

[19] Other groups benefit from specific policies, e.g. subsidized stadia benefit the construction industry, and bidding for mega-events benefits public relations and other media companies. Among potential negative side-effects are the increased opportunities for corruption.

[20] The caveat 'among democracies' is to exclude comparisons with autocracies spending huge amounts on prestige events, such as the 2014 Sochi Winter Olympics.

[21] The Australian Sports Party won a West Australian seat in the Senate in 2013, but failed to retain it in the re-run election of 2014. The single-issue party faced little opposition on sports; its only controversial moment followed release of an election poster featuring a topless female jogger.

with a powerful, secretive, and paternalistic government. The state promotes and spends money on elite sports to an extent unparalleled in other democracies, and the AIS and similar state-level projects have few international parallels since the end of European communism. Australia's lack of regulatory interference and generous public subsidies for professional team sports are also extreme in the twenty-first century, when sports industries in other jurisdictions (and especially their formerly idiosyncratic labour markets) are becoming more like other sectors of the economy. Elsewhere, sports management has become increasingly professional, while in Australia there is a contrast between high levels of technical professionalism but ultimate economic decision-making often being in the hands of a self-perpetuating clique. In sum, the sports industry offers a mirror of Australian Exceptionalism, but little explanation of the phenomenon.

References

ABS (Australian Bureau of Statistics). 2012. *Sport and Physical Recreation: A Statistical Overview, Australia*, 4156.0. Canberra: Australian Bureau of Statistics.

Booth, R. 1997. 'History of player recruitment, transfer and payment rules in the Victorian and Australian Football League', *Australian Society for Sports History Bulletin*, no. 26, pp. 13–33.

Booth, R. 2004. 'The economics of achieving competitive balance in the Australian Football League, 1897–2004', *Economic Papers*, vol. 23, no. 4, pp. 325–44.

Borland, J. and Lye, J. 1992. 'Attendance at Australian Rules football: a panel study', *Applied Economics*, no. 24, pp. 1053–8.

Borland, J., Chicu, M., and Macdonald, R. 2009. 'Do teams always lose to win? Performance incentives and the player draft in the Australian Football League', *Journal of Sports Economics*, vol. 10, no. 5, pp. 451–84.

Chesterton, R. 2007. *100 Years of Rugby League*. Sydney: Hachette Livre Australia.

Coates, D. 2007. 'Stadiums and arenas: economic development or economic redistribution?', *Contemporary Economic Policy*, vol. 25 no. 4, pp. 565–77.

Cook, J. and Davies, C. 2012. 'Free agency and the Australian Football League', *Bond Law Review*, vol. 24, no. 2, pp. 64–100.

Czarnitzki, D. and Stadtmann, G. 2002. 'Uncertainty of outcome versus reputation: empirical evidence for the first German football division', *Empirical Economics*, vol. 27, no. 1, pp. 101–12.

Dabscheck, B. 2004. 'The imperfect market for players', *Economic Papers*, vol. 23, no. 4, pp. 345–54.

Davies, C. 2011. 'Salary cap scandals in Australian professional team sports', *International Sports Law Review*, vol. 9 no. 2, pp. 30–6.

Davies, C. 2012. 'Australian sport and the Commonwealth constitution', *Bond University Sports Law eJournal*, pp. 1–8.

Donihue, M., Findlay, D., and Newberry, P. 2007. 'An analysis of attendance at major league baseball spring training games', *Journal of Sports Economics*, vol. 8, no. 1, pp. 39–61.

Forbes, D. 2014. 'Is the AFL obeying our corporations and tax laws?', 9 May, <http://davidforbes.com.au/blogs/12.%20> (accessed 20 November 2015).

Giesecke, J. and Madden, J. 2011. 'Modelling the economic impacts of the Sydney Olympics in retrospect: game over for the bonanza story?', *Economic Papers*, vol. 30, no. 2, pp. 218–32.

Haigh, G. 1993. *The Cricket War: The Inside Story of Kerry Packer's World Series Cricket*. Melbourne: Melbourne University Press.

Huberman, M. and Minns, C. 2007. 'The times they are not changin': days and hours of work in Old and New Worlds, 1870–2000', *Explorations in Economic History*, no. 44, pp. 538–67.

Jolly, R. 2013. 'Sports funding: federal balancing act', Background Note, Department of Parliamentary Services, Canberra.

Klugman, M. 2012. 'AFL and tanking: the cure might be worse than the disease', *The Conversation*, 4 August.

Lenten, L. 2009a. 'Unobserved components in competitive balance and match attendances in the Australian Football League 1945–2005: where is all the action happening?', *Economic Record*, vol. 85, no. 269, pp. 181–96.

Lenten, L. 2009b. 'Towards a new dynamic measure of competitive balance: a study applied to Australia's two major professional "football" leagues', *Economic Analysis and Policy*, vol. 39, no. 3, pp. 407–28.

Mehra, S. and Zuercher, T. J. 2006. 'Striking out "competitive balance" in sports, antitrust, and intellectual property', *Berkeley Technology Law Journal*, no. 21, pp. 1499–545.

Pomfret, R. and Wilson, J. K. 2011. 'The peculiar economics of public policy towards sport', *Agenda: A Journal of Policy Analysis and Reform*, vol. 18, no. 1, pp. 85–98.

Shanahan, M. and Wilson, J. K. 2013. 'Labor market outcomes in settler economies between 1870 and 1919: accounting for differences in labor hours and occupations' in C. Lloyd, J. Metzer, and R. Sutch (eds.), *Settler Economies in World History*. Leiden: Brill.

Siegfried, J. and Zimbalist, A. 2006. 'The economic impact of sports facilities, teams and mega-events', *Australian Economic Review*, vol. 39, no. 4, pp. 420–7.

Szymanski, S. and Zimbalist, A. 2005. *National Pastime: How Americans Play Baseball and the Rest of the World Plays Soccer*. Washington, DC: Brookings Institution.

Taylor, B. and Trogdon, J. 2002. 'Losing to win: tournament incentives in the National Basketball Association', *Journal of Labor Economics*, no. 20, pp. 23–41.

Taylor, M. 2013. 'The global ring? Boxing, mobility, and transnational networks in the Anglophone world, 1890–1914', *Journal of Global History*, vol. 8, pp. 231–55.

Vamplew, W. 1992. 'Sports crowd disorder: an Australian survey' in J. O'Hara (ed.), *Crowd Violence at Australian Sport*. Sydney: Australian Society for Sports History Inc., University of Western Sydney.

Ward, T. 2009. 'Early sports 1860–1900', *Soccer and Society*, vol. 10, no. 5, pp. 584–98.

Wilson, J. K. and Pomfret, R. 2009. 'Government subsidies for professional team sports in Australia', *Australian Economic Review*, vol. 42, no. 3, pp. 264–75.

Wilson, J. K. and Pomfret, R. 2014. *Public Policy and Professional Sports: International and Australian Experiences*. Cheltenham: Edward Elgar.

12

The Industrialist, the Solicitor, and Mr Justice Higgins

Some Biographical Insights into the Harvester Case of 1907

Peter Yule

The Harvester Case of 1907 was the key case in the development of Australia's unique industrial relations system.[1] Essentially, the case determined that Australia should have a minimum wage set, not by market forces, but a judicial determination of the needs of workers and their families. The uncoupling of wage fixing from the laws of supply and demand, or even a general assessment of economic conditions, was the single most dramatic step that established Australia's special path in industrial relations early in the twentieth century, and it still resonates in Australian public policy debate in the early twenty-first century.

This chapter provides a biographical appreciation of the actors behind this key piece of 'institutional' history.

12.1 Three Irish Families

The story of the Harvester Case is bound up with the history of three Protestant families from Ireland, the Higginses, the McKays, and the Shaws. Henry Higgins, Hugh McKay, and George Shaw were central figures in the case, and a study of their attitudes, beliefs, and actions helps to explain how Australia's unique industrial relations system was shaped.

[1] *Ex Parte H V McKay* 2 CAR 1 1907.

The Higgins family came from the strongly Catholic town of Ballina in County Mayo on the west coast of Ireland.[2] The family had been Catholic but, probably in search of social and economic advantage, became members of the established Church of Ireland in the late eighteenth century. In 1841, however, John Higgins, then aged in his early twenties, converted to Methodism and announced his intention to become a travelling preacher. This led him, and, after his marriage in 1848, his wife and family, to a peripatetic life of relative poverty in a country recently devastated by the Great Famine. Their second of nine children, Henry Bournes Higgins, was born in Newtownards in County Down in 1851. The family continually moved around the Methodist circuits and young Henry was frequently confronted with the brutal realities of extreme poverty in post-famine rural Ireland.

A delicate child, who developed a stammer at a young age, Henry was educated at a Wesleyan boarding school in Dublin, but left school at the age of 14 due to poor health. He worked for some time as a shop assistant before, in 1869, the whole family decided to migrate to Australia, primarily for the healthier climate rather than perceived economic advantages. After arriving in Melbourne, Henry worked as a schoolteacher and began studying law at the University of Melbourne. In his twenties, Higgins abandoned the Wesleyan faith he had been raised in, becoming a 'spiritual agnostic', but he always retained the strong social conscience and commitment to social justice typical of Methodism. He was also a public supporter of Irish home rule, an unpopular position in Protestant circles in Victoria. After graduation, he went to the bar, where he overcame his stammer and quickly prospered. In 1894, he was elected to the Victorian parliament as a 'small l' liberal and supporter of a land tax. He was a Victorian delegate to the Federal Convention of 1897 that framed the Australian Constitution, although he was deeply dissatisfied with the result, regarding the document as rigid and oppressive. Although a good friend of Alfred Deakin, he was always sympathetic to the Labor movement and, in 1901, was elected to the federal parliament for Northern Melbourne, a working-class constituency, and served as attorney-general in the first Labor government in 1904. Higgins was appointed to the High Court in 1906, and the following year became president of the Commonwealth Court of Conciliation and Arbitration. The Harvester Case was the first case Higgins heard as president (Rickard 1984).

In contrast with the southern Irish and Wesleyan Higginses, the McKay and Shaw families were Ulster Presbyterians who had been friends and neighbours for generations. In 1851, the depressed Irish economy, following the famine, prompted the families to sell their farms and other businesses and migrate to

[2] The chief source for this account of the Higgins family is Rickard (1984).

Victoria, arriving in Melbourne on the *Joshua* in January 1852. The first gold rushes in Victoria had begun in mid-1851, and family tradition had always held that the Shaws and McKays came in quest of gold. However, the news of the gold discoveries did not reach Ireland until well after they had left, so it appears that it was just good luck that they arrived in Melbourne in January 1852. They could not have chosen a better time. It is not often talked about these days but Victoria was the Saudi Arabia—or perhaps, more accurately, the Norway—of the 1850s. Gold mining made Victoria enormously wealthy. On a per capita basis Victoria was probably the richest place in the world from the 1850s to the early 1890s.[3] And it was a wonderful place to be a worker. Labour was scarce so wages were high and unemployment low, factors which account for Australia leading the world in the introduction of the eight-hour day (from the mid-1850s) and legislation regulating working conditions (first introduced in Victoria in 1873 (Gollan 1960)).

The first generation of Shaws in Australia did very well. George Shaw, the author's great-grandfather, spent a short time on the gold diggings at Ballarat but he quickly realized that, barring a lucky strike, there was more money to be made in selling provisions to the miners than being a miner. With his brothers he began buying goods cheap in Melbourne and selling dear in Ballarat and Bendigo. The business flourished and, by the 1860s, he was a wealthy man with large shops in Melbourne and the goldfields. In my largely teetotal family it was always said that George Shaw sold groceries, but his newspaper advertisements from the 1860s and 1870s show that he was primarily a wine, spirits, and tobacco merchant.[4] The McKays, on the other hand, persisted longer with mining without ever striking it rich, and then settled on a farm near Raywood in central Victoria in the 1860s. The two families always remained close, and in 1869 George Shaw, then aged 41, married 29-year-old Eliza McKay. They built a large house in East Melbourne and settled down to raise their family of eleven children. Eliza's brother, Nathaniel McKay, and his wife, Mary, had twelve children in their little farmhouse near Bendigo, the fifth being named Hugh Victor, more commonly known by his initials H. V., who was born in 1865.

The Shaw children were educated at private schools in Melbourne, with the boys either entering the professions—medicine or law—or being settled by their father on large grazing properties in western Victoria. In stark contrast, their cousin H. V. McKay left school at the age of 13 to work on the family farm. During the 1870s and 1880s, the wheat industry in Victoria was growing rapidly, but farm labour was expensive and in short supply. Consequently,

[3] During this period Australian gross domestic product (GDP) per capita was perhaps 25 to 30 per cent above the USA and up to 20 per cent above the UK (McLean 2013, p. 12).

[4] A lively, but not altogether accurate, history of the Shaw family is Shaw (1976).

there were strong economic incentives to mechanize farming processes and the government even offered prizes for successful new mechanical harvesters. In 1883, when he was just 18 years old, H. V. McKay built a stripper-harvester using bits and pieces lying around the farm (Lack 1986).

McKay's machine was efficient and effective and he quickly took out a patent. He approached local farmers for financial backing and though he received many knock-backs—notably from Charles Hyde, a prominent Raywood wheat farmer—he gained enough support to set up a factory in Ballarat and began making and selling harvesters. Charles Hyde's decision not to invest in McKay's harvester quickly looked like a mistake as business boomed in the late 1880s. However, he would have felt less foolish when McKay's business was one of thousands that failed in the crash of the early 1890s. Most businesses that failed in the depression of the 1890s never recovered, but McKay successfully restructured his business and, as the economy recovered, it grew at an amazing rate—he sold twelve harvesters in 1895, fifty in 1896, 500 in 1901, and nearly 2,000 in 1906. In 1901 he began exporting harvesters to South Africa, Argentina, and other countries. McKay even made a sales trip to Russia in 1911, but the First World War intervened before he was able to make significant sales. A family tale records that his original booking included a transatlantic voyage on the maiden voyage of the *Titanic*, but he changed his plans not long before the ship sailed to its doom.

By 1904 McKay was Australia's largest exporter of manufactured goods. In real terms his overseas sales were probably greater than any Australian manufacturer before or since. He employed over 500 workers—the number eventually rose to 3,000—and his profits made him a rich man. He installed modern plant and equipment, developed assembly line processes, and ran a business that was highly efficient by world standards. Nonetheless, competition from North American companies such as International Harvester and Massey Harris was fierce, and McKay argued strongly for high tariff protection for his industry.[5]

H. V. McKay had strong views on industrial relations and wage fixing. He believed that market forces should determine wage levels and, at the factory level, he believed in individual bargaining between employer and worker. He was strongly opposed to trade unions and to wages being set by tribunals or arbitration, and in 1904 moved his factory from Ballarat to the outer western Melbourne suburb of Braybrook after obtaining secret undertakings from the Victorian government that the jurisdiction of wages boards and

[5] McKay set out his case for protection in evidence to the Tariff Commission in April 1905. ('Harvesting Machinery. American Competition. Prohibitive Duty Suggested' 1905. See also Lack 1986, pp. 292–3.)

other industrial tribunals would not be extended to his new factory.[6] In spite of this, he was a paternalistic employer, providing his employees with good conditions by the standards of the day and generally paying his workers above-average wages. In 1906, he paid his unskilled workers six shillings a day, while the average for unskilled workers was 5/6d a day (Lack 1986, p. 292).

Today a business of the size of H. V. McKay's would have a team of in-house legal counsel as well as giving large amounts of legal work to the big law firms. In those simpler times, all of McKay's legal work was done by his cousin, George Shaw, the oldest son of George and Eliza Shaw (and the present author's great-uncle). Shaw had completed his law degree in the darkest days of the depression of the 1890s, and set up as a solicitor in Melbourne. He did well and, by the early 1900s, had built up a thriving practice, with McKay as his most important client and industrial law as his main area of practice.[7]

12.2 The Judgement

In 1903 Alfred Deakin became prime minister, and it is Deakin whose name is most closely associated with the Australian 'special way', with the Deakinite Settlement being the name given to the series of measures enacted in the early years of Federation that set out in legislation the basis of Australia's special path. These were the White Australia Policy, protection of Australian industry, and a centralized framework for the arbitration of industrial disputes.[8] Long a protectionist, Deakin described his policy while prime minister as the New Protection—the old protection simply erected tariffs to protect industries from overseas competition, but he believed the New Protection could spread the benefits of tariff protection to workers and even consumers.[9] In 1906, his government passed two related Acts as part of the New Protection policy—the Customs Tariff Act and the Excise Tariff Act. The Customs Tariff Act increased the existing tariff and the Excise Tariff Act introduced a matching new excise on products manufactured in Australia. However, manufacturers would be entitled to a remission of the excise if they paid 'fair and reasonable' wages and reduced the price of their products. The legislation did not define what

[6] 'Mr McKay's Reply' (1904); 'The Factory Act. Sunshine Harvester Works. A Question in Parliament' (1904), 'Sunshine Harvester Works' 1905.

[7] Information about George Shaw junior in this chapter is based primarily on extensive discussions of his son, the late Professor A. G. L. Shaw, with the author.

[8] For an excellent summary of the Deakinite Settlement see Kelly (1994, pp. 5–12), and La Nauze (1965, ch. 18).

[9] For Deakin's own description of the New Protection, see 'Mr Deakin's Third Address. New Protection Scheme. Angling for Labour. Fair Returns and Fair Conditions. Social Legislation. Admiration for Germany' (1906).

'fair and reasonable' wages were, but left this to the new Commonwealth Conciliation and Arbitration Court to decide.

H. V. McKay applied to the Court for remission of excise on his products and the president of the Court, Justice Henry Bournes Higgins, selected his application for a test case to decide what 'fair and reasonable' wages really were.

When the hearing of the Harvester Case began in Melbourne in 7 October 1907, George Shaw set to work to prove that McKay's existing wages were fair and reasonable, while the Agricultural Implement Makers Union, which represented a minority of McKay's workers (most were not union members), argued that wages were far too low. The case ran for twenty days and forty-nine witnesses gave evidence, most of them called by the union.[10]

The union's leaders instructed their barrister to seek wage justice on the basis of McKay's huge profits, but Justice Higgins refused to accept this approach. Rather, he insisted that the case was not about profit-sharing but about the payment of wages before profits were calculated. Higgins believed that an employer who could not pay fair and reasonable wages should not be in business.

Higgins began exploring what the cost of living was in Melbourne in order to ascertain what a fair and reasonable wage should be. His research was amateurish. He took some calculations of the weekly budget of a family of five by Vida Goldstein (1907), a prominent socialist, Christian Scientist and feminist, and then prompted the union to produce the budgets of eleven supposedly random households to show how much it cost for a family to live.

While the case was being heard, George Shaw wrote a letter to a friend:

> I have come to the conclusion that we are sure to have our wages put up. Between you and me I would not be particularly sorry at the result, if I were not battling for McKay. I do not think he could support the wages he pays if he had all the KCs [King's Counsels] in the world. (Shaw 1963, p. 166)

Shaw's anticipation that he would lose the case was correct. Justice Higgins found that the wages paid by McKay to his unskilled workers were not fair and reasonable. He then set about defining 'fair and reasonable'. He consciously and deliberately took no account of market forces or profitability in deciding the case. The judge reasoned that the Act specified that employers should pay 'fair and reasonable' wages and that these words must mean something more than the level set by what he saw as the 'barbarous higgling of the market'. Higgins concluded: 'I cannot think of any other standard than the normal needs of the average employee, regarded as a human being, living in a civilised community.'[11] He argued that:

[10] A good account of the progress of the Harvester Case is in Lack and Fahey (2008).
[11] See 'Harvester Excise. Mr Justice Higgins' Decision' (1907).

> He would not think that an employer and a workman contracted on an equal footing, or made a fair agreement as to wages, when the workman submitted to work for a low wage to avoid starvation or pauperism . . . for himself and his family, or that the agreement was reasonable if it did not carry a wage sufficient to ensure the workman food, shelter, clothing, frugal comfort, provision for evil days, etc.[12]

Using the small survey of household expenses presented as evidence during the case, and guessing (inaccurately) that the average household consisted of a husband, wife, and three children, Higgins ruled that the minimum living wage should be 7 shillings a day.

Although George Shaw was not surprised by this decision and, indeed, privately welcomed it, his cousin was outraged. McKay was even angrier when the Commonwealth followed up with a demand for £20,000 in excise on the grounds that his wages had not been fair and reasonable, even though he had increased his wages to 7s a day following Justice Higgins' judgement. George Shaw realized that the only way out was to challenge the validity of the Excise Tariff Act. In March 1908, when the case was heard by the High Court, McKay's barristers argued that the Act was unconstitutional. The High Court agreed by a majority of three to two (with Higgins one of the dissenters), and in late June the Act was thrown out.[13]

However, while this decision saved McKay from having to pay excise, the principles set out in the Harvester judgement were maintained by the Conciliation and Arbitration Court and became the foundation of the Australian industrial relations system for many decades. The basic wage was set as the minimum wage for an adult male to support himself and his family in frugal comfort, and, on top of this, there developed a complicated system of margins for skill, hard physical labour, and so on.

12.3 The Context

The Harvester judgement struck a strong chord with public opinion in Australia. The belief that the state had a role in adjudicating wages, rather than leaving the matter to the 'higgling of the market' and the 'unequal contest' between employer and individual worker was not new—state wages boards had been introduced from the 1880s. But Higgins' declaration that a minimum 'fair and reasonable' wage should be an absolute amount reflecting a family's cost of living was something quite new.

The fact that George Shaw agreed with the Harvester decision goes a long way towards explaining its quick and widespread acceptance. George Shaw

[12] See 'Harvester Judgement. "Fair and Reasonable Remuneration"' (1907).
[13] For the High Court decision, see '"New Protection" Invalid' (1908, p. 12).

was in most ways a very conservative man. He was a member of the Royal Melbourne Golf Club and the Melbourne Club—he died in his favourite armchair in the Melbourne Club in 1953—and he lived in a large house in Toorak, then, as now, Melbourne's most exclusive suburb. He was strongly partisan in his politics, always voting for the non-Labor parties, which he simply called 'our side'. So why would such a man—and many more conservatives—support the establishment of a legal minimum wage based on the needs of workers and their families rather than leave wage-setting to the operation of market forces?

I think the answer goes back to the depression of the 1890s and the industrial relations turmoil that accompanied it.

The depression of the 1890s was a great shock to contemporaries. Australia had enjoyed sustained economic growth almost without interruption from the discovery of gold in 1851 until the end of the 1880s. Wool and gold were the basis of a highly successful export-oriented economy that gave Australians the highest per capita income in the world. Wages were high because there was a near permanent shortage of labour. During the 1880s, high export prices, the discovery of rich new mines at Mt Morgan and Broken Hill, and rising capital inflow from Britain led to an economic boom across most of Australia. In Melbourne, the boom turned into a frenzied bubble. In 1887 and 1888, prices for city and suburban land doubled, trebled, even quadrupled over a matter of months, share prices soared, and mansions were built for the paper millionaires.[14]

Every boom is followed by a bust and the bust of the early 1890s was of epic proportions. From 1890, most of the economic trends which had caused the boom of the 1880s went into reverse, leading to the most severe depression in Australia's history. The only colony to escape the depression was Western Australia, due to the discovery of gold at Coolgardie and Kalgoorlie. Tens of thousands fled Melbourne and headed west—the population of Melbourne fell from 486,000 in 1891 to 417,000 in 1901, and streets of houses built in the boom stood empty.[15]

The early 1890s saw a massive wave of industrial unrest as workers tried to maintain wages and employment as the economy collapsed, while employers tried to force wages down to keep their businesses afloat. The shearers' strikes and the maritime strike were the largest and most violent, but strikes and lockouts occurred in many other industries. Given the high unemployment it was almost inevitable that the strikes failed, with the result that wages were

[14] The origins of the boom of the 1880s, and particularly the land boom in Melbourne, are discussed in Hall (1968, pp. 117, 126); Davison (1978, pp. 13, 155, 158); Blainey (1958, pp. 130); Boehm (1971, ch. 9); and Cannon (1995, pp. 18–21).

[15] For detailed analyses of the causes of the depression of the 1890s, see Boehm (1971, chs 8, 9, and 10); Blainey (1958, pp. 136–43); Davison, (1978 pp. 167–8); and McLean (2013, ch. 6).

cut and hard-won conditions removed (Gollan, 1960, ch. 8; Blainey 1980, pp. 264–77; Svenson 1989).

The industrial chaos of the early 1890s led to a widespread acceptance of the need for alternative ways of resolving industrial disputes. Discussions of various systems of conciliation and arbitration were a major theme of public policy debate throughout the 1890s and early 1900s. George Shaw frequently spoke of the turmoil of 1890 when shearers, sailors, miners, and other key groups of workers were all on strike or locked out, and enormous demonstrations took place in central Melbourne. Living through this period had a strong impact on him and left him—and many like him—open to new approaches to industrial relations. H. V. McKay was in a minority in maintaining his commitment to settling wages and conditions by direct bargaining between employers and employees.

At a broader level, too, the crash of the 1890s was seen by many as demonstrating the failure of the free market, and there was an increasing acceptance of state intervention in the economy. Socialism was not yet damned by the failure of communism and it attracted increasing support among workers and intellectuals. But even many of those who remained wedded to capitalism supported the extension of state ownership of such things as transport systems, electricity generation, and even, in Queensland, a chain of butchers shops, as well as active state promotion of irrigation and land settlement (Eggleston 1932; Blainey 1994, pp. 125, 141). W. L. Baillieu of the 'Collins House group' was one of Australia's leading industrialists, a co-founder of the Zinc Corporation (now Rio Tinto), the Herald & Weekly Times, Carlton & United Breweries, and many other major companies, and his views largely reflected those of the business establishment of his time. Baillieu was also a Cabinet minister in Victoria from 1909 to 1917. As minister for public works, he advocated the establishment of government-owned cool stores, and responded when it was suggested that this investment should be left to private enterprise:

> Honourable members were now up against the old familiar controversy of Government *versus* private enterprise, but he thought they had lived long enough to realise that there were many things that the State had done with great advantage, and many more things that the State would have to do. (Baillieu 1910, p. 3803)

When a Farmers Union member interjected that 'The withering hand of Government kills everything it touches', Baillieu replied,

> While he admitted that it was difficult in some matters to get the same management under the Government as could be got in connexion with private affairs, he also felt bound to say that, take it in the lump, the management of Government business was more satisfactory than the management of a good many people outside. (Baillieu 1910, p. 3803)

In the early 1900s, as the economy slowly recovered from the depression, two of the major issues facing the new Commonwealth were how to minimize class conflict and maintain Australia as a high-wage economy. The result was the Deakinite Settlement, based on the exclusion of non-European labour, high tariffs, and a conciliation and arbitration system with a high minimum wage. The economic costs of the Deakinite Settlement were not ignored in the first half of the twentieth century. They were clearly pointed out in the 'Brigden Report' of 1929, in Edward Shann's eloquent and despairing *Economic History of Australia* (Shann 1930), and by the various farmers' organizations. In spite of this, a solid majority of the Australian electorate and both major political parties remained firmly wedded to Deakin's principles until the 1960s. Significantly, in the 1930s when the Wheat Growers Union was campaigning for fixed prices for wheat, they based their claims on the Harvester decision, arguing that 'Wheatgrowers, in common with the wage earners, have a right to a normal standard of living equal to the normal needs of a human being living in a civilised community. In common with manufacturers, they have a right to their costs of production, plus a reasonable margin of profit' ('Fixing Wheat Prices by Arbitration' 1935).

Even after the White Australia Policy was abandoned in the 1960s and 1970s and tariff protection for industry dismantled in the 1970s and 1980s, the concept of a legal living minimum wage, set independently of the laws of supply and demand, has remained a strong feature of Australian public policy. Under the Keating government's Industrial Relations Reform Act 1993, a 'safety net' was mandated in terms reminiscent of Justice Higgins' Harvester judgement (Isaac 2008, p. 298). The rhetoric of 'fairness' was removed from wage fixing under the Howard government's 'WorkChoices' policy, but rapidly restored following the defeat of the government in the 2007 election. It appears that, over a century after the Harvester judgement, the Australian electorate remains wedded to the principles set out by Justice Higgins in 1907.

12.4 The Aftermath

Higgins remained president of the Conciliation and Arbitration Court until 1920 when he resigned in protest against what he saw as the Hughes government's undermining of the arbitration system, although he remained on the High Court until his death in 1929. On the Arbitration Court he always maintained the principle he established in the Harvester Case, and as a member of the High Court he resisted the narrow federalism of the first Chief Justice, Sir Samuel Griffith, advocating a far broader interpretation of Commonwealth power.

At the turn of the century, Higgins had been a lonely voice in Australian public life in opposing the Boer War, but in 1914 he could see no alternative to fighting Germany and he did not try to prevent his only son, Mervyn, from enlisting. Mervyn's death in action in 1916 was a devastating blow from which Higgins never recovered. After the war Higgins paid for his nephew, Esmonde, to follow Mervyn's path in studying at Oxford, and he showed remarkable tolerance as Esmonde became a fanatical Marxist and began to attack his uncle as a tool of the capitalist system. In 1922, when Higgins published a book on the conciliation and arbitration system, *A New Province of Law and Order*, Esmonde wrote a shattering review from a socialist perspective. While most unions and almost all employers had seen Higgins as a 'friend of labour', to his nephew, the Arbitration Court under Higgins' leadership had 'emasculated' unionism, broken down class consciousness, acted as 'a mere convenience of capitalist social order', and made labour 'mutely content with a subordinate status' (Rickard 1984, p. 263). Higgins' response was to pen a mild and understanding letter arguing that he had 'of necessity, worked within the system, "under existing facts" in the interest of "workers who in the meantime ought to be fed properly and treated as civilized beings"' (ibid.).

H. V. McKay's business continued to prosper in the years after the Harvester Case, and for many years the Sunshine Harvester Works was the largest factory in Australia. A succession of new products and technological innovations (notably the world's first self-propelled harvester in 1924), together with rising tariff protection, helped the business ward off fierce competition from North American competitors. McKay maintained complete personal control of the business at both a managerial and financial level, and his anti-union and anti-socialist views became ever more strongly entrenched as he aged. He worked hard to keep unions out of his factory, defeating and almost destroying the Agricultural Implement Makers Union after a lengthy strike in 1911. To counter the attraction of unions, he invested heavily to make the suburb of Braybrook—later renamed Sunshine—into 'a model community of worker freeholders opposed to militant unionism' (Lack 1986, p. 293). As well as selling houses to workers on favourable terms, McKay provided the suburb with a public hall, library, public gardens, and electricity, and planted trees and provided land for schools. He also gave his workers generous holiday leave, a contributory accident fund, and a personal loan scheme. McKay believed that these measures would provide 'a loyal, diligent and politically moderate workforce', and, following the defeat of the strike of 1911, industrial relations at the Sunshine Harvester Works appear to have gradually improved (ibid.).

McKay also attempted to promote his views on industrial relations and protection through political action. In 1913 he won the Liberal Party nomination to contest the federal seat of Ballarat when Alfred Deakin, who had held the seat since Federation, retired from politics. McKay was one of the first candidates to use a car for campaigning, touring the electorate in his chauffeur-driven Prince Henry Vauxhall. His speeches emphasized defence and national development, including the need for a 'scientific tariff', and generally avoided industrial relations, although heckling often brought out his strong anti-union beliefs. The campaign was bitterly fought (as evidenced by the subsequent libel actions!), with McKay being narrowly defeated in spite of a nationwide swing to the Commonwealth Liberal Party. His demands for a recount were rejected.[16] The weekly journal *Table Talk* argued:

> Mr. McKay had one great handicap, and that was that he employs labor. Mr. Deakin, his predecessor, had not that black mark against him, and again Mr. Deakin had a high political reputation and unequalled gifts of speech. On the whole, therefore, Mr. McKay's achievement can be put down as remarkably fine.
>
> ('The Week' 1913, p. 4)

Although he was still spoken of as the likely Liberal candidate for Ballarat until late 1913, he did not contest the seat in the 1914 elections.

McKay's decision not to pursue a seat in parliament did not indicate a lessening of his commitment to industrial relations reform. In 1922 McKay and Guillaume Delprat, the recently retired general manager of BHP, launched the 'Single Purpose League', which aimed at the abolition of compulsory arbitration. It is evidence of the general acceptance of the Deakinite vision of industrial relations as symbolized by the Harvester Case that the League failed to gain support even from employer associations, and it petered out by 1924 (Plowman 2011).

McKay and his family lived in a modest house at Sunshine until 1922, when he fulfilled a long-held ambition by purchasing one of Victoria's grandest mansions, Rupertswood, at Sunbury. H. V. McKay died of cancer in 1926 aged only 60. He left an estate valued for probate at £1,448,146, one of Australia's largest fortunes of the early twentieth century, and probably Australia's most significant fortune derived from manufacturing.

In most industrial nations, manufacturing has been the basis of many long-lived family fortunes—Ford, Du Pont, Krupp, Michelin, and Siemens come quickly to mind, and in the field of agricultural machinery, the McLintock family of International Harvester.[17] Yet in Australia the long-lasting fortunes have come from pastoralism, mining, media, city real estate, and retailing.

[16] This account of McKay's candidacy for Ballarat is based on articles such as 'Men of the Moment' (1913), 'Election Irregularities' (1913), 'Political Libel Cases' (1913), 'Ballarat Contest. Recount Refused' (1913), 'Personal' (1913).

[17] A valuable comparative study of the sources and longevity of great family fortunes is Rubinstein (1980). A useful Australian study is Fleming, Merrett, and Ville (2004). Few manufacturing companies feature.

This reflects the structure of the Australian economy, in which the drivers of economic growth have always been a combination of primary industries oriented to export markets and capital formation in the large cities on the eastern seaboard. Manufacturing has been a relative sideline, nurtured by the state to provide employment and supply the domestic market. Without support from tariffs or subsidies, large-scale manufacturing in Australia has always struggled with the problems of a small domestic market, high costs of production, and distance from export markets. Examples of family fortunes derived from manufacturing in Australia are scarce, particularly in the metals and machinery category, in which H. V. McKay and Henry Holden were unusual as successful entrepreneurs in a field dominated by large companies, many of them foreign—significantly, both McKay's and Holden's businesses were bought by North American companies. In other areas of manufacturing, success stories such as those of the Nicholas ('Aspro'), and Ramsay ('Kiwi') families have been rare. A revealing case study is that of Helena Rubinstein, whose globally successful cosmetics manufacturing business had its origins in Coleraine in the Western District of Victoria in 1902, but who moved her entire operations overseas in 1908.

Following McKay's death, the Sunshine Harvester business was run by his brother and then his son, neither of whom came close to matching H. V.'s entrepreneurial flair and business acumen. At the height of the depression in 1930, the business merged with one of its main competitors, the Canadian company Massey Harris, which eventually purchased the McKay family's remaining interests in 1955. The McKay family remained wealthy, but no longer had any ties with the business H. V. had founded, and it has since faded from public life. Agricultural machinery continued to be made at Sunshine until the reduction of tariffs and the rise of foreign competition in the 1970s led to the factory being gradually closed down. Manufacturing ended in the late 1980s and the last section of the factory was sold off in 1992. Much of the factory has been demolished, but the former bulk store, factory gates, clock tower, pedestrian footbridge, factory gardens, and head office complex have been preserved and are listed on the Victorian Heritage Register.

George Shaw continued to act as solicitor for the Sunshine Harvester Works until about 1939, and he was an executor of H. V. McKay's will. Shaw's son, Alan, recalls that his father did not learn to drive until late in life and he would take the train to Sunshine every Friday to deal with the Harvester Works' legal affairs. He was the archetypal city solicitor in the days before specialization and he had a prosperous and highly regarded general legal practice. Alan Shaw was originally destined to study law and join his father's practice, but at university he found he far preferred history to law and, after some family tensions, his father agreed he could concentrate on history. After studying at Oxford in the late 1930s, Alan Shaw had a successful academic career at

Melbourne, Sydney, and Monash Universities, publishing widely on Australian and British imperial history, with perhaps his most notable book being his last, *A History of the Port Phillip District: Victoria before Separation* (Shaw 1996). He had a prodigious and accurate memory and remained lucid until his death in 2012. I was fortunate to be able to spend many hours with him in the decade before his death and we talked extensively about our family history. He had vivid recollections of his father's stories of H. V. McKay and the Harvester Case, and these have provided much of the background for this chapter.

By the time the Harvester Case was heard, Charles Hyde, the Raywood farmer who had rejected young H. V. McKay's plea for financial support in 1884, was considering moving with his family to Australia's new agricultural frontier, the wheat lands of Western Australia. In 1910 he selected land at Dalwallinu, 260 km north-east of Perth, and through hard work and good luck with the seasons and prices he built up a highly successful farming enterprise. By 1929 he owned over 10,000 acres, with 2,900 acres planted for wheat.[18] His grandson, John Hyde, farmed his share of the family properties before turning to politics, where he became famous as a leader of the 'dries' in the Liberal Party, who campaigned strongly for free-market policies during the 1970s and 1980s. The two central planks of the dries' agenda were the dismantling of tariff protection for Australian industry and the freeing up of Australia's rigid and centralized industrial relations system. While they encountered strong resistance from both sides of politics, many of their ideas were taken up by Paul Keating, John Howard, Peter Reith, and others, and they came to dominate Australia's public policy for much of the late 1980s and through the 1990s. As tariff barriers were dismantled and the Chinese economy began its export-driven boom, Australian manufacturing's lack of competitiveness was revealed and the sector rapidly contracted. The Sunshine Harvester Works was just one of the victims. How might recent Australian history have been different if John Hyde's family had taken up and retained a large holding in H. V. McKay's harvester business?

References

Baillieu, W. L. 1910. *Victorian Parliamentary Debates. Legislative Council*, vol. 126, Melbourne: John Ferris.

'Ballarat Contest. Recount Refused'. 1913, *Australasian*, 21 June, p. 35.

Blainey, G. 1958. *Gold and Paper: A History of the National Bank of Australasia*. Melbourne: Georgian House.

Blainey, G. 1980. *A Land Half Won*. Melbourne: Macmillan.

[18] *Western Mail* (Perth), 31 January 1929, p. 49.

Blainey, G. 1994. *A Shorter History of Australia*. Melbourne: William Heinemann.

Boehm, E. A. 1971. *Prosperity and Depression in Australia, 1887–1997*. Oxford: Oxford University Press.

Cannon, M. 1995. *The Landboomers: The Complete Illustrated History*, 2nd paperback edition. Melbourne: Melbourne University Press.

Davison, G. 1978. *The Rise and Fall of Marvellous Melbourne*. Melbourne: Melbourne University Press.

Eggleston, F. W. 1932. *State Socialism in Victoria*. London: P. S. King & Son.

'Election Irregularities'. 1913. *Argus*, 6 June, p. 7.

'Fixing Wheat Prices by Arbitration'. 1935. *Hillston Spectator and Lachlan River Advertiser*, 28 March, p. 7.

Fleming, G., Merrett, D., and Ville, S. 2004. *The Big End of Town: Big Business and Corporate Leadership in Twentieth-Century Australia*. Melbourne: Cambridge University Press.

Goldstein, V. 1907. 'Socialism of to-day: an Australian view', *Nineteenth Century and After*, vol. 62, pp. 406–16.

Gollan, R. 1960. *Radical and Working Class Politics: A Study of Eastern Australia, 1850–1910*. Melbourne: Melbourne University Press.

Hall, A. R. 1968. *The Stock Exchange of Melbourne and the Victorian Economy, 1852–1900*. Canberra: Australian National University Press.

'Harvester Excise. Mr Justice Higgins' Decision'. 1907. *Argus*, 9 November, p. 18.

'Harvester Judgement. "Fair and Reasonable Remuneration"'. 1907. *Sydney Morning Herald*, 9 November, p. 13.

'Harvesting Machinery. American Competition. Prohibitive Duty Suggested'. 1905. *The Argus*, 28 April, p. 9.

Isaac, J. 2008. 'The economic consequences of Harvester', *Australian Economic History Review*, vol. 48, no. 3, pp. 280–300.

Kelly, P. 1994. *The End of Certainty: Power, Politics and Business in Australia*, revised edition. Sydney, New South Wales: Allen & Unwin.

Lack, J. 1986. 'McKay, Hugh Victor' in *Australian Dictionary of Biography*, vol. 10. Melbourne: Melbourne University Press.

Lack, J. and Fahey, C. 2008. 'The industrialist, the trade unionist and the judge: the Harvester judgement of 1907 revisited', *Victorian Historical Journal*, vol. 79, no. 1, pp. 3–18.

La Nauze, J. A. 1965. *Alfred Deakin: A Biography*, vol. 2. Melbourne: Melbourne University Press.

McLean, I. W. 2013. *Why Australia Prospered*. Princeton, NJ: Princeton University Press.

'Men of the Moment'. 1913. *The Argus*, 2 June, p. 11.

'Mr Deakin's Third Address. New Protection Scheme. Angling for Labour. Fair Returns and Fair Conditions. Social Legislation. Admiration for Germany'. 1906. *Sydney Morning Herald*, 28 April, p. 11.

'Mr McKay's Reply'. 1904. *The Argus*, 10 October, p. 5.

'"New Protection" Invalid'. 1908. *Sydney Morning Herald*, 27 June, p. 12.

'Personal'. 1913. *Table Talk*, 30 January, 6 March, 5, 12, and 26 June.

Plowman, J. D. 2011. 'Industrial arbitration and the Single Purpose League', *Journal of Industrial Relations*, vol. 53, no. 2, pp. 209–24.

'Political Libel Cases'. 1913. *Argus*, 6 September, p. 9.

Rickard, J. 1984. *H. B. Higgins: The Rebel as Judge*. Sydney: Allen & Unwin.

Rubinstein, W. D. (ed.). 1980. *Wealth and the Wealthy in the Modern World*. London: Croom Helm.

Shann, E. 1930. *An Economic History of Australia*. Cambridge: Cambridge University Press.

Shaw, A. G. L. 1963. 'The Harvester Case: a personal note,' *Journal of Industrial Relations*, no. 5, p. 166.

Shaw, A. G. L. 1996. *A History of the Port Phillip District: Victoria before Separation*. Melbourne: Miegunyah Press.

Shaw, M. P. 1976. *The Shaws of Tullyvallin*. Melbourne: National Press.

Svenson, S. 1989. *The Shearers' War: The Story of the 1891 Shearers' Strike*. Brisbane: University of Queensland Press.

'Sunshine Harvester Works'. 1905. *The Argus*, 6 February, p. 6.

'The Factory Act. Sunshine Harvester Works. A Question in Parliament'. 1904, *The Argus*, 9 November, p. 4.

'The Week'. 1913. *Table Talk*, 5 June, p. 4.

13

Barons versus Bureaucrats

The History of the Grain Trade in North America and Australia

Nick Cater

The pioneers of American industrialization get a bad press. The sobriquet 'robber barons' carries an imputation of theft, and reflects the widespread view that their wealth was accumulated dishonourably at the expense of the common good. The innovation, growth, and prosperity they stimulated seems easily forgotten.

In Australia, economic expansion in the late nineteenth and early twentieth centuries relied less on individual initiative and more heavily on state sponsorship. Infrastructure was paid for with government borrowings, wages and conditions were heavily regulated, and key industries were state controlled. As in the USA, 'the motive power of human progress' (Menzies [1942] 1980, p. 60) was individual ambition, but colonial governments in Australia assumed a central role in national development.

The expansion of grain production in North America and Australia, beginning in the second half of the nineteenth century, allows us to compare contrasting approaches to developing the New World. One might be characterized as baronial; the other bureaucratic. In America, risk-takers took advantage of a lightly regulated economy and pushed back the boundaries of the frontier. They invested in technology, developed sophisticated trading systems, and embraced competition, to drive down margins and costs.

In Australia, by contrast, a system of 'colonial socialism' emerged in the eastern colonies between 1860 and 1890. The railways that made large-scale cultivation of grain feasible were financed, built, and operated by government, an arrangement uncommon at the time (Ergas and Pincus 2015). Australian farmers looked to the benevolence of the state to protect their interests to a much greater extent than in the USA. Farming cooperatives, which became dominant players in the Canadian grain market, were largely absent in the eastern states.

The extent to which these structural differences influenced the fortunes of the grain trade is the subject of this chapter. Did the hunger of profit-seekers give the North Americans a competitive edge? Had these super-capitalists taken to the field in Australia, would grain have made a greater contribution to national prosperity? Or did Australia's peculiar geographical and climatic situation demand a paternalistic, interventionist state?

It is contended here from the outset that North America's dominance of the international grain market was not predetermined. Australia's challenges of climate and distance were not insurmountable. Indeed, the harsh sub-Arctic conditions of the Canadian interior posed their own difficulties. North America's advantage was largely achieved in grain *handling* rather than growing. The introduction of central trading, mechanised handling systems, and efficient transportation was driven by entrepreneurs. The Australian grain-handling system, on the other hand, relied on state investment, socialized marketing, and central planning. A shortage of capital, the absence of political will, and vested self-interest account for the strange delay in the introduction of bulk handling of grain in Australia—epitomized by the concrete grain elevator. Not until after the First World War—and after the Second World War in some states—was this innovation embraced, by which time North American pre-eminence was entrenched.

A century later, the consequences of these divergent paths can be seen in the global dominance of North American agribusiness corporations. The emergence of these corporations as players in the Australian market in recent decades may represent the final triumph of the barons over the bureaucrats.

13.1 'Bread enough to Spare'

The conversion of grassland to grain-land in the New World was an agricultural transformation of epic proportions. Vast swathes of uncultivated land in America, Australia, Canada, Argentina, and elsewhere were turned over to cultivation to supply expanding international markets. The boundaries between wilderness and civilization were pushed further into continental interiors. Innovation, mechanization, the development of efficient supply chains, the expansion of free trade, and the frontier spirit of adventurous migrants expanded human settlement at a previously unimaginable pace.

The demand for imported wheat grew rapidly in nineteenth-century Britain as the Industrial Revolution drove urbanization and population growth. In part it was encouraged by an early, bold experiment in free trade—the repeal in 1846 of the Importation Act of 1815 (55 Geo.3c.26)—the Corn Laws—that had imposed steep import duties on cereals. International trade in perishable goods was becoming less hazardous and less costly. Transportation by sea became faster and cheaper with the development of clippers and the introduction of steam. The use of hardwood and iron offered better protection for biodegradable cargoes. Improvements in agricultural technology in the second half of the nineteenth century would make broadacre farming feasible in pioneering colonies where labour was in short supply.[1]

Australia's early settlers, like their North American predecessors, had struggled to make unfamiliar and seemingly lifeless soils productive, a task driving them at times to the point of despair. But in the space of two generations, Australia's prospects had been transformed. The new colony of South Australia had developed a new system of settlement, enticing migrants with the promise of land. Its early success was remarkable. In 1847, a mere eleven years into the life of the newly-founded colony, the editor of the *South Australian Register*, John Stephens, wrote an open letter to his former countrymen in the motherland inviting them to emigrate to 'one of the most favoured portions of the Great Southern Land' (Stephens 1847, p. 1). His letter described the bounty:

> The settlers may be said to lack for nothing, for, by the blessing of the Most High upon their labours, they have not only bread enough to spare, but their garners are so full that those who cultivated for the supply of thirty thousand souls, have lately been able to send over sea, to British ports, more than thrice thirty thousand bushels of wheat which challenge a comparison with any grown in any other part of the world; and still they have thousands of superfluous bushels to sell. 'We are', say the growers, 'compelled to send it away for a market, because people do not flock here fast enough to eat our bread stuff'. (Stephens 1847, p. 1)

Australia was at the forefront of agricultural innovation in the second half of the nineteenth century, spurred by the challenge of overcoming the continent's soil, climate, and geography, and the shortage and expense of labour. Mechanical innovation, such as the invention of the stump-jump plough, Ridley's stripper, and the Sunshine harvester, increased efficiency and lowered costs. Yet by 1914, Canada and the USA were firmly established as Britain's principal suppliers of wheat, with Australia running a distant third. Canada, a relatively late developer in grain production, began to open up a gap in terms of wheat production in the first decade of the twentieth century. Until the 1880s, Canadian and Australian wheat production grew at a similar pace. Subsequently, Canadian production grew at a much faster rate than Australian production, and by

[1] Broadacre farming: 'the farming of large tracts of land as a single operation resulting in economies of scale' (Broadacre Farming 2013, p.244).

Table 13.1 Annual Wheat Production in Australia and Canada, 1875–1913
Ten-Year Averages

	Australia, million bushels	Canada, million bushels	Australia as percent of Canada
1875	13.6	21.2	64
1880	16.5	21.7	76
1885	21.8	30.1	73
1890	26.6	38.5	69
1895	28.7	42.7	67
1900	29.3	49.3	59
1905	35.9	65.3	55
1910	52.6	95.4	55
1913	65.3	128.4	51

Source: O'Connor 1970.

1913 Canada was typically producing twice as much wheat each year (Table 13.1).[2]

The romance of taming 'a sunburnt country' looms large in the Australian imagination. It is the narrative that invites the celebration of success achieved against the odds. But it also offers an excuse for failure. While the challenges of farming in Australia may be different from those in other New World territories, it is hard to argue that climate, soil, or geography are the only reasons why Australia has been less successful as a grain producer and exporter than Canada or the USA. Australian dominance of the wool trade, and its later success in the supply of frozen meat, has shown that the 'tyranny of distance' between supplier and consumer can be overcome.

For ease of settlement, Australia ranked far above Canada for the prospective migrant. A British journalist noted in 1905:

> The rich chocolate soil of Tasmania, the fertile belts of Gippsland, etc., are not surpassed even in the choicest selection of New Ontario, the coming boom land of Canada. Winter in Canada continues throughout half of the year, during which time the lakes are ice-bound, the woods are silent and the earth is covered with a mantle of frozen snow...
>
> Many false impressions exist in Great Britain about Australia, encouraged by exaggerated accounts of drought, expensive living, wild dogs and cannibals. Personally I am prepared to recommend Australia in preference to Canada.
>
> ('Australia and Canada' 1905, p. 5)

It is the parallels in their general environments, and not the differences, that are striking in the comparison of Australian and North American wheat lands. Thus Donald W. Meinig's 1959 study comparing the wheat regions of the Columbia interior of the American Pacific Northwest and the northern wheat

[2] In the five years ending in 1913, wheat production in Australia was just 44 percent that of Canada, the lowest percentage of any quinquennial period between 1870 and 1913.

lands of South Australia notes that both the northern expansion of wheat-growing in South Australia and the eastward expansion in America from the Willamette River pushed settlers into areas that were widely believed to be too dry for agriculture. The landscapes were similar; rolling hills with a summer-dry climate, ranging from sub-humid to semi-arid. Rapid colonization occurred at the same time—the 1870s and 80s—under similar economic conditions. In both, cultivation was 'an experimental folk process' (Meinig 1959). In both areas, wheat varieties evolved to suit local conditions. The Federation cultivar was developed in Australia, capable of resisting the onset of rust in warm, moist conditions. In Canada and the USA, hard varieties of red spring and winter wheat were developed, together with milling technology capable of breaking it. Indeed, all other things being equal, Australian soft wheat was a superior product to the 'hard' winter wheat of North America.

Neither was there any significant gap in technology. Pioneers on both sides of the Pacific were ingenious in developing machinery to master local conditions. The counterpart of the chilled steel mould-board plough used to turn the tough prairie sods of America was the stump-jump plough that tilled the Mallee lands of South Australia. As Meinig notes, 'the reaper and the stripper and the remarkably different harvesters were prominent examples of near simultaneous, yet independent inventions' (1959, p. 208).

While Australia's arid interior imposed natural limits on the advance of the plough, an equal if not greater challenge was the efficient delivery of grain to market. It was here that America gained its vital competitive advantage. Australian producers had demonstrated they could satisfy distant markets with a high value-to-weight product like wool. Transporting a high-volume, low-value commodity like wheat, however, required capital investment, astute decisions, and a healthy appetite for risk. It would require not just grit, but raw animal spirit. Nowhere in the second half of the nineteenth century was the spirit of enterprise more alive than in the American Midwest, where innovations in trade and mechanics would transform the supply of grain.

13.2 Inventing a Grain Market

The introduction of bulk handling in the American Midwest in the second half of the nineteenth century transformed the supply chain into a river, with tributaries feeding main arteries and eventually flowing to the sea. From the start of the export trade, the North American grain industry was geared to bulk handling. Australia was slow to adopt the innovation. Bulk handling was not introduced in New South Wales (NSW) until after the First World War, and another forty years again passed before the process was adopted in every state.

Bulk handling was preceded by two innovations in trading.

The first innovation was the establishment of the Chicago Board of Trade in 1848, moving transactions from offices, warehouses, and bars to a central location (Cronon 1992, p. 115). Traders began to take samples to the board, where they would arrange contracts between buyers and sellers. The larger the volume of wheat traded and the greater the number of trades, the more efficient the market would become.

The second trading innovation occurred in 1856 when the board began regulating the quality of wheat. The introduction of three grades—white winter wheat, red winter wheat, and spring wheat—would, according to historian William Cronon, 'forever transform the grain trade of the world' (Cronon 1992, p. 116). At a stroke, one of the greatest logistical challenges for shippers—separating consignments from each producer and tracking their progress through to sale—was overcome. Farmers would deliver their harvest to the warehouse and would be issued with a receipt for the value of the same quantity of equally graded grain. As Henry Crosby Emery notes: 'the development of a system of grading and of elevator receipts is the most important step in the history of the grain trade' (Emery 1896, p. 38). Cronon observes that the development would 'sever the link between ownership rights and physical grain, with a host of unanticipated consequences' (Cronon 1992, p. 116).

One result was better grain, since farmers and shippers had a financial incentive to improve the quality of their wheat. Dirty wheat, or consignments bulked out with oats or chaff, became less common. The Board developed its own rigorous inspection programme, which in time would be recognized by civil courts. Grading also served as means of inventory control that made bulk handling possible. It allowed the introduction of elevators; vertical warehouses storing loose grain located adjacent to railways, no more than a day by horse power from the farm. Bagging would become redundant. Transporting loose grain in railway box cars was less laborious and more efficient. Faster loading reduced the amount of down time for rolling stock.

An agreed standard for graded wheat encouraged greater financial complexity. Traders could sell not just physical wheat but wheat that was yet to be harvested. When the telegraph arrived in Chicago in 1848, the transmission of commodity prices quickly became its core business. Eastern and western markets began to operate in tandem. In time, the development of an active futures market, formalized by the Board of 1865, would be a source of grievance for producers, who saw speculative traders deriving undeserved profits from the products of their labour. Yet the futures market brought considerable benefits to farmers and shippers alike. First, it helped reduce the fluctuations between glut and scarcity, thereby stabilizing prices. Second, it increased the availability of credit, since the standardization of grades regulated by boards of trade gave certainty to contracts. Farmers and dealers had easy access to cash by borrowing against elevator receipts and contracts. Third, the risks of deterioration and fluctuating prices were no longer concentrated on the owners, but were transferred from the growers to the traders, who could bear them more easily. Fourth, the sheer size of the Chicago market gave it an insatiable appetite for grain. It gave railway companies and elevator operators the confidence to pursue speculative extensions into uncultivated regions in the Northwest and into Canada. They were prepared to do so on the grounds that they might achieve an effective 'line monopoly', allowing them to receive a reliable return on their capital investment.

13.3 'A Buckler to Defend Villainy'?

The growth of the grain trade in the Midwest occurred organically, with only a light interventionist touch from the courts and legislatures. When the courts were asked to adjudicate, their broad inclination was to interfere as little as possible. As Jonathan Lurie observes, the judiciary was inclined to trust the Board of Trade's capacity to self-regulate. It was essentially a private club, but one which understood the workings of the markets and had a vested interest in preserving their integrity. The Board of Trade, says Lurie:

> acted like a legislature in passing certain rules and regulations that were binding upon its members. It acted like a judge when it heard complaints, issued penalties and tried to mediate disputes. In enforcing the rules it adopted, the Board demonstrated executive authority. (Lurie 1979, p. 9)

A robust challenge to unregulated markets came from the agrarian movement, which gathered a head of steam in the 1890s. Farmers laboured in a world remote from the commodities market, where distrust of potential speculative abuses festered. There was particular anger about the so-called bucket shops, unofficial trading floors which blurred the line between speculation and gambling. The agrarians crusaded for anti-option legislation, in an attempt to forbid the trade in non-existent grain. A petition to Tennessee Senators Isham Harris and William Bate from the 'farmers and citizens of Shelby County' offers a taste of their complaint against 'these great combines, trusts and monopolies' that 'obstruct legitimate commerce by inextricably blending and interweaving future contracts' and thereby 'kill off the real article':

> Senators! God never made a richer land than ours . . . but the hands of men exerted and extended from afar in evil combination are robbing us of our industry and plundering us by the capitalistic ledgerdemain of 'futures' . . .
>
> Through the subtle and devilish perversions of reasoning practiced by the brightest prostituted minds of the age, retained and employed as paid attorneys and lobbyists by evil capitalistic syndicates with sinister designs, the Constitution

> is now used as a cloak to hide rascality, a shield to protect fraud, a buckler to defend villainy. (Cited in Lurie 1979, p. 114)

In 1891, William Hatch of Missouri presented an anti-option bill to the US House of Representatives. But after four years of political wrangling it was finally rejected in 1895, reaffirming the ascendancy of speculation and the unregulated market.

Thus, the judiciary and legislators provided the conditions in which entrepreneurialism would flourish. They allowed for the construction of private railway networks—the arteries of the grain trade—and gave trading companies the confidence to invest heavily in infrastructure in the pursuit of market dominance. Their investment was the driving force in the expansion of wheat-growing in North America.

13.4 The Barons

The buccaneering, self-reliant industrialists, who were a feature of North American life in the late nineteenth century, played an indispensable role in the growth of the North American trade. They were risk-takers who balanced debt and reinvested profits to grow their businesses rapidly and dominate the market. The empires they created laid the foundation for the twentieth-century corporation.

Economic historians have sometimes portrayed the so-called robber barons as immoral and rapacious. Yet the success of the North American grain trade forces us to reassess this one-dimensional stereotype. Their contribution as agents of growth is rarely acknowledged; it is clear that the nineteenth-century tycoons created far more wealth than they accumulated.

Principal-owner-controlled companies with no dread of risk provided the motive power for the growth of the wheat industry in Canada and the USA. Had it not been for the railway and wheat barons, large swathes of the Northwest may never have been settled.

When the potential of rail haulage to improve the value of farmland became apparent in the first half of the nineteenth century, the open question in both America and Australia was whether the capital investment could be recovered. Receipts from passengers and agricultural freight by themselves, even on the most optimistic projections, were unlikely to generate sufficient profit. Private investors would need land holdings that would offer capital gain when the amenity lifted land values.

In North America, subsidies and land grants were offered to encourage private entrepreneurs to push back the boundaries of the frontier by building railways that encouraged settlement and released the economic potential of land. This build-and-they-will-come model of infrastructure-led development was followed in virtually every corner of the expanding New World in the late nineteenth and early twentieth centuries, with private entrepreneurs, rather than governments, carrying most of the risk. Australia was the exception. Its reliance on government-driven infrastructure, notably railways, had a profound influence on the continent's human geography and economic development. In Australia, railways would chiefly service existing communities; in North America, railways would forge a passage into the wilderness to encourage new settlement.

The role of the rail barons in driving the expansion of wheat farming in North America is illustrated in the life of James J. Hill. As a shipping clerk in Minneapolis–Saint Paul, Hill developed an interest in the potential of the undeveloped territory between Minnesota and Washington state. In 1878, with the support of Canadian investors, he bought the bankrupt St. Paul and Pacific Railway and began to extend it into North Dakota, empty and unsettled territory. He offered settlers a $10 passage on the condition they settle near his railway. The company established experimental farms and sponsored agricultural competitions to encourage innovative farming. It courted investors to construct elevators along the track.

Hill's Northern Pacific competed with the government-assisted Union Pacific (UP) and Central Pacific that had been granted land and subsidies for each completed mile of track. The rush for subsidies led the rail builders to cut corners. Workmanship was substandard; rails laid in the frozen winter months had to be rebuilt in the spring; the tracks meandered circuitously into wastelands, driven by the lure of working capital rather than any considered plan for settlement. In the drive to court politicians, the UP spent lavishly on hospitality, to no obvious benefit to its shareholders or customers.

Hill, on the other hand, directed his efforts to build efficient railways taking the most economical path: 'What we want is the best possible line, shortest distance, lowest grades and least curvature that we can build. We do not care enough for Rocky Mountains scenery to spend a large sum developing it' (cited in Malone 1996, p. 249). The Northern Pacific grew incrementally, nurturing new settlements and realizing a return on capital before forging further west.

In was in Hill's interest that the farmers should succeed. He promoted dry-farming to increase yields, and gave away 7,000 cattle imported from England to encourage diversity. He subsidized the fares of settlers, telling immigrants, 'we are in the same boat as you, we have got to prosper with you or be poor with you' (Folsom 1987, p. 27).

While the federally-assisted transcontinental projects were obliged to use American steel, Hill bought higher-grade steel from Britain and Germany, giving the Northern Pacific lower fixed maintenance costs. Unlike his competitors, Hill was under no obligation to carry mail at a loss. Finally, Hill's Northern Pacific could build branch lines without congressional approval, enabling it to push north across the Canadian border as far as Manitoba, with a series of spurs along the way. Thus, the Northern Pacific's network came to resemble a riverine system with a vast number of tributaries, each joining the main current that flowed like a mighty river into the heart of Minneapolis–Saint Paul.

In Australia, the political and economic climate made it difficult for entrepreneurs like Hill to flourish. Thomas McIlwraith, a Scottish-born engineer, surveyor, politician, embryonic shipping magnate, and the eighth premier of Queensland, was arguably the closest Australia came to a rail baron. McIlwraith proposed a privately funded 2,000 km transcontinental line in Queensland, linking the Darling Downs with the Gulf of Carpentaria, which would form a freight corridor for pastoralists and a putative grain trade. It would unlock the interior, encourage settlement and migration, and link south-east Queensland with an imagined port in the Gulf of Carpentaria, shortening travelling times from Europe to the Australian continent.

The Railway Companies Preliminary Act of 1880 made possible land grants to private railways, a model that had already proved successful in the USA and had recently been adopted by the Canadian federal government for the construction of a transcontinental line. The following year the *Brisbane Courier* cited the North American experience where private interests had 'made available for profitable occupation millions of acres which would have otherwise lain waste' (*Brisbane Courier* 1881, p. 4). The promise of land had attracted a better class of migrant; 'the cream of pioneer populations, and worthy of the highest praise for their eminent respectability and their standing in imparting character to the country'.[3]

Opposition to the proposal was strong, however. *The Telegraph* objected to the granting of land at a knock-down price to 'dummiers and landsharks'.

> It is proverbial that large companies have no conscience and are mercilessly cold-blooded... The only place in which land grant railways have been constructed as yet is the United States of America, and they have been gigantic swindles from beginning to end. ('The Telegraph' 1881, p. 2)

Pastoralists from the north and west of the state joined forces with McIlwraith's political opponent, Samuel Griffith, to block the proposal. While the dream of a Queensland transcontinental railway lived on until the early twentieth century, in reality it was a lost cause. Political parochialism played a part in the failure of McIlwraith's scheme, and investors may well have been nervous at the fragile business case. Waterson (1986) highlights the

[3] *The Brisbane Courier*, 6 August 1881, p. 2.

problematic climate and the onset of drought. The company had limited knowledge of the land or its economic potential. The potential to build a port in the shallow coastal waters of the Gulf was limited, to say the least.

Yet other attempts to facilitate private investment through the land-grant model supported by government guarantees failed to get off the ground in NSW and Victoria, forcing the burden for railway development onto the state (Ergas and Pincus 2015).

Government entry into railways in Australia to the exclusion of private can be explained in ad hoc terms (Butlin 1959, p. 40). The consequence for the pattern of railway development, however, was profound, as John Foster Fraser observed in 1911. In Australia, railways followed settlement; in North America it led it.

In 1891 the Victorian Minister for Lands told the Select Committee upon the Settlement of the Mallee Country:

> I am afraid it is hardly practicable that the railway should precede settlement.... The country has been always anxious to have some guarantee that there would be a fair traffic when the line is opened, but I think they should go on simultaneously... there would be no difficulty in getting an increased price for the land where there was a guarantee of railway construction and water conservation. (Cited in Dunsdorfs 1956, p. 163)

Political, rather than economic, considerations came to the fore. 'The taxpayer has to find the money; naturally he wants the railway to come near him', wrote Fraser (1911, p. 163). Variations in rail gauges, in some cases even within states, presented a further obstacle to national development:

> The present lines were constructed with as little consideration for the benefit of the whole continent as a railway in Finland would be built with consideration for the benefit of Italy...
>
> That the confusion of present system is detrimental to pastoralists, agriculturalists and traders generally will not deny. As there is no competition, there is no choice of routes, and the State Government does much as it likes.
>
> (Fraser 1911, pp. 109–11)

Cost, logistical barriers, and the failure to use railways to drive new settlement meant that, by the turn of the century, Australia was far less able than the USA and Canada to adapt to bulk handling.

13.5 Elevator Tycoons

The contrast in railway development in the two continents is matched by a closely connected contrast in the deployment of grain elevator.

The story of grain elevators in the USA might be said to start with Frank H. Peavey arriving in Sioux City, Iowa, in 1866 with a dollar in his pocket, and using it to trade grain. In 1874 he joined the Minneapolis Millers Association, where he conceived of an audacious plan to divert the flow of wheat away from Iowa and through Minneapolis. He persuaded the company to build a network of warehouses and elevators along the Chicago–Minneapolis–Saint Paul Railway, and then extended his network along other rail lines (Morgan 1979, pp. 54–5).

Building the capacity to store grain in quantities that would allow the barons to influence the market was technologically challenging. Since their introduction in the mid-1800s, elevators have been constructed using combustible timber. By the end of the nineteenth century, the risk of fire made them virtually uninsurable. In early 1899, Peavey and engineer Charles F. Haglin began investigating the possibility of using reinforced concrete, a relatively new material, to construct grain elevators.

Their prototype, the Peavey–Haglin Experimental Concrete Grain Elevator, was completed in 1900 in St Louis Park, Minnesota, alongside the tracks of the Northern Pacific. The success of the experiment encouraged Peavey's company to commit to the construction of a 34-metre-high concrete elevator at Duluth, Minnesota, on Lake Superior, at the western end of the St Lawrence Seaway. With a capacity of 3.5 million bushels it would have been capable of storing a third of South Australia's annual wheat crop. Within a decade, a network of majestic concrete elevators spanned the Midwest plains like rural skyscrapers.

An Australian visitor to the USA marvelled at the efficiency of the competitive grain-handling system:

> There are no fewer than 36 elevator companies in Minneapolis, controlling 1,862 country elevators with a combined capacity of nearly 50,000,000 bushels of wheat . . .
>
> These elevators are distributed along nearly every railroad line touching Minneapolis, and they form a network of business enterprise covering five States. Every part of every system vibrates in instant sympathy with the controlling head at Minneapolis, and deals are made with a rapidity fairly dizzying to the outsider.
>
> The manager of a local house may buy a thousand bushels a day. The central office at Minneapolis is immediately informed of the amount by telegraph, and within an hour every bushel is sold on the floor of the Chamber of Commerce . . .
>
> Perhaps no one thing so simplifies and facilitates the movement of wheat as the present rigid system of inspection and grading. In former times a load of grain must needs be carefully examined by every prospective purchaser, were he miller or commission man; and if this buyer sold again, a second examination became necessary, with its attendant disagreement as to quality.
>
> The business of wheat-buying, indeed, was full of time-consuming details, and in the end neither party to a trade was likely to be satisfied.
>
> As a consequence, the state government, or, in some primary markets, the local chamber of commerce, stepped in, and assumed charge of the whole system of

> grading and inspection; and now no portion of the great wheat business moves with more ease and efficiency, a degree of care and accuracy simply amazing to the outsider being constantly maintained. (Baker 1900, p. 46)

The Northern Pacific was thus able to forge a symbiotic relation with the grain handlers, who would compete to build elevators along the route and vast storage elevators in Minneapolis–Saint Paul to tap the river of grain.

The theory that the private rail companies exploited line monopolies to collude with grain traders against the interests of producers has become part of the robber baron folk law. It is true that the high capital costs of entry present a formidable barrier to entry, and that competition was narrowed further by what might euphemistically be termed sharp practices. Yet the competition between the transcontinental hauliers on both sides of the 49th parallel had a measurable bearing on price. In Australia, where the parochial fanning of rail networks from state capitals and eclectic mix of rail gauges enforced a form of interstate protectionism, there would be next to no competition in rail transport for another century. Australian railways were expensive to build and expensive to run by international standards. Fraser notes the average freight charge in NSW of 1.62d per mile was six times higher than that on the Chicago–New York route (Fraser 1911, p. 115).

The robber baron narrative takes no account of the interest shared by producers, hauliers, and traders in a maintaining a vigorous market for grain. Their relationship was not, as writers like Morgan seem to insist, between the exploiter and the exploited. It was one characterized by the mutual dependency that arises with the division of labour in a modern, industrialized economy.

Grain-handling efficiency reached its zenith in Canada where three forces—an enlightened colonial state, a vibrant free market leeching across the border, and entrepreneurial farmers' cooperatives—worked in harmony. Bulk handling was already established practice in the USA in the 1880s when construction of the transcontinental Canadian Pacific Railway (CPR) began, and the requirement for grain-loading facilities influenced its physical and economic design. The proximity of the US market introduced an element of competition, as grain was drawn south into the Minneapolis trading system. Hill's Great Northern pushed north of the border in search for new sources of grain, which was funnelled from Manitoba via St Vincent into Minneapolis.

The CPR was privately built with a generous subsidy from the Canadian government of $25 million and a grant of 100,000 square kilometres of land. The land parcels would give the CPR a share of the uplift in land values, thus giving the company an incentive to ensure that settlement succeeded.

The CPR issued licences to private companies for the construction of wooden elevators along the route. It offered free land rental but enforced construction standards with a minimum capacity of 25,000 bushels. By 1890 there were ninety elevators—so-called Prairie sentinels—in western Canada, with a total capacity of 4.3 million bushels. Many of these were built speculatively by small investors. Districts looking for settler farmers would use their 'elevator rows' as a draw.

In 1897 western Canadian wheat began to be traded at the Winnipeg Grain and Produce Exchange. It became the nucleus of the prairie grain business, introducing futures trading from 1904. Between 1896 and 1911, Manitoba quadrupled its wheat harvest, producing 60 million bushels—equivalent to two-thirds of the wheat harvested in Australia that year.

The CPR was obliged to compete for traffic with the US railways from its inception, keeping freight costs in check to the benefit of farmers and traders. In 1884, for instance, CPR introduced a special east-bound grain rate with the express intention of drawing trade from the cross-border route (Innis 1923, p. 179). It faced further competition from the Canadian Northern Railway, completed in 1900, that linked the prairies to the Great Lakes though the port of Thunder Bay, 300 km north of Duluth, Minnesota.

The heirs to Peavey's US grain empire entered the Canadian boom by building a network of fifty elevators along the Canadian Pacific in Saskatchewan. But from 1910 onwards there was increasing political pressure from farmers demanding government intervention to curb the power of what they regarded as local private monopolies. State governments largely resisted the calls for nationalization, instead offering assistance for the establishment of farmers' cooperatives (Storey 2006). Thus, the Canadian grain market came to be dominated by growers' cooperatives for the next eighty years, notably the Saskatchewan Wheat Pool. Crucially, however, the bulk-handling stream was well established by 1910, influenced by the model developed in the USA and thanks to heavy private investment—albeit with government incentives—to establish a network of large-scale, efficient elevators across the prairies. The proximity to the American Northwest and the expansion of railways across the border, including Northern Pacific, introduced an element of competition, driving down freight prices and giving farmers some choice in the market. The effect was to ensure that Canadian producers, like their American neighbours, could benefit from the maximization of prices thanks to futures trading and the ability to store large quantities of grain. While prices fluctuated, the dominance of the Canadian export market and its competitive handling costs allowed producers the assurance of steady demand in good years and bad.

By the end of the 1920s Canada was producing more than a third of world grain exports. Even more so than in the USA, the Canadian grain-handling system operated as a complete and integrated whole. There were 5,400 country elevators with a capacity of 180 million bushels. The thirty-eight public elevators could store half as much again. They were linked seamlessly by

66,000 km of railway and a huge fleet of ships able to navigate the inland waterways.

13.6 Why Were There No Grain Elevators in Australia?

By contrast, wheat handling in Australia at the start of the twentieth century was a laborious, wasteful, and piecemeal process. Wheat was shovelled in hessian sacks imported from India, sown by hand, and then loaded and unloaded multiple times in their journey from farm to mill.

Among the factors inhibiting the introduction of bulk handling was the lack of a sophisticated grading system. A trusted and reliable wheat multiple-grade system had operated in the USA since 1856 and in Canada since 1900. In Australia there was just one grade, fair average quality, or f.a.q., adopted in Victoria in 1891, NSW in 1899, and Western Australia in 1905. The stubbornly egalitarian measure of f.a.q. referred not to the grain's baking quality but the milling quality, which tolerated a level of dirt and impurity. Despite its obvious failings, opposition to its replacement by a multi-grade system was still ferocious in the mid-1920s. In their 1926 book, *The Wheat Industry in Australia*, Callaghan and Millington seem sympathetic to the arguments in favour of retaining f.a.q.:

> If a new system were adopted, it is argued, oversea millers would want to buy only one or two classes for blending purposes and in consequence our wheats would immediately come into open competition with 'graded' wheats of other origins. This could quite easily react to the detriment of Australian growers. There is a possibility that the classes wanted by oversea millers would command a premium on present f.a.q. prices but this advantage could be more than offset by the discount it would be necessary to accept on the other classes.
>
> (Callaghan and Millington 1926, p. 363)

Yet the failings of the measure had been clear. Professor Lowrie, the principal of Roseworthy Agricultural College, writing more than a quarter of a century earlier, claimed:

> The standard is generally fixed so low that good farmers suffer . . . I have heard many farmers express surprise and disgust when shown the 'standard sample' going out as representative of the Colony's wheat. It has certainly contained a percentage of rubbish that should not be there—drake, wild oats, chaff, shriveled and broken grain and also other impurities such as barley, small pellets of stone, etc. If wheat merchants in London pay attention to this sample it must affect disadvantageously the reputation of our wheat. (Lowrie 1899, p. 572)

In 1915–16, according to one estimate, £216,720 was spent on transporting waste, dirt, and screenings mixed with wheat to export markets. As Griffiths writes: 'The farmer says "But I was paid wheat price for that." So he was... because whatever he sends, however clean it may be, he gets only f.a.q. price' (Griffiths 1920, p. 3). With no reliable method of determining quality, bulk handling was impossible.

The bulk-handling question was a matter of considerable enquiry before the First World War, but recommendations for its introduction were 'received with apathy', according to the compilers of the 1953 *Commonwealth Year Book* (ABS 1953, p. 954). Yet with Argentina's transition to bulk in 1900, the competitiveness gap between Australia and the American continent was clear. The cost of landing a bushel of wheat in England from South Australia in 1910 was 7½d, compared to 4d from Argentina, 1½d from Canada, and 1d from the Atlantic ports of the USA ('Wheat in Bulk' 1910, p. 9). A South Australian Royal Commission in 1908 recognized that the gap was only partly accounted for by the length of the journey. They heard evidence from NSW that it cost 1½d in Australia merely to bag a bushel of wheat and load it on a truck:

> One only has to see a vessel being loaded with bags of wheat, with a large number of men laboriously employed, and then imagine the grain poured into it like water, to be convinced that a considerable saving of cost could be effected by the latter method, and a substantial saving of time to the vessel. ('Wheat in Bulk' 1910, p. 9)

In a paper delivered to Victorian farmers in 1910, W. G. McRoberts said economic grain handling in Australia was imperative:

> If we intend to settle a vigorous and hardy population of wealth producers and real nation-builders, also to develop, with the best results, the hidden wealth lying untouched in our almost limitless and unequalled agricultural areas, and, if we intend to compete with other grain-producing countries, in the effort to supply the human race with that important natural food product, we must adopt the bulk and elevator system of our competitors, which has built up their immense trade, and made them so successful in settling and developing their agricultural lands, by means of which they are leaving us far behind, although we enjoy much better and, indeed, unsurpassed natural conditions of life.
>
> ('Handling of Wheat in Bulk' 1910, p. 3)

'The losses are appalling under the present bag handling arrangement—you can't call it a system', thundered H. A. Griffiths in Western Australia's *Merredin Mercury* in July 1920. It cost Western Australian farmers £16,000 a year in freight alone to import the sacks, which were simply slashed open with a knife when they were unloaded in the UK: 'All the farmers' labour in sewing the bags and ramming the wheat and his 1s 6d paid for the bag goes to waste.'

Griffiths compared the Australian market unfavourably with Saskatchewan, where the Co-Op Elevator Company was handling 30 million bushels a year:

> Bulk-handling will release an army of men to engage in work of a productive nature. Would it not be far better if those men were engaged in growing wheat, rather than carrying it? Let mechanical and electrical appliance and gravitation move your wheat about and find these men something easier. (Griffiths 1920, p. 3)

The impetus for the introduction of bulk handling in NSW, the first Australian state to adopt the process, was the deterioration of supplies of wheat during the First World War. Huge reserves of bagged wheat had been stacked in the open at railheads and sidings, only to be destroyed by mice and weevils because of a shortage of shipping and labour. During the great rodent plague of 1916, 33,000 mice were said to have been poisoned in one night at Port Pirie in South Australia (Anderson 1958, p. 2). The losses prompted the Commonwealth to establish the Wheat Storage Commission in 1917 and pass the Wheat Storage Act, making almost £3 million available to the states to finance the installation of bulk handling.

In the aftermath of the war, NSW adopted a £2 million plan to build seventy grain silos across the state, with a large facility at White Bay on Glebe Island which had a projected capacity of 5.6 million bushels. By the time commercial ships began loading at White Bay in 1921, the cost had increased to £2.6 million, part of a wider scandal that contributed to the ousting of Premier W. A. Holman from office.

In Victoria, John Monash, later General Sir John Monash, had been a prewar advocate of concrete grain silos. Monash's Reinforced Concrete & Monier Pipe Construction Company built the first concrete silo at Rupanyup, Victoria, in 1907 for flour miller George Frayne, based on Monash's innovative 1904 design for concrete tanks for Carlton Brewery. Yet it was not until 1934 that the Victorian parliament passed the Grain Elevators Act, introducing bulk handling.

In Western Australia, the Westralian Farmers' Co-Operative Ltd reached an agreement with the Commonwealth in 1921 to install bulk handling, but in West Australia a mixed system of bags and bulk continued into the 1950s.

South Australia was the last state to change to bulk handling in the mid-1950s, a full ninety years after the system had begun to develop in North America. The chaotic nature of South Australian wheat handling was exposed by a Royal Commission in 1908. Rail carried bagged wheat to the four main ports, but at others, like Port Wakefield and Port Victoria, wheat was hauled down to the ports and loaded, sack by sack, onto lighters. Much of it was taken to Port Adelaide where it was shipped over the side to ocean ships. If arrangements failed, and the trans-shipment could not be carried out directly, the sacks would be loaded on to the wharves to wait until a ship became available.

Among the vested interests resisting bulk handling were the 'lumpers', a unionized cohort of heavy manual labourers who frequently took strike action in support of better wages and conditions. There were other complaints about the price of bags, which further reduced the return on wheat. Rail-side storage sheds offered poor protection against the elements and vermin. There was opposition too from some traders and millers, who, the commission found, had established cartels operating against the interests of farmers. 'The price is fixed by traders acting in unison, and not in competition', the commission found. The 'honourable understanding', as the traders preferred to call it, kept farm-gate prices consistently below those in other states.

The absence of competition was, to some extent, enforced by the pattern of railway development. D. W. Meinig's comparative study of the South Australian and Columbia Basin railnets illustrates how the free-wheeling North American capitalism delivered a far more efficient and competitive system than the paternalistic state. The systems were constructed in much the same period to link farming districts with tidewater, but the differences are striking. Wheat growers in the Columbia Basin were served by five inter-regional trunk lines to competing Pacific ports at Puget Sound and Portland. There were four trunk lines leading to Chicago and the East. A web of competitive branch lines gave many farmers a choice of two services, with some districts serviced by three.

In South Australia, by comparison, lines were constructed on the assumption that wheat would be fed to the nearest of five ports. Port feeders were narrow gauge, while the metropolitan system servicing Adelaide was broad gauge. Break-in-gauge points at Hamley Bridge and Terowie were deliberately chosen to prevent Port Adelaide competing with local ports. Of the three agricultural districts served by rail, only a small portion of one, the west-central portion of the Lower North, had a choice of port destinations. With the construction of the standard-gauge Commonwealth Transcontinental to Perth in 1917, Port Pirie achieved the dubious distinction of being the junction of three different rail gauges.

It is little wonder that the 1908 Royal Commission was 'much impressed' with the case for a transition to bulk handling, which would provide considerable efficiency savings: 'Against this, however, are the difficulties in connection with the adaptation of shipping and business methods... Such a vital change should not be recommended without the most complete investigation' ('The Wheat Commission' 1908, p. 10).

Legislation to introduce bulk handling was brought before the South Australian parliament, but failed to pass on at least three occasions, in 1922, 1925, and 1937. It was not until 1952 that the first bulk-handling terminal was completed in South Australia, built by the Wheat Board at Ardrossan. Frustrated growers formed the South Australian Co-operative Bulk Handling

Ltd company in 1955, completing a bulk-handling terminal in Wallarroo in 1958 and Port Lincoln soon after.

13.7 Arrested Development

Like much else that is odd about Australia, the objections to bulk handling stood upon the supposed peculiarity of Australian conditions. Australia's wheat fields, it was argued, were closer to the coast than those on the American continent, making the rail component of the journey less easy to streamline than on the vast steel arteries that span the American continent. Australia's climate was more capricious and harvests were more variable, while capital was harder to raise, and, with lower volumes of wheat, would take longer to pay off.

While these factors undoubtedly played a part, it is clear that progress in the grain industry was inhibited by state intervention. Government railway bureaucracies proved unresponsive to the requirements of the freight market. Driven by political rather than economic demands, they were reluctant to expand into uncultivated zones where they may have become the catalyst for settlement.

Putting aside questions about the availability of private sector capital, the chief argument for public ownership and management of infrastructure over private investment is that it better serves the public good. The baron's interest in feathering his own nest is imagined to be in conflict with the greater good. It is assumed that the technocratic expertise of disinterested bureaucrats will be directed towards the provision of better nests all round.

Yet the evidence suggests that the self-interested capitalists of the USA were better at promoting the public good than the disinterested bureaucrats in Australia. There was synergy between private ambition and the public good. The perceived tension between interests of the pioneering industrial tycoon and the pioneering farmer are largely imagined. Both rely on the success of the other for their own prosperity.

Hence, the rail and wheat barons played close attention to the viability of farmers, directing their rail tracks and building their silos into territory in which they judged there was the best opportunity for growth. That discipline was further honed by their finite capital, and their personal exposure to borrowing. The flow of capital, therefore, followed paths dictated by the market, unrestricted by the limited knowledge of central planners.

The morality of the sharp business practices in which tycoons engaged in the America of the late nineteenth and early twentieth centuries, and the reticence of the judiciary or legislatures to interfere, warrants further discussion. The regulation of business and finance is intended to protect the public good. Yet, judged over time, the damage to the public good of local private monopolies and insider manipulation of the commodity market is of marginal significance to the tycoon's contribution to economic, technical, and social progress.

13.8 The Past and the Present

The comparison between the bureaucratic and baronial patterns of industrial development can provide clarity to some contemporary debates in Australia.

It helps to explain the general weakness of Australian agribusiness and the absence of domestic corporate strength and financing. The North American grain empires established by the self-made entrepreneurs of the late nineteenth and early twentieth centuries laid the foundation for the corporations that dominate the wheat trade today. The Food and Agriculture Organization of the United Nations (FAO) reported, in 2003, that 60 per cent of the world's grain-handling facilities were in the hands of four corporations: Cargill, CHS, Arthur Daniels Midland, and General Mills. All four began life in Minneapolis during the grain boom.

General Mills began life as the Minneapolis Milling Company in 1856, founded by Illinois Congressman Robert Smith, and was bought by flour baron Cadwallader Colden Washburn, who built a dam, canal, and water tunnels to feed a network of mills. William Cargill, a Scottish immigrant sea merchant, established the Cargill Elevator Company in Minneapolis in the late 1880s, and grew his business by establishing a network of elevators along the tracks built by James Hill's Great Northern. It is now the largest privately held corporation in America and the main competitor to Arthur Daniels Midland, which began life as the Arthur-Daniels Linseed Company in Minneapolis is 1923. CHS is the descendant of the North Pacific Grain Growers' cooperative, established in Minnesota in 1929.

The Saskatchewan Wheat Pool in Canada became a private corporation in 1996 and launched a successful takeover of its Winnipeg-based competitor, Agricore United, in 2007. It now operates as Viterra—a wholly owned subsidiary of Glencore—and is the major grain handler in South Australia and western Victoria.

The landscape of the Australian grain industry today is a consequence of the triumph of the baronial model over the bureaucratic model of wheat handling in a contest played out a century ago. Its lessons should not be allowed to go to waste.

References

ABS (Australian Bureau of Statistics). 1953. *Official Year Book of the Commonwealth Australia*, cat. 1301.0. Canberra: Australian Bureau of Statistics.

Anderson, H. 1958. *Wheat Handling*. Melbourne: Macmillan.

'Australia and Canada; The South the Better Land'. 1905. *The Advertiser*, 9 August, p. 5.

Baker, R. S. 1900. 'The movement of wheat', (Adelaide) *Chronicle*, 13 January, p. 46.

Brisbane Courier 1881. 6 August, p. 4.

Broadacre Farming. 2013. *Macquarie Dictionary*. Sydney: Macquarie Dictionary Publishers.

Butlin, N. G. 1959. 'Colonial socialism in Australia' in H. G. J. Aitken (ed.), *The State and Economic Growth*. New York: Social Research Council.

Callaghan, A. R. and Millington, A. J. 1926. *The Wheat Industry in Australia*. Sydney: Angus & Robertson.

Cronon, W. 1992. *Nature's Metropolis: Chicago and the Great West*. New York: W.W. Norton.

Dunsdorfs, E. 1956. *The Australian Wheat Growing Industry, 1788–1948*. Melbourne: Melbourne University Press.

Emery, H. C. 1896. *Speculation on the Stock and Produce Exchanges of the United States*. New York: Columbia University Press.

Ergas, H. and Pincus, J. 2015. 'Infrastructure and colonial socialism' in S. Ville and G. Withers (eds.), *Cambridge Economic History of Australia*. Melbourne: Cambridge University Press.

Folsom, B. W. 1987. *The Myth of the Robber Barons: A New Look at the Rise of Big Business in America*. Herndon, VA: Young America's Foundation.

Fraser, J. F. 1911. *Australia: The Making of a Nation*, 3rd edition. London: Cassell & Company Ltd.

Griffiths, H. A. 1920. 'Bulk handling of grain: some telling arguments in its favour', *Merredin Mercury*, 1 July, p. 3.

'Handling of Wheat in Bulk'. 1910. *West Australian*, 4 August, p. 3.

Innis, H. A. 1923. *A History of the Canadian Pacific Railway*. London: P.S. King & Son.

Lowrie, W. 1899. 'The standard sample of wheat', *Journal of Agriculture and Industry of South Australia*, vol. 2, pp. 572–4.

Lurie, J. 1979. *The Chicago Board of Trade, 1859–1905: The Dynamics of Self-Regulation*. Urbana: University of Illinois Press.

Malone, M. P. 1996. *James J. Hill : Empire Builder of the Northwest*. Norman: University of Oklahoma Press.

Meinig, D. W. 1959. 'Colonization of wheatlands: some Australian and American comparisons', *Australian Geographer*, vol. 7, no. 5, pp. 205–13.

Menzies, R. G. [1942] 1980. 'The Forgotten People', radio broadcast (originally broadcast 22 May 1942), in G. Starr (ed.), *The Liberal Party of Australia: A Documentary History*. Melbourne: Drummond Heinemann.

Morgan, D. 1979. *Merchants of Grain: The Power and the Profits of the Five Giant Companies at the Center of the World's Food Supply*. New York: Viking Press.

O'Connor, M. A. 1970. 'World wheat supplies 1865–1913', Discussion Paper No. 12, Woodrow Wilson School, Princeton University, Princeton.

Stephens, J. 1847. 'Address to the starving or suffering millions of Great Britain and Ireland', *South Australian Register*, 21 July, p. 1.

Storey, G. 2006. 'Grain elevators', *Encyclopedia of Saskatchwan*, Canadian Plains Research Centre, <http://esask.uregina.ca/entry/grain_elevators.html> (accessed 11 July 2014).

'The Telegraph'. 1881. *The Telegraph*, 29 July, p. 2.

'The Wheat Commission'. 1908. *The* [Adelaide] *Register*, 4 November, p. 10.

Waterson, D. B. 1986. 'Pastoral capitalism and the politician Thomas McIlwraith and two land companies, 1877–1890', *Royal Historical Society of Queensland Journal*, vol. 12, pp. 401–15.

'Wheat in Bulk: The Elevator System'. 1910. *The Argus*, February, p. 95.

14

Australia's Distinctive Governance

Westminster, Ottawa, and Canberra Contrasted

J. R. Nethercote

The practice of Westminster governance throughout the world resembles observance of traditions within the various provinces of the Anglican Church. According to Article 34 of the Articles of Religion, 'It is not necessary that Traditions and Ceremonies be in all places one and utterly alike; for at all times they have been divers, and may be changed according to the diversities of countries, times, and men's manners . . .'. This chapter is an exploration of that diversity in the realm of government and politics, highlighting that which is particular to Australia (mainly the Commonwealth), but showing how it is distinguished from similar practice elsewhere, notably in the UK itself and Canada, the other great federation of the Westminster world. It is especially by reference to the UK and Canada that the distinctiveness of Australia's framework and structures can be most clearly revealed. The approach here tends to highlight the contrasts and differences between the major Westminster polities, rather than the more usual practice that stresses comparison, likeness, and similarity.

Australian government is usually regarded, with good reason, as being derived from that of Westminster and modelled upon it. As at Westminster, the defining characteristic of government in Australia, in the states as well as the Commonwealth, is the selection of the principal executive officers of government, the ministers of state (by whatever designation), from the parliament. Other features of Australian government, such as a non-partisan public service, also reflect those of Britain. But the essential, Westminster nature of the regime stems from the intimate relationship between the legislature and the executive, and the formal dependence of the latter upon the former.

It is equally conventional to observe that there are notable differences between 'Westminster in Australia' and 'Westminster at Westminster'. Of these, the most prominent is the federal structure of Australian government and its parliamentary manifestation, the Senate, the elected second chamber of the Commonwealth parliament; whereas, at least until recently, the UK was viewed as a unitary state, and its Upper House, the House of Lords, a mainly appointed body.

It is the purpose of this chapter to explore this conventional wisdom more broadly and precisely. It is based on a view that Australia is basically in the Westminster mould, but not markedly British.

There is one important preliminary observation. That there are significant differences in Westminster practice between the various jurisdictions is not surprising; indeed, it would be surprising if it were otherwise. The UK polity has evolved over more than a millennium and has a history which pre-dates even the Norman Conquest. Canada, on the other hand, derives from French and British settlements in North America dating from the sixteenth century; it secured self-government in the middle decades of the nineteenth century, in the first phase of such developments in the post-American British Empire. All Australian colonies except Western Australia achieved self-government at that time; the Australian Federation itself represents a later, indirect phase of imperial development. Australia, of all the British settlements of this era, was the most affected by convictism.

14.1 The Development and Alteration of Constitutions

The Constitution is the appropriate starting point for any examination of Australian government. It was drafted in Australia at conventions initially elected by several but not all of the colonial legislatures but, in later stages, by the voters themselves. The text adopted at the second convention was later approved at referendum by the colonies and taken to London where, after some changes, it was embodied, as section 9, in the Commonwealth of Australia Constitution Act 1900 of the UK parliament (63 & 64 Victoria, ch. 12).

One especially significant provision was the last, section 128, 'Mode of altering the Constitution'. It set out a wholly Australia-based procedure for amending the Constitution, embracing two stages, a parliamentary stage followed by submission to the voters. Initiative in the procedure was vested in the parliament of the new Commonwealth and included the possibility that one House alone could activate the procedure (this has occurred only once, in 1974). For the change to proceed, it requires support of the majority of those voting nationwide and majorities in a majority of the states.

This provision has been fully activated on forty-four occasions; on eight such occasions the proposed change has succeeded with the voters. There have been several occasions when proposed changes have been supported by a majority of voters but without securing majorities in a majority of the states. (The section 128 procedure relates to what can be described as entrenched provisions of the Constitution; there are many unentrenched provisions where the parliament itself is authorized to make a change, signalled by such words as, 'until the Parliament of the Commonwealth otherwise provides . . . '.)

The Australian Constitution does not tell the full story of the law governing the government of Australia, and certainly not the full story of how Australia is governed; it provides the essential framework. There are a host of other laws, which include electoral legislation and legislation concerning ministers of state and other office-holders, which are also relevant.

The UK famously does not have a written constitution and has never had one, even when there have been major changes in government such as abolition of the monarchy in 1649; its restoration little more than a decade later; and the so-called revolution of 1688–9. There are, however, many laws concerning the monarchy, executive government, the parliament, and elections. These laws form part of the ordinary law and may be altered by normal legislative process. In addition, the British also have resort to conventions to a much more conspicuous degree than is to be found in either Australia or Canada.

Canada was constituted by the British North America Act 1867 (30–31 Victoria, ch. 3); it is now referred to as the Constitution Act. Its text was prepared by the leaders of the provinces of Canada (Upper Canada and Lower Canada), Nova Scotia, and New Brunswick, working first in Canada and later in London. Though, according to the preamble, the union was to be federal, the constitution was expressly to be 'similar in Principle to that of the United Kingdom'. Its provinces are formally subordinate to the Dominion government. For this reason, they have lieutenant governors who have been appointed by the Governor General of Canada on the advice of the prime minister (see Section 14.2).

The Commonwealth of Australia was much more directly a creation of the self-governing Australian colonies. Although the imperial power had an interest in a supra-colonial body, whereas Canada effectively assumed a range of imperial functions in British North America when the Dominion was created in 1867, the Commonwealth, by contrast, was not created to stand in for the imperial power. There is no undertaking in the Constitution of Australia for it to be 'similar in Principle to that of the United Kingdom', and any desire of this type would probably have been resisted; it was certainly resisted by the Senate in its earliest days when it refused a proposed standing order that, in the event of doubt about procedure, guidance would be sought in the practice of the UK House of Commons (Reid 1987, chs 1 and 2). The Australian colonies retained their identity and, upon formation of the Commonwealth, became states (Commonwealth of Australia Constitution Act 1900, section 6); each state retained its governor, who continues to be appointed by the Queen (in her new capacity as Queen of Australia) on the advice of the premier of the state. Ironically, Canada's provinces have been, certainly in the past half-century, decidedly more robust in asserting their own identity than have the Australian states. In Australia, the Federation in this period has been increasingly marked by centralization of finance and homogenization of public policy.

Just as there was little public participation in Canada in the composition or adoption of the British North America Act, neither did it contain any provision for such subsequent amendment as may be desired. For more than a century, formal amendment was possible but it required a journey to Westminster. It is only since 1982 that it has been possible for Canadians alone to amend the Constitution Act, but there is no express provision for popular participation or approval.

In both adoption and amendment of the Australian Constitution there is a distinctively democratic (participatory) quality which is not to be found in the constitutional arrangements of the UK or Canada. That Australia took this course is partly a consequence of the breadth of research underlying the framing of the Constitution by participants such as Alfred Deakin and Andrew Inglis Clark; a readiness to search beyond British practice (both Deakin and Clark visited the USA); and the general liberalism of the federal era.

Since the Second World War, the referendum has been used very occasionally in the UK and Canada, invariably in a plebiscitary manner. But it remains an ad hoc mechanism that has to be reactivated for each use. A positive result, when achieved, is not indisputably binding as in Australia.

14.2 The Governor-General and the Monarch

The Australian Constitution provides that 'A Governor-General appointed by the Queen shall be Her Majesty's representative in the Commonwealth' (section 2). It also states that the 'executive power of the Commonwealth is vested in the Queen and is exercisable by the Governor-General as the Queen's representative, and extends to the execution and maintenance of this Constitution, and of the laws of the Commonwealth' (section 61).

There is no comparably concise constitutional statement of the Governor General of Canada's role. On other specific matters in relation to, for instance, summoning and meetings of parliament, the two documents contain comparable provisions.

An interesting contrast can be found in relation to command of the naval and military forces. The Australian Constitution states that 'The command in chief of the naval and military forces of the Commonwealth is vested in the Governor-General as the Queen's representative' (section 68). The British North America Act simply stated: 'The Command-in-Chief of the Land and Naval Militia, and of all Naval and Military Forces, of and in Canada, is hereby declared to continue and be vested in the Queen' (section 15). By Letters Patent issued in 1947, however, the Governor General has also been styled 'Commander-in-Chief in and over Canada'.

There is very little comparison between Governors-General and the Queen. The Queen, since ascending the throne in February 1952, has had twelve prime ministers and attended six changes of government as a consequence of an election. Her representatives in Australia rarely witness more than one change of government or prime minister (and two, Sir Zelman Cowen and Bishop Peter Hollingworth have seen neither; and Sir Peter Cosgrove has, thus far, presided only over a change of prime minister). Moreover, the heir apparent, the Prince of Wales, has had several decades of a partial participation in government affairs of a kind which future Governors General are unlikely to have had. Nor has there been any instance, either in Australia or Canada, of a Governor General establishing the kind of confidential relationship with a prime minister exemplified in the weekly meetings which the Queen has with her prime minister of the day. Australian prime ministers, indeed, have treated some Governors-General fairly peremptorily.

The procedure for selecting and advising on appointment of the Governor General in Australia has remained the same since adoption of the Statute of Westminster, 1931: it is a tightly held prerogative of the prime minister. Peter Costello, Treasurer (1996–2007), said that were he to become prime minister, advising on an appointment of a Governor-General would be, along with that of Chief Justice of the High Court and governor of the Reserve Bank of Australia, among his most important responsibilities.

Canada has, however, recently established a procedure for advice on selection. First used in 2010, the Advisory Committee on Vice-Regal Appointments has now been placed on a permanent footing and used for Governor General and lieutenant governor appointments, and also commissioners of Canadian territories.

In Australia, the federal structure is activated when it is necessary to have a temporary occupant during absence of a Governor-General. Administrators of the Commonwealth invariably come from the ranks of state governors, usually the most senior, though several hold the necessary commissions. In Canada, for absences of more than a month, a Justice of the Supreme Court of Canada will fill in. For an opening of parliament, if there is no Governor General or the Governor General is indisposed or otherwise unavailable, the Chief Justice stands in.

Australian-born Governors-General have come from four of the six states (Victoria, New South Wales (NSW), Western Australia, Queensland). Five have previously been parliamentarians and ministers, two at state level; four have been superior court judges; two have been academic lawyers; and two have had an army background. All but one have been men. Two (Sir John Kerr and Bishop Hollingworth) have left office early, in controversial circumstances, but the most obvious adjective to describe the quality which seems to be sought in Governors-General of Australia is 'sound'.

A conspicuous feature of Canadian practice has been an almost studied alternation between those with an English-speaking background and those from a French background. In this respect, the governor generalship has been utilized to recognize and address national unity concerns. When Governors General were first appointed from within Canada they brought diplomatic experience; one was actually drawn from the diplomatic service. Thereafter, there were several from politics; three had been presiding officers (two Speakers of the House of Commons and another, a Speaker of the Senate), two ministers, and another a provincial premier. The last three appointees have included two journalists, both women and both born outside Canada, and an academic lawyer and administrator, who had held top posts at universities in both Quebec and Ontario.

14.3 The Federal Executive Council and the Privy Councils

The Federal Executive Council is a further illustration of the sparseness of Australian government institutions, especially in contrast to its illustrious UK counterpart, Her Majesty's Most Honourable Privy Council. The Constitution deals briskly with the Executive Council: 'There shall be a Federal Executive Council to advise the Governor-General in the government of the Commonwealth.' Members are 'chosen and summoned' by the Governor General and 'hold office during his pleasure' (section 62). The following section states that 'The provisions of this Constitution referring to the Governor-General in Council shall be construed as referring to the Governor-General acting with the advice of the Federal Executive Council' (section 63).

Under section 64, officers appointed by the Governor-General to administer departments 'shall be members of the Federal Executive Council, and shall be the Queen's Ministers of State for the Commonwealth'. Today, parliamentary secretaries are also appointed to the Executive Council.

In the history of the Commonwealth, no one apart from a minister, assistant minister, or parliamentary secretary has ever been appointed to the Federal Executive Council. A number of judges of the High Court have been members but only because they have previously been ministers; but, like a number of Governors-General, quite a few have, however, been members of the UK Privy Council, which enabled them to sit on the Judicial Committee when it was still part of the Australian court system. Nor has there ever been a full meeting of the Executive Council, even for a ceremonial purpose. Its entire existence revolves around the business for whose despatch it was created.

The Council generally meets fortnightly, sitting at a small dining table at Government House, Yarralumla; refreshments or even lunch may follow. It is chaired by the Governor-General (not a member except when previously appointed) and attended by two ministers, usually of junior rank. It is serviced by a secretariat located in the Department of the Prime Minister and Cabinet (DPMC).

In the UK, Her Majesty's Most Honourable Privy Council, the formal body of advisers to the sovereign, is a much grander institution. Its main membership is drawn from the ranks of senior politicians on both sides of the House of Commons. The Leader of the Opposition is immediately sworn of the Privy Council if not already a member. Others, apart from members of the royal family, include the two archbishops and the Bishop of London; the private secretary to the sovereign; the Lord Chamberlain; the Speaker of the House of Commons and the Lord Speaker; numerous judges; and a small number of senior officials. Particular individuals may be appointed, for example, so that they may sit on an enquiry into some public matter. The Clerk of the Privy Council heads an independent unit within the Cabinet Office.

The Privy Council meets once a month wherever the Queen is residing. She stands at meetings. The Lord President, a Cabinet minister, reads a list of Orders to which the Queen simply says: 'Approved'. At the Demise of the Crown and the succession of a new monarch, the Privy Council is especially active.

Canada also has a Privy Council. The nomenclature itself indicates that Canada modelled its government more closely on that of the UK than Australia ever attempted to do. The British North America Act stated: 'There shall be a Council to aid and advise in the Government of Canada, to be styled the Queen's Privy Council for Canada' (section 11). In a section which may have been influential in drafting the Australian Constitution, 'The Provisions of this Act referring to the Governor General in Council shall be construed as referring to the Governor General acting by and with the Advice of the Queen's Privy Council of Canada' (section 13).

As with the UK Privy Council, others, apart from ministers and senior politicians (but only occasionally parliamentary secretaries), may be appointed—provincial premiers, senior officials and prominent Canadians, government and Opposition whips, and the Speakers of the Senate and the House of Commons upon retirement. Members of the parliamentary Security

Intelligence Review Committee must, by law, be privy councillors. Both Prince Philip, the Duke of Edinburgh, and the Prince of Wales are members of the Privy Council of Canada, appointed respectively in 1951 and 2014; in 1916, the Prime Minister of Australia, W. M. Hughes, was made a member. He has been described as an honorary member but the meaning of this is unclear, as being a privy councillor of itself does not attract any remuneration.

The office of President of the Queen's Privy Council for Canada has been described as the 'closest thing to a sinecure' in Ottawa; it is often held in conjunction with other ministerial posts.

Canada's Privy Council is supported by a Privy Council Office (PCO), headed by the Clerk of the Privy Council, who also has the titles of Secretary to the Cabinet and, by statute, Head of the Public Service. Except in relation to statutory instruments and orders-in-council, the PCO does not seem to have much to do with the Privy Council. The PCO describes itself as 'the hub of non-partisan, public service support to the Prime Minister and Cabinet and its decision-making structures... [it] helps the Government implement its vision and respond effectively and quickly to issues facing the government and country'.

14.4 The Cabinet

The Cabinet is the centrepiece of a Westminster government. It embodies the essential characteristic, namely, the intimacy of the legislature and the executive; as Walter Bagehot wrote, the Cabinet is 'a hyphen which joins, a buckle which fastens, the legislative part of the state to the executive part of the state' (Bagehot 1867, p.15). The Cabinet is unknown to the Australian Constitution. But, whereas in the UK it is designated as a committee of the Privy Council, and, in Canada, of the Privy Council of Canada, the nearest the Australian Cabinet comes to an organic link with the Federal Executive Council is a rule, not of great moment, that meetings of the Executive Council have precedence over Cabinet meetings!

The Cabinet, in all jurisdictions, is as elusive as it is pervasive. Much government business and decision-making has a Cabinet wrapping. All ministers are bound by Cabinet decisions but, even if very senior, they may not have been present when they were made.

In Australia, the Cabinet is currently composed of nineteen ministers. Other ministers, eleven in number, and parliamentary secretaries, of whom there are twelve, may attend specified items. The Cabinet 'meets in the Cabinet room at Parliament House, Canberra, in most weeks of the year' (DPMC 2015, p. 53). It has a substantial agenda, 'matters of public interest, importance, or controversy... only in emergencies will significant decisions not go to the Cabinet'

(DPMC 2015, p. 64). Selection of ministers is generally a key prerogative of the prime minister (though it would be misleading to say that they had a free hand: apart from addressing the claims of leading figures in the party, in both Australia and Canada it has been wise for prime ministers to have regard for the federal distribution). The big exception has been the century-long practice of the Australian Labor Party (ALP). From the second Labor government, the Fisher government, 1908–9, ministers in Labor governments have been elected by the party caucus. This practice was abandoned in 2007 by newly elected leader, Kevin Rudd. However, following Rudd's return to the party leadership (and prime ministership) late in 2013, he established a method of electing the party leader which included party members as well as the parliamentary party; at the same time, election of ministers was returned to the caucus. Under both systems, allocation of portfolios remained a prerogative of the prime minister.

Since 1949, Cabinet decisions have been issued by a Cabinet Secretary who attends meetings. From 1949 until 1968, and from 1971 until 1996, the Cabinet Secretary has been the head of the Prime Minister's Department (Prime Minister and Cabinet from 1971). In the interval there was a separate Department of the Cabinet Office whose secretary was also Secretary to the Cabinet.

In 1996, the newly installed Howard government appointed a separate Cabinet Secretary under the Members of Parliament (Staffing) Act 1984; this practice was resumed under the Abbott government when it took office in 2013. From September 2015, the Turnbull government appointed a minister as Cabinet Secretary. In the Labor governments 2007 to 2013, a minister performed the role. Notwithstanding these innovations, the head of DPMC and other senior officials continue to attend and service Cabinet meetings.

Practice in the UK and Canada is different from Australia, and, in terms of governmental orthodoxy, much more conventional. Cabinet meetings are shorter in both; more business is carried out by committees of the Cabinet. Second, in both countries the Cabinet Secretary is the top civil (public) servant and, among other roles, is the adviser to the prime minister on top civil (public) service appointments (as is the Secretary to the Department of the Prime Minister and Cabinet in Australia). In the UK, the Cabinet Secretary has been, from 1956 until 1963, and since 1981, usually head of the Home Civil Service; and has been so by statute in Canada in recent decades. There is no comparable title in Australian government though it is sometimes attached to the Secretary to the Department of the Prime Minister and Cabinet with the adjective, 'effective' (or 'de facto').

Heads of the DPMC in Australia are not invariably drawn from the public service itself. In the past four decades, four have been appointed from outside. All had previously been in the public service, two of them at a senior level. Another rose from a senior post, having joined the public service at age 40 from a university. Of the career appointees, several had prior experience in the department; two have come from the Treasury and two have headed Finance; two recent appointees have had significant experience at high levels in defence and diplomacy.

Since Sir Maurice Hankey retired from the post in 1938, no Secretary to the UK Cabinet has been appointed from outside the civil service. Apart from the present occupant, Sir Jeremy Heywood, all have made their careers in the Treasury and most have had significant private office experience; two were head of the Home Office prior to appointment to the Cabinet Office. Sir Jeremy is the only appointee to have spent some time in the City. Canada is more like Australia; deputy ministers of Finance (counterpart of Treasury) do not move to the PCO, though half a century ago one head of PCO subsequently took the reins at Finance; most have had previous experience in the PCO combined with time in line agencies. The older pattern of drawing people from the Foreign Affairs department also ended decades ago.

Only in Canada have women been appointed to these top jobs, and it has happened there on two occasions.

14.5 Houses and Senates

It is in the structure of the parliament that the distinctiveness of Australian government is clearest. Two features of the Australian parliament, and the interaction between them, mark its character. The first is the brief maximum three-year term of the House of Representatives. The second is the existence of an elected second chamber, the Senate, with virtually co-equal powers (differences between the two are procedural, not substantial). The effect of these features is sharpened by the limited number of sitting days each year (markedly less than the number in either Westminster or Ottawa).

Both the UK and the Canadian Houses of Commons are elected for terms of five years (fixed five years in the UK). Apart from a small number of hereditary peers in the House of Lords, both upper houses are appointed; senators in Canada must retire at 75 years.

The powers of the House of Lords were curtailed as a consequence of the battle over the Budget in 1909–10; money bills do not need the concurrence of the House of Lords and become law a month after passing the Commons; there is a suspensive veto of one year on other legislation. As a consequence, there is no need for the parliament at Westminster to have a dispute resolution procedure. UK governments, if they have a workable majority in the House of Commons, can have reasonable certainty that their legislation will pass; this is not inevitable, however—in the late 1960s the Wilson Labour government, with a majority of around a hundred, had to abandon controversial legislation on industrial relations in the face of backbench protest.

The Canadian Senate is, in law, co-equal with the House of Commons, with the usual qualifications concerning financial legislation. Clashes between the two Houses are rare, but have been overcome, in extreme situations, by appointment of additional senators. There is no formal dispute resolution procedure and, as the Senate cannot be dissolved, there can be no simultaneous refreshment of the membership of the two Houses as in Australia.

Members of the Australian House of Representatives are elected by single-member electorates as occurs for the Houses of Commons in the UK and Canada. In Australia, voting is compulsory and preferential. In both the UK and Canada, voting is voluntary and first-past-the-post. The effect of the two approaches is difficult to specify but it does appear that the Australian approach means smaller swings of the pendulum so far as parliamentary seats are concerned; this, however, is a proposition which needs to be tested further as distribution of the vote may be a factor in the smaller swings.

In Australia, both the Senate and the House of Representatives have been elected on an adult franchise virtually since their inception (and certainly from the second federal election in 1903). The Senate is elected on a state-wide basis (or territory-wide in the case of the two territories). Unless there is a double dissolution, senators from the states have fixed terms of six years; half the Senate is elected every three years. Senate elections must be held in the year preceding commencement of senators' terms and usually coincide with general elections for the House of Representatives (separate periodical elections of senators have only been held in 1953, 1964, 1967, and 1970). Membership of the Senate in Ottawa is by appointment; the House of Lords retains a small hereditary component.

All three second chambers have been the subject of much debate throughout the twentieth century. For half a century, 1920 to 1978, the ALP's platform included abolition of the Senate. It now favours simply limiting the Senate's powers relating to appropriation legislation, in particular as a consequence of the dismissal of the Whitlam government in November 1975, when the Senate refused to vote on appropriation legislation until an election was called.

For the first half-century of the Commonwealth, the method of electing senators saw the creation of some very lopsided Senates; in 1913 the Liberal government had only seven seats in a thirty-six-seat Senate, the remainder were all held by the ALP. The numbers were reversed after the Great War, with the Nationalist government holding thirty-five of the thirty-six seats; and from 1947 to 1949, the Labor government held thirty-three seats.

In 1948 a system of proportional voting was adopted at the time when the number of seats in the Senate was increased to sixty (it is now seventy-six, including two senators each from the two territories whose terms are aligned with those of the House of Representatives). In the first instance, this created very closely divided Senates, government majorities rarely exceeding five. Subsequently, the major parties (ALP, Liberal, and National) have seen their virtual monopoly of Senate seats disappear at the hands of a succession of minor parties (Democratic Labor (1955–74), Australian Democrats (1978–2007), and Greens (since 1990)) and independents. As at 2015, apart from the territory senators, a quarter of the seats in the Senate are held by various cross-benchers, of whom the Greens is the largest group.

The elective quality of the Australian Senate has, in the past three decades, been eroded as a consequence of an amendment to the Constitution in 1977 (new section 15). Under that amendment, where a vacancy arises in the Senate, whether as a consequence of death or resignation, the replacement must be a nominee of the previous senator's party and serves the entirety of the remainder of the term. Previously, under proportional representation (PR), there was a gentlemen's agreement to fill vacancies from the former (late) senator's party until the next general election for the House of Representatives or periodical election of senators; the gentlemen's agreement was not always observed, conspicuously with regard to not filling a vacancy in Queensland in 1975 arising from death of a Labor senator.

The consequence is that resignations from the Senate, which previously ran at half the rate of those from the House of Representatives, now run at twice the rate or more; this is because a resignation does not put a seat at risk. It is a classic instance of Machiavelli's precept that it is rare, in human affairs, that in remedying one deficiency we do not create another. The House of Representatives remains an exclusively elected House; the only method of entry is by election, whether at a general election or a by-election.

In the UK, as a consequence of the Budget controversy of 1909–10, the powers of the House of Lords were significantly curtailed, leaving it with only a suspensive veto over non-financial legislation. In 1958 a system of life peerages was adopted, bringing extensive and continuing expansion of the House's membership. Under the Blair government, all but a handful of hereditary peers were removed from the House, and various non-partisan appointment procedures have been developed.

The Canadian Senate is a federal chamber, as in Australia and the USA. But unlike Australian and American counterparts, the provinces of Canada are not represented equally. The aspiration to equality in the Canadian Senate is expressed regionally. Each of the four designated regions—Maritimes (Nova Scotia, New Brunswick, Prince Edward Island); Quebec; Ontario; and Western (Manitoba, Saskatchewan, Alberta, British Columbia)—has twenty-four senators. The remainder of Canada, including Newfoundland, a former dominion which joined Canada in 1949, has nine seats.

Appointment to the Senate is a prime ministerial prerogative. To be eligible for appointment to the Senate it is necessary to be 30 years of age; own property in the relevant province worth $C4,000 and live in the province; and have a net worth of $C4,000; these requirements have remained unchanged since 1867. An interesting aspect of the Senate's history is that, in 1928, the Supreme Court of Canada ruled that women were not eligible for appointment to the Senate, not being 'persons' within the meaning of the British North America Act; the case went to the Judicial Committee of the Privy Council where the Supreme Court decision was reversed. Appointment was initially for life but, since 1965, senators retire at age 75.

There has been a great deal of debate about the Canadian Senate. One of the major themes around which debate has centred is creation of a Triple-E Senate—elected, equal, and effective. Most conspicuous advocates of change appear to come from Western Canada, notably Alberta. Various schemes for electing senators and involving the provinces in selection have been promoted but none has come to fruition. Alberta has even had a provincially run election of senators, but Ottawa declined to appoint those elected when vacancies arose.

An instructive comment on the membership of the Canadian Senate is provided by the Senate itself:

> The Senate was created to counterbalance representation by population in the House of Commons. In recent years, the Senate has come to bolster representation of groups often underrepresented in Parliament, such as Aboriginal peoples, visible minorities and women. (<http://sen.parl.gc.ca/portal/about-senate-e.htm>)

The method of electing senators in Australia has had something of the same effect. For several decades women found it easier to win a seat in the Senate than the House of Representatives (Harris 2005, p. 206); or, more precisely, to win major party preselection for the Senate than for a winnable seat in the House. Likewise, there have been several Aboriginals in the Senate but only one so far in the House. In 2013–15, both the leaders of the Government and the Opposition in the Senate migrated to Australia as children.

The Australian Senate is a fully fledged House of Parliament, exemplified by election of its own presiding officer, the president. The president, in order to preserve the equality of state representation, has a deliberative, not a casting vote; if voting is equally divided, the Roman principle applies: 'when the votes are equal the question shall pass in the negative' (Constitution of Australia, section 23).

By contrast, in the House of Lords until 2006, the Lord Chancellor (a Cabinet minister and judge) was the Speaker; the House of Lords now elects its own Speaker, limited by convention to two terms. The Speaker of the Canadian Senate is appointed by the Governor General on the advice of the prime minister.

The Australian parliament has largely abandoned ceremonial attire. Neither presiding officer wears robes but, for a short time in 2011, Peter Slipper, who had left the Liberal Party to take the speakership when a vacancy arose, restored some of the traditional wardrobe and also instituted a Speaker's procession during his brief tenure. Nor do the various officers of the chambers robe, with the exception of clerks at the table in the House of Representatives, who wear black gowns and previously also wore a wig until instructed by the Speaker in 1995 to cease doing so (Harris 2005, p. 206). On ceremonial occasions the Sergeant-at-Arms wears appropriate court dress (Harris 2005, p. 208). Traditional parliamentary office in the Senate is so diminished that *Odgers' Australian Senate Practice* no longer pays any special attention to the Usher of the Black Rod.

Party organization and activity is a relatively undocumented aspect of parliamentary life and proceeding. In Australia, what is clear, from newspaper reports, is that parties have been very active and organized from the inception of the parliament in 1901. The Australian parliament is not a parliament which has had some pre-party golden era where members freely debated the great topics of the day and voted on the merits of the arguments put. The first parliament, elected in March 1901, had three parties, none of whom had a majority in the House of Representatives or the Senate: Protectionists, who formed the government; the Labor Party, which sat on the cross bench but generally supported the government; and the Free Traders, the Opposition. Deakin wrote of the 'three elevens'. The leaders of the government and the Opposition, Edmund Barton and George Reid, both veterans of the parliament of NSW, seem to have assumed their leadership positions. Labor had an election.

Leadership has since been a matter for the party room (including senators) on all sides of politics until Labor, in 2013, introduced a method of electing leaders which involved the party membership on a 50–50 basis with the parliamentary party; Labor's new practice has been included in caucus rules but not in the party constitution. When prime ministers have died in office (1939, 1945, and 1967), replacements (invariably deputy prime ministers) have been appointed on a caretaker basis until the succession has been settled. On two occasions, 1939 and 1967, the prime minister so chosen was leader of the Country Party in a Coalition government and thus not a contender for the post; in 1945, the prime minister was a candidate for the succession in the Labor Party but was beaten.

In the UK it was not until 1965 that the Conservative Party elected a leader; the choice historically was made by what one Tory MP (Iain Macleod) called the 'magic circle'. Whereas, in Australia, a simple majority is sufficient to elect a leader (and, indeed, to have the leadership declared vacant), a victor in a Conservative Party ballot needed a specified plurality over all other contenders to win; this applies even to an incumbent prime minister, as was evident when Mrs Thatcher was successfully challenged in 1990.

Subsequently, the Conservative Party followed Labour in involving the party membership in leadership elections, although the field is settled by the parliamentary party. Leaders of the Labour Party were elected by the parliamentary party throughout the twentieth century until 1980, when voting was turned over to the membership.

Canadian political parties have used party conventions to elect party leaders since the end of the Great War. The initial rationale, in the case of the succession following the death of Sir Wilfrid Laurier in 1919, the Liberal leader, was that the party in the House of Commons was too small for the task; American methods of choosing presidential candidates presumably provided something of a model. On a number of occasions, the Progressive Conservative Party has elected leaders who did not have a seat in the House of Commons. Two Liberal leaders who became prime minister were not in the House of Commons when they won the party leadership, John Turner in 1984 and Jean Chrétien in 1990, but they soon entered the House (in both cases, as Leader of the Opposition).

Party solidarity is very marked in Australia. Lord Norton of Louth has been able to write two substantial volumes about party dissent in the UK House of Commons. There has even been a certain latitude in the Canadian House of Commons, if not especially in recent decades. But in Australia, unless a party split is involved, party dissent could be exhaustively disposed of in a very brief research note.

Perhaps the most conspicuous illustration of the party essence of the Australian parliament is the speakership of the House of Representatives. The first Speaker, Frederick Holder, a former premier of South Australia, was elected unanimously to what Deakin described as 'one of the highest appointments in the gift of the new Government' (cited in Nethercote 2015). A protectionist, he was the Barton government's choice for the post because another former premier of South Australia, Charles Cameron Kingston, had joined the ministry. When Holder died whilst presiding over vigorous debate in the House, a long and even more vigorous debate marked the contested choice of a successor.

The Labor Party supported one of its own, the chairman of committees. But Deakin, the prime minister, preferred one of his own supporters and used the majority of the Fusion government to secure the election. His argument was that a member of the Labor Party, used to caucus practice, where the will of the majority bound the whole, could not shed such loyalties simply by ascending the Speaker's chair. The Labor leader, Andrew Fisher, unsuccessfully contended that loyalty to the party platform did not affect impartiality in the chair (Reid 1987, ch. 2).

The speakership has ever hereafter been an object of partisan contest. The governing party has only ever had one nominee when the post was vacant; the speakership has always changed with a change of government except in the unusual circumstances of the divided wartime parliament of 1940–43, when the Speaker remained in the chair after the Labor government came to office until, in mid-1943, the government was challenged. Speaker Sir Littleton Groom, who refused to support the Bruce–Page government in the vital vote which brought it down, won little sympathy for his clear and explicit adherence to Westminster practice.[1] Very occasionally, the Opposition, holding a Speaker in sufficient regard, has not nominated anyone in an election at the beginning of a new parliament.

The presidency of the Senate has likewise gone with the government (but within the schedules of Senate terms). In the last three decades, however, there has been a view, not always followed, that the president should be drawn from among government senators and the deputy president from the Opposition.

The Speaker of the UK House of Commons is usually a parliamentarian of some distinction but not one who has followed a ministerial path, though there have been exceptions. The Speaker usually serves two terms, even if there is a change of government along the way. Upon retirement, Speakers are normally elevated to the peerage.

Though the speakership of the Canadian House of Commons has usually gone to a member of the governing party it does not seem to have been a party prize as in Australia. For a time, Speakers were nominated by the prime minister and seconded by the Leader of the Opposition. Since 1986, the Speaker has been elected by secret ballot, everyone being a candidate unless a minister, Opposition office-holder, or members who have excluded themselves. There are often several ballots before anyone secures a majority.

Another indication that the Australian parliament has always been a party institution is the office of Leader of the Opposition. When the Commonwealth was established, with Edmund Barton as prime minister, his Free Trade rival simply took the title of Leader of the Opposition. There was no office as such at the time.

Canada also acknowledged a role for the principal contender for office at an early stage and, in 1910, arranged a salary for the occupant of the post based on constitutional arguments about the role of an Opposition leader in a Westminster-style parliament. Since 1950, the Leader of the Opposition has

[1] The Bruce–Page government was defeated when the House was in committee, but still in the chamber, in a little-used stage in the legislative process between the second and third readings when bills are discussed in detail. The Speaker does not traditionally participate in this committee stage, and Littleton Groom did not participate.

had an official residence, Stornoway. Australia instituted an allowance for the Leader of the Opposition in 1920. The explanation in this instance placed much emphasis on the volume of extra work which fell to the Opposition leader (a work value rationale not surprisingly put by the Prime Minister, W. M. Hughes, a former trade unionist). The UK did not follow suit until 1937 (an allowance which, until the 1970s, used to cut out upon the dissolution of the House of Commons unless the occupant was also a former prime minister).

No appraisal of the Australian parliament would be complete without reference to its architecture. There are two critical points in which it differs from those of the UK and Canada. The first has marked both of the two buildings the parliament has occupied in Canberra since 1927. The current building is more than all-embracing. It includes the two chambers of the Houses. This is typical of Anglosphere parliaments and legislatures and a contrast with continental practice where the Houses often have separate buildings; in Paris, the Palais Luxembourg (Sénat) and the Palais Bourbon (Assemblée Nationale) do not even share a metro line.

Parliament House also accommodates the executive branch of government, including the Cabinet room as well as the offices of the prime minister, all ministers, and parliamentary secretaries; ministers only very occasionally, and then almost invariably ostentatiously, work in the departments. In this sense, its design is an unusual physical manifestation of Bagehot's precept about the joining of the legislative and executive parts of government. (The building also draws on Bagehot in the sharpness with which the dignified—perhaps better seen as the rowdy—and the efficient parts of the government are separated.)

Though the judiciary has a separate building of its own, down the hill on the shores of Lake Burley Griffin, the fourth estate—newspapers, radio and television, and related media—have a floor of their own on the top of the Senate side of the building.

Such physical concentration of the apex of the political life of a nation is unmatched in either London or Ottawa, or many other parliamentary jurisdictions. In London, even members of the House of Commons do not necessarily have offices in the Palace of Westminster. The Cabinet itself meets at No. 10 Downing Street, half a kilometre away, where the prime minister's office is located. Ministers have their main offices in departments. The media in its various forms is accommodated in numerous buildings around Westminster and elsewhere in London.

In Ottawa, what can be found in one building in Canberra is spread around the Parliament Building itself, East and West Block, and various buildings along Wellington Street. The media is accommodated further down the hill, in buildings along Sparks Street Mall.

The second feature is the modernity of Parliament House, Canberra. It is just a quarter-century old. Indeed, this anniversary passed almost without notice, indicating a certain imperviousness on the part of Australians to historical landmarks. The preceding Provisional Parliament House deliberately sought to emphasize its derivation from Westminster and other parliaments of the empire, symbolized by the Speaker's chair fashioned from timbers from HMS *Victory*. The new Parliament House—opened in 1988 and intended to have a life of two centuries—is defiantly Australian. Except for marble imported from Italy, all the building materials are local. And there is plenty of space. The chambers of the two Houses are so large that even when everyone is present, they still seem half-empty. Churchill's dictum of October 1943, that chambers should be designed so that business is readily transacted in an atmosphere of discussion and conversation, has been assiduously ignored. Internal TV means that all proceedings can be followed in the spacious suites of senators and members.

The parliaments of Westminster and Ottawa are built in the Gothic style. They may once have been fit for purpose but such a claim is rarely made these days. Functionality, so stark in Canberra, is barely obvious in these dignified, graceful buildings. Walking their corridors is like a walk through history. Both buildings are said to be badly in need of very major and extremely expensive repair.

It is nearly seventy years since the Palace of Westminster was rebuilt after the Commons side had been bombed during the Second World War. And it is nearly a century since the Parliament Building in Ottawa was rebuilt after the Great War and the fire of 1919. Plans in the 1990s to gut the building in two phases did not proceed and so the task is yet to be undertaken.

14.6 The Public Service and the Civil Service

Soon after Federation, the Commonwealth parliament passed a Public Service Act. Even at the time there was no strong sentiment that Australia was following a British path. There were, undeniably, some similarities. Official heads of departments were called 'secretaries', more or less after the Whitehall style, and the public service itself was meant to be politically impartial with recruitment based on merit, not patronage (or spoils). But the new service, in many respects, was extensively influenced by North American practice. The spirit of scientific management, the 'new science of management', permeated the legislation and the manner in which the service was shaped by its formidable commissioner, Duncan McLachlan. It was a stark illustration that the new nation was not dominated by British legacies and was conspicuously open to adaptation of practice elsewhere.

The reasons for this course were several. First, the public service was a grandchild rather than a child of Whitehall. Most of its early staff came from colonial public services which themselves took shape before the merit-based Northcote–Trevelyan civil service had taken root in Whitehall. They had also had a fair share of the inefficiencies and corruptions of that period. Several of the services, but most notably that of NSW, had already been reorganized to reduce (if not eliminate) political influence by the establishment of a public service board, introducing open competition for employment, and applying scientific management techniques to the organization of work, classification and remuneration of staff, and methods of operation.

The public service differed from that of the Home Civil Service in several ways. First, there was comprehensive public service legislation covering employment, classification, and remuneration of staff. Public service management was vested in a statutory official; the public service commissioner was appointed for a seven-year term. The British relied on orders-in-council. The Civil Service Commission, a Crown agency, was responsible only for recruitment; other functions came under the Treasury. In Australia, the Treasury (like its state counterparts) was essentially a budget and accounting office until Keynesianism brought in a modern economics orientation.

The egalitarian spirit was strongly in evidence. Except for professional work (lawyers, engineers, doctors), there was no provision for graduate recruitment. The general administrative ranks were to be filled by school leavers (university entrance qualification), whereas the higher-level posts in the UK civil service were substantially a graduate preserve. Australian unions resisted graduate recruitment until well into the 1960s, even though a door was partially opened in 1935 at the behest of General Sir John Monash, Chancellor of the University of Melbourne.

The Dominion of Canada took over the civil service of Upper Canada (Ontario), and it was not until after the Second World War that nationwide integration was perceptibly accomplished. In the first four decades there were periodical attempts to establish a government-wide administrative framework for personnel management. This was partially achieved in 1908 in a form strongly reminiscent of UK arrangements.

The Great War proved a watershed for all three public services. In the aftermath, there were various reviews; acrimoniously by businessmen in Australia; top officials in the UK; and management experts from the USA in Canada. New structures were created, in a different form in each jurisdiction, but with efficiency as much as control the leitmotif. Australia and Canada each established a three-member body by statute to oversee the personnel and management of the public service. In the UK, a distinct command with comparable functions was created in the Treasury, individual personnel selection remaining a responsibility of the Civil Service Commission.

It is in the handling of management–staff relations that the different natures of the three public services are revealed, with the unions gaining their strongest foothold in Australia.

One of the most distinctive features of the Commonwealth was the early and formidable influence of organized labour. The Labor Party was, as it still is, a trade-union-based party. It was successful in rapidly establishing itself in the new parliament, and Labor was not alone in its sympathy with collectivism and state interventionism: it had a number of willing allies among the Protectionists. It is not therefore surprising that a part of the early legislative programme created a new Court of Conciliation and Arbitration that amounted to a substantial and very formal intervention of the state into the business and industrial life of the nation. The significance of this realization of Commonwealth power is underlined when it is recognized that the judges on this new labour court were drawn for several decades from the bench of the High Court of Australia. There was no parallel to this institutional arrangement in either the UK or Canada. Even when, later, there were similar interventions, they were much less formal and lacked the sustaining force of judicial prestige. Canada followed the US practice of direct bargaining between management and labour; third-party arbitration was a feature of the structure but it was engaged after negotiation between the parties and did not involve anyone with judicial rank or titles. It was not until 1948 that the Canada Labour Code was adopted.

The passage of the conciliation and arbitration legislation through the Australian parliament was contentious and the occasion for defeat and resignation of the first two governments, the Protectionist ministry in April 1904 followed by Watson's Labor government in August. The Protectionist defeat was expressly on the question of access of government employees to the proposed Court of Conciliation and Arbitration.

In 1910, Labor won majorities in both Houses for the first time in Commonwealth history, and public servants won access to the Court of Conciliation and Arbitration. So great was the workload from the public service that, in 1920, a separate arbitration jurisdiction (the public service arbitrator) was created and lasted for more than half a century.

The UK civil service resisted formal structures for management–staff relations until after the First World War. There was resistance for a time on the basis that the Crown did not negotiate with its servants, but eventually the consensual Whitley philosophy provided a framework in which honour was maintained but the right to negotiate effectively conceded.

The Canadian public service, though there were discussions between management and employees about remuneration and employment conditions, held out in a formal sense until 1967. In that year, as part of a major restructure of the public service, a legalistic collective bargaining regime was introduced. Personnel selection based on the merit principle was exempted from the new framework, and this continues to be contentious.

Canada's changes in 1967 largely brought public service management back within the remit of direct ministerial supervision through a statutory committee of the Cabinet, the Treasury Board, which combined budget and administrative management with that of the public service. In 1981, the Civil Service Department in the UK, as the Treasury command concerned with personnel and management had become (in 1968), was abolished, expenditure functions returning to the Treasury, the remainder forming an office within the Cabinet Office. In 1987, the Public Service Board in Australia was abolished, though a limited number of personnel functions found a home under a public service commissioner. Australia's distinctiveness in the field of public service management was largely at an end, notwithstanding expanded responsibilities vested in the commissioner in 2012.

14.7 Conclusion

It has been the major aim of this chapter to identify and describe distinctive features of Australian (national) government as it evolved during the twentieth century, drawing extensively on comparison and contrast with practice in Westminster and Ottawa. In concluding, it is worth addressing, albeit briefly, how this distinctiveness is viewed and what difference, if any, it makes.

The distinctiveness has not in general been well regarded or even well acknowledged. This was, perhaps, most conspicuously exemplified in the 1975 parliamentary crisis, which culminated in the dismissal of the Whitlam government, and the simultaneous dissolutions of the two Houses of the Australian parliament. Throughout the crisis, the embattled prime minister, Gough Whitlam, who usually was most brazen in boasting his nationalism, readily fell back on British rhetoric in defence of his parliamentary situation, as if he were in a remake of the UK Budget crisis of 1909–10. In this, he reflected fairly pervasive Labor thinking hostile to the Senate and the federal structure of which it was a major feature. Whitlam was, in his thinking, an unrepentant unificationist and unicameralist. He was hardly alone in these dispositions.

The three-year term of the House of Representatives is partly an inheritance of Chartism (which favoured annual parliaments). It has been, for many decades, under attack as an impediment to long-term policy-making and planning, largely at the hands of executive-oriented analysts who favour decisiveness over the discussion and debate favoured by the relatively few advocates of parliamentary proceeding and values.

The Governor-General as an institution seems, ironically, to be an admired part of the body politic. There has, intermittently, been a campaign to replace the monarchy in Australia with a presidency. But the proposed change, when it went to referendum, took the form of advocating a presidency in form similar to the Governor-General, in effect a recasting and renaming of the current office. Such a change would require new methods of selection and appointment but there have otherwise been few calls for alteration. The recent changes in Canada concerning vice-regal office have not attracted any interest in Australia.

It has lately been realized that Cabinet government is livelier and more active in Australia than in the UK or Canada. There is no inclination to wind it back. Cabinet government, in its present form, has wide-ranging political strengths apart from any considerations of doctrinal integrity. It facilitates fostering high-level cohesion among ministers and provides a regular forum for communication on the central questions at particular times.

The Constitution, and the method of amendment, has always been the target of criticism. The Whitlam government, for example, sought to reduce the state requirement for amendment from four to three, but there have been few other specific suggestions for change. It is certainly the case that judicial interpretation has proven to be more influential in adaptation (innovation) than formal amendment; there have, however, been a number of other cases where decisions of the Court have undone measures which, in practice, have been effective; such an example is the Court's decision in the late 1960s concerning state revenue-raising. But many other apparent problems have proven resolvable when there is political agreement. The art of forging political agreement has lately been overlooked in Australia.

Answering questions about what differences Australia's distinctive institutional structures make presents greater difficulties. The course of public policy in Australia, the UK, and Canada has been broadly similar throughout the twentieth century, which suggests that the impact of particular institutional arrangements is neither especially discernible nor decisive. Or, to put it another way, perhaps general, sustained opinion is more influential than the institutional framework. Parliament, ideally, is an important forum for articulation of opinion; but it is not the only forum. Features (op-ed) pages of newspapers have won a significant place in this respect. And current affairs programmes on both radio and TV perform similarly, if not always with perceptible benefit.

Whether a particular set of institutional structures works well depends upon several considerations, including the policies being advocated and the interests seeking representation. The Australian Senate furnishes an illustration. For many years Labor sought its abolition, seeing it as an obstacle to what it deemed to be progressive legislation. But, under the Coalition governments led by John Howard and Tony Abbott, it has been something of a bulwark against change in the form of resisting measures to reduce the range and scope of government, notably in the fields of welfare, higher education, and labour relations. This, together with the growing cross-bench, gives rise to questions about the continuing adequacy of the parliamentary dispute resolution procedures under the constitution. (At present, it would seem likely that only by proceeding to a joint sitting of the two Houses could disputes be settled.)

What can be said of all three jurisdictions covered by this chapter is that the continuing concentration on second chambers is excessive. Such concentration is mostly motivated by a desire to strengthen the position of executive government in an unproven if not mistaken belief that decisiveness is more important than wisdom. More attention to the role and vitality of the primary chambers in legislatures has much to commend it.

References

Bagehot, W. 1867. *The English Constitution*. London: Chapman Hall.

DPMC (Department of the Prime Minister and Cabinet). 2015. *Cabinet Handbook*, 8th edition. Canberra: Commonwealth of Australia.

Harris, I. (ed.). 2005. *House of Representatives Practice*, 5th edition. Canberra: Department of the House of Representatives.

Nethercote, J. R. 2015. 'MPs choosing a Speaker: Alfred Deakin's flawed legacy', *The Age* August 5 2015, p. 29.

Reid, G. S. 1987. 'Chronology of the federal parliament, 1901–1986', National Library of Australia, MS 8371.

15

Australia and New Zealand

Parallel and Divergent Paths

Keith Rankin

The thesis of Australia's exceptionalism contends that Australia has a distinctive social, economic, and political history, which has created an informal yet confident strategic personality, and forged a distinctive development path reflecting a political culture of pragmatic interventionist government. Has New Zealand conformed to this Australian path? Has it, in fact, originated aspects of such a path? Or has New Zealand deviated from Australia's course? Is New Zealand exceptionally exceptional?

Australian political exceptionalism is commonly linked to the development roles of 'the state' (and the 'states'), and to early working-class assertiveness. Australia emerged from the financial, economic, and drought crises of the 1890s with a Commonwealth government that presided over a national 'settlement', which Castles (1985, p.8) has called 'working-class welfare'. The political narrative in New Zealand, in contrast, has revolved less around the juxtaposition of labour and capital, and more around equitable land settlement and income security. New Zealand, which defederated well before Australia federated, arguably exceeded Australia in its levels of economic intervention. Several aspects of a trans-Tasman exceptionalism were pioneered in New Zealand, through nationalism expressed within a British imperial geopolity, through the use of government to substantially modify resource allocation and distribution (albeit within a general commitment to classical political economy), through visions of 'utopian' improvement, and through the early adoption of social security measures.

15.1 Exceptional Anglo-Western Expansion

James Belich (2009) emphasizes a pervasive British connection. While there are other regions of recent resettlement (South America, South Africa, Siberia, Manchuria), it is only the Anglo-wests that experienced explosive growth in the nineteenth century. Australia, New Zealand, Canada, and the UK constituted a 'Greater Britain' that, in the course of history since around 1840—the year of New Zealand's founding Treaty, and Canada's Act of Union—had been more or less apparent as a single cultural and supra-political identity. Belich sees Australia, New Zealand, and Canada as neo-Britannic, 'Anglo-wests', parallel to (but distinct from) the various Anglo-wests that constitute the American union. By this analogy, New Zealand would be equivalent to California, a 'farthest-west'.[1] Melbourne projects as a close analogue of Chicago.

From this point of view, neither the 'wests' of Greater Britain nor of the USA are uniquely exceptional, but considered together are exceptional. Canada now references itself more to its southern neighbour and less to its British origins, leaving only Australia and New Zealand as Britain's authentic and ongoing new wests. The exceptional differences between American and Greater British western expansions arose from timing, the extent of geographical distance, and in the different contributions of government to their respective development processes.

Before the railway age, when oceans were connectors rather than dividers, the actual extent of distance should not be overstated. Australia, an eastern 'far west', remained conceptually and culturally near-west; and, by sea, closer to London than San Francisco was to New York.[2] Nevertheless, physical distance does matter. And that is the first point of Australasian exception. New Zealand—like Australia—feared Asia to the north, much nearer than London, always sensing that Austral-Asia was mislocated. While Australia and New Zealand resolutely retain the symbolism of Greater Britain through their blue ensigns, the stars of the Southern Cross represent their antipodean distance.

While antipodean physical detachment from their metropole was an Australasian reality quite different from that of an Atlantic-focused America

[1] Belich (2009, p. 69) imagines a map of Canada, Australia, and New Zealand as if they were in the Atlantic Ocean; an alternate Scotland, Wales, and Ireland. In his map of the Atlantic, New Zealand sits between Australia and England. Perhaps he should have placed New Zealand to the west of Australia: the Belich analogy works best with the 'newer wests' (California and New Zealand) also being the 'farther wests'.

[2] New York to San Francisco via Cape Horn is 24,000 km. The problem of distance in the USA eased dramatically following the 1869 completion of the Pacific Railroad. While this opened up a shorter and faster passenger route from New Zealand to Britain (by steam rather than sail), the opening of the Suez Canal in the same year also reduced the effective distance from Australia to Europe.

with its receding land frontier, it was a reality quite familiar to early California. And a reality that would, in all cases, involve conflict with indigenous populations. Here, Australasia and the USA did have much in common: frontier conflicts, even if Australia does not name its settlement conflicts 'wars'. For the American West, as in New Zealand, treaties were negotiated between indigenous peoples and colonizers. In New Zealand, the Treaty of Waitangi serves as a founding national document. Nevertheless, as in the USA, treaty observance was often shallow. Frontier conflict was unambiguously 'war' over land.

The Belich new-west thesis is essentially a boom-bust, commodity-export growth model. The boom is migrant-driven, and the number one facilitator of migration is falling transport costs. Malthusian demand for new lands was ever present, and was prone to erupt, in peacetime, in response to favourable price signals. Capital followed. Significant busts occurred in New South Wales (NSW) in the 1840s, New Zealand and South Australia in the 1880s, and Victoria in the 1890s. Export recoveries tightened the economic bonds within Greater Britain, especially the bonds between each antipodean new-west and their parent old-east. New Zealand's reforged bond to its metropole tightened most, thanks to a proportionately larger impact of dairy farming and refrigeration and, later, to the Panama Canal. Australia and New Zealand became rivals for Britain's favours. Back to back, they faced each other.

Though eclipsed by Australia when viewed from London, in its nineteenth-century political imagination New Zealand relished an exceptionally great sense of Britishness, carrying the banner 'Britain of the South' (Belich 1996, p. 302). It was Americans, with a newly-acquired Pacific lens, who came and discovered that New Zealand offered lessons in 'progressive' policy-making (Coleman 1987). In reciprocation, significant influences on New Zealand thought before the turn of the century included Henry George (Sinclair [1959] 2001, p. 180) and Edward Bellamy. The Pacific Ocean was a point of New Zealand connection with America, just as the Tasman Sea connected Australia. And Pacific Polynesia was seen as New Zealand's special backyard, not an ambiguous part of Australasia (Mein Smith 2009, p. 298).

During its export-recovery phase, from the 1890s to the 1920s, New Zealanders' self-image as new southern Britons gave way to a martial 'better British' (Belich 2001) rivalry with Australia; understated in tone, yet deep-seated in the belief that white New Zealanders really were the best of the best.[3] Much of twentieth-century policy-making—epitomized by the Reform

[3] In parallel came the conviction that brown New Zealanders were 'better blacks'. For example, Belich (1997, p. 11) notes: 'People like the Aboriginal Australians were never forgiven for their lack of interest in Europe; peoples like Māori were congratulated for their interest.' Indeed, Māori embraced 'trade' in both its manufacturing and export-import senses (Monin 2009).

Party governments of 1912 to 1928—was about fostering grasslands' science and primary produce marketing, to entrench the trade lifeline with Britain. Sinclair noted ([1959] 2001, p. 248) that 'the premise of [Prime Minister] Massey's political philosophy, a cliché of the 1920s, was that New Zealand was the "Empire's outlying farm" '. Over the full extent of its export-facilitated expansion, New Zealand developed a truly exceptional neo-British economy from 1882 (first successful shipment of frozen meat to London) to 1972 (Britain's entry into the European Economic Community (EEC)), with up to 80 per cent of exports and 60 per cent of imports (Briggs 2003) being shipped literally from one point on the planet to its geographic opposite.

15.2 Geography as Politics before Australian Federation

New Zealand was always apart from New Holland, NSW, and Van Diemen's Land; more a smaller and greener alternate than a one-seventh part of an embryonic Australian nation. Tasmania, only semi-detached, was a coherent part of that Australia, by virtue of its geography as part of a continental landmass that physically separated after human settlement. Australia, Tasmania, and New Guinea are of Sahul, a partially drowned continent off South-East Asia.

New Zealand, a part of Polynesia, belongs to a separate largely submerged continental mass, Zealandia (Campbell 2011, p. 25). Australia was the fabled southern continent, fantastically different in its geography, botany, and zoology. New Zealand, a land of birds seemingly waiting to be settled by British bipeds and quadrupeds,[4] offered a way to be British in a new land. For the most part, New Zealand was to be settled directly from Britain, with the principal exception being a reflux from Victoria's gold rush. Many neo-British intellectuals were geographic Darwinists (Belich 1997, p. 356). There was a tendency in New Zealand to see Australia's climate as too languid to present proper fitness challenges to settler manhood (Macmillan Brown 1933). New Zealand, though more antipodean than Australia, would be less exceptional, more British; forged—as the Britons were—by wind and rain, not heat.

Five of New Zealand's earliest Anglo-settlements were facilitated through Edward Gibbon Wakefield's New Zealand Company and (with John Robert Godley) the Canterbury Association. As in *The New British Province of South Australia* (Wakefield 1834) a few years before, financial reality quickly intervened. Yet the high expectations behind the New Zealand settlements remained a driving force. Settlers planned their towns and villages through social lenses polished in England and Scotland. The important Otago

[4] It seems likely that, about 25 million years ago, Zealandia was close to fully submerged, resulting in the subsequent creation of a new ecosystem (Campbell 2011, p. 160).

settlement (1848) carried a utopian vision that reflected the evangelical political economy of Thomas Chalmers (Hilton 1985), architect of the 1843 Disruption of the Presbyterian Church. These Free Church founders of Dunedin (Edinburgh in Gaelic) likened themselves to the Pilgrim Fathers, who sailed to New England in the *Mayflower* two centuries earlier (Brooking 1984).[5]

The five planned settlements of Wellington (1840),[6] New Plymouth (1841), Nelson (1842), Otago/Dunedin (1848), and Canterbury/Christchurch (1850), along with Auckland and its estuarine hinterland, defined what would become in effect a federal system of government. Following what the Crown understood as the Māori cession of sovereignty through the Treaty of Waitangi and a brief period as a dependency of NSW, New Zealand's venture into quasi-federalism began in 1841 with a division 'by Royal Charter' of the North, Middle, and Stewart Islands into the notional provinces of New Ulster, New Munster, and New Leinster (Moon 2010, p. 66; Paterson 1966).[7] As a colonial project, New Zealand was visualized from afar as New Ireland, a sea passage from NSW.[8]

In 1846, with the actualization of the provincial system, New Leinster was discarded and Wellington joined New Munster. Auckland remained the seat of colonial government. Two provincial superintendents were appointed. The New Ulster Assembly never sat; and New Munster only once. When New Zealand became a self-governing colony in 1853 (Moon 2010, p. 74), the governance of New Zealand was restructured around six 'fishing village' settlements (Palenski 2012, p. 17).[9] These provinces had by 1873 become ten (Lenihan 2015, p. 24), with the additions of Southland, Marlborough, Hawkes Bay, and, finally, Westland. Whereas the Tasman Sea connected Westland with eastern Australia during the 1860s gold rush, the Southern Alps divided it from its own provincial capital of Christchurch.

Between 1853 and 1876 New Zealand was, then, an effective Federation, with hands-on government taking place at the provincial level, and a quasi-federal colonial government in Auckland, functioning as the political conduit with London. This was a sub-imperial administration which negotiated the

[5] This may form an exceptional founder basis for 'a particularly virulent form of Puritanism' widely depicted by 'fiction writers in the middle decades of the twentieth century' (Fairburn 2008, p. 30).

[6] The eight-hour working day was introduced in Wellington in October 1840, thanks to advocacy on this issue by Samuel Parnell. Labour Day was first celebrated fifty years later in 1890, and became a public holiday in 1899.

[7] Middle Island officially became South Island only in 1907.

[8] The names New Britain and New Ireland were already gazetted as islands in Melanesia by British navigators William Dampier in 1700, and Philip Carteret in 1767 (*Encyclopaedia Britannica*; Old Maps Online; 1826 Map, <http://www.oldmapsonline.org/map/rumsey/0096.049> (accessed 20 November 2015)).

[9] Belich (1996, p. 188) reports that these were sometimes known as the 'six colonies of New Zealand'.

interface between settler and indigenous New Zealand. As the weight of settler numbers and expectations increased, those mediations failed. The central North Island descended into frontier warfare from 1861 to 1864. While individual battles were evenly contested, the wars could only have one outcome: Māori lands confiscated and opened for resettlement. King Country became a quasi-autonomous Māori region of the central North Island (King 2003, p. 216),[10] which would eventually open up with the completion of the Auckland–Wellington railway in 1908. The settlement of the North Island interior from the 1870s[11] constituted a double frontier (south from Auckland and north from Wellington) to which Frederick Jackson Turner's explanation of American identity by its frontier could be applied, though not necessarily affirmed. These North Island re-settlers would underpin New Zealand's distinctive physiocracy—rule by small farmers who 'lay above the threshold of peasantry' (Bertram 2009, p. 554)—in the first two-thirds of the twentieth century.

Impractical access to Auckland in the 1860s sailing ship era (Brooking 1996, p. 41) meant that, once the North Island conflicts were 'resolved', the seat of colonial government would be shifted in 1865 to the still-small Wellington settlement (Moon 2010, p. 80). Wellington policy was to connect the provinces, by standardizing time, creating a national telegraph system (Palenski 2012), and borrowing on London to build steamship facilities and interprovincial railways. The political mastermind here was the Colonial Treasurer, Julius Vogel (Dalziel 1986).[12] Vogel was a persuasive business progressive who became renowned for large-scale borrowing on the London market to finance national infrastructure and immigration. The enhanced revenue-collecting capacity of central over provincial government was intrinsic to the financial deals Vogel was negotiating. Debt service would also be facilitated by extensive growth as a consequence of Vogel's scheme of subsidized immigration. The bold 'think big' programme of the 1870s formed the economic basis of New Zealand's nationhood.

With national connectedness progressing fast, economies of scale came to favour unified central government. The abolition of provincial government formed the political basis for New Zealand nationhood within the British

[10] Named in reference to the Kīngitanga (Ballantyne 2009, p. 113) movement, made up mainly of *iwi* (tribes) who did not sign the Treaty of Waitangi. While the Māori King (or Queen) retains a significant ceremonial role in New Zealand's increasingly formally bicultural constitution, big *iwi* such as Ngāpuhi and Ngāti Porou contribute little to Kīngitanga. These *iwi* clashed with the Kīngitanga over, for example, First World War conscription. Māori within government rejected Māori exemption from conscription (<http://www.nzhistory.net.nz/war/maori-in-first-world-war/resistence-to-conscription> (accessed 20 November 2015)).

[11] In general, the term 'land selection' is much less common in New Zealand than Australian historiography, though it was used (e.g. Brooking 1996, p. 70).

[12] His vision was presented in the 1870 Budget. Vogel later became premier (1873–75, 1876).

Empire.[13] Already New Zealand was building what would become quite an exceptional track record of domestic constitutional change.[14] For all practical purposes, on 1 January 1877, New Zealand became a coherent nation—as a unitary state—whereas the Australian colonies were clearly a part of a separate inchoate whole. While New Zealand-resident neo-Britons might readily resettle across the Tasman Sea, there was no appetite in New Zealand for government from Australia. The year 1877 was to New Zealand what 1901 was to Australia.

Government further matured in 1890 with the election of the Liberal Party, otherwise known as Liberal–Labour, on account of a strengthening trade union movement becoming one of the party's key stakeholders. The decade came to be known for 'radical' land and labour reforms,[15] piloted by John McKenzie and William Pember Reeves respectively. Reeves drew much of his labour legislation from Charles Kingston's compulsory arbitration proposals for South Australia (Mein Smith 2009, p. 301). 'State experimentation' meant an unusually high extent of departure from classical hands-off orthodoxy.

New settlement lands acquired as part of the Liberal government's land reforms coincided with financial crisis in Australia. North Island frontier lands attracted settlers from the South Island, directly and indirectly (via in particular Victoria). Further, infrastructure projects and industry attracted many young male immigrants from Australia. This cohort of Australians would feature prominently in New Zealand's 1935–49 reformist Labour government. Sinclair ([1959] 2001, p. 278) suggests that Australian radicals were particularly attracted to New Zealand in the years immediately after Australian Federation, believing the Australian Constitution had created too many points through which radical policy might be snuffed out.

15.3 The Presbyterian Connection

There is a significant Scottish dimension to New Zealand settlement and immigration. Scots, mostly of one or other variation of the Presbyterian

[13] The legislation was passed fifty-two to seventeen in July 1875, during Daniel Pollen's premiership, while Vogel was in England, 'detained by ill health' (Morrell 1933, p. 116).

[14] New Zealand, with surprising ease, and under conservative administrations, dispensed with the provinces (1876); the Legislative Council, an appointed second chamber modelled loosely on the British House of Lords (in 1950); and the British 'first-past-the-post' electoral system (1993). It switched the 'federal' capital from Auckland to much smaller but centrally located Wellington in 1865. New Zealand was the first national polity to grant women the vote (1893), and was the first colonized nation to grant the vote to indigenous men. Indeed, 'Māori men achieved universal suffrage 12 years before European men', in 1867, after four special Māori seats were created to ensure Māori representation in the colonial parliament (Ballantyne 2009, p. 116). Today there are seven Māori seats.

[15] Including graduated land taxes. The Liberals were influenced by the land nationalization writings of John Stuart Mill and Alfred Russel Wallace (Coleman 1987, p. 31; Sinclair [1959] 2001, p. 180).

faith, came to New Zealand early and often. In addition, a significant proportion of Irish immigrants to New Zealand were from the northern (more Scottish) counties of Ireland (Phillips and Hearn 2008). Scots comprised a substantial portion of early business leaders, pastoralists, and political leaders. The founders of Auckland (John Logan Campbell and William Brown), Christchurch (John and William Deans), and Dunedin (William Cargill and Thomas Burns) were Scots.

Richard Seddon, New Zealand's longest-serving prime minister (1893–1906), while born in Lancashire, was a 'north Briton' strongly influenced by his Scottish mother (Brooking 2014, p. 12). Significant prime ministers,[16] or premiers, had Scottish or Northern Irish heritage: Robert Stout, John Ballance, William Ferguson Massey, Peter Fraser, Keith Holyoake, Jenny Shipley, Helen Clark. From 1885 to 2015 these leaders (including another Scot, Thomas McKenzie, and Seddon) led New Zealand for a combined total of fifty-nine years.[17] In addition, William Downie Stewart, Jr, Arnold Nordmeyer, and Donald Brash became important financial leaders. Refugee highlander John McKenzie became New Zealand's pre-eminent land reformer. Other leaders were non-conformists. Harry Atkinson, though himself Anglican, had strong Unitarian connections. Walter Nash, an English-born Labour finance minister and prime minister, was a Christian Socialist. David Lange and Roger Douglas were Methodist; Robert Muldoon was Baptist. Norman Kirk had a Salvation Army background. Of New Zealand's important prime ministers, three had Irish Catholic roots (Ward, Savage, Bolger).[18] Gordon Coates, George Forbes, Sid Holland, and Bill Rowling were Anglican.

Otago (comprising Dunedin and Port Chalmers) was a Free Church of Scotland settlement, with puritan leanings. After the gold rushes commenced in 1861, Dunedin's Scottishness broadened. The population influx from Victoria was heavily infused with the socialistic ideas that circulated at Bendigo and Ballarat. Chartism was important (Brooking 1996, p. 41). Miners coming via California would have been exposed to the statist ideas of German-American Friedrich List.[19] John Carruthers, the Scot whom Vogel employed to become New Zealand's first chief engineer, was strongly influenced by John Ruskin's antipathy towards classical economics (Smith 1996). He would go on to present, in Wellington, tightly argued critiques of Mill's *Principles of Political*

[16] While the actual title was formally changed from premier to prime minister in 1907, when New Zealand gained Dominion status, Seddon's preference for the term 'prime minister' dates back to 1900 (McLintock 1966).

[17] While less prominent in national politics before 1885, Scots made significant early contributions to provincial politics.

[18] Ward and Savage were both born in Victoria. Bolger's parents immigrated from Ireland in 1930.

[19] Eldred-Grigg (2008, p. 234) notes California as a source of gold-seeking immigrants, many by way of Victoria.

Economy (Rankin 1993). Later, back in the UK as a member of William Morris's Socialist League, Carruthers would criticize the Liberal's state reforms as half-baked.

It was another Scottish-born Otago engineer, William Newsham Blair (Rankin 1993), whose economic policy prescriptions represented an outline of what Blyth (1966) would later call the 'Kiwi vision'. It was a story of pragmatic protectionist intervention, in line with the writings in the *Age* by David Syme (Macintyre 1991), yet another Scot, whose views were emblematic of Australian progressive exceptionalism.

This non-conformist mix of egalitarian and socially conservative influences was comparatively undiluted by Irish Catholicism.[20] New Zealand's more permissive Presbyterian legacy may have formed a basis for its political and cultural distinctiveness from Australia. New Zealand became a country with a dry egalitarian culture; a state of welfare with emphasis on comprehensive education, health care, and income support that would be applicable to farmers as well as to wage workers.

15.4 Dominions of Debt

Scots have a reputation for being concerned with financial matters, and this clearly shows through the contributions to financial governance of a number of those Presbyterian-influenced politicians. Scottish personal thrift would be offset by deficits in business ventures and government. Both private and public-sector debt featured substantially in New Zealand's growth model; New Zealand became an exceptional 'Dominion of Debt' (Schwartz 1989). Public debt expanded overtly in the early 1870s, covertly during the conservative Reform era of the 1920s, and out of necessity in the Muldoon era (1975–84) when external shocks hit New Zealand particularly hard. In other periods, such as the late 1870s, early 1920s, late 1930s, and the 'neoliberal' period after 1984, private indebtedness soared to fund land purchases or imports.

New Zealand's circumstances, going back to the era of provincial government, ensured that these governments would competitively borrow for local development, with full expectation that progress and rising asset values would offset that public debt. Subsequent national leaders such as Julius Vogel and Joseph Ward carried on the tradition of borrowing on the London market to a degree seen by many as incautious (King 2003, p. 277).[21]

[20] The early Catholic Church in New Zealand was French in origin, through Bishop Pompallier (The Catholic Church in Aotearoa New Zealand; <http://www.catholic.org.nz/our-story/> (accessed 20 November 2015)) and the Marist Brothers. The New Zealand Sisters of Compassion was founded by Suzanne Aubert, a candidate to become New Zealand's first saint.

[21] The Australian-born Ward became colonial treasurer in 1893 at the age of 37, and was personally bankrupt three years later. Ward was prime minister and finance minister from

New Zealanders and Australians continue to be exceptional today in their capacity to absorb debt (Rankin 2014b). On public debt in recent decades, fiscal conservatism has prevailed, however. 'Getting back into surplus' has become a principal policy commitment made by both National and Labour parties. Fiscal conservatism was entrenched in New Zealand in 1994 with the Fiscal Responsibility Act, now embedded within the Public Finance Act. This quasi-constitutional statute requires governments to prioritize the public debt to gross domestic product (GDP) ratio over other claims on public revenue.

While New Zealand does not lack financially austere people, twenty-first-century New Zealanders nevertheless have a high propensity to incur debt, especially (but not only) in the form of mortgages. Both Tasman countries have currencies that are bought and sold at unusually high levels relative to the sizes of their economies; the Australian dollar has been the fifth most traded in the world, and the New Zealand dollar the tenth (BIS 2013; Gaynor 2013). New Zealanders spend substantially more than their per capita share of creditor nations' savings. This reflects an exceptional degree of optimism, and Australasian willingness to invest in—and draw enjoyment from—global economic growth. And it is an integral part of a very new relationship with Asia.

15.5 Political Economy before the Second World War

Divisions between rural and urban interests precipitated the effective formation of a party political system in New Zealand in 1890. The Liberals principally represented the urban interest, while the Reform League promoted the interests of the growing numbers of farmers, especially those settling on newly available land in the North Island (Gardner 1966). William Ferguson Massey would become the early champion of these increasingly numerous farmers who favoured freehold tenure.[22] The Reform movement, answerable to the new dairy farmer interest, became the parliamentary Opposition and, from 1912, the government.[23]

1906–11, minister of finance in the Coalition War Cabinet (from the Opposition benches; 1915–19), and again prime minister and finance minister in 1928–30. Ward was by no means the only senior politician who had to leave office as a result of financial scandal. Another, Āpirana Ngata, whose policies helped many *iwi*, but his own Ngāti Porou more than most, was forced to leave parliament in 1934 on account of financial irregularities. Nevertheless, his contribution was such that he appears on New Zealand's $50 note.

[22] This contrasts with the Liberal land reforms of the 1890s, which favoured long-term leases over freehold tenure (Brooking 1996).

[23] See Sinclair ([1959] 2001, p. 215) for further explanation of the creation of both a Country Party and a Farmers' Union in the early 1900s. The Country Party was soon absorbed into the broader Reform Party, a freehold-farmers' party, which incorporated urban capital interests. Gaining power in 1912 through a successful no-confidence vote in a 'hung parliament', one of Reform's first actions was to reinstate the first-past-the-post electoral system. Elections of 1908 and

Reform had become a multi-interest party by the 1920s. An explicit 'Country Party' could not achieve prominence in New Zealand as it had in Australia, thanks to the electoral system. A new 1920s Country Party eventually morphed into the Social Credit Political League (Gully 1966). Political opinions in rural New Zealand railed against foreign 'middlemen' and foreign-owned New Zealand banks before and during the Great Depression (Sinclair [1959] 2001, p. 262). Returning soldiers had acquired farms, at inflated prices, with low interest loans. Many new farms in remote North Island locations were, at best, marginal. With the British shipping strike in 1926 and the more general deterioration of the terms of trade in the late 1920s, New Zealand's small farmers were struggling well before the world depression hit during 1930. These farmers, plus many owners of small businesses in the rural service towns, looked towards Social Credit for solutions, as many Canadian farmers and small businesses had. With a different rural–urban balance, Australia seems to have been somewhat less affected by this form of agrarian radicalism.

With the rise of the Labour Party, the hitherto 'left' Liberal Party became more like the Australian Liberal Party. Liberal (renamed United), now mainly a South Island party, 'won' a three-cornered election in 1928. To keep Labour from benefiting from a split right-of-centre vote, Reform and United effectively merged in 1931; contesting two elections under the 'Coalition' banner before adopting the name 'National'. The merger did keep Labour at bay in 1931. Absorbing the monetary reform message, Labour swept to power in 1935 thanks to a transfer of allegiance on the part of the credit-starved provincial and rural self-employed.[24] A new splinter group on the 'far right' (Sinclair [1959] 2001, p. 277)—the Democrat Party—split the conservative vote, and Labour ruled until 1949. The rise of the Democrat Party was a response to the pragmatic recovery policies of 1933–35 finance minister (and former prime minister, 1925–28) Gordon Coates, who had gathered around him a small 'brains trust', of young economists, who, some thought, had 'communist sympathies'.[25] His recovery policies included devaluation, and the establishment of the Reserve Bank of New Zealand.

1911 had been conducted under a two-ballot system; effectively a preferential voting (PV) scheme, that has otherwise been rare in New Zealand.

[24] Social Credit advocates supported Labour in the period of Savage's leadership. Social Credit contested elections as a stand-alone political party from 1954 to 1990. As the Democrat Party within the left-wing Alliance Party (1991–2002), it held executive posts in the 1999–2002 Labour-led government.

[25] One of these young economic advisers was W. B. Sutch (Easton 2001, chs 7 and 10), a significant author of political economy texts such as *Colony or Nation?* and *The Quest for Security in New Zealand*. In the 1950s and 1960s, mainly under National administrations, Sutch was a significant public servant, as permanent secretary for the Department of Industries and Commerce. In 1975 Sutch was prosecuted under the 1951 Official Secrets Act, by New Zealand's then Labour Government, for passing documents to an emissary of the Soviet Union. Although acquitted, he died a few months later. Sutch remains one of the more enigmatic figures in New Zealand's history.

15.6 Post-Second World War Political Economy

New Zealand retained its 'Senate' (Legislative Council) until 1950, when it was euthanized by the newly-elected conservative National government; an echo of the abolition of the provincial assemblies in 1876. The resulting unicameral system has been likened to an 'elected dictatorship'; an ability for governments to legislate with minimal checks. A referendum in 1967 to extend the parliamentary term to four years was soundly defeated. For four decades, the short parliamentary term was New Zealand's only constitutional check on the abuse of power.

Political and economic life in the two countries was conducted in parallel. Defence alliances in the form of the Australia, New Zealand, United States Security Treaty (ANZUS) and the Southeast Asia Treaty Organization (SEATO) meant that a military relationship was retained, albeit under the USA's oversight. Australia's military contribution to South-East Asian regional conflicts was greater than New Zealand's, and Australia's alliance with the USA was somewhat tighter. This is shown by the substantially different scales of involvement in the Vietnam War, and in New Zealand's somewhat casual (in Australian eyes) departure from ANZUS in 1985. Australia sent conscripts to Vietnam, New Zealand did not; a reversal of the First World War, when New Zealand conscripted and Australia did not.[26]

There was some economic convergence from 1965, starting with the hopeful New Zealand Australia Free Trade Agreement (NAFTA) and currency decimalization, though most facilitated by the devaluation in 1967 of the New Zealand dollar and by Britain's entry into the EEC in 1972. The devaluation, in particular, extended the Australian market for New Zealand's manufactured goods. In the 1970s and 1980s, that period of exceptionally 'stormy seas' (Easton 1997), New Zealand policy initiatives reoriented the export economy towards Asia, creating unusually strong relationships with China from the late Maoist period, the Soviet Union during that period of Cold War intensification, and with revolutionary Iran in the years around 1980. New markets were found for those staples formerly sold almost exclusively to Great Britain, while new export industries emerged. 'Closer Economic Relations' with Australia in 1982 followed (CEDA 1985) the China, Soviet, and Iranian initiatives, substantially extending market opportunities for New Zealand manufacturers.

Australia and New Zealand came to see Asia as an opportunity rather than as a threat. And they rediscovered each other. Economic tensions remained, however, most visibly through the Ansett Airlines collapse in 2001 (and the subsequent blockading of the New Zealand Prime Minister in Melbourne

[26] Conscription also operated in the Second World War, legislated for by Prime Minister Peter Fraser, who himself had been imprisoned as a conscientious objector in the First World War.

Airport), and most prolonged in relation to the apple fire blight issue (Bertram 2009, p. 544). Fundamentally different natural environments meant there would always be tensions over biosecurity. Both countries are exceptional in terms of their histories of extreme caution over biosecurity matters.

The 'neoliberal policy' revolution (dubbed 'Rogernomics' after Roger Douglas, Labour Finance Minister 1984–88) was framed as a reaction to a stifling National Party 'statism' that allegedly reached its apex in the second and third terms (1979–84) of the Muldoon-led government.[27] The reality is that while Robert Muldoon exhibited a divisive and at times brutal political style—he probably had to in order to prevail in the 1978 and 1981 elections—he was a cautious liberalizer over a period of nearly two decades of stormy international political and market forces.[28] Through 1978–84 New Zealand's economic growth was above the Organisation for Economic Co-operation and Development (OECD) average and inflation rates were high, but not exceptionally so. Unemployment, hitherto exceptionally low, increased. But it remained low by OECD standards throughout the stagflation of the early 1980s.

Both external and government debt increased substantially, but could easily have been much higher had Muldoon's trade and import substitution initiatives not taken place. A significant proportion of that debt reflected a countercyclical 'Think Big' investment initiative—reminiscent of Julius Vogel 110 years earlier—that focused on reducing New Zealand's imported oil requirements, and on using hydroelectricity and iron-sands to produce exportables such as aluminium and steel. These developments gave a substantial economic boost to provincial New Zealand, Muldoon's power base. It is difficult to envisage counterfactual policies for the early 1980s that could have achieved higher growth for New Zealand's tradable sector.

Bertram (2009) summarizes twentieth-century economic policy-making as following three major epochs. The first quarter of the century was essentially a farmer-led policy environment, with support for arbitrated family wages in the 'sheltered' domestic sector. The middle third of the century was dominated by the interests of the tradable sector as a whole, including substantial

[27] Labour Prime Minister David Lange (1984–89) likened the 1975–84 New Zealand economy to a Polish shipyard ('His views' 2005, p. 13; Goldfinch and Malpass 2007, p. 120), implying that it had controls comparable to those of an Eastern-bloc nation in the then-Cold War era. Castles, Gerritsen, and Vowles (1996, p. 219) perpetuate the myth in describing Muldoon's prime ministership as 'nine years in office, with extreme statist solutions across the board imposed by steamroller tactics'. The 'Polish shipyard' image facilitated the acceptance in New Zealand of neoliberal policy reforms, much as Paul Keating's 1986 'banana republic' comment did in Australia.

[28] See Gould (1985), Goldfinch and Malpass (2007), Rankin (2014a) for various perspectives on Muldoon. Liberalizations relate to official secrecy, the removal of import licensing, restrictions on Saturday shopping, restructuring of protected industries, and freight transport. With cautious reform and a commitment to welfare principles established in 1938, New Zealand was not a dirigiste society in 1984.

protection for secondary industries.[29] The 1984 disjuncture represented an alleged Treasury-supported 'coup' on the part of the interests of the urban-based non-tradable sector, with special reference to the growing finance industry.[30]

The trade-off for rapid economic liberalization, by a Labour government, was policy concession elsewhere. For this reason, politicians and business leaders backing 'Rogernomics' supported an exceptional set of 'nuclear-free' foreign policies, getting New Zealand into serious political difficulties with the governments of the USA, the UK, and France.[31] Even property developer and boxing promoter Bob Jones—whose New Zealand Party's presence in the 1984 election would ensure a substantial defeat for Muldoon—astounded voters by proposing an essentially pacifist defence policy (Trotter 2013).[32] These policies led to New Zealand's suspension from the ANZUS defence pact.

Labour governments which came to power in Australia (1983) and New Zealand (1984) were able to implement new sets of policies by presenting the previous decade's challenges as cases of government failure. Castles, Gerritsen, and Vowles (1996, p. 2) note the exceptionalism of Labour governments becoming 'neoliberal' midwives, when hitherto these kinds of policies had been associated with radical conservative governments led by, for example, Margaret Thatcher and Ronald Reagan. Labour governments in the twenty-first century have matured rather than disavowed these respective 1980s policy directions.

15.7 Parallel though Not Always Together

Immigration control was a central Federation issue in Australia in 1901. New Zealand policy was more nuanced than the overt 'White Australia' legislation. No dictation tests were imposed in European languages other than English (O'Connor 1968, p. 305). While Chinese 'Asiatics' became a particular bogey,

[29] These are represented, respectively, by Blyth (1966) as the 'competitive model, welfare style' ('colonial vision') and the 'growth model' (industrial and planning styles; 'kiwi vision'). The post-1984 epoch would represent a strong version of Blyth's preferred 'competitive model; efficiency style'.

[30] Bertram (2009, p. 559) says: 'State agencies not aligned with the new political economy were simply abolished, and those that were so aligned (particularly Treasury and the Reserve Bank) were strengthened.'. McKinnon (2003, p. 289) says 'officials were determined to wean ministers from Keynesian thinking', and discusses the Treasury's relationship with Roger Douglas (p. 318).

[31] In 1985 the French government covertly sank the Greenpeace ship *Rainbow Warrior* in Auckland, with the loss of one life.

[32] Jones had already become popular with urban liberals by sponsoring ballet in New Zealand (Dalglish 2005). While few social liberals voted for his party in 1984, Jones's crossover defence policy facilitated the subsequent acceptance of economic liberalism by 'sixties generation' Labour supporters.

New Zealand generally complied with British wishes to accept Indians as British subjects. Indeed, in the racial hierarchy of the day, Indians were more 'Aryan' than Chinese. While immigration policy strongly favoured Britons, an important special case was Pacific Polynesia, seen as New Zealand's own sub-imperial domain. Ethnic kinship with Māori exempted Polynesians from some racial prejudice.

'White Australia' was a unification project; creating a European bulwark in an antipodean hemisphere of brown, yellow, and black. Australia's nationalism has been more formal, more contrived, than that of New Zealand. Australian citizenship became both a prized status and a set of formal responsibilities. While voting eligibility was tight, it became compulsory to exercise that right. Australia became a land of opportunity-seeking denizens amidst privileged citizens. In the twenty-first century, a very large number of those denizens are immigrants from New Zealand. Australian citizens, on the other hand, continue to hold full residence rights in New Zealand. While trans-Tasman migration has always been sensitive to differences in each country's business cycle (Rankin 1992), immigration policy asymmetry is a twenty-first-century phenomenon.

New Zealand's 'big-four' banks are now entirely Australian-owned. And since federation Sydney has remained an important cultural centre for New Zealanders; a sort of London-lite (Fairburn 2008). Australian magazines were always readily available and popular in New Zealand. Professional bodies shared activities, though mostly in Australia. Entertainment exchanges continued through the twentieth century, from Nellie Melba's tour in 1903, to Kiri Te Kanawa's visits to Australia towards the end of the century. Regular visits to New Zealand of Australian circuses, such as Bullens, became part of the fabric of New Zealand life in the 1950s and 1960s. Popular music bands, such as Split Enz, sojourned in Australia. The 'Tasman World' was ongoing, in reality, if not always in perception.

While general New Zealand news stories today seem conspicuous by their absence in the Australian press, a random 'citing' of one country newspaper ((Rockhampton) *Morning Bulletin*, 1 July 1947) showed two New Zealand front page stories. While sporting links were strong in some cases—rugby in particular —Australians chose not to play test cricket with New Zealand for many decades,[33] despite New Zealand vying with the rest of the cricket-playing empire. Horse racing, like rugby, was a significant shared activity, especially through the Melbourne Cup and the Inter Dominion pacing championship. New Zealand continues to be a nursery for Australian thoroughbreds. Carbine

[33] The year 1973 was the second ever test match; 1974 the year of New Zealand's first victory over Australia.

and Phar Lap—Melbourne Cup winners in 1890 and 1930—remain among the most famous of many Australian horses from New Zealand.

When practically necessary, New Zealand teamed up with Australia, in tennis and athletics before the First World War, and in Albany and Cairo during that war. There has always been a suspicion, though, that Australia gives little recognition to the 'NZ' in 'Anzac'. Indeed, in Ausflag's pictorial essay on the Australian red ensign 'people's flag',[34] pairings with New Zealand's blue flag are remarkable by their absence, even where Australia's red flag was shown alongside allied flags. When Robert Menzies disavowed Australia's red flag in 1953, there appears to have been little awareness or concern that the full adoption of the blue flag might undermine the separate identity of Australia's Anzac partner.

In policy-making, politicians and public servants (including those in Australian states) naturally turned to their Tasman partners for inspiration about how or how not to meet a particular challenge (Mein Smith 2012). The two economies grew in parallel with similar living standards—give or take cyclical variations—until the 1980s. However, the strong similarities in the formation of welfare states from 1890 diverged in the 1930s. Labour and National/Liberal administrations prevailed in each country at different times. With regard to Michael Joseph Savage, the Labour prime minister of New Zealand from 1935 to 1940, who represented the face of New Zealand social security, the *New Zealand Herald* stated it 'greatly admired the man himself as the epitome of the New Zealand character, even though he had been born in a foreign land', to the extent of making him their person of the year in both 1937 and 1938:

> An Australian by birth, but a New Zealander by 28 years' adoption, Mr Savage has none of the easy optimism and irresponsibility with which popular belief endows the typical 'Aussie'.... In temperament he so far conforms to the accepted New Zealand pattern that he has been able to win the almost instinctive respect and liking even of those to whom his political creed is anathema.
>
> ('Mr Savage's Career' 1935, p. 14)

Castles (1985, p. 8) wrote of Australasian exceptionalism in the context of workers 'welfare state'. In both countries 'working class' assuredly would not mean 'lower class'. Thus the early welfare states that emerged from the state experiments of the 1890s and 1900s would take on a form in Australia that would remain exceptional, albeit on account of its limitations compared to many post-Second World War welfare societies.[35] Here Australia is the exemplar of a 'selective' welfare state. New Zealand state experiments in social

[34] See: <http://www.ausflag.com.au/red_ensign.asp> (accessed 20 November 2015).

[35] Castles does not address the early welfare structures in Argentina and Uruguay, which shared some commonalities with the Australasian model (Easton 2001).

security more often preceded those of Australia. From 1938 welfare policy diverged in areas of health care, retirement income, and per-child family benefits without means tests. One important feature of the comprehensive 1938 social security reform was the 'universal superannuation' demogrant (Castles 1985, p. 27), payable to persons over 65 not receiving the higher means-tested age benefit.[36]

In 1974, New Zealand Labour established an insurance-based earnings-related pension that would replace universal superannuation (McLure 1998, p. 191). McClure notes that Labour's new insurance-based scheme was unlike anything in New Zealand's welfare traditions. New Zealand, before 1974, had never had any form of income support that related positively to past earnings. This became the big issue of the 1975 election campaign, and contributed to Labour's defeat (McLure 1998, p. 193).[37] From 1977, welfare practice in New Zealand diverged from Australia through the restoration and extension of universal superannuation in its more generous guise as National Superannuation.[38] Labor in Australia, having eschewed universal pensions, implemented, in the 1980s, a workers' funded pension, not unlike New Zealand Labour's short-lived scheme.

The language and assumptions of tax and welfare policies vary markedly between the two countries. Income taxation also diverged from the 1970s, when New Zealand, in 1974, replaced allowances and exemptions with a personal tax rebate (Rankin 2006).[39] When the rebate was abolished in 1978, it left an income tax structure that required persons to pay tax on every dollar earned. This flattening of the tax scale at the bottom end was extended to the top end in 1988 (Rankin 2014a).[40] The sharemarket crisis of 1987 hit New Zealand much harder than it hit Australia, a result of a sharemarket bubble reflecting the very rapid financial deregulation in 1985.[41]

[36] The 1938 grant was payable to all persons over 65 not receiving the higher age benefit. It was funded with the help of a 7.5% hypothecated tax, which was merged with general income taxation in 1967 (Rankin 2014a).

[37] McLure commits a whole chapter ('Generous Years') to the 1972 Royal Commission of Inquiry on Social Security which recommended a substantial expansion of welfare support along the universalist principles first enunciated by Savage in 1938. This commitment, wholeheartedly embraced by Robert Muldoon (Rankin 2014a), represents a divergence in welfare principles between New Zealand and Australia.

[38] The 1977 National Superannuation payment fully replaced all previous age benefits. But until 1986 payments to high earners were substantially clawed back through marginal tax rates in excess of 50 per cent. Inflation brought many more people into these higher tax brackets.

[39] The current technical name for such a rebate is 'non-refundable tax credit'; a payment that offsets income tax but cannot exceed liable tax. It effectively extended the tax-free income bracket. This contrasts with a demogrant, which is an example of a 'refundable tax credit' or 'negative income tax'.

[40] In a sense, the exceptional flattening of the income tax scale at both ends echoes the one tier political structure created through the abolition of provincial governments and the Upper House.

[41] While, in Australia, the liberalization process was more restrained, there was a banking crisis there, too, in 1990 and 1991 (Rankin 2014b). The Bank of New Zealand failed twice (and was twice rescued) in 1988 and 1990. The latter failure was due to its Australian operations.

The policy disjuncture in New Zealand is clearly dated to 14 July 1984, when the Muldoon-led National government was defeated by the Lange–Douglas Labour Party. On welfare and tax matters, this led to increased selectivity or 'targeting' of cash benefits—a return to the Australian tradition of selective welfare as a working-class safety net—and the progressive replacement of universal child benefits with tapered 'tax credits', some of which (for example, the present in-work tax credit) applied only to families in substantial employment. National Superannuation—becoming a 'guaranteed retirement income'—was subjected to an indirect means test. However, as New Zealand Superannuation, it became universal again in 1998 due to the influence of Coalition Treasurer Winston Peters, a political disciple of Robert Muldoon. While there is no strong present-day movement to extend universal welfare provision, those forms that exist, including the restored New Zealand Superannuation, are more resolutely defended than they were in the 1980s and 1990s.

The return to universal retirement pensions was made possible by the introduction of the mixed member proportional (MMP) electoral system in 1996, following referendums in 1992 and 1993. Lower House proportional representation (PR) is exceptional in the Anglo-world, although it does exist (albeit through different voting mechanisms) in Ireland, Tasmania, and, more latterly, Scotland. The process in New Zealand of adopting a new voting system was a reaction both to the National Party's ability to rule from 1978 to 1984 despite Labour gaining more votes, and to the post-1984 policy revolution that took New Zealand voters by surprise. Efficiently implemented, and endorsed by a further referendum in 2011, New Zealand proudly owns its exceptional electoral system, which combines local representation with proportionate outcomes, much as it owns its exceptional demogrant system of publicly sourced retirement income.

15.8 Reflection

New Zealand is both a unique British 'far-west' and a Polynesian 'south west'. Its circumstances of geography and brief human history—discovered and settled across the ocean by Polynesians, rediscovered and settled by people from its antipodes—ensure that. But has New Zealand been exceptionally exceptional? Maybe it is different from Australia due to its mix of Polynesian and British settlers. New Zealanders differ from their own source populations by virtue of those journeys made; they are adaptive in policy, as in the economic techniques of surviving and prospering. Australian immigrants made many of the same journeys, although in different Anglo-Celtic mixes and, in Australia's early years, in more coercive circumstances.

New South Britons came to land with established populations too easily discounted as 'primitive'. Australian and New Zealand immigrants settled as communities of imported social and financial capital. The development of collective governance cultures among these settlers was a natural adaptation to these novel far-flung environments. Each nation has its own unification story, and each remained connected to the other as sibling rivals within an ongoing British imperial polity. Both societies forged egalitarian development paths which encouraged risk-taking, and aspired to be ruled democratically by a propertied hard-working class.

Organized labour was an important institution in both societies, though in New Zealand the balance was more towards petit-bourgeois farming and farmer-servicing small businesses. The Farmers' Union ruled through the Reform Party in the 1910s and 1920s. Export-dependent policies tied New Zealand closely to its distant Anglo-parent. In consequence, the country was less diversified than Australia in 1970, so the troubled waters of global economic turbulence and changing British priorities forced a very rapid re-evaluation of New Zealand's relationship with Asia. This happened in Australia as well. In the process—thanks in large part to cheaper air-fares—the two Anglo-wests rediscovered each other.

Welfare states emerged at similar times, developing similarly in the 1890s and differently from the 1930s to the 1980s. Public income-support mechanisms remain works in progress, despite both countries being among the first in the world to embrace them. New Zealand was able to make constitutional changes more quickly—maybe too quickly—having removed the upper and lower tiers of its initial political structure. When the 1980s ushered in a global policy climate best understood as a return to laissez-faire, both countries responded with distinctly different variations of this path, albeit, exceptionally, under the auspices of Labour governments. A former parity of incomes gave way to a significant income gap, meaning that substantially more New Zealanders migrated to Australia than vice versa. With echoes of New Munster in the nineteenth century, in this century New Zealand has indeed become Australia's Ireland.

New Zealand's journey since the 1970s has increasingly been one of Asian and Polynesian themes, not British. Australia likewise is much more ethnically diverse than its early twentieth-century founders could ever have imagined. In the 1990s, Prime Minister Jim Bolger said 'we are all Asians now' (O'Sullivan 2003). Geography, trade, and economic growth have created dramatically new post-colonial realities for both. The markets for the dominant food staples of New Zealand behave differently from those for Australian staple mineral exports, and are less subject to the vagaries of global fixed capital investment. For people of Asian birth, New Zealand is an emigrant destination in its own right, not simply Australia-lite. Once-exceptional Tasman paths have now become enmeshed within a globalized order. New cosmopolitan middle and lower classes displace almost everywhere the yeoman and working classes of nineteenth- and twentieth-century Australasia. Australia and New Zealand have matured to become distinct 'new wests' in the Far East.

References

Ballantyne, T. 2009. 'The state, politics and power' in G. Byrnes (ed.), *The New Oxford History of New Zealand*. Melbourne: Oxford University Press.

Belich, J. 1996. *Making Peoples: A History of the New Zealanders from Polynesian Settlement to the end of the Nineteenth Century*. Auckland: Penguin.

Belich, J. 1997. 'Myth, race and identity in New Zealand', *New Zealand Journal of History*, vol. 31, no. 1, pp. 9–22.

Belich, J. 2001. *Paradise Reforged: A History of the New Zealanders from the 1880s to the Year 2000*. Auckland: Penguin.

Belich, J. 2009. *Replenishing the Earth: The Settler Revolution and the Rise of the Anglo World*. Oxford: Oxford University Press.

Bertram, G. 2009. 'The New Zealand economy 1900–2000' in G. Byrnes (ed.), *The New Oxford History of New Zealand*. Melbourne: Oxford University Press.

BIS (Bank of International Settlements). 2013. *Triennial Central Bank Survey. Foreign Exchange Turnover in April 2013: Preliminary Global Results*. Basel: BIS.

Blyth, C. 1966. 'The special case: the political economy of New Zealand', *Political Science*, vol. 18, no. 1, pp. 38–51.

Briggs, P. 2003. *Looking at the Numbers: A View of New Zealand's Economic History*. Wellington: New Zealand Institute of Economic Research.

Brooking, T. 1984. *And Captain of their Souls*. Dunedin: Otago Heritage Books.

Brooking, T. 1996. *Lands for the People: A Biography of John McKenzie*. Dunedin: University of Otago Press.

Brooking, T. 2014. *Richard Seddon: King of God's Own. The Life and Times of New Zealand's Longest Serving Prime Minister*. Auckland: Penguin.

Campbell, H. 2011. *In Search of Ancient New Zealand*. Auckland: Penguin.

Castles, F. 1985. *The Working Class and Welfare in Australia and New Zealand*. Wellington: Allen & Unwin.

Castles, F., Gerritsen, R., and Vowles, J. (eds.). 1996. *The Great Experiment*. Auckland: Auckland University Press.

CEDA (Committee for Economic Development of Australia). 1985. *Closer Economic Relations: A View from Both Sides of the Tasman*. Wellington: New Zealand Institute of Economic Research.

Coleman, P. J. 1987. *Progressivism and the World of Reform: New Zealand and the Origins of the American Welfare State*. Lawrence, KS: University Press of Kansas.

Dalglish, K. 2005. 'Bob Jones: my property world', *Scoop*, 7 September, <http://www.scoop.co.nz/stories/HL0509/S00091.htm> (accessed 20 November 2015).

Dalziel, R. 1986. *Julius Vogel, Business Politician*. Auckland: University of Auckland Press.

Easton, B. 1997. *In Stormy Seas: The Post-War New Zealand Economy*. Dunedin: University of Otago Press.

Easton, B. 2001. *The Nationbuilders*. Auckland: Auckland University Press.

Eldred-Grigg, S. 2008. *Diggers, Hatters and Whores: The Story of the New Zealand Gold Rushes*. Auckland: Random House.

Fairburn, M. 2008. 'Is there a good case for New Zealand exceptionalism?', *Thesis Eleven*, no. 92, pp. 29–49.

Gardner, W. J. 1966. 'Reform party' in A. H. McLintock (ed.), *An Encyclopaedia of New Zealand*. Wellington: Government printer.

Gaynor, B. 2013. 'Why everyone likes trading in our money', *New Zealand Herald*, 21 December, p. 16.

Goldfinch, S. and Malpass, D. 2007. 'The Polish shipyard: myth, economic history and economic policy reform in New Zealand', *Australian Journal of Politics and History*, vol. 53, no. 1, pp. 118–37.

Gould, J. 1985. *The Muldoon Years: An Essay on New Zealand's Recent Economic Growth*. Auckland: Hodder & Stoughton.

Gully, J. S. 1966. 'Social Credit Political League' in A. H. McLintock (ed.), *An Encyclopaedia of New Zealand*. Wellington: Government printer.

Hilton, B. 1985. 'Chalmers as political economist' in A. C. Cheyne (ed.), *The Practical and the Pious*. Edinburgh: Saint Andrew Press.

'His Views'. 2005. *New Zealand Herald*. 15 August, p. 13.

King, M. 2003. *The Penguin History of New Zealand*. Auckland: Penguin.

Lenihan, R. 2015. *From Alba to Aotearoa*. Dunedin: Otago University Press.

Macintyre, S. 1991. *A Colonial Liberalism: The Lost World of Three Victorian Visionaries*. Melbourne: Oxford University Press.

McKinnon, M. 2003. *Treasury: The New Zealand Treasury 1840–2000*. Auckland: Auckland University Press.

McLintock, A. H. 1966. 'The title "premier"' in A. H. McLintock (ed.), *An Encyclopaedia of New Zealand*. Wellington: Government printer.

McLure, M. 1998. *A Civilised Community: A History of Social Security in New Zealand 1898–1998*. Auckland: Auckland University Press.

Macmillan Brown, J. 1933. 'Epilogue' in *Cambridge History of the British Empire*, vol. 7, part 2. Cambridge: Cambridge University Press.

Mein Smith, P. 2009. 'The Tasman world' in G. Byrnes (ed.), *The New Oxford History of New Zealand*. Melbourne: Oxford University Press.

Mein Smith, P. 2012. *A Concise History of New Zealand*, 2nd edition. Melbourne: Cambridge University Press.

Monin, P. 2009. 'Māori economies and colonial capitalism' in G. Byrnes (ed.), *The New Oxford History of New Zealand*. Melbourne: Oxford University Press.

Moon, P. 2010. *New Zealand Birth Certificates; 50 of New Zealand's Founding Documents*. Auckland: AUT Media.

Morrell, W. P. 1933. 'The constitution and the provinces' in *Cambridge History of the British Empire*, vol. 7, part 2. Cambridge: Cambridge University Press.

'Mr Savage's Career'. 1935. *New Zealand Herald*. 28 November, p. 14.

O'Connor, P. S. 1968. 'Keeping New Zealand white: 1908–20', *New Zealand Journal of History*, vol. 2, no. 1, pp. 41–65.

O'Sullivan, F. 2003. 'Losing track of the tigers'. *New Zealand Herald*. 3 August.

Palenski, R. 2012. *The Making of New Zealanders*. Auckland: Auckland University Press.

Paterson, D. 1966. 'New Leinster, New Munster, and New Ulster' in A. H. McLintock (ed.), *An Encyclopaedia of New Zealand*. Wellington: Government printer.

Phillips, J. and Hearn, T. 2008. *Settlers: New Zealand Immigrants from England, Ireland and Scotland 1800–1945*. Auckland: Auckland University Press.

Rankin, K. 1992. 'New Zealand's gross national product: 1859–1939', *Review of Income and Wealth*, vol. 38, no. 1, pp. 49–69.

Rankin, K. 1993. 'Three nineteenth-century New Zealand contributions to economic thought', *Seventh History of Economic Thought Society of Australia Conference*, 13–15 July 1993, Wollongong, NSW.

Rankin, K. 2006. 'New Zealand income tax policy 1973–1982 and its legacy', *New Zealand Journal of Taxation Law and Policy*, vol. 12, no. 1, pp. 10–18.

Rankin, K. 2014a. 'New Zealand's income tax in the rollercoaster Muldoon years: 1967–84', *2014 Asia-Pacific Economic and Business History Conference*, 13–15 February, Hamilton, New Zealand.

Rankin, K. 2014b. 'Private sector financial balances 1980–2012', *2014 Asia-Pacific Economic and Business History Conference*, Hamilton, 13–15 February New Zealand.

Schwartz, H. M. 1989. *In the Dominions Of Debt: Historical Perspectives on Dependent Development*. New York: Cornell University Press.

Sinclair, K. [1959] 2001. *A History of New Zealand*. Auckland: Penguin.

Smith, C. 1996. 'The political economy of John Ruskin', MA thesis, Victoria University of Wellington.

Trotter, C. 2013. ' "Putting the neo back in neo-liberal": Matthew Hooton goes in search of a new Bob Jones', *Daily Blog*, 11 December.

Wakefield, E. G. 1834. *The New British Province of South Australia*. London: Knight.

Index

Index